American Literature
and the Destruction
of Knowledge

American Literature and the Destruction of Knowledge ■

Innovative Writing in the Age of Epistemology ■ Ronald E. Martin

Duke University Press ■ Durham and London

© 1991 Duke University Press
All rights reserved
Printed in the United States of America
on acid-free paper ∞
Library of Congress Cataloging-in-Publication Data
appear on the last page of this book.

For Barbara,
who shared the ideas
and all the sweet time it
took to work them out

Contents

Acknowledgments

For the considerable encouragement, understanding, and help they offered over the long haul of this project, I thank my most recent succession
of department chairmen, Zack Bowen, Jerry Beasley, and Carl Dawson.
Thanks, too, to Maria Frawley, who as a graduate assistant provided accurate and intelligent help with the research on Hemingway and Crane; also
to Lydia Anderson, who as part of her undergraduate Humanities Fellow-
ship contributed substantially to research on the chapter on the visual
arts. For the considerable amount of research I was able to do while on
sabbatical in Vienna in 1984, I thank Waldemar Zacharasiewicz and his
assistants at the Institut für Anglistic und Amerikanistic der Universität
Wien and Roswitha Haller and her staff at the America Haus Library for
their helpfulness. I also thank Susan Brynteson and her staff at the University of Delaware Morris Library for a first-class job of providing materials, facilities, and assistance for so complex a project. Reynolds Smith of
Duke University Press provided me with notable support and advice for a
second time here, and I thank him. Thanks too to the manuscript's readers, as yet unknown to me, for their judicious readings and very helpful
suggestions.

■ ■ ■

The poems of Emily Dickinson are reprinted by permission of the pub-
lishers and Trustees of Amherst College from *The Poems of Emily Dickinson*,
Thomas H. Johnson, ed., Cambridge, Mass.: The Belknap Press of Harvard University Press, copyright 1951, 1955, 1979, 1983 by the President
and Fellows of Harvard College.

Hemingway quotes are reprinted with permission of Charles Scibner's
Sons, an imprint of Macmillan Publishing Company. From *The Sun Also
Rises*: copyright 1926 by Charles Scribner's Sons, renewed 1954 by Ernest
Hemingway. From *Death in the Afternoon*: copyright 1932 by Charles
Scribner's Sons, renewed 1960 by Ernest Hemingway. From *A Moveable*

Feast: copyright 1964 by Mary Hemingway. From "Mr. and Mrs. Elliott" from *In Our Time*: copyright 1925 by Charles Scibner's Sons, renewed 1953 by Ernest Hemingway.

The quotes from Whitman are reprinted from *Walt Whitman, Poetry and Prose*, published by the Library of America, 1982, by permission.

Niels Bohr is quoted from *Atomic Theory and the Description of Nature*: Cambridge University Press, 1934, by permission.

Rudolph Carnap is quoted from *Logical Structure of the World and Pseudoproblems in Philosophy*, ed./trans. Rolf George, copyright 1967 Rudolph Carnap. By permission of The University of California Press.

Jayne L. Walker is quoted from *The Making of a Modernist*, 1985, University of Massachusetts Press, by permission.

Melville's *Pierre*, ed. Harrison Hayford, Hershel Parker, and G. Thomas Tanselle, is quoted from *The Writings of Herman Melville*, Northwestern-Newberry Edition, vol. 7 (copyright 1971), by permission.

Dos Passos's *U.S.A.* is quoted by permission of Mrs. Elizabeth Dos Passos.

Stephen Crane is quoted from *The Complete Works of Stephen Crane*, ed. Fredson Bowers (1969–75), by permission of the University Press of Virginia.

William Carlos Williams is quoted by permission of New Directions Publishing Co. from *Collected Poems of William Carlos Williams 1909–1939*, copyright 1938 by New Directions; *The Farmer's Daughters*, copyright 1933 by William Carlos Williams; *The White Mule*, copyright 1939 by New Directions; *The Autobiography of William Carlos Williams*, copyright 1951 by William Carlos Williams; *Imaginations*, copyright 1970 by Florence H. Williams; *The Embodiment of Knowledge*, copyright 1974 by Florence H. Williams; *Selected Essays*, copyright 1951 by New Directions.

Gertrude Stein's Four in America (1947), and Selected Letters of Conrad Aiken, ed. Joseph Killoran (1978), are quoted by permission of Yale University Press. *Selected Writings of Gertrude Stein*, ed. Carl Van Vechten (1962), is quoted by permission of Random House Inc.

Wallace Stevens's works are quoted by permission of Alfred A. Knopf Inc.: *The Necessary Angel* (1951); *The Palm at the End of the Mind*, ed. Holly Stevens (1972); The Collected Poems of Wallace Stevens (1954), Opus Posthumous, ed. Samuel French Morse (1957); and Letters of *Wallace Stevens*, ed. Holly Stevens (1967).

Preface

This book* is a study of the literature produced by a number of nineteenth- and twentieth-century American writers who acted on the deep conviction that the principal obstacles to real understanding of experiential reality were the culture's certified knowledge and the habits and techniques by which that knowledge was customarily produced. The destruction of concepts and patterns, of literary and linguistic forms, was for them a precondition of knowing. Their assault was on nothing less than the linguistic order of their world.

The kind of radical repudiation to which I refer was not stock anti-intellectualism; it was often more probing, more exacting than intellectualism itself. Also it was an activity that took place outside the traditional dialectic of cultural debate. It was not just another step in the round of philosophical confutations or even in the shift of paradigms, for it challenged fundamental notions of how philosophies and paradigms are constructed, questioned the basic connections in the circuit of reality, experience, perception, language, representation, and interpretation. At its most extreme it impugned, at least by implication, the possibility of attaining any understanding by verbal means. As one characteristic Wallace Stevens poem says,

> Pfttt. . . . In the way you speak
> You arrange, the thing is posed,
> What in nature merely grows.[1]

And as William Carlos Williams urged in one of his typically hyperbolic exhortations, "We must go back to the beginning; it must all be done over; everything that is must be destroyed."[2]

That proposition still sounds incredible—an impossibility and a vio-

---

*Throughout this book numbered footnotes are used only for documentation. Substantive notes appear at the bottoms of pages.

lation of all our civilization's myths of knowledge since Prometheus—but it is based in two very profound recognitions, born in the nineteenth century and matured in the twentieth. First, there was a recognition of the inadequacy of the regnant verbal representations and interpretations of the world, a distrust of explanatory concepts and systems that don't explain the primary data of experience. As Conrad Aiken says of one of his early protagonists, "It occurs to him that the possibility of knowledge is itself limited: that knowledge is perhaps so conditioned by the condition of the knower that it can have little but a relative value."[3] Gertrude Stein insists, "One cannot come back too often to the question what is knowledge and to the answer that knowledge is what one knows"[4]—not what is comfortably generalized and conventionally accepted. And, as Ezra Pound puts it, " 'Thought' as Browning understood it—'ideas' as the term is current, are poor two-dimensional stuff, a scant, scratch covering. 'Damn ideas, anyhow.' An idea is only an imperfect induction from fact."[5]

Second, there was a recognition of the arbitrary and relative nature of language itself. The writers I am characterizing as knowledge destroyers knew or suspected that language was not just a simple and absolute medium for the representation of experience and its underlying rationale. They could see language as relative to the milieu, the moment, and even the individual using the words. As Emily Dickinson recognizes, "The Queen, discerns like me—/Provincially."[6] Gertrude Stein pushes farther, more insistently into the realm of language's relativity and arbitrariness: "I found myself plunged into a vortex of words, burning words, cleansing words, liberating words, feeling words, and the words were all ours, and it was enough that we held them in our hands to play with them; whatever you can play with is yours, and this was the beginning of knowing."[7]

This book is a study of the varieties of literature produced out of extreme dedication to the destruction of the old and the creation of radical, individualistic new knowledge. It is about the specific assumptions and insights about perception, language, and understanding manifested by individual knowledge destroyers; and it is about the particular innovations in literary form and technique that were the correlatives of their knowledge destroying behaviors.

These behaviors had significance well beyond the realm of imaginative literature. They served to advance certain conceptual possibilities, certain potential approaches to discourse and thought, to semantics and form, that are still being explored, especially in the realms of social and textual theory. The destructionist writers impugned, by implication at least, social and political as well as literary and philosophical regimes. They pioneered an absolute skepticism about the language of ideology and of social control, and that attitude has been invaluable to subsequent social movements arguing against race- and gender-based oppression. They undermined customs of genre, text, and linguistic representation in ways that foreshadowed subsequent Deconstructionist thought. If such knowledge destruction be nihilism—the denial of an objective basis for truth—this episode in our cultural history provides a case study in the constructive uses of nihilism. Even the destructionist writers themselves were able to discover new centers of meaning and confidence. But then that had all along been the purpose of the destruction.

Historical context is essential to an understanding of these behaviors, and the story I mean to tell has as an underlying assumption that deeply inherent in the tradition of American letters there is a fundamental negativeness, a destructiveness toward what is known, established, and believed, and that this destructiveness suddenly flourished in the early twentieth century. In capsule the argument of my book is as follows. In the nineteenth century the knowledge destroying impulse was manifested partly in an anti-old-world stance, and partly in the personal experiential empiricism of a few especially imaginative writers. The influence of nineteenth-century science added force and direction to the impulse, and the results are most noticeable in turn-of-the-century realism, itself a revolt against conventional "truths," but a revolt that nevertheless maintained a naively rationalistic conception of thought processes and language. Epistemological notions from twentieth-century science introduced new instabilities into conventional views of knowledge, and science's influence, along with that of a number of other fields—most especially visual art—encouraged a widespread recognition of the arbitrariness and relativity of all perspectives and all systems of knowledge. Twentieth-century literature, partly as result and partly as cause, manifested special propensities for mind-bending, form-breaking originality and for rigor in the repudiation of convention. One of my unprovable convictions is that this cultural tide of void-making, of indiscriminate mind-liberating, enabled some writers of relatively limited talent to produce some powerful and original work.

Part I explores the backgrounds of twentieth-century knowledge destruction in American literature of the nineteenth century, and for that purpose I select four writers with the strongest tendencies toward the repudiation of the accepted wisdom of their day—Emerson, Whitman, Melville, and Dickinson—scrutinize their work for its most radical epistemological elements, and attempt to analyze the rationales and the literary products of their individualistic repudiations. Emerson set the tone and established the precedent, fashioning out of a variety of borrowed ideas and original intuitions a myth of knowledge in the new world. His myth involves, most conspicuously, a belief in the necessity of throwing off the cultural baggage of Europe and creating something entirely original, entirely experiential; but it goes well beyond that in many of its formulations, into realms of phenomenalism and relativism such as would later and from much different sources become startling new insights of the twentieth century. Whitman, determined to liberate himself from rationalism and even rationality, attempted to plunge into the particulars of his world and to generate a language and a style directly expressive of his experience of the inherency of things. Melville and Dickinson were keenly aware of the gap between experience and the language of explanation and rationalization. A number of their works specifically challenge and negate the philosophical and religious truths of their day—beliefs that they saw as projecting ego, sentiment, and a priori optimism, or as offering answers and assurances that close off inquiry into the particular experiential matters most in need of careful analysis and understanding. Each of these nineteenth-century writers carried on the destructionist crusade individualistically and alone, each armed only with his or her own doubts and the (often very considerable) verbal and conceptual power he or she was able to muster. Experience was their watchword. Experience —personal or interpersonal, practical or mystical—was the standard by which every conception, every creation was to be judged.

Part II of my study surveys some of the specific scientific developments and philosophies that affected literary knowledge destruction. There is discussion of nineteenth-century issues of objectivity and mechanism, of twentieth-century issues of relativity and indeterminacy, and of the philosophical dimensions of the science of Einstein, Bohr, and others. The logical positivism of such thinkers as Dewey, Russell, and Wittgenstein is explored, as is the process philosophy of Bergson, James, and Whitehead. The ideas and perspectives of these various scientifically oriented epistemologists provoked new awarenesses of the relationships of mind, experience, and language, and often relate interestingly (and sometimes directly) to various experiments of the American modernist writers; I have arranged and slanted my treatment of them to show that.

Nineteenth-century science impressed secularism, naturalism, and causal determinism on American literary culture. Pragmatically irrefutable in the midst of the spectacular burgeoning of technology, it put considerations of abstract ideals and teleological purposes virtually into the realm of the old-fashioned. Its practitioners developed a system intended to maximize empirical, demonstrable, quantifiable, and (above all) objective criteria. Its system could authoritatively discredit notions not in keeping with its methodology or its current understandings. Thus while a good deal of nineteenth-century literature (its nature poetry especially) headed in quite the opposite direction, science provided a set of possibilities—a discipline, actually—for minimizing factors of self-projection, anthropomorphism, teleology, and value-bias in the act of knowing. Its debiasing was also, however, necessarily a dehumanizing of knowledge. As long as science was conceived of as a body of immutable, absolute laws, arrived at through a methodology modeled on mechanics, the universe it projected was deterministic, reducible to matter and motion, and basically mechanical in all its operations.*

There were, however, nineteenth-century approaches to scientific epistemology that were more sophisticated, and shortly after the turn of the century such approaches became more dominant—especially by way of twentieth-century physics. This new epistemological influence undermined the absolutism and mitigated the presumption of pure objectivity of the earlier vision. A new emphasis on science as *process* modified the simpler conception of it as a body of immutable laws and called attention to the ways that scientific concepts, meta-concepts, and paradigms interrelate, alter, and die. The triumph of Einstein's theory of relativity was an influential event for twentieth-century thinkers: not only did it supplant Newtonian theory, fundamentally changing our picture of the universe, but it also changed our idea of how we arrive at knowledge, changed our notions of empiricism, rationality, and imagination. Relativistic physics—or at least the intellectual discussion it stimulated—opened the floodgates of possibility for thinking about knowing: if scientific certainty could be destroyed, and by what seemed to be an incredible sally of the imagination, then other habitual modes of thought that were impeding rather than facilitating knowing might be similarly jettisoned. The new epistemology of science (however it might be understood or misunderstood) was highly likely to impact any impulse toward knowledge destruction.

Part III, on the early cultural effects of the new science, focuses on realism in two discrete but contemporaneous and clearly analogous forms: that of the literary theorists and that of the philosophers. The discussion

*Elsewhere I've termed it a "universe of force" and shown the ambivalent attempts of the writers to whom it was most congenial—Adams, London, Norris, and Dreiser—to accommodate to it. See *American Literature and the Universe of Force* (Duke University Press, 1981).

shows the growing difficulties of maintaining a belief in an absolute and reliably describable external world in a milieu increasingly preoccupied with ideas of knowledge and method. Although both types of realists were attuned to many of the new intellectual tendencies, most of their theories involve, as I see it, a relatively unsophisticated notion of the relationship of language and experience, and cultural conditions no longer favored such notions. In studying the epistemologically oriented work of Stephen Crane and Robert Frost, I explore two literary approaches on the cusp—approaches that presuppose realism's actual and describable world, yet strive to explore and control their culture's conventional tendencies toward self-projection and rationality-projection and to imagine a de-anthropomorphized universe.

It was not just the physical sciences that stimulated the new epistemological sophistication. At and after the turn of the century the story is similar in the visual arts, history and the social sciences, psychology, philosophy, linguistics, Biblical study, and even biography. The relativity and hypotheticalness of basic perceptions and fundamental laws seems to have been a virtually simultaneous discovery in many different fields. And it soon became a fascination and a preoccupation for many practitioners. Historians increasingly focused on the arbitrariness of any given method of studying history, sociologists on the variant models of social analysis and their variant ideological bases, philosophers on the ways in which language embodies meaning. The twentieth century became a period of probing, questioning, redefining, and theorizing about knowledge and perception—an age of epistemology.

Modernist visual art, the subject of Part IV, is especially crucial to the literary epistemological revolution. Many modernist writers associated with artists and identified with their works, and many of those artists were dedicated, in a variety of ingenious ways, to the destruction of conventions. Greatly concerned with the problems and paradoxes of perception and representation, these artists developed very self-aware approaches to method. Collectively they shattered the traditional sense of the perceptual event, the stock moment of relationship between artist, subject, and medium; collectively they introduced a sense of a wider event that could on any given occasion comprise milieu or medium, personality or perspective, or any multiple or combination thereof. I survey some specific theories and developments in the visual arts that parallel the intentions and techniques of the literature. Some connect quite directly to the literature, and others merely provide suggestive correlations.

The First World War, too, profoundly affected the writers' relationship to the knowledge of their day. Many of them experienced the war as the end of a culture based on futile and hypocritical principles, and what they came to know about the invalidity of those principles—indeed about the inconceivability of there being *any* value-laden principles inherent in experience—affected their works profoundly. It certainly changed their conceptions of knowledge and knowing. As the young John Dos Passos wrote in his diary in a trench near the front in France: "How damned ridiculous it all is! The long generations toiling—skimping, lashing themselves[,] screwing higher and higher the tension of their minds, polishing brighter and brighter the mirror of intelligence to end in this—My God what a time—All the cant and hypocrisy, all the damnable survivals, all the vestiges of old truths now putrid and false infect the air, choke you worse than German gas."[8] And of course Hemingway, Pound, Cummings, and many others came away from the war years with similar motives to destroy the knowledge, the forms, and the traditions by which humankind had been so trapped.

In Part V I give full-dress demonstrations of my concepts and hypotheses, focusing on several twentieth-century writers, their specific approaches to the destruction of knowledge and tradition, and the particular qualities of the works that ensued. The writers I put in the foreground are Stein, Pound, Hemingway, Aiken, Stevens, Williams, and Dos Passos. I choose these writers to represent a variety of salient examples of knowledge destruction. My purpose is to find the shape of a cultural current, not to describe it comprehensively; thus I do not survey all writers conceivably categorizable as epistemologically destructionist (like Marianne Moore, E. E. Cummings, Henry Miller, Nathanael West, or William Faulkner), and there is an element of arbitrariness in my choices. Nor do I furnish full estimations of the work of the writers I do study, but rather my treatment features those works and aspects of works most related to destruction and experimental creation. It emphasizes the literature's bizarreness, its outrageousness, and finds manifestations of new knowing or perception in those qualities. It also emphasizes the individual characteristics of each of the writers and the amazing variety of their verbal imaginings. Irrepressibly individualistic, these writers were never identified as comprising a "movement," even in an age with a strong tendency to package and promote writers in that fashion, and none of them attained the preeminence that would make her or him recognized by the others as their leader or guide. They did not even share a consensus about what exactly needed destroying, thus the appropriateness of emphasis on their individuality.

Although their work has considerable epistemological significance, the poets and fiction writers of the early twentieth century generally encountered the new age in very personal and immediate terms. They had little or no sense of participation in an epistemological paradigm-shift of drastic proportions, such as Wittgenstein and Whitehead, or Einstein and Bohr had. But despite their disengagement from (and in some cases incompetence with) explicit epistemology, their works make implicit epistemological statements, as do the works of psychologists and painters, physicists and anthropologists. Thus I compare and juxtapose and align literary with nonliterary works, sometimes pointing up direct influences and other times working with what I call cultural analogues. These latter (if not overstated) are useful in revealing contemporary ideas and assumptions, while at the same time marking the differences in disciplinary context and significance.

I do not give separate and explicit treatment to the various British and continental writers and literary theorists who shared the epistemological preoccupation and drove it to new, radical lengths. The experimentation of British novelists like Conrad, Joyce, Lawrence, and Woolf, of French poets like Apollinaire, Valéry and Cendrars, of dadaists and imagists and such, encouraged American writers in their own experiments with perspective and syntax, image and word. I note some of the Americans' specific indebtednesses within the discussions of individual writers but leave the larger comparative literature approach for other commentators.

I try to represent the writers' destructions, both theoretical and practical, in the terms in which they themselves understood them. Of course there is no real escape from the historical and interpretive preconceptions of our own time, but I believe we can learn more from a past age by trying to imaginatively recreate its ways of behaving and thinking than we can by applying our (conceivably superior) categories to its travails. I am leaving period-comparisons to my readers, then, as well as the application to this material of specific interpretive theories. Although I have undoubtedly been sharpened in some of my awarenesses by recent Deconstructionist and feminist critical theories, and although I find a comparison of this historical literature with those critical movements fascinating, I do not mean this book to go into that, nor do I mean to take any theoretical stance that might distract me from attempting to understand what these writers thought they were trying to do.

Neither do I involve the kind of critical approach devoted to defining or diagnosing "modernism" or the general temper of the times, although critics taking such an approach often focus on concepts such as I treat here. Irving Howe, for instance, says in *The Idea of the Modern in Literature and the Arts*, "In much modernist literature one finds a bitter impatience with the whole apparatus of cognition and the limiting assumption of rationality."[9] I will focus more on the performance than the underlying temper, more on the works than theory about text or society, insofar as those are separable concerns.

A number of interesting cultural themes develop in the course of the discussion of the twentieth-century writers. Consistent with their epistemological impulse, they persistently explored the relationship of the perceived and the perceiver, testing the boundaries of the self and the other. Repeatedly, of course, they returned to themes of the blocking, distorting, inhibiting effect of conventional habits of perception. They were vividly aware of the effects of their culture's prevailing mind-sets and philosophies, of conventional literary genres and traditions, of patterns of thought and expression, and of conventions of language, any and all of which could determine and limit one's ability to access and represent experience. At the same time, in various ways and to various degrees they questioned the extent to which any and all perceptions are really projections. For a number of them the destruction of the knowledge of the past was a rejection of the simple and un-self-aware reflexiveness of much of what passed for thought and literature in their day, and for some the self's permeation of perception exerted an inescapable yet indeterminate force upon every experience.

They tried to strike a course between conventionality and solipsism, and their attempts were bound to involve some radical revisions in common understandings of the world and the place of a sentient individual in it. The extreme variety of perspectives and points of view they employed comprises in itself nothing less than a literary version of relativity. In addition, conventional notions of time and identity yield, in the works of several of them, to new senses of process and moment-by-moment mutability. The knowing consciousness itself is even seen as indeterminate, a transient process. And the most basic of intellectual/aesthetic criteria —what in an experience is significant enough to be worth literary treatment—is in some instances drastically modified by what these writers do. The point of a work might even be its own coming-into-existence, rather than some mimetic or teleological significance.

The techniques by which these writers attempted to realize their programs were often ingeniously innovative but at the same time individualistically, almost desperately, improvised. Their heritage offered little guidance, quite naturally, given their desire to obliterate heritage; there was no reliable repertoire of routines for recreating the order of the world, even only linguistically. Their whole endeavor was impossible, romantically paradoxical: the creation of knowing counter to knowledge, the contrivance of linguistic escapes from the trammels of language, the discovery of an anti-order order of things. Yet they possessed a strongly willed sense of discipline (of words and style, of emotion, and of knowing); a self-awareness, with a special awareness of the powerful innate inclination toward self-projection; and a conscious concentration on method. *Imagination* was the term most of them used for the faculty by which they created; what they meant by that was variously the ability to picture and to de-picture, to word and to de-word, to invent new realities and to empathize into old ones. And they had language and what they could make it do.

Language, these writers were especially aware, could determine, inhibit, and conventionalize experiences, thoughts, and feelings, or it could liberate and express them, and they found that verbal ingenuity could lead to new pathways of expression and representation. Some writers had vivid understandings of the artifactuality of language; others still had yearnings to make their words correspond inevitably with their experience. But the urge to experiment, to redefine the boundaries of what language could do, to make it somehow new, was always there. The products, as we shall see, were experiments with pure literalness, free invention, nonreferentiality, discontinuous syntax, deliberate ambiguity, and so forth.

Every one of the destructionists took on his or her job as a kind of moral mandate, in terms of the language, the literature, the individual and his or her knowing. The culture was perceived as being hypocritical —compromised and betrayed by its literature and its other expressive forms—and the road to regeneration was through the reconstitution of the relationship of the individual person to the written word.

Of course the destructionists' fundamental notion of what they were doing was a colossal mythic vision, an imagined projection of themselves against the backdrop of history and contemporary culture that gave their creative adventures great significance. Yet aren't all philosophies of knowledge myths, and don't they all function similarly—the Promethean, the Platonic, the Augustinian, the Faustian, the Darwinian, the Einsteinian? In the case at hand, at half a century's remove we can see a good deal of outright naïveté in the rationale of the myth of the destruction of knowledge, an element of almost childlike self-admiration—"yes, Western Culture has gone off in the wrong direction, and I've got to cancel out all that and put it on a right path." Still, however pretentious and paradoxical an anti-knowledge knowledge, an anti-order order might be, the activity of these proponents of the myth has, I think, a real cultural function.

This is why I think so; this is the myth that underlies my particular presentation: the whole category of order-versus-chaos is, I maintain, a human projection. Chaos is an invention of the human mind, existing nowhere in nature but invented to symbolize human insecurity about what is uncontrollable and incomprehensible. Order is only a way we have of thinking about things; positing chaos is a way of expressing our fear that we haven't got a way to think about them. Chaos, in other words, exists only relative to some particular system of order. Systems of order are all inventions, are all ultimately inadequate, and the knowledge that constitutes them is exclusionary, acting to close off certain other possibilities of perception or apprehension. Thus an attack on knowledge can be a constructive act, an opening of possibilities.* Furthermore, language and other symbol systems by which we represent and presume to understand experience—the embodiments of our knowledge—are essentially crude, biased, and approximate. Thus it is best not to place too much credence on any particular formulation and reasonable to tolerate or even welcome its possible destruction. Moreover, since conceptual categories, semantic conventions, and forms of discourse are instrumentalities of mental and social control, an awareness of their fallibility and their functioning can be an important component of freedom.

Thinking along these lines, we can see how the basically epistemological-literary efforts of the destructionists were in effect assaults on the centers of power in their society. Dos Passos dealt explicitly with political issues at times, as did Pound in his later career, but for Stein, Stevens, Aiken, Hemingway, and Williams the assault was nearly wholly implicit, albeit, I would assert, for all of them it took place on a level deeper than that of the issue or even of the philosophy. If questions about linguistic and expressive forms are indeed prior to questions about the society that such forms frame and embody, then epistemological nihilism has a decisive and revolutionary effect *infrapolitically*. If all ideologies, concepts, principles, abstractions, even language itself, are revealed as fundamentally arbitrary, then political systems and their rationales are left without an authoritative conceptual infrastructure. We can understand, especially rec-

---

*Morse Peckham, in *Man's Rage for Chaos* (Schocken, 1965), maintains that the essential function of all art is to dis-order systems of order and that this function is what defines art's role in our biological survival. Peckham's largest generalizations are too sweeping and reductionist for me, although I found much in his attempt to reorient aesthetic philosophy congenial and stimulating when I was in the finishing stages of this study.

ognizing the tendency in Hemingway, Williams, and Stein to particularly target language and concept-systems dedicated to order and restraint, how the destructionist writers might legitimately have felt that the process of societal regeneration might indeed begin with the reconstitution of the relationship of the individual and the word. Significantly, the European dadaists were explicitly advocating a similar program of cultural destruction and regeneration at this same time.

Consider for a moment a comparison between the writers I have characterized as epistemological nihilists with their contemporaries who had (to varying extents) radical sociopolitical agendas but no particular epistemological orientation. Take, for example, Afro-American writers like Claude McKay, Jean Toomer, or Langston Hughes, or feminist writers like Kate Chopin, Edna St. Vincent Millay, or Katherine Anne Porter; in the production of their art these writers carried out their often quite considerable campaigns against racism and sexism explicitly on occasion, but more customarily they urged their radical ideas through indirection, implication, and innuendo, through silences and signifying. Some of their techniques and insights tended to disrupt the canons of official knowledge, but for the most part they played within the epistemological conventions of the literary game. The modes and approaches they chose undeniably counteracted specific usages of society's authority structure but often on a conventionally ideological level, leaving intact the infrastructure of prevailing sociopolitical discourse. In fact, for a writer of the period between the world wars to attempt to advance a specific sociopolitical agenda would probably necessitate his or her establishing a conventional sort of credibility with a relatively conventional audience in order that his or her message could have some chance of acceptance. The protest sonnet and the rationally crafted story of social inequity certainly had fully appropriate historical socio-literary roles.

But literary conventions, like the conventions of political discourse, have certain entailments, certain biases. It takes, as I have indicated, an awareness of the arbitrary elements of language and expressive forms to counteract the influence of those entailments, and this awareness is what the literary knowledge destroyers of the twenties and thirties give us; this is how they induce revolution on the infrapolitical level. Their assaults were broader and less well-defined than those of other reform-minded writers. They intentionally disrupted the canons of credibility, striving for insight-through-surprise, askance understanding. They were method-oriented rather than issue-oriented, deeply concerned with the *means* of knowing and representing. And they were indomitably personal rather than generic in their reference. Politically, within the literary culture the destruction-of-knowledge phenomenon functioned as the radical democratization of access to reality.

Afro-American and feminist liberation movements lay ahead, as did absurdism and a radical revolution in literary theory, and although the sociopolitical applications and postwar effects of the knowledge destroying behaviors fall outside the bounds of this study, an acknowledgment of them will serve to indicate the far-reaching significance I see in this epistemological orientation.

Epistemological nihilism has become endemic among postmodernist writers; many commentators see it as a defining characteristic of postmodernism. For those writers who deal substantially with the indeterminate, relativistic, fabricated qualities of truth, perception, language, and form—for example, Barth, Pynchon, and Barthelme—the similarity to the destructionism of the twenties and thirties is clear and obvious: the epistemological motif frequently becomes a central preoccupation of the work. For those writers who direct their works toward social causes like racial and gender liberation—for example, Amiri Baraka and Adrienne Rich—their epistemological sophistication enables them to approach their work on the infrapolitical as well as the political level. Any linguistic form can be used, from street talk to semantic analysis, and the myths of culture —whether myths of our contemporary culture, myths of traditional cultures, or myths invented by a writer to express or re-form our culture —are seen and presented as myths.

The infrapolitical destruction of knowledge may well have influenced the postideological character of postmodernist literature. Ralph Ellison provides a good example of a writer transmitting the infrapolitical message of the thirties to the literary culture of the fifties. Ellison, a syncretist, second-generation modernist, brings together in *Invisible Man* radical narrative techniques such as he saw in Joyce and the American modernists; a deep sense of folk history, folk myth, and folk language; and a bizarre personal history that made sense only in light of what he saw as an essential lesson of both modernism and folk history: epistemological nihilism. The idea of the arbitrariness of all language, all patterning, all justification pervades literature after the Second World War in ways such as this.

I would propose too that the destructionist writers of the twenties and thirties can be seen as an indigenous American influence on the poststructuralist theory of the past two decades. Although American Deconstructionists, for instance, customarily trace the explicit genealogy of their ideas to continental sources, the epistemological insights of Stevens and the semantic experiments of Stein were familiar to them, certainly, and quite possibly played some role, at least in preparing the way for Derrida. The pervasive skepticism about absolutes and conventions dealing with texts and their usages and natures and the resistance to conceptual closure and adventitious authoritativeness are certainly themes of the earlier knowledge destroyers that resonate in later literary critics and theorists.

Clearly, many of the ideas, images, and approaches of the knowledge destroyers have become deeply infused in our culture and have become part of what we are; paradoxically, their anti-orthodoxy has become a new orthodoxy, their anti-style a new style. In a familiar cultural pattern the avant-garde has evolved the new guard.

With a sense of these cultural consequences hovering in the background, let us move into this study of the destruction of knowledge in the years between world wars, the impulses and traditions behind it, and the possibilities it presented. What I hope the study provides is an understanding of some of the goals of the most venturesome of our early twentieth-century writers and some new interpretive insights into their writings. But I also mean it to establish, by way of exploring the American literary community's involvement in the age of epistemology, a framework for understanding and appreciating the whole culture's struggle with and utilization of the concepts of the reflexiveness of perception, the fallibility of symbolic media, and the relativity of standpoint and representation.

I The Destruction of Knowledge in the Prescientific Literary Imagination

The destruction of knowledge in nineteenth-century American literature was carried out principally by Whitman, Melville, and Dickinson in their most radically skeptical mind-frames, motivated by their deep dissatisfaction with much of the wisdom of their age. They could see that its insights were often little more than naive self-projections, its concepts and categories often obstructions or egregious oversimplifications of the truth, and its language often an instrument of biased perception, facile rationalization, and social control. They were highly individualistic in their attacks on conventional knowledge and ways of knowing. They headed into uncharted waters, developing, in the process, some new and unproven techniques of literary navigation. And they arrived in no safe haven of consensus: the result of their rejection and reformulation of knowing—the reality their works projected—was often an unresolvable ambiguity, a provoking bewilderment, or an affirmation so ineffable as to seem willful, exclusively personal, mystic. They installed the individual imagination as absolute arbiter and interpreter; and in so doing they discovered much about the limits of the self and the self's knowing. They took the risk that the products of their imaginations might be eccentric, solipsistic, not sane —the risk that they were substituting perverse and complex self-projections for normal and simple ones.

Their literary activities took place in the context of both a traditional American reverence for knowledge and a traditional American skepticism.

Americans energetically founded colleges; they published and disseminated the world's great literature and its great religious and secular thought; they established ambitious lecture programs; and they reverenced men and women of learning. At the same time many Americans were proud to acknowledge the questioning of orthodoxy and authority as a national characteristic. That habit of questioning had as its intellectual and literary manifestation a highly developed tradition of skepticism about standard wisdom, best embodied in Franklin, continued in Hawthorne, and raised to the level of a (relatively) systematic philosophy by Emerson. Collectively and at its best it projected a judicious, sophisticated view of authority and tradition. As a response to the overbearing intellectual authority of Europe, as an attempt to make intellect in America a pragmatic and populistic force, and as an attitude both democratic and sensibly conservative, American skepticism served to prepare the way for American philosophies of knowledge.

The destructionists were the radical fringe of skepticism. At times what they were doing seemed sheer negativism, indiscriminate anti-intellectualism. Their destruction of knowledge was a conscientious and strenuous pursuit, however, not to be confused with run-of-the-mill anti-intellectualism. Whitman, Melville, and Dickinson destroyed knowledge not out of contempt for or bias against knowing, but out of a desire to know more than could be contained in the standard modes and categories of knowledge. They had no bias against using specifically intellectual powers (along with others) to pursue their ends. While it is undoubtedly true that anti-intellectualism existed in nineteenth-century America at the grass-roots level—basically as a bias against highbrows and theoretical and abstract thought and as a bias for practical know-how, material reality, and/or the God of our Fathers—and while it is true that this attitude does indeed destroy knowledge too, and on a vast scale, it has very different characteristics. It is provincial, complacent, and exclusionary; it involves an abiding faith in a stable consensus of practical folk and in a simply described universe, material or spiritual. Faulkner and William Carlos Williams make some interesting uses of folk anti-intellectualism, but the nineteenth-century knowledge destroyers shared only its confidence in the right of an individual to stand outside impressive intellectual constructs and make his or her own judgments.

(African-American expressive traditions of the nineteenth century were apparently unknown to the knowledge destroyers, although several of those traditions had strong authority-subverting tendencies. The conscious utilization of the seemingly ingenuous, stereotypical persona for the dual purpose of self-concealment and social satire, for example, and the "signifying" use of language to trick and insult an unwitting audience* worked to preserve blacks' individual and group integrity against an overwhelming set of racist beliefs. Such sophisticated folk strategies would come together powerfully with the intellectual tradition's epistemological nihilism in the explicitly liberationist literature of the 1940s and later.)

The nineteenth-century writers' destruction of knowledge can be seen as a part of our American mythos: it can be characterized as a kind of intellectual frontierism, an egalitarianism of the life of the mind, a philosophical impulse both independent and revolutionary. It can also be seen as a striving toward a connection with what is real behind the screen of concepts and categories, a casting away of cultural intermediation, the liberation of the questing self from the trammels of convention and secu-

---

*For a discussion of the former strategy, especially the minstrel trope, see Houston A. Baker, Jr., *Modernism and the Harlem Renaissance* (University of Chicago Press, 1987), 25–47. For discussions of "signifying" see Geneva Smitherman, *Talkin and Testifyin* (Houghton Mifflin, 1977), 47–50, 118–128; and Henry Louis Gates, *The Signifying Monkey* (Oxford University Press, 1988), 44–124.

rity; the context of Romanticism is thus a congenial one for this strange nineteenth-century anti-epistemology. The knowledge destroyers were by no means early phenomenalists or deconstructionists, although some of their techniques and motifs did tend toward those distant directions. I classify their imaginations as "prescientific" here, despite the fact that several of them were acquainted with various aspects of the theory and achievement of the science of their day, because for them science did not have a role as a dominant force in destroying and reformulating basic conceptions.

However we integrate the efforts of these writers with our interpretive categories, their own demonstrable destructionist motives are: (1) a dissatisfaction with the categories, ideas, explanations, theories, and even the language of the discourse of their day; (2) a special respect for experience; and (3) a vast confidence in the ability of the individual imagination to get beyond not only the complacent society's reflexive self-projections, but those of the self-aware knowledge destroyer as well.

1   The Emersonian Myth of Knowledge
in the New World

From his position as acknowledged sage of the northern states, Emerson articulated a philosophy that offered a good deal of support, direct and hortatory as well as subtle and implicit, for the destruction of knowledge. The statements and insights about knowledge that are sprinkled liberally throughout his works comprise a new American knowledge-myth; they not only suggest to his countrymen and -women procedures for destroying certain kinds of knowledge and repudiating certain ways of knowing, but they legitimize the whole endeavor as well, sanctioning it in nearly sacred terms. His thought is not really consistent on the subjects of knowledge and perception, however (actually it is consistent on only a relatively few subjects), so his knowledge myths are multiple. Overall he seems paradoxical—a Platonist with a passion for the particular, an absolutist with a relativistic imagination; nonetheless he proposes some ideas with intriguing potential for writers with deeper and more self-aware minds.

Whatever the tendency of his thought in other areas, epistemologically Emerson is anticonservative. First of all, nationalistically his was the strongest voice, providing the climax of a radical movement for a nonimitative national literature.* "We have listened too long to the courtly muses of Europe," he insists, and encourages a new-world breakaway. But nationalism is only one aspect of his conception that knowledge needs to be up-to-date, continually newly created: "Each age, it is found, must write its own books; or rather, each generation for the next succeeding. The books of an older period will not fit this."** In "The American Scholar"

---

*That movement had been established and promoted by Francis Calley Gray, Edward Tyrell Channing, Edward Everett, and others, largely in the pages of the *North American Review*. See James M. Hutchisson, *Paper Wars: The Literary Manifesto in America* (Ph.D. dissertation, University of Delaware, 1987).

**"The American Scholar," *Essays and Lectures*, ed. Joel Porte (Library of America, 1983), 70, 56–57. Parenthetical page numbers in this chapter refer to this volume.

he avows respect for the knowledge embodied in the books of past ages, and throughout his essays he draws freely and frequently on the wisdom of the past—on Plato and Pythagoras, Shakespeare and Swedenborg—but the dominant message of his myth of new knowledge is its newness.

In many of his formulations this rage for newness is part of an even more radical motif: an unwillingness to accept any sort of cultural mediation between the individual knower and the thing known. "The foregoing generations beheld God and nature face to face; we, through their eyes. Why should not we also enjoy an original relation to the universe?" (7) he asks in *Nature*, and in "The Poet" asserts that "every thought is also a prison; every heaven is also a prison" (463) from which we need liberating. Language too is a prison: "The poets made all the words and therefore language is the archives of history, and, if we must say it, a sort of tomb of the muses. . . . The etymologist finds the deadest word to have been once a brilliant picture. Language is fossil poetry" (457). Thus Emerson, like a number of other writers of his day, claimed a special appreciation for vividly up-to-the-minute language:

> The language of the street is always strong. What can describe the folly and emptiness of scolding like the word *jawing*? I feel too the force of the double negative, though clean contrary to our grammar rules. And I confess to some pleasure from the stinging rhetoric of a rattling oath in the mouth of truckmen and teamsters. How laconic and brisk it is by the side of a page of the *North American Review*. Cut these words and they would bleed.[1]

Even rationality itself could be a prison, Emerson sometimes asserted. He maintains in "The Over-Soul" that the highest and deepest questions are not even posed by the understanding (393), and in "The Poet" he explains how the best use of the intellect is in the abandonment of its controlled rationality:

> It is a secret which every intellectual man quickly learns, that, beyond the energy of his possessed and conscious intellect, he is capable of a new energy (as of an intellect doubled on itself), by abandonment to the nature of things; by unlocking, at all risks, his human doors, and suffering the ethereal tides to roll and circulate through him. . . . The poet knows that he speaks adequately, then, only when he speaks somewhat wildly, or 'with the flower of the mind'; not with the intellect, used as an organ, but with the intellect released from all service, and suffered to take its direction from its celestial life. (459)

Striving for disengagement from tradition and from the ideas, language, and rationality that culture interposed, the knower, according to Emerson's new-world myth, needed to establish personal experience as the basis of knowing. Only through immersion in the immediacy, the multifariousness, the spontaneity of firsthand experience could a person hope to know the world in its essential otherness. Along this line of thought, Emerson seems to have felt that our traditional conceptually oriented perception was unable to get beyond conventions and stereotypes and into new insights; the flux of experiences, however, could evade or overwhelm our categories and surprise us with new revelation. "I know that the world I converse with in the city and in the farms, is not the world I *think*," he says. "I observe that difference, and shall observe it. One day I shall know the value and law of this discrepance" (491–492). In that famous exhortation "The American Scholar," using himself as the implied model knower, he advocates the plunge into multifarious otherness in these terms:

> The world,—this shadow of the soul, or *other me*, lies wide around. Its attractions are the keys which unlock my thoughts and make me acquainted with myself. I run eagerly into this resounding tumult. I grasp the hands of those next me, and take my place in the ring to suffer and to work, taught by an instinct, that so shall the dumb abyss be vocal with speech. I pierce its order; I dissipate its fear; I dispose of it within the circuit of my expanding life. So much only of life as I know by experience, so much of the wilderness have I vanquished and planted, or so far have I extended my being, my dominion. (60)

I expect that the implicit metaphor of western expansion, of annexation and domination, is more than a rhetorical ploy here. In a very real sense (as we shall soon see) the act of knowing was for Emerson an act of imposing the self of the knower on the nature of the thing known. That notwithstanding, the pattern he advocates, of a knower overwhelming his conceptual categories in a flood of perceptual data, prevails, as in his famous "transparent eyeball" passage in *Nature*:

> Standing on the bare ground,—my head bathed by the blithe air and uplifted into infinite space,—all mean egotism vanishes. I become a transparent eye-ball. I am nothing; I see all; the currents of the Universal Being circulate through me; I am part or particle of God. The name of the nearest friend sounds then foreign and accidental: to be

brothers, to be acquaintances, —master or servant, is then a trifle and a disturbance. (4–5)

Of course his advocacy of experiencing the new things and the commonplace things of the world is a key part of this program for expanding knowledge. And his appreciation of science is another aspect of this knowledge-myth, as exemplified by the beauty he can find in "the galvanic battery, the electric jar, the prism, the chemist's retort" (in, it is worth noting, his essay "Art") (440).

The act of knowing is an individual act—so runs this myth. Knowledge is genuine only when the individual knower comes to know it for himself, in his own specific way: "We are always coming up with the emphatic facts of history in our private experience, and verifying them here. All history becomes subjective; in other words, there is properly no history; only biography. Every mind must know the whole lesson for itself, —must go over the whole ground. What it does not see, what it does not live, it will not know" (240). The individual knower needs to pursue the act of knowing with all faculties and capacities—emotional and instinctual as well as rational; peculiar and personal as well as universal. "I need my fear and my superstition as much as my purity and courage, to construct the glossary which opens the Sanscrit [sic] of the world," he affirms to himself in his journal,[2] and "trust the instinct to the end, though you can render no reason" he exhorts his readers in his essay "Intellect" (419). Emerson's ideas of perception and knowledge are based on a faith that the individual mind, liberated to follow its own particular impulses, will somehow shape to the contours of the outside world:

> As the traveller who has lost his way, throws his reins on his horse's neck, and trusts to the instinct of the animal to find his road, so must we do with the divine animal who carries us through this world. For if in any manner we can stimulate this instinct, new passages are opened for us into nature, the mind flows into and through things hardest and highest, and the metamorphosis is possible. (460)

There could hardly be a faith more destructive of conventional knowledge.

In its literary applications the Emersonian myth puts the highest premium on originality. It casts poets as "liberating gods" and asks for radically individualistic writing: "I think nothing is of any value in books, excepting the transcendental and extraordinary. If a man is inflamed and carried away by his thought, to that degree that he forgets the authors and the public, and heeds only this one dream, which holds him like an insanity, let me read his paper, and you may have all the arguments and histories and criticism." As examples of extraordinary writers he cites Pythagoras, Paracelsus, Kepler, and Swedenborg, and as liberating conceptual systems, he specifies magic, astrology, palmistry, and mesmerism —although he is writing an essay on the poet (462). (The presence of a physical scientist on this list is of interest, adumbrating, perhaps, the next century's view of scientific originality.)

The extremest reaches of Emerson's philosophy of knowledge lie in a realm of radical relativism. Uncharacteristic of much of the rest of his thought and of nineteenth-century thought generally, they more resemble the uncertain terrain of the twentieth century. At times his universe seems indeterminate, and all approaches to knowledge arbitrary. "The highest minds of the world have never ceased to explore the double meaning, or, shall I say, the quadruple, or the centuple, or much more manifold meaning, of every sensuous fact" (447), he states, giving a free reign to the possibility of variant perceptions; and at times he even proposes a view of nature as having no basic identity to which a true idea of things can correspond. "There are no fixtures in nature. The universe is fluid and volatile. Permanence is but a word of degrees" (401), he says; and again, "Nature . . . resents generalizing, and insults the philosopher in every moment with a million of fresh particulars. . . . You are one thing, but nature is *one thing and the other thing*, in the same moment" (581).

But even the knower seems not "one thing" to him at times, further multiplying the ambiguity of knowledge: "Illusion, Temperament, Succession, Surface, Surprise, Reality, Subjectiveness, —these are the threads on the loom of time, these are the lords of life. I dare not assume to give their order, but I name them as I find them in my way. I know better than to claim any completeness for my picture. I am a fragment, and this is a fragment of me" (490–491). As would be the case with Ahab's doubloon, the meaning of anything is strictly relative to the individual, transient state of its beholders:

> History and the state of the world at any one time [are] directly dependent on the intellectual classification then existing in the minds of men. The things which are dear to men at this hour are so on account of the ideas which have emerged on their mental horizon, and which cause the present order of things as a tree bears its apples. A new degree of culture would instantly revolutionize the entire system of human pursuits. (407–408)

For Emerson in these relativistic frames of mind it would seem that there is no possibility whatever of direct knowledge of reality, however strong his urgings toward pure or unmediated experience. The key that he offers to knowing in this intermediate universe is metaphor. Figurative seeing is the way to translate life into truth:

> We are symbols, and inhabit symbols; workmen, work, and tools, words and things, birth and death, all are emblems; but we sympathize with the symbols, and, being infatuated with the economical uses of things, we do not know that they are thoughts. The poet, by an ulterior intellectual perception, gives them a power which makes their old use forgotten, and puts eyes, and a tongue, into every dumb and inanimate object. (456)

But no particular figurative insight has any finality, Emerson says; our truth changes over time. Humankind's process of truth-seeking thus consists of passing through a temporal succession of metaphoric approximations—each new metaphoric insight gets us closer to reality, but none will ever give us its precise picture. This the poet knows, claims Emerson, and the mystic does not:

> the quality of imagination is to flow, and not to freeze. . . . Here is the difference betwixt the poet and the mystic, that the last nails a symbol to one sense, which was a true sense for a moment, but soon becomes old and false. For all symbols are fluxional; all language is vehicular and transitive, and is good, as ferries and horses are, for conveyance, not as farms and houses are, for homestead. (463)

So much for the hypothesis of Emerson as radical epistemologist. I have selected ideas and quotations for this segment with a purpose of seeing how much like a post-Machian, post-Whiteheadian thinker Emerson could seem, trying to reveal those elements in his myth of new-world knowledge that could have encouraged his contemporaries onto paths that would lead to the epistemological realms of Wallace Stevens or William Faulkner. It would be a mistake, however, to identify Emerson as especially prescient of the science-steeped, post-phenomenalist thought of the twentieth century. It would be a mistake because, in the first place, he was relying on literary, theological, ethical, and aesthetic traditions of thought rather than investigative, scientific ones. To him science was facts generalized, names, paraphernalia, historic discoveries, or, in its highest levels, it was physical nature entirely transcended. It wasn't method, process, or specialized mental discipline. His concept of knowledge as developing out of a succession of metaphorical approximations is closer in origin to the rhetoric of Shakespearian and Metaphysical lyric poetry, of the standard nineteenth-century sermon, or of the King James Bible than it is to the scientists' pattern of formation, testing, and relegation of hypothesis. (Did he even know that the explanation of heat in terms of caloric had quite recently been supplanted by the theory of molecular motion? Was he aware that a momentous new theory of universal force conservation was proposed in the early 1840s? He certainly knew of Coleridge's theory of the imagination.) In the second place it would be a mistake to propose Emerson as a father of twentieth-century epistemology and knowledge destruction because most of the main tendencies of his thought are in a different and entirely uncongenial direction.

For one thing Emerson was an irrepressibly didactic writer, and his didacticism assumed a teleological, absolutistic universe. Every perceptual detail had to have an interpretation, had to teach a lesson. "Let me see every trifle bristling with the polarity that ranges it instantly on an eternal law," he asks in "The American Scholar," and we will see that "one design unites and animates the farthest pinnacle and the lowest trench" (69). The interpretive design has to be there, final and fulfilled, in the trifle before we look at it; our apprehension of the eternal law "instantly" turns our perceptive act into a deductive exercise. We begin (as he does in *Nature*) with the question "to what end is nature?" and, as answer and conclusion, "we apprehend the absolute" (37); there is nothing relative, hypothetical, or even figurative about it in many of Emerson's statements. The knower can even have the deep assurance that "in going down into the secrets of his own mind, he has descended into the secrets of all minds" (64)—there is a Truth and it is the same for all.

This teleological current in Emerson's thought inevitably carried him toward a quasi-mystical Platonism, a philosophy of knowledge utterly unlike his radical conception of absolute truth as inconceivable, generalizations as metaphoric approximations, and the tide of particular sensations as the surest guide to the real. In his Platonist frame "the world of any moment is the merest appearance" (64), and the individual deed or detail is a "dull grub" which needs to be "raised, transfigured" by the contemplative mind to become "an angel of wisdom" (61). In *Nature* he asserts that in the process of true knowing the philosopher, like the poet, "animates nature with his own thoughts": "It is, in both cases, that a spiritual life has been imparted to nature; that the solid seeming block of matter has been pervaded and dissolved by a thought; that this feeble human being has penetrated the vast masses of nature with an informing soul, and recognized itself in their harmony, that is, seized their law." And he goes on with an erroneous description of scientific method that eventually adds physicists too to the vanguard of Platonist poets:

> In physics, when this is attained, the memory disburthens itself of its cumbrous catalogues of particulars, and carries centuries of observation in a single formula.
>
> Thus even in physics, the material is degraded before the spiritual. . . .
>
> Intellectual science has been observed to beget invariably a doubt of the existence of matter. . . . It fastens the attention upon immortal necessary uncreated natures, that is, upon Ideas; and in their presence, we feel that the outward circumstance is a dream and a shade. (36–37)

Finally, it is the naive reflexiveness of Emerson's thought that allies it with older, less epistemologically sophisticated forms. His concept of perception is incorrigibly human-centered, and it seems to have no inbuilt way of controlling self-projection. In fact he seems to glory in self-projection. "All the facts in natural history taken by themselves, have no value, but are barren, like a single sex. But marry it to human history, and it is full of life" (21), he claims, and implicitly recommends this perspective as an essential aspect of inquiry: "Sensible objects conform to the premonitions of Reason and reflect the conscience. All things are moral; and in their boundless changes have an unceasing reference to spiritual nature" (28). Perception seems to feed directly back on itself in this system; we look for signs of our spirituality in the lineaments of our world, and sure enough, we find them. And not surprisingly, the higher the level of this self-projective perception, the more its object takes on the aspect of the creative imagination of the writer:

> As the eyes of Lyncaeus were said to see through the earth, so the poet turns the world to glass, and shows us all things in their right series and procession. For, through that better perception, he stands one step nearer to things, and sees the flowing or metamorphosis; perceives that thought is multiform; that within the form of every creature is a force impelling it to ascend into a higher form; and, following with his eyes the life, uses the forms which express that life, and so his speech flows with the flowing of nature. All the facts of the animal economy, sex, nutriment, gestation, birth, growth, are symbols of the passage of the world into the soul of

man, to suffer there a change, and reappear a new and higher fact. (456)

If we look at this passage from "The Poet" as metaphysics, we see Emerson explaining his belief in the fundamental unity of all types of creativity in the universe—they all basically involve a process of metamorphosis from a lower to a higher form. But if we look at it as knowledge theory—an explanation of "that better perception" and how it is comprised—we see that he is not really prepared to observe any of "the facts of the animal economy" except insofar as they illustrate a process very like the one by which he is generating that very insight. The disadvantage of humanistic thought which has this quality of unself-aware, uncontrolled reflexiveness is that it may be offering us in the guise of an orderly, comprehensible, and moral universe only a reflected image of our own orderly and benign mind at work.

And its risks are greater than the petty sins of tautology and self-admiration. High-minded social intolerance and religious bigotry are rooted here. Take one of Emerson's diverse ethical ideas, the concept of compensation, as a case in point; criticizing a common reaction to the slave trade he said:

> A tender American girl doubts of Divine Providence whilst she reads the horrors of "the middle passage:" and they are bad enough at the mildest; but to such as she these crucifixions do not come: they come to the obtuse and barbarous, to whom they are not horrid, but only a little worse than the old sufferings. They exchange a cannibal war for the stench of the hold. They have gratifications which would be none to the civilized girl. (1294)

Now this is horrendous nonsense, not very typical of Emerson as an ethical thinker, and I admit in all sincerity that I am maligning him seriously by quoting it without putting it in the context of the full body of his ethical thought. It is an idea he had and saw fit to publish, however, and I think that the lesson it teaches with regard to reflexive thinking is more important than the slight to his reputation. Let me put it in terms of a comparison, a question-and-answer that will foreshadow a bit of what will follow and begin to suggest some of the constructive value of a more thorough and self-aware destruction of knowledge than Emerson's. Question: why didn't Herman Melville or Emily Dickinson have this sort of moral insight? Answer: because they did not have Emerson's need to hold up his own open-minded benignity as the principle of the workings of the universe.

Naive self-projection was widespread in American literature of the earlier nineteenth century. Emerson was, as I say, following a very conventional line in investing all nature with his own values and feelings. Nineteenth-century American nature poetry especially, from Bryant's "To a Waterfowl" to Lanier's "The Marshes of Glynn" (and with very few exceptions) seems almost single-minded in its effort to "marry" natural history to human history the way Emerson recommends, to "animate" nature (a very curious idea from our perspective) with the thoughts and feelings of the poet. The approach has not lasted well. In our post-Darwinian world, pictures of an idealized, benevolent, teleological, ethical nature seem quaint and naive, and I think they would appear so now even if there had never been a Charles Darwin or a theory of evolution to destroy their simple anthropocentric view. The reflexive approach shapes seeing too directly to the poet's own needs and desires, framing the details of the subject to fit the themes and issues the poet presupposes, resolving in a self-confirming closed circuit. Lovely lines and vivid images are not rare in nineteenth-century American nature poems, but frequently their observation of nature is tautology and their reassurance meaningless, other than to say to us "this is how I can feel about using these natural details to exemplify my ideas."

Take Emerson's poem "The Rhodora" as an example of this particular relationship of perception, poet, and poem, keeping in mind the differences of his culture and ours.

The Rhodora
On Being Asked, Whence Is the Flower?

In May, when sea-winds pierced our solitudes,
I found the fresh Rhodora in the woods,
Spreading its leafless blooms in a damp nook,
To please the desert and the sluggish brook.
The purple petals, fallen in the pool,
Made the black water with their beauty gay;
Here might the red-bird come his plumes to cool,
And court the flower that cheapens his array.
Rhodora! if the sages ask thee why
This charm is wasted on the earth and sky,
Tell them, dear, that if eyes were made for seeing,
Then Beauty is its own excuse for being:
Why thou wert there, O rival of the rose!
I never thought to ask, I never knew;

But, in my simple ignorance, suppose
The self-same Power that brought me there brought you.[3]

Presumably a poem about a particular Rhodora and its place in the scheme of things, its real signification concerns idealized personal emotions and the kind of comfort an immersion in them can bring. The Rhodora itself is no sooner introduced when (in line four) it is imbued with the poet's own emotions, his senses of purpose and beauty. From that point on the descriptive portion of the poem (which lasts only through the next quatrain —this sonnet seems in a rush to get to its philosophical interpretation by the midway point) is dominantly reflexive. Not only does anthropomorphized water have its beauty made gay, but the red-bird arrives to find refreshment in this spot (like the poet coming upon the Rhodora) and (like the poet writing his poem) to court the flower with a somewhat less beautiful "array." Nineteenth-century naturalists and nature-observers would not be so naive as to accept this as literally descriptive of bird-motivation and bird-behavior, and the conventions of the genre (poetic license?) and the reassuring resonance of the climactic aphorisms in lines 11–12 and 16 would have acted to exempt the statement from naturalistic cavils.

The philosophical reassurance grows quite comfortably out of the soft, self-projective thinking. The process is inevitable, but only because the aesthetic-religious philosophy was there in the poet's mind dominating his thought from the very beginning; he simply projected beauty and purpose into the flower, bird, and brook as part of the act of perception that the poem purportedly represents. The poem is disingenuous insofar as it implies any searching or inductiveness or new understanding of the world; it invests nearly its whole significance in reflexive thought that is utterly naive and conventional, trusting in the reliability of simple concepts of perception and symbol, language and intellection.

Whatever simplifications dominated his poetic practice, Emerson did introduce some new questions and ideas about knowledge and knowing into American culture. He was not a prophetic forerunner of twentieth-century epistemology, not a premature postmodernist so much as an eccentric enthusiast of ideas with a genius for turning them every which way in a search for provoking, probing, sonorous utterance. He was instrumental, however, in projecting a new-world myth of knowledge that prepared the way for the more consistently radical knowledge destroyers who would establish that practice as a national literary tradition.

2 Walt Whitman and the World Beyond Rationalism

Perhaps indeed the efforts of the true poets, founders, religions, literatures, all ages, have been, and ever will be, our time and times to come, essentially the same—to bring people back from their persistent strayings and sickly abstractions, to the costless average, divine original concrete. —Walt Whitman, *Specimen Days**

Whitman's conception of knowledge, its uses and its destruction, was similar to Emerson's. Many of its features were borrowed or were codiscovered out of the same assumptions and context of impulses. A principal difference, however, is in the far greater capacity Whitman shows in his works to submit to that multifarious "costless average, divine original concrete," to risk an encounter with chaos, with perceptual uninterpretability. Emerson's habit of explicitly and intellectually interpreting every detail seems to have been one of the habits Whitman felt ought to be broken, and this attitude makes Whitman more significant as a forerunner to some of our century's most venturesome writers.

We begin a study of Whitman's knowledge-myth with caveats about consistency similar to those we had to recognize in considering Emerson: Whitman too was not a consistent thinker, and he had no consistent method of observing his world and making meaning out of his experience. He had a general program, to be sure, but it is so vast and so inclusive of manifold ideas and approaches that to explain its destructions and reconstructions one needs to select and separate, winnow and systematize—to fashion, in fact, an artificial consistency. One even needs to interpret Whitman's words—often vague, idiosyncratic, slapdash utterances—with one's own coherent Whitman myth in mind, or some of them can mean anything or nothing. Another caveat: although Whitman speaks at times like a nominalist, naturalist, or phenomenalist, one must keep steadily in mind that theism is a fixed star of his firmament. For him the highest benefit of literature is the sense it can give us of "its development, from the eternal bases, and the fit expression, of absolute Conscience, moral soundness, Justice."**

---

*Walt Whitman, *Complete Poetry and Collected Prose*, sel. and intro. Justin Kaplan (Library of America, 1982), 926. Parenthetical page numbers in this chapter refer to this volume.
***Democratic Vistas*, 982. The deconstructionist view of Whitman in Paul A. Bové's

Whitman's range of literary techniques was broad and original —beyond that of any of his contemporaries—but he was nevertheless capable of a good many conventionally sentimental, trite, and bombastic poetic effects, too, and he set a good deal of stock in some of them. Thus his works, even his best, are odd mixtures of original and trite elements, just as they are mixtures of sensitivity and caricature, of candor and fakery, of great subtlety and mightily proclaimed obviousness. But it is the techniques he developed relative to the destruction and reconstitution of knowledge that make the best case for his originality and for his influence on twentieth-century literature.

Whitman rebelled against the knowledge he inherited because he felt that, in the first place, it was backward-oriented, enshrining European philosophies and art, and, in embodying essentially feudal assumptions about the individual and society, it was likely to make people (citizens all) deferential toward civil and intellectual authority. Furthermore, the literature inspired by that knowledge from the past was largely out of contact with the real present—it belittled, in fact, the significance of the acts and experiences of living Americans. In the second place, the prevailing knowledge was stiflingly cerebral, rationalistic, static in its vision of life. Not that intellectual, rational approaches in themselves were dead wrong (he would generally admit), but the exclusiveness they maintained over knowing was wrong; there was much more to reality than they could access.

"We see that almost everything that has been written, sung, or stated, of old," he asserts in *Democratic Vistas*, "with reference to humanity under the feudal and oriental institutes, religions, and for other lands, needs to be re-written, re-sung, re-stated, in terms consistent with the institution of these States, and to come in range and obedient uniformity with them" (993). At times he shows a level-headed patience about urging this process, as in the 1855 Preface to *Leaves of Grass* where he states "America does not repel the past or what it has produced under its forms or amid other politics or the idea of castes or the old religions . . . [America] accepts the lesson with calmness . . . perceives that the corpse is slowly borne from the eating and sleeping rooms of the house . . . that it was fittest for its days" (5); and he even envisions the greatest poet of the new age saying to the past "Rise and walk before me that I may realize you" (13). At other times the need for destruction seems more urgent; in *An*

Deconstructive Poetics (Columbia University Press, 1980) interestingly and quite appropriately presents the absolutist strain in Whitman's work as a consistent limit to his premodernist, deconstructionist tendencies.

American Primer, during an exhortation concerning education in classical mythology, he states: "Because, what is America for?—To commemorate the old myths and the gods?—To repeat the Mediterranean here? Or the uses and growths of Europe here?—No;—(Na-o-o) but to destroy all those from the purposes of the earth, and to erect a new earth in their place."[1] The same recommendation is made in section 41 of "Song of Myself," in which he presents the gods of other lands and other times, from Kronos through Buddah to Mexitiki, as being of less consequence than the ordinary American citizen—

> Discovering as much or more in a framer framing a house,
> Putting higher claims for him there with his roll'd-up sleeves driving
> the mallet and chisel . . .
> Lads ahold of fire-engines and hook-and-ladder ropes no less to me
> than the gods of the antique wars, . . .
> . . . the mechanic's wife with her babe at her nipple interceding for
> every person born.
> (233–234)

As part of the same campaign Whitman urges that "the United States themselves are essentially the greatest poem" (5) and charges the poet to "flood himself with the immediate age as with vast oceanic tides" (23). In reflecting on the sources of his own poetic inspiration he was wont to discover the same message, as here in *Autumn Rivulets*:

> I WAS looking for a long while for Intentions,
> For a clew to the history of the past for myself, and for these chants
> —and now I have found it,
> It is not in those paged fables in the libraries, (them I neither accept
> or reject,)
> It is no more in the legends than in all else,
> It is in the present—it is this earth to-day.
> (512)

Whitman attacked what he saw as the tendency of the prevailing rationalistic knowledge to influence literature in the direction of conventionality, false consistency, and simplistic closure. He clearly felt that great literature should unsettle its readers. They should feel challenged to doubt authority and received opinion, to think for themselves, and to discover new ways of doing the thinking. The writer should not assume the role of spokesperson and representative of authority, not present readers with the standard rationalistic simplifications as an authentic picture of reality:

"a heroic person walks at his ease through and out of that custom or precedent or authority that suits him not. . . . The cleanest expression is that which finds no sphere worthy of itself and makes one" (14), he insisted, and claimed that when the writer abandoned the role of pedagogue, of telling the readers how and what to think, "that were to make a nation of supple and athletic minds, well-train'd, intuitive, used to depend on themselves, and not on a few coteries of writers" (983). "A great poem is no finish to a man or woman but rather a beginning."[2]

As Whitman saw it, the cerebral quality of conventional knowing closes one off from the fuller, more substantial messages of things; its exclusively rational quality belies the real relationships of things; and its abstractive, idealizing, time-denying tendencies obscure the vivid flow of actuality. The attitude in "When I Heard the Learn'd Astronomer" is typical: his speaker has listened to the astronomer's lecture, with its proofs and figures, charts and diagrams and "much applause," but

> How soon unaccountable I became tired and sick,
> Till rising and gliding out I wandered off by myself,
> In the mystical moist night-air, and from time to time,
> Look'd up in perfect silence at the stars.
> (410)

Rationalistic knowledge, which is so methodical, has such authority, and is so widely appreciated, is simply not complete enough or essential enough to keep his model persona interested; he must go out and know the stars in his own superrational way. (Science might, as he says in other contexts, contribute significantly to our understanding; however, it also can narrow our perceptions and divert our inquiry away from the fullest knowing.)

"Present literature," Whitman charged in *Democratic Vistas*, "while magnificently fulfilling certain popular demands, with plenteous knowledge and verbal smartness, is profoundly sophisticated, insane, and its very joy is morbid. It needs tally [sic] and express Nature, and the spirit of Nature, and to know and obey the standards" (983). Their "plenteous knowledge" brought the writers of his day nowhere near "the spirit of Nature."

Whitman's effort to approach the spirit of Nature involved his reconstructing knowledge along the lines of his own poetic process. His most prominent and explicit insights concerned concreteness, abstraction, epiphany, and the intricate and mysterious relationship of the self to the other. Less obvious though still important were his insights about process, spontaneity, and idiom.

The "divine original concrete" is the basis of Whitman's concept of knowing. Typically in his poetry the vivid force of concrete description supercedes generalized knowledge and transcends judgmental knowledge —his repesentations of teamster and runaway slave, of matron and prostitute, effectively put aside our social and moral categories through the power of their particularity. Similarly, our cerebral knowledge is often confounded in a tumult of physical, sexual imagery. The characteristic accumulation and savoring of images and details in his poems, the multitude of lists, descriptions, and vignettes, are all signs of his revision of knowledge along anti-abstractionist lines. Verisimilitude often becomes a prime objective of his technique; details must be vivid and true:

> The artillery, the silent cannons bright as gold, drawn along, rumble
>   lightly over the stones.
>
> (417)
>
> From the stump of the arm, the amputated hand,
> I undo the clotted lint, remove the slough, wash off the matter and
>   blood,
> Back on his pillow the soldier bends with curv'd neck and side-
>   falling head,
> His eyes are closed, his face is pale, he dares not look on the bloody
>   stump,
> And has not yet look'd on it.
>
> (444)

Many times, however, his attempts to elicit an unconventional contemplation of the concrete actual involve his simply saying the names of things, of places, of activities, events, or persons. Frequently in such passages he is not merely using the designative function of the naming-word —not even, I would maintain, merely the designation-with-connotations. He is attempting a kind of object-evocation, in which the independent *otherness* of the object is his main concern—and additionally, perhaps, some more deeply infused quality. Take, for example, this meditation (from *Specimen Days*):

> Here is one of my favorites now before me, a fine yellow poplar, quite straight, perhaps 90 feet high, and four thick at the butt. How strong, vital, enduring! how dumbly eloquent! What suggestions of imperturbability and *being*, as against the human trait of mere *seeming*. Then the qualities, almost emotional, palpably artistic, heroic, of a tree; so innocent and harmless, yet so savage. It *is*, yet says nothing. . . .

One lesson from affiliating a tree—perhaps the greatest moral lesson anyhow from earth, rocks, animals, is that same lesson of
inherency, of *what is*, without the least regard to what the looker on
(the critic) supposes or says, or whether he likes or dislikes. (789–790)

In this spontaneous impression we see Whitman apparently groping, on
the spur of the moment, for a way to describe the otherness of the tree
—reflexively attributing to it various qualities (emotional, artistic, heroic)
in an attempt to articulate its greater significance, and then in effect canceling all describability by acknowledging the tree principally as *being*, as
inherency, as *what is*.

Inherency can't be directly accessed by description or explanation
because language itself is a mediating factor. One can only point to the
inherency, invoke it with its name, and let it come across in itself. "*Names
are magic,—*" he says in *An American Primer*, "One word can pour such a
flood through the soul."[3] One thinks of the passages naming the parts of
the body in "I Sing the Body Electric" and the regions of the country in
"Starting from Paumanok" as evocations of this sort; even the chanted
sounds of the naming-words are a fascination, an invitation to contem-
plate these things in their uniquenesses:

> Upper-arm, armpit, elbow-socket, lower-arm, arm-sinews, arm-
>   bones,
> Wrist and wrist-joints, hand, palm, knuckles, thumb, forefinger,
>   finger-joints, finger-nails,
> Broad breast-front, curling hair of the breast, breast-bone, breast-side.
> (257)

Whitman conceived of things-in-their-actuality as being ultimately
beyond any conceptualization or linguistic representation. In his technique of object-evocation the poet names the thing or the act, and it conveys its own inherent significance. Thus in "From Pent-Up Aching Rivers" he refers to "the act-poems of eyes, hand, hips and bosoms" and in
"A Song of the Rolling Earth" he says,

> Were you thinking that those were the words, those upright lines?
>   those curves, angles, dots?
> No, those are not the words, the substantial words are in the ground
>   and sea,
> They are in the air, they are in you. . . .
> Human bodies are words, myriads of words. . . .
> Air, soil, water, fire—those are words. . . .

> The truths of the earth continually wait, they are not so conceal'd
> either,
> They are calm, subtle, untransmissible by print,
> They are imbued through all things conveying themselves willingly.
> (362–364)

The things of this world, the acts and processes of this world, reveal their own inherency; the poet, dwelling in a state of continual wonder, continual epiphany ("WHY, who makes much of a miracle?/As to me I know of nothing else but miracles" [513]), by naming the things lets their revelation shine through. And such revelation is in no way inferior to the grand myths of the past: "As if the beauty and sacredness of the demonstrable must fall behind that of the mythical!" (6). As Whitman sees it, denotation becomes revelation through the magic evocative power of the inherently imperfect word.

Whitman had an abiding, absorbing interest in the ways the self relates to the other, and he had a complex set of insights into that relationship and its impact on the attempt to realize life's inherencies. He was quite sensitive to the fallibility of anthropomorphic and self-reflexive perception, while at the same time feeling that self-projection was essential to the act of knowing.

He poses the general question this way in *Specimen Days* (preparatory to launching a woolly discussion of Kant, Schelling, and Hegel): "What is the fusing explanation and tie—what the relation between the (radical, democratic) Me, the human identity of understanding, emotions, spirit, &c., on the one side, of and with the (conservative) Not Me, the whole of the material objective universe and laws, with what is behind them in time and space, on the other side?" (175). The natural world rejects humankind's simple anthropomorphism, he felt, as he indicates here in "A Song of the Rolling Earth":

> The earth does not argue,
> Is not pathetic, has no arrangements,
> Does not scream, haste, persuade, threaten, promise,
> Makes no discriminations, has no conceivable failures,
> Closes nothing, refuses nothing, shuts none out,
> Of all the powers, objects, states, it notifies, shuts none out.
>
> The earth does not exhibit itself nor refuse to exhibit itself.
> (364)

Another of the American archadvocates of experience, Whitman set high standards for that best type of knower, the poet: "Latent, in a great user of words, must actually be all passions, crimes, trades, animals, stars, God, sex, the past, might, space, metals, and the like—because these are the words, and he who is not these, plays with a foreign tongue, turning helplessly to dictionaries and authorities."[4] In his own work facts from anywhere, skills or perspectives from anywhere, the lingo of any profession, the sound or feel of any activity, can come into a poem and create new accesses, fill in essential parts of the enormous picture. One of his personae (as we noticed earlier) walks out on the learned astronomer into a larger realm of experience, but another sings

> Hurrah for positive science! long live exact demonstration! . . .
> This is the geologist, this works with the scalpel, and this is a
>   mathematician.
>
> Gentlemen, to you the first honors always!
> Your facts are useful, and yet they are not my dwelling,
> I but enter by them to an area of my dwelling.*

In the same spirit he appropriated techniques and structural forms from music, concepts from politics, perspectives from painting and sculpture, intuitions from mystic religions; his eclectic, omnivorous, impromptu approach to poetic technique shows what a multiplicitous, unpreprogrammed activity he thought knowing should be. In Whitman's view a poet might need any or all possible knowledge bases to give him the perspectives necessary to approach reality's inherencies.

With all experience—immediate and vicarious, emotional and intellectual, subjective and objective—teeming within him, the poet needed to establish a subtle relationship with the world's details. Whitman generally presents details noninterpretively, his speaker-persona detached from them intellectually but in no other way. The great poet, he says, "judges not as the judge judges but as the sun falling around a helpless thing" (9) and in a language that "seldomer tells a thing than suggests or necessitates it" (999). In the last half of "Sparkles from the Wheel," a city scene

---

*"Song of Myself," *Complete Poetry*, 210. Robert J. Scholnick has recently demonstrated an extensive connection between Whitman and the science of his day, a connection resulting not only in Whitman's acknowledgment of science's legitimacy, but in his accommodation of its general vision in his representation of the monistic, dynamic, interactive qualities of the universe and of his persona as well. See "'The Password Primeval': Whitman's Use of Science in 'Song of Myself,'" *Studies in the American Renaissance* (1986), 385–425.

focused on an itinerant curbside knife-grinder, he demonstrates this relationship between scene, observer, and interpretation:

> The scene and all its belongings, how they seize and affect me,
> The sad sharp-chinn'd old man with worn clothes and broad
>   shoulder-band of leather,
> Myself effusing and fluid, a phantom curiously floating, now here
>   absorb'd and arrested,
> The group, (an unminded point set in a vast surrounding,)
> The attentive, quiet children, the loud, proud, restive base of the
>   streets,
> The low hoarse purr of the whirling stone, the light-press'd blade,
> Diffusing, dropping, sideways-darting, in tiny showers of gold,
> Sparkles from the wheel.
> (514–515)

In the presence of the scene's inherency the knower-poet must ignore all culturally induced tendencies to explain or interpret, but he needs an observer-self "effusing" throughout the scene. Thus what the reader witnesses is not ersatz-objectivity, not slice-of-life realism, but a word-version of an event in the process of being experienced. Depiction, like perception, involves both fact and imagination. The inherency of things that shines through Whitman's poems is often times transmitted through his poet-persona.

Perception was an active, participatory, self-projective process for Whitman, and he was persistent, resourceful, and subtle in finding ways to locate the persona of the perceiving self within his poems. Thus, Whitman's practice knowingly avows a kind of relativity in approaches to knowing that Emerson's theories glimpse only in their most radical moments. "Song of Myself" is of course the most prominent (and most commented upon) collection of his self-projective accounts of perception. The work itself is a celebration not only of heterogeneous, self-revealing reality, but also of a participating, observing, celebrating persona who ranges in relationship to his subject from the imaginative reteller of the story of John Paul Jones (227–229), to the reportorial observer who notes how "the little one sleeps in its cradle" and "the suicide sprawls on the bloody floor of the bedroom" (195), to the vivid empathizer for whom "agonies are one of my changes of garments, . . . I am the mash'd fireman with breast-bone broken. . . . I lie in the night air in my red shirt, the pervading hush is for my sake" (225).

For Whitman knowing involves a reciprocity, an intermerging of external presence and subjective sentience. Like Emerson he believed that the imagination was instrumental and even necessary in "animating" nature and, reciprocally, that nature could and did nourish the imagination. On the individual imagination's animating power, he said:

> Whatever may have been the case in years gone by, the true use for the imaginative faculty of modern times is to give ultimate vivification to facts, to science, and to common lives, endowing them with the glows and glories and final illustriousness which belong to every real thing, and to real things only. Without that ultimate vivification —which the poet or other artist alone can give—reality would seem incomplete, and science, democracy, and life itself, finally in vain.[5]

It is the epistemological equivalent of a love affair, this reciprocity of imagination and reality, and it seems even more so when accompanied (as it often is) by the idea of the yearning for direct contact of the sentient self and the actual:

> Houses and rooms are full of perfumes, the shelves are crowded
>   with perfumes,
> I breathe the fragrance myself and know it and like it,
> The distillation would intoxicate me also, but I shall not let it.
> The atmosphere is not a perfume, it has no taste of the distillation,
>   it is odorless,
> It is for my mouth forever, I am in love with it,
> I will go to the bank by the wood and become undisguised and
>   naked,
> I am mad for it to be in contact with me.
> (188–189)

The non-mental avenues of knowing, the reciprocity of self and other, and the yearning for absolute contact—these three epistemological motifs come together in much of Whitman's sexual imagery. Faced with the inadequacy of conventional systems of knowledge, he seems to have seized on the sexual paradigm as a model for many aspects of the mysterious act of knowing.

Spontaneity seemed to Whitman the seal of genuineness in the self-other relationship. Even more so than Emerson, Whitman wanted the knower/creator to be someone who "throws the reins on the horse's neck," who submits to the cosmic/instinctive tide. Thus while his lists and his extended seria of parallel instances function as strings of individual denotative epiphanies and as revelations of collective, conglomerated inherency, their structure is also a flow, a spontaneity of sheer accumulation. A Whitman list is generally guided only by association, with no categories of exclusion, hierarchy, priority or such. Its lack of logic constitutes a kind of destruction of knowledge, its spontaneity a kind of true-to-life vitality. It seems randomly inclusive and is meant to sound like improvised composition—not a set piece, but a newly discovered path—the conventions of composition being overthrown in this moment-to-moment accretion:

> In Tennessee and Kentucky slaves busy in the coalings, at the forge,
>   by the furnace-blaze, or at the corn-shucking,
> In Virginia, the planter's son returning after a long absence, joyfully
>   welcom'd and kiss'd by the aged mulatto nurse,
> On rivers boatmen safely moor'd at nightfall in their boats under
>   shelter of high banks,
> Some of the younger men dance to the sound of the banjo or fiddle,
>   others sit on the gunwale smoking and talking;
> Late in the afternoon the mocking-bird, the American mimic, singing
>   in the Great Dismal Swamp,
> There are the greenish waters, the resinous odor, the plenteous
>   moss, the cypress-tree, and the juniper-tree;
> Northward, young men of Mannhatta, the target company from an
>   excursion returning home at evening, the musket-muzzles all bear
>   bunches of flowers presented by women;
> Children at play, or on his father's lap a young boy fallen asleep,
>   (how his lips move! how he smiles in his sleep!)
> The scout riding on horseback over the plains west of the Missis-
>   sippi, he ascends a knoll and sweeps his eyes around;
> (320–321)

"Always the free range and diversity—always the continent of Democracy," Whitman had said as part of the prologue to this portion of "Our Old Feuillage," prefiguring its conglomeration and liberating its free associative flow from any intermediating intellectual categories.

Like all destroyers of knowledge, Whitman battled against the conventions of language and the limitations of thought inherent in those conventions. Matthiessen's *American Renaissance* reveals a good deal about Whitman as a language-innovator, devoting a substantial portion of its treatment of him to that subject, and especially citing his shifting among levels of diction, his substitution of parts of speech, his affinities for slang, for onomatopoeia and for foreign borrowings, and his coinages. There is no need to reproduce such a demonstration here; we need only under-score the liberating and enriching effects of such practices and acknowl-edge, with Matthiessen, the excesses and pointless barbarisms to which Whitman's linguistic liberation often led.

Whitman's cadences and syntaxes (also much commented on in the scholarship) can be seen for our purposes both as an assault on those kinds of thinking that are confined by a subject-verb-object system of logic and as an increment of spontaneity. Flux, richly interconnected diversity, and continuous epiphany are far more appropriately represented in dis-tended, accumulative structures such as Whitman gives us than in more conventional modes. In breaking down habitual syntactical relationships, Whitman is able to suggest new ideas about how things connect, how they reveal themselves to us, and where we stand in relation to them and to each other. As one example, his extended series of syntactically equiva-lent clauses is indeed a fitting grammar of democracy.

Despite the variety of techniques Whitman developed for destroying knowledge and developing new pathways of knowing, his thought was deeply imbued with an Emersonian Platonism that located the ultimate reality in a transcendental realm beyond human experience. The inheren-cies of all things and all people were coherent, he believed, unified in a single purposeful scheme which ought to be the objective of inquiry and imagination. Experiential details should be used primarily to inquire beyond experience, he insists in *Democratic Vistas*: "the elevating and ethe-realizing ideas of the unknown and of unreality must be brought forward with authority, as they are the legitimate heirs of the known, and of real-ity, and at least as great as their parents" (985). In another mood, in "To Think of Time," it seems to him that without belief in ultimate essence we are lost in a world of mutable, decaying particulars; the transcendental is our only hedge against death:

> I have dream'd that the purpose and essence of the known life, the
>   transient,
> Is to form and decide identity for the unknown life, the permanent.
>
> If it all came but to ashes of dung,
> If maggots and rats ended us, then Alarum! for we are betray'd,
> Then indeed suspicion of death.
> (556)

At times Whitman could be quite pessimistic about our possibility of knowing and representing this ultimate level—as in "As I Ebb'd with the

Ocean of Life," where his deeper self, "the real Me," confronts his persona amidst the

> chaff, straw, splinters of wood, weeds, and the sea-gluten. . . .
> Pointing in silence to these songs, and then to the sand beneath. . . .
> I perceive I have not really understood any thing, not a single object,
>   and that no man ever can.
> (395)

Similarly, in "Out of the Cradle Endlessly Rocking," as the only answer to the romantic question-beyond-experience, the sea "Lisp'd to me the low and delicious word death" (393).

In other frames of mind, no less self-projective, the Whitman persona could receive a message as reassuring as these were not. I quote the whole of a rather long meditation here (from *Specimen Days*) because it shows the process of thought that takes Whitman from experience to transcendence. Especially notable are the concrete precision of the observation (an empirical, virtually unadorned encounter with the night's otherness), the unpredisposed quality of the experience (its events surprise him, he expected a storm and not a perfect night), and the sudden lift — without intermediate steps or stages — to the vastest of epiphanies. It is a transitionless leap from concrete night to absolute ineffable, the only two levels on which Whitman's mind found significance.

> July 22d, 1878 —
> Living down in the country again. A wonderful conjunction of all that goes to make those sometime miracle-hours after sunset — so near and yet so far. Perfect, or nearly perfect days, I notice, are not so very uncommon; but the combinations that make perfect nights are few, even in a life time. We have one of those perfections to-night. Sunset left things pretty clear; the larger stars were visible soon as the shades allow'd. A while after 8, three or four great black clouds suddenly rose, seemingly from different points, and sweeping with broad swirls of wind but no thunder, underspread the orbs from view everywhere, and indicated a violent heat-storm. But without storm, clouds, blackness and all, sped and vanish'd as suddenly as they had risen; and from a little after 9 till 11 the atmosphere and the whole show above were in that state of exceptional clearness and glory just alluded to. In the northwest turned the Great Dipper with its pointers round the Cynosure. A little south of east the constellation of the Scorpion was fully up, with red Antares glowing in its neck; while

dominating, majestic Jupiter swam, an hour and a half risen, in the east—(no moon till after 11). A large part of the sky seem'd just laid in great splashes of phosphorus. You could look deeper in, farther through, than usual; the orbs thick as heads of wheat in a field. Not that there was any special brilliancy either—nothing near as sharp as I have seen of keen winter nights, but a curious general luminousness throughout to sight, sense, and soul. The latter had much to do with it. (I am convinced there are hours of Nature, especially of the atmosphere, mornings and evenings, address'd to the soul. Night transcends, for that purpose, what the proudest day can do.) Now, indeed, if never before, the heavens declared the glory of God. It was to the full the sky of the Bible, of Arabia, of the prophets, and of the oldest poems. There, in abstraction and stillness, (I had gone off by myself to absorb the scene, to have the spell unbroken,) the copiousness, the removedness, vitality, loose-clear-crowdedness, of that stellar concave spreading overhead, softly absorb'd into me, rising so free, interminably high, stretching east, west, north, south—and I, though but a point in the centre below, embodying all.

As if for the first time, indeed, creation noiselessly sank into and through me its placid and untellable lesson, beyond—O, so infinitely beyond!—anything from art, books, sermons, or from science, old or new. The spirit's hour—religion's hour—the visible suggestion of God in space and time—now once definitely indicated, if never again. The untold pointed at—the heavens all paved with it. The Milky Way, as if some superhuman symphony, some ode of universal vagueness, disdaining syllable and sound—a flashing glance of Deity, address'd to the soul. All silently—the indescribable night and stars —far off and silently. (825–826)

Observing intently, experiencing fully, and avoiding the categories of intellection and rationalization (the categories that make up our heritage of knowledge and prevent our apprehension of the real), that is what gives us whatever access we can have to the ultimate grand inherency. And the existence of that unifying inherency is what ensures our connection with the real world, our real selves, and the real selves of others. Ultimate knowledge is faith, and relativism is, after all, only a matter of different individual situations and approaches.

There is no question but that Whitman took Emerson's destruction of knowledge farther and deeper. He was far more willing and eager to suspend categorization of experience, to delay or even forestall interpretation in his works, and to leave the making of the deep, complete picture to the reader. He went much farther too in destroying the myth of the objectivity of knowing, showing the individual sentient self—active, projective, empathetic—as the locus of all significance. The middle range of abstractions and generalizations (such as were the repository of most knowledge) he shunned and repudiated. He thoroughly abandoned unified systems of thought (like Emerson) in the conviction that knowing is a fluid, manifold endeavor. He thought of knowing as democratic, nonauthoritarian, spontaneous. Still, he had the transcendentalist's faith in ultimate purpose and in the unanimity of truth: the ultimate significance of things is out there in those things and will be discovered to be an absolute unity by anyone who inquires and is truly and freshly attentive. The knower-artist is protected from misconception, delusion, and simple reflexiveness by his *candor*, Whitman thought: be true-to-self and true-to-experience and you will be true-to-nature. And true-to-nature is the highest art; Whitman said it in his 1855 Preface in a way that echoes down through American literary theory to the present: "to speak in literature with the perfect rectitude and insousciance of the movements of animals, and the unimpeachableness of the sentiment of trees in the woods and grass by the roadside, is the flawless triumph of art" (13).

3   Herman Melville and the Failure of Higher Truth

I have written a wicked book, and feel spotless as the lamb.
—Letter to Hawthorne about *Moby-Dick*

It was Herman Melville and Emily Dickinson who took the destruction of knowledge beyond Whitman's sticking point of a belief in the objective uniformity of higher truth. Many of their works are aimed at giving glimpses of a universe without an ascertainable higher order, a universe in which death and circumstance are imposingly actual, but in which an individual, self-biased metaphor system is the only instrument for comprehending and coping. They destroyed not merely some specific and precious concepts, conventional sources of reassurance and affirmation, but all hope of consensus on the deepest questions of the human soul. Their aggressive conscientiousness, their purity in the pursuit of truth and the practice of their art, put them on the path to artistic and social isolation, under a cloud of solipsism and psychic delusion. However spotless-as-the-lamb Melville felt in the first flush of Hawthorne's favorable reaction to *Moby-Dick*, he would learn to feel a lot worse in time. Dickinson, with a Higginson rather than a Hawthorne to whom to show her works, never seems to have felt very confident about the reactions the more challenging of them might draw.

Broadly speaking, Melville's concept of knowledge had two main aspects: a deep and straightforward respect for specific, factual, practical knowledge, and a complex fascination-distrust for more general and speculative knowledge—for the psychology, philosophy, and theology of his day. Practical knowledge was always very real for Melville—that was one of the bases of his assaults on knowledge of the other kind. One might suspect Emerson (and even Whitman at times) of a somewhat theoretical allegiance to practical fact, but for Melville it is always evident that the operation of things, their physical characteristics, behavior, and usages are subjects of real and primary concern. On the higher level of generality, however, the whole system of knowledge failed him. Questions of motive, morality, meaning, and purpose he saw as evoking the biases and limitations of the culture and the (all too) human mind, and nothing more.

Melville seems to have used his art to confront his age's religio-philo-sophical concepts with their own inadequacies, to break their claim on credence, cancel the solutions and reassurances they too facilely provided.

The focus of his work shifted in the course of his career from the things he knew and could trust to the things he deeply doubted but could not help wondering about. His early novels—*Redburn, Typee, White-Jacket*—are nearly documentaries about how it was to be there, concretely and practically—on a first Atlantic crossing, on a South Seas isle, on a man-of-war. Ships and oceans, cities and mountains and valleys are reliably and physically knowable, and knowledge of the craft of seamanship, of the layout of Liverpool, of the practices and customs in a native village or aboard a man-of-war is well worth the considerable effort to acquire. "The object of this work is to give some idea of the interior life in a man-of-war," Melville wrote in his preface to the first English edition of *White-Jacket*,[1] and the burden of the work is indeed the information it conveys—about the construction, equipment, personnel, routines, and regulations aboard the man-of-war, from the casual habitat the tops provide ("quite spacious and cosy")[2] to the horrendous practice of "flogging through the fleet." For certain broader purposes, such as comprehending the man-of-war as a whole, Melville employed a metaphoric act of imagination—it's "a city afloat," "a lofty, walled, and garrisoned town, like Quebeck," "a three-story house in a suspicious part of the town, with a basement of indefinite depth, and ugly-looking fellows gazing out at the windows"[3]—but there is no creative indefiniteness about the ship's specific functions or usages, at least once one has learned the ropes.

Early or late in his career, Melville often developed the theme of the ironic contrast between the deep intricacy of the actual and the simple provinciality of the conceptual. In reading his works we are persistently put in mind of the fallibility of our knowledge, the weakness of our facul-ties of knowing, and the pettiness of our preconceptions. In simplest form, most characteristically in his early works, characters have woefully inade-quate knowledge to deal with the situations they encounter. They have only their culture's shallow nonsense to use in interpreting experience: the myth about the Typees serves a runaway sailor in the Marquesas no better than preconceptions about aristocratic Spanish captains will serve Captain Delano aboard the San Dominick, or Redburn's mantelpiece frig-ate, antique Liverpool guidebook, and his mother's teachings will serve him on his first voyage. The naïveté of knowledge-before-experience, whether comical or near-woeful in its results, seems to be a condition of human existence, but a correctable one for a person able to learn. More characteristically in his later works, the problem is no mere matter of correcting some anticipatory misconceptions, however; in several it is a problem that inundates the narrator as well as the characters in a realization that one doesn't know what he knows even after he's had the experience. As Ishmael says of the whale,

> Dissect him how I may, then, I go but skin deep; I know him not, and never will. But if I know not even the tail of this whale, how understand his head? much more, how comprehend his face, when face he has none? Thou shalt see my back parts, my tail, he seems to say, but my face shall not be seen. But I cannot completely make out his back parts; and hint what he will about his face, I say again he has no face.*

Here the epistemological problem gets deeper: real meaning is not just beyond previous knowledge, it is beyond understanding altogether. And when Melville's subject is human, presumably with human character and motives such as would be comprehensible in Whitman's scheme of things, our access to the actual is far less certain. It doesn't matter whether the interpreter be character or narrator, reader or author—Bartleby the scrivener stands before us all, in his own way as faceless as the whale. And the springs of Pierre's behavior are well beyond where any interpreter can go: "Deep, deep, and still deep and deeper must we go, if we would find out the heart of a man; descending into which is as descending a spiral stair in a shaft, without any end, and where that endlessness is only concealed by the spiralness of the stair, and the blackness of the shaft."** All knowledge leads back to the self, the *Pierre* narrator claims in another passage, and the self is fathomless. When Pierre mistakenly turns to books to try to get knowledge, the narrator lectures us that not even "all great works," "federated in the fancy" would teach him about life:

> He did not see, that even when thus combined, all was but one small mite, compared to the latent infiniteness and inexhaustibility in himself; that all the great books in the world are but the mutilated shadowings-forth of invisible and eternally unembodied images in the soul; so that they are but the mirrors, distortedly reflecting to us

Moby-Dick, ed. Harrison Hayford and Hershel Parker (W. W. Norton, 1967), 318. Parenthetical page numbers in discussions of this novel refer to this edition.
**Pierre, or the Ambiguities*, ed. Harrison Hayford, Hershel Parker, and G. Thomas Tanselle (Northwestern University Press and Newberry Library, 1971), 288–289. Parenthetical page numbers in discussions of this novel refer to this edition.

our own things; and never mind what the mirror may be, if we would
see the object, we must look at the object itself, and not at its reflection.
(284)

But where is this "object itself," where is Truth in that hall of mirrors and
shadows? Could one conceivably know it undistortedly if he knew himself and subtracted that factor from the remainder? But knowing the self
is the worst of the problems: "Appalling is the soul of a man! Better might
one be pushed off into the material spaces beyond the uttermost orbit of
our sun, than once feel himself fairly afloat in himself!" (284). Granted
the possibility that Melville probably meant to be determinedly, melodra-
matically obfuscating in *Pierre*—still, a question once asked can't be un-
asked, and he clearly had moments when he could suggest that not even
the fixed perspective of the self could be established. He warns Hawthorne in the same letter in which he gloats over having written a wicked
book, "This is a long letter, but you are not at all bound to answer it.
Possibly, if you do answer it, and direct it to Herman Melville, you will
missend it—for the very fingers that now guide this pen are not precisely
the same that just took it up and put it on this paper. Lord, when shall we
be done changing?"[4] In the farthest reaches of his destruction of knowledge, then, Melville saw the would-be knower of general truth as caught
between unresolvable uncertainty and inescapable reflexiveness—between
a shadow and a mirror.

Three of his novels best represent his attack on the linguistic order of
the world and the possibility of higher truth—*Moby-Dick*, *Pierre*, and *The
Confidence-Man*—and each of the three is a strikingly original work in its
own right, with a unique approach to humankind's epistemological predicament. *Moby-Dick* is the broadest, the richest, and by far the most successful, and it uses a great variety of techniques to demonstrate and insin-
uate the fallibility and relativity of general knowledge. *Pierre* is more
direct and single-minded about exposing the ambiguity, arbitrariness,
and harmfulness of what is commonly taken to be wisdom. *The Confidence-Man* is the least explicit of the three, a complex set of narrative
screens which tacitly constitute a kind of epistemological parable of lost
bearings.

As epistemological myth, *Moby-Dick* is a symphony of themes,
motifs, and voices, and its ground-bass is factual accuracy. Whatever
difficulties narrator Ishmael senses in the interpretation of natural symbols, his passion for getting the measurable, verifiable facts right is undeniable:

In length, the Sperm Whale's skeleton at Tranque measured seventy-two feet; so that when fully invested and extended in life, he must have been ninety feet long; for in the whale, the skeleton loses about one fifth in length compared with the living body. Of this seventy-two feet, his skull and jaw comprised some twenty feet, leaving some fifty feet of plain back-bone. Attached to this back-bone, for something less than a third of its length, was the mighty circular basket of ribs which once enclosed his vitals. (377)

Ishmael seems to feel that whales and whaling must be understood in such commonly verifiable ways, in such predominantly literal language, for the significance of his tale to be appreciable. He is intolerant of misinformation, contemptuous of inaccurate pictures of whales that make them look like a "squash" or an "amputated sow" (227). Melville also shows Ishmael, anxious about the believability of his tale, inserting an "Affadavit" chapter to give historical evidence that whales can indeed escape with harpoons in them, that several whales have indeed become individually recognizable to whalemen, that the same whale could be battled more than once by the same sailor, and that a sperm whale can indeed intentionally sink a large ship (175–182).

Like the earlier works, *Moby-Dick* also develops the motif of the initiation into a new realm of fact and activity. As he narrates the tale, Ishmael has already been through the whole experience, and the image he projects of himself before the voyage is one of a typical novice—naive, ill-equipped, and obtuse, confident about the wrong things and alert to the wrong clues. With respect to what he is about to get into, the wisdom of his civilization has equipped him to be an ignorant man—and this is true psychologically, philosophically, and morally, not just in terms of the practical techniques of whaling. It is experience, not knowledge, that educates Ishmael.

Narrator Ishmael has come to understand the relativity and the reflexiveness of the act of knowing. He can represent in his narration the fundamental differences between individuals' perceptions, catch the nuances of difference in what people experience when they witness the same phenomenon, reveal subtly and persistently the inescapable determining element of self-projection in everything we see or know. Take, for example, a quiet moment, when Ishmael feels toward the placid ocean "a certain filial, confident, land-like feeling," regarding it as "so much flowery earth." Ishamel sees Starbuck and Stubb both looking at the same phenomenon—Starbuck reliving his own inner struggle with his faith:

"Loveliness unfathomable, as ever lover saw in his young bride's eye!—Tell me not of thy teeth-tiered sharks, and thy kidnapping cannibal ways. Let faith oust fact; let fancy oust memory; I look deep down and do believe"; and Stubb rehearsing a complacent little chant, "I am Stubb, and Stubb has his history; but here Stubb takes oaths that he has always been jolly!" (405–407). The famous chapter 99, "The Doubloon," is of course another paradigm of relativistic, reflexive perception. And the vengeful pursuit of Moby-Dick itself, which is to Ahab an assault upon "some unknown but still reasoning thing [that] puts forth the mouldings of its features from behind the unreasoning mask" of the visible, is to Starbuck simply "vengeance on a dumb brute . . . that simply smote thee from blindest instinct! Madness!" (144). As Edward H. Rosenberry pointed out in 1955, "circumstance and point of view are the only determinants with meaning. . . . On all questions of significance the prior question becomes: Seen by whom, in what mood, and in what light?"* There is no general truth in *Moby-Dick*, then, because each man's perception is his own—this is Melville's monumental blow against the naive reflexiveness of the knowledge of his day.

Melville had no faith that intellect could overcome or mitigate simple reflexiveness. He had no real acquaintance with contemporary developments in scientific methodology or with epistemology grounded in method and language—no sense that there might be a procedural discipline of intellectual discovery, as there were procedural disciplines of sailing and of whaling. The intellect for him was merely a rationalistic justifier of belief-systems, and that was a baggage he felt he needed to jettison; Ishmael says as much in drawing the lesson from the precarious trim of the Pequod with an enormous whale-head fastened to a hoist on either side:

> As before, the Pequod steeply leaned over towards the sperm whale's head, now, by the counterpoise of both heads, she regained her even keel; though sorely strained, you may well believe. So, when on one side you hoist in Locke's head, you go over that way: but now, on the other side, hoist in Kant's and you come back again; but in very poor

---

Melville and the Comic Spirit (Harvard University Press, 1955), 105. The theme of relativism in *Moby-Dick* has been very well studied in Melville scholarship, from Charles Fiedelson, Jr., *Symbolism and American Literature* (University of Chicago Press, 1953), to some excellent more recent studies like Paul Brodtkorb, Jr., *Ishmael's White World* (Yale University Press, 1965), and Robert M. Greenberg, "Cetology: Center of Multiplicity and Discord in *Moby-Dick*," *ESQ* 27:1–13.

plight. Thus, some minds for ever keep trimming boat. Oh, ye foolish! throw all these thunderheads overboard, and then you will float light and right. (277)

For Ishmael, instinct can come closer to touching ultimate reality than can intellect, as the New England colt senses a menace in the musk of a fresh buffalo robe, as the sailor likewise senses in the whiteness of the whale, "by its indefiniteness," that "it shadows forth the heartless voids and immensities of the universe" (169). And Melville, concurring with Hawthorne's anti-intellectualism in "Ethan Brand," declares, "I stand for the heart. To the dogs with the head! I had rather be a fool with a heart, than Jupiter Olympus with his head. The reason the mass of men fear God, and *at bottom dislike* Him, is because they rather distrust His heart, and fancy Him all brain like a watch."[5]

Paul Brodtkorb, Jr., makes the interesting point that *Moby-Dick*'s anti-intellectualism springs from the realization that "thought-forms, systems of analysis, deal in categories, and categories are static, while nature—that to which the categories are applied—is always in process." Thus the whole whale can never be known categorically, although direct experience can put one in actual touch with it; Brodtkorb quotes Ishmael: "only in the heart of the quickest perils; only when within the eddyings of his angry flukes; only on the profound unbounded sea, can the fully invested whale be truly and livingly found out."[6] It is Ishmael's strong commitment to experience and to instinct and his rejection of a priori philosophical categories that make him the exceptionally effective narrator that he is for these events. A humanistic bias and a relativistic approach equip him to see the conflicts between different men's worldviews, between their beliefs and their experience, and to see them nonpedantically, nonjudgmentally. He is a new kind of knower, aware of the impossibility of absolute knowledge and aware of the distortion of men's vision that comes from their self-justifying belief systems. Enough of a participant in life to have been temporarily infected with the fervor of Ahab's quest, he is yet enough of a self-observer to see what had happened to him and to understand something of the cause: "a wild, mystical, sympathetical feeling was in me; Ahab's quenchless feud seemed mine. With greedy ears I learned the history of that murderous monster against whom I and all the others had taken our oaths of violence and revenge" (155). He knows, when the fit passes, that there are many other ways of looking at the whale. "Ishmaelian truth," as Brodtkorb has pointed out, "is the truth of relativity."[7]

The contrast to Ahab's style of knowing is extreme. Ahab persists in absolutism, persists in believing in personal, anthropomorphic motivations and inherencies, and insists that others share his vision.* As closed to experience as Ishmael is open, he prefers, at least in the latter stages of the voyage, to talk with characters who speak inconsequentialities —mundane things, like the carpenter, or mad things, like Pip—into which Ahab can read his own symbolism. He is not thinking so much as talking to himself, the whole outside universe serving only as a reflector of the intricacies of his own mad a priori vision. His is the reflexive mode of thought at its extreme, the absolutism of his imagination expressed in the absolutism of his oppressive dominance over the ship's officers and men. It is his metaphysical surety that wreaks calamity on the Pequod and its men. The novel viewed in this light seems like a cultural allegory about a major shift in styles of knowing: the self-projective absolutistic style seen in the act of destroying itself in a multifarious and unknowable universe in which only the least self-involved, least presumptive, most openly democratic style is able to survive.

Ishmael, in disclaiming all absolute general knowledge, even renounces the possibility of ultimately understanding Ahab, couching his explanations as "surmises" (182–184) and admitting that "Ahab's larger, darker, deeper part remains unhinted. But vain to popularize profoundities, and all truth is profound" (161). However, he has empathy (itself ideally a kind of reverse self-projection) and a strong sense of the tragic significance of what he observes: "God help thee, old man, thy thoughts have created a creature in thee; and he whose intense thinking thus makes him a Prometheus; a vulture feeds upon that heart forever; that vulture the very creature he creates" (175). Ishmael's whole strategy and style of narration is an extended assault against absolutistic thinking, Ahab's and others' —an attempt to keep us constantly aware of the fallibility of knowledge and the vastness of the universe.

The whole world of conventional metaphysical knowledge and discourse is subverted in a narrative specifically designed to confound the canons of Truth and swamp the canons of relevance. Rational argument is

---

*Charles H. Cook, Jr., in "Ahab's 'Intolerable Allegory,'" *Boston U. Studies in English*, 1 (1955–1956), 45–52, worked out a similar contrast between an Ishmael-Melville who knows that "philosophical significance is chiefly a matter of human creativity" and an Ahab who sees the world in the terms of an "intolerable allegory"; Brodtkorb in *Ishmael's White World*, 127, notes that Ahab's "will to absolute, ultimate knowledge" contrasts with Ishmael's "compulsive mental integrity that must admit all contradictory speculation."

decided not rationally but by charisma and power. Starbuck, urged by Ahab to "the little lower layer" of understanding, finds his straightforward Christian responses baffled by the force of his captain's imagination and by the authority of his rank. But no view, however cogent or charismatic, could maintain its sway ultimately in a world in which each captain (like every individual man) is pursuing his own vision—Boomer and his surgeon Bunger drinking and enjoying life on the Samuel Enderby, Mayhew and his "Archangel" Gabriel spooking at every omen on the Jeroboam, and Gardiner on the Rachel preoccupied with the loss of his son. As compelling as Ahab's vision might be on "the little lower layer," in a broader context it simply dissipates into inconsequentiality: Ahab seems merely crazy to Captain Boomer, a blasphemer to Mayhew's Gabriel, and coldly inhuman to Captain Gardiner. A single metaphysical vision cannot be sustained across the whole ocean of human preoccupations and fates and concerns: the message had been implicit from the novel's beginning and the Sub-Sub Librarian's barrage of multifarious "Extracts."

And the multifariousness is exacerbated by the multiplicity of languages in which the novel takes place. From Queequeg's honest injun English to shipowner Bildad's scripture-spiced commercialism to Father Mapple's seastruck salvationism to the arcane technicalities of the quoted cetologists to Ahab's Shakespearian rant, the novel presents us with a linguistic bazaar, each lingo a different implicit view of the world. The "Extracts" again set the tone, heaping together the languages of memoir and scripture, technical report and drama, chronicle and song. Ishmael's narrative voice, retrospective and ironic, gives the whole a convincing framework—his past experience is the chosen presentational locus of all this multiplicity—but the rhetorical approaches, also presumably his, focus our attention extremely variously, by means of drama and poetry and every variety of expository mode. The innocent first-time reader, trying to penetrate the book's meaning, finds him/herself awash in what seems like an ocean of distracting material without adequate authorial assistance. Contemporary reviewers indeed often reacted this way: Melville's good friend Evert A. Duyckinck characterized the novel (in a really very commendatory review) as "an intellectual chowder," and George Ripley said (likewise in a basically positive review) "on this slight framework [the Ahab revenge story], the author has constructed a romance, a tragedy, a natural history, not without numerous gratuitous suggestions on psychology, ethics, and theology."[8]

We are subjected to a glut of information, significances, viewpoints, languages, and approaches in *Moby-Dick*, and the net effect, with respect to Melville's campaign against higher knowledge, is to swamp any hope of metaphysical answers in a sea of qualification and alternative possibilities. The authorial strategy of diverse inclusiveness even swamps the canons of customary relevance. The basic plot-line is clear, of course, but the multitude of details and aspects have too many potential significances; the reader is willy-nilly put in a situation in which *any* interpretation of general meaning involves a leap over a good deal of material that does not pertain, to some extent an arbitrary imposition of the reader's own sense of purpose on the novel. In a way this is of course what any reader does to any work of literature—or any observer to any real event, for that matter—but Melville's construction specifically and pointedly forces the situation on his reader as if he had a lesson to teach him or her. Hershel Parker and Harrison Hayford's ingenious anthology of criticism, *Moby-Dick as Doubloon*,[9] vividly demonstrates the extent to which generations of critics have projected their sundry personal visions into the novel.

Melville seems fascinated, as does Whitman, with the idea of the immersion of the mind in the multiplicity of the world, of the escape from concepts and categories by giving oneself over to the flux of unmediated experience. Unlike Whitman he sees alienation and great peril in the urge, and no assurance—no chance, even—of fulfillment and concord with the nature of things. But he does see a necessity and a romantic nobility in it. In Chapter 23, "The Lee Shore," he describes the Pequod running in a winter storm away from the shore—that place of comfort and safety that would (paradoxically) wreck the ship in the storm—and the ship is being steered by a sailor named Bulkington, who earlier had no sooner landed safely from one dangerous voyage than he unexplainably embarked on another. For both the sailor and the ship, the only salvation is in breasting the perils of the howling ocean, and Melville makes psychological and epistemological application of this symbol by asking:

> Know ye, now, Bulkington? Glimpses do ye seem to see of that mortally intolerable truth; that all deep, earnest thinking is but the intrepid effort of the soul to keep the open independence of her sea; while the wildest winds of heaven and earth conspire to cast her on the treacherous, slavish shore?
>
> But as in landlessness alone resides the highest truth, shoreless, indefinite as God—so, better is it to perish in that howling infinite, than be ingloriously dashed upon the lee, even if that were safety: For worm-like, then, oh! who would craven crawl to land! Terrors of the terrible! is all this agony so vain? Take heart, take heart, O

Bulkington! Bear thee grimly, demigod! Up from the spray of thy ocean-perishing—straight up, leaps thy apotheosis! (97–98)

There is self-dramatization of the author of *Moby-Dick* here, and an urging of the reader toward an adventure away from shore-categories and knowledge-haven. The novel's unassimilated amplitude also inclines the reader that way.

So too does the author's use of the madness of characters to reveal flashes of truth. Melville saw the technique as basically Shakespearian and one for which he regarded the works of Hawthorne as especially profound:

Now it is that blackness in Hawthorne . . . that so fixes and fasci-nates me. . . . [As with Shakespeare,] it is those deep far-away things in him; those occasional flashings-forth of the intuitive Truth in him; those short, quick probings at the very axis of reality. . . . Tormented into desperation, Lear the frantic King tears off the mask, and speaks with the sane madness of vital truth.[10]

Pip's speeches, for example, loosed from logic and the inhibiting catego-ries of commonplace causality can reveal the howling metaphysical wil-derness mankind inhabits and the self-destructive fates men precipitate for themselves therein. The "white squalls" Pip feels himself within (the white men, their white God, and their white whale all on a rampage), the doubloon that he sees as the ship's navel (unscrew it and your ass falls off), and the "velvet shark-skin" of Ahab's hand (Pip's fateful "man-rope" of safety and concern) all give us insight beyond ordinary knowledge. Ahab too in his dark maunderings can attain illuminations as in this ex-change with the ship's carpenter, who, seemingly oblivious to the irony, is fitting out Queequeg's coffin to be a life buoy; Ahab speaks enigma, as did Lear, touching on the nature of music, the world, and mortality:

"Hark ye, dost thou not ever sing working about a coffin? The Titans, they say, hummed snatches when chipping out the craters for volca-noes; and the grave-digger in the play sings, spade in hand. Dost thou never?"

"Sing, sir? Do I sing? Oh, I'm indifferent enough, sir, for that; but the reason why the grave-digger made music must have been be-cause there was none in his spade, sir. But the calking mallet is full of it. Hark to it."

"Aye, and that's because the lid there's a sounding-board; what in all things makes the sounding-board is this—there's naught beneath.

And yet, a coffin with a body in it rings pretty much the same, Carpenter." (432)

Melville's particular method of building symbols is another way he overwhelms knowledge with relativity, irreducible diversity, and illuminating irrationality. The ocean, the whale as a creature, the act of whaling, Moby-Dick himself, and his very whiteness ("not so much a color as the visible absence of color, and at the same time the concrete of all colors" [169]) are all symbols rife with possibilities, rational and irrational, yet ultimately indefinable. Melville/Ishmael's narrational style is irrepressibly metaphoric, yet, even more so than Emerson's most radical technique of successive metaphoric approximations, it figures for us a complex and undeterminable world, glimpsed only indirectly, fitfully—never definitively.

But *Moby-Dick* is such a large and inclusive book that it contains elements at odds even with its own basic philosophy of knowledge-destroying inclusiveness. (Every schematization of the novel is inadequate, including this one.) Ishmael indulges in a good deal of simple and reflexive metaphor-making in the middle parts of the novel, drawing lessons and parables out of details of whaling, whale anatomy, and so forth, as his language and his wit play over the intricate material. The prophesies are another disparate element. As Brodtkorb has pointed out, fate implies teleology or a single, meaningful, underlying order;[11] prophesy would be accurate foreknowledge of a single predestined line of truth—a metaphysical situation negated in numerous ways in the novel. Many of Pip's and Ahab's prophetic insights could be read naturalistically, as brilliant intuitions, but Fedallah's haunting prophesy—that Ahab couldn't die until two hearses were seen on the sea and until Fedallah had gone before him as his pilot—is too specific to be read as anything but real foreknowledge. Melville, for whatever dramatic purpose or out of whatever literary enthusiasm, seems to have laced his epistemological agnosticism with some antithetical Shakespearian omen-mongering. At an earlier point Ishmael had even portrayed the omen-conscious crew of the Jeroboam as superstitious fools in a very practical world.

Moby-Dick then is a multiple attack on the knowledge and the patterns of rationality and belief of Melville's day. A "wicked book" indeed, it resolves none of the epistemological problems it poses. What's known is truly known—the physiology of whales, the techniques of whaling, the events that men experienced. The rest—the significances and ultimacies —are left to settle any way they will once "the great shroud of the sea rolled on as it rolled five thousand years ago" (469).

A universe so little knowable can seem an alien place for humans. Stephen Crane, Robert Frost, and other writers would point this out some decades later, but Melville's vision of the otherness, the nonhumanness of the sea pioneered in conveying the sense of desolate alienation:

> In hollows of the liquid hills
>   Where the long Blue Ridges run,
> The flattery of no echo thrills
>   For echo the seas have none;
> Nor aught that gives man back man's strain—
> The hope of his heart, the dream in his brain.

Melville also had a sense, however—like Whitman's in *Specimen Days* and anticipatory of Robinson Jeffers, Ernest Hemingway, and Theodore Roethke—of a healing, curative power accessible by connecting with this alien otherness:

> Healed of my hurt, I laud the inhuman Sea—
> Yea, bless the Angels Four that there convene;
> For healed I am even by their pitiless breath
> Distilled in wholesome dew named rosmarine.[12]

In *Moby-Dick*, Melville showed such a keen sense of the relativity of perception and meaning, and such an ability to manipulate the masks of language with their various inherent assumptions, limitations, and possibilities of revelation, that it seems unusual for him to come back just a year later in *Pierre* with such a disastrously artificial novelistic approach. In subject *Pierre: or, the Ambiguities* seems to be a narrowly focused moral exemplum, the story of a youth, noble of aspect, demeanor, and sentiment, who destroys himself and his loved ones through an action in keeping with the highest moral ideals. The novel's ostensible intent is to challenge our moral thinking with a radical example of things working out counter to our expectations and sense of justice. In presentation, however, it is as contrived, didactical, and figuratively ornamented a tale as has been told since *Euphues*. Pierre's situation is exaggeratedly idyllic in the book's early chapters, and it is exaggeratedly desperate in the late chapters; the main plot is moved by a series of stark accidents and coincidences, and it is embellished by a heavily ironic subplot (of the illicit lower-class lovers Ned and Delly) and by an ample sprinkling of ironic ornaments (such as the name of the intolerant minister Dr. Falsgraveor and the fork Pierre's mother blindly hurls that sticks in the breast of her own painted portrait); the narration is heavily and complicatedly metaphori-cal, lavishly allusive, digressively didactic; and the language is pseudo-archaic, virtuosic, overdone. Contrary to Melville's practice in *Moby-Dick* and also to that book's messages about the fallibility of wisdom, personal and societal, *Pierre* is delivered to us by a knowing narrator, who spins the tale, interprets it to us, tisks knowingly at the characters' shortsighted-ness, gives us some sincere nihilistic philosophizing, and does some sty-listic handstands and cartwheels along the way. Fallibility is for other folks.

Interestingly (for those who think a further complication is interest-ing at this point) *Pierre*'s narrator explicitly attacks the artificiality of nov-els. There are a number of different motifs in the following excerpt, but several of them can certainly be construed to apply to this very novel we are reading—the "schematizing" of "unsystematizable elements," the spin-ning of "vails of mystery" to be later cleared up, and so forth:

> Like all youths, Pierre had conned his novel-lessons; had read more novels than most persons of his years; but their false, inverted at-tempts at schematizing eternally unsystematizable elements; their au-dacious, intermeddling impotency, in trying to unravel, and spread out, and classify, the more thin than gossamer threads which make up the complex web of life; these things over Pierre had no power now. . . . He saw that human life doth truly come from that, which all men are agreed to call by the name of *God*; and that it partakes of the unravelable inscrutableness of God. . . . [W]hile the countless tribes of common novels laboriously spin vails of mystery, only to complacently clear them up at last; and while the countless tribe of common dramas do but repeat the same; yet the profounder emana-tions of the human mind, intended to illustrate all that can be hu-manly known of human life; these never unravel their own intrica-cies, and have no proper endings.(141)

We have, in *Pierre* then, a paradox: a set piece that attacks set pieces. Does Melville thus intend to produce a kind of negative-example parody that will explode the whole form of the "common novel"?

Much but not all of the technique strongly suggests parody. A mock dedication sets the parodic tone at the very outset; it is the usual petition-ing tribute, not, however, to a notable and wealthy person but to an awe-inspiring mountain, before whose "most bounteous and unstinted fertil-izations" the narrator kneels and presumes to "render up my gratitude, whether, thereto, The Most Excellent Purple Majesty of Greylock benig-nantly incline his hoary crown or no." Not only does the dedication satirize authors' patrons, and the queer system by which society supports (or doesn't support) literary endeavor, but it immediately suggests the asympathetic otherness of outer reality (in the dedication it's a mountain, but in the novel it will be God, society, reality) before which humankind plays out its whole desperate drama of love and hope, commitment and denial. The novel continues in both of these veins—heavy-handed parody (in the rigged plot, the forced symbolism and thundering ironies, the authorial lectures and the ornate writing) intermixed with moral earnestness (in the representation of characters struggling against their hostile fates in a coldly neutral world). The mixture doesn't work very well—the aggressive artificiality of the presentation occasionally lapsing into dull caricature and tending overall to vitiate the moral earnestness (or is it the moral earnestness that weighs down the parody?)—although with the mixture Melville offers a radical challenge to this whole mode of discourse and especially to its arbitrariness. He shows that it is as easy to rig a novel with this anti-idealism as it is with the idealism of the "common novel." He shows that in this literary form a case can be hypothesized that will confound judgment as much as the run of "common novels" falsely facilitates it.

With God characterized as "unravelable inscrutableness," knowledge comes in for a good deal of disparagement; in keeping with the confrontational strategy of the novel, much of the disparagement is audacious. Pierre himself, in determinedly setting out to write a truthful book, is at first represented as "ignorant that in reality to a mind bent on producing some thoughtful thing of absolute Truth, all mere reading is apt to prove but an obstacle hard to overcome" (283); and he later discovers for himself "the everlasting elusiveness of Truth; the universal lurking insincerity of even the greatest and purest written thoughts. Like knavish cards, the leaves of all great books were covertly packed. He was but packing one set the more" (339). According to our narrator, philosophers who claim to have gotten an answer out of "that profound Silence, that only voice of our God" are soon discovered to be self-deluded, and "those philosophers and their vain philosophy are let glide away into practical oblivion. Plato, and Spinoza, and Goethe, and many more belong to this guild of self-imposters, with a preposterous rabble of Muggletonian Scots and Yankees, whose vile brogue still the more bestreaks the stripedness of their Greek or German Neoplatonical originals" (208). The narrator's attack on theology as a body of thought and the church as a contemporary institution is no less outrageous—it is merely presented more cagily, symbolized in the narrator's description of the Church of the Apostles, formerly an active institution in the center of town, now because of the dynamics of urban growth, a rooming house turned artists' colony in the depths of a warehouse neighborhood:

> Such, then, was the present condition of the ancient Church of the Apostles; buzzing with a few lingering, equivocal lawyers in the basement, and populous with all sorts of poets, painters, paupers and philosophers above. A mysterious professor of the flute was perched in one of the upper stories of the tower; and often, of silent, moonlit nights, his lofty, melodious notes would be warbled forth over the roofs of the ten thousand warehouses around him—as of yore, the bell had pealed over the domestic gables of a long-departed generation. (269–270)

With ultimate truth inaccessible and finite knowledge subject to decay, the plight of the would-be knower was not yet quite complete for *Pierre*'s narrator. As in *Moby-Dick*, the characters suffer from predispositions and situational limitations, and the narrator is quick to draw the lessons of human fallibility: a youth disillusioned will always come to see the world as "saturated and soaking with lies" (231), and a man with vague doubts about his theory of life will instinctively reject any new ideas that tend to challenge his views (233). Furthermore, life invariably forces these situations and their accompanying attitudes on people: youth *must* be won over by the beauty of Christian morality, and it *must* be shocked by morality's virtual absence in the functioning of professedly Christian societies, claims the narrator. New and unsettling ideas *must* come along. From the narrator's all-knowing perspective, humankind's earnest quest for truth, preprogrammed with its internal obstacles and bounded by its absolute limit, is as predictable as puppetry.

Like *Moby-Dick*, *Pierre* offers several broadly ambiguous symbols on which the characters and readers can exercise their parochial and ultimately futile understandings. Significance is projected, not discovered, the narrator implies, and, persistently and perversely cynical, he adds the element of indeterminacy—even with hints of narrative unreliability—to the mixture. In one passage he prefaces an extended description of a mountain range to which Pierre returns in his dreams, searching for consolation and guidance, with this attack on the Emersonian sort of nature philosophy: "Say what some poets will, Nature is not so much her own ever-sweet interpreter, as the mere supplier of that cunning alphabet, whereby selecting and combining as he pleases, each man reads his own peculiar lesson according to his own peculiar mind and mood" (342). The highest, most prominent of the peaks had been named the Delectable Mountain, an appellation that seemed to suit either its Bunyanesque-religious aspect, if that was how one were minded, or its aesthetic beauty, if one were poetically inclined. But those are both long-vista perspectives; as we journey to and up the mountain, the narrator shows us that "long and frequent rents among the mass of leaves revealed horrible glimpses of dark-dropping rocks, and mysterious mouths of wolfish caves" (showing, presumably, the romantically iconoclastic inclination of *his* fancy). Pierre in a sky-assaulting mood dreams of the mountain as a wild Titan. The Delectable Mountain is *Pierre's* doubloon.

The novel's most complex, ambiguous, and important symbol is Plotinus Plinlimmon, together with his disquisition, "Chronometricals and Horologicals." The disquisition itself, positioned as a kind of interpretive centerpiece for the novel, is audacious in content and insidious in tone. The outrageous lesson it teaches is that whatever the example and teachings of Christ, "A virtuous expediency . . . seems the highest desirable or attainable earthly excellence for the mass of men, and is the only earthly excellence that their Creator intended for them." It argues, with respectful dignity and utter disingenuousness, that "no average son of man" ever went to the extreme of turning the other cheek or giving all that he had to the poor, and that the history of Christendom for the last 1800 years shows that the uncompromising Christian ideal "has proved entirely impracticable"; after all, "in spite of all the maxims of Christ . . . history is . . . just as full of blood, violence, wrong, and iniquity of every kind, as any previous portion of the world's story." "In things terrestrial (horological) a man must not be governed by ideas celestial (chronometrical)," the lecture teaches; "when [people] go to heaven, it will be quite another thing. There, they can freely turn the left cheek, because the right cheek will never be smitten. There they can freely give all to the poor, for *there* there will be no poor to give to" (214–215).

The disquisition is sheer audacity, especially couched as it is in the form of a straightforward mid-nineteenth-century lecture on morality. As Melville presents it, however, it is entirely hedged with ambiguities and disclaimers. The question of who, really, is saying these things is virtually unanswerable—it disappears in a complex of narrative screens, shifts in fictional level, and ambiguous symbols; and the question of what the disquisition is doing here in this novel is no more clearly determinable.

The author has quite gratuitously put it into the novel. Pierre finds it by accident down between the linings of a secondhand overcoat he's been reduced to wearing. The manuscript is unprepossessing, but since he's come across it while taking a long, dull coach journey, he feels (with no sense of portentousness) that he might as well read it to pass the time. The narrator not only reports the event of Pierre's reading it, but he quotes the whole text, saying with mock diffidence, "each person can now skip, or read and rail for himself" (210). The narrator acts (or pretends to act) as if the manuscript has an independent existence: his comments about it distance him from it, although they indicate ambiguity of intent. He describes it insistently as a "thin, tattered, dried-fish-like thing" (206), a "pamphlet-shaped rag" (207), a "sleazy rag pamphlet" (209), "a very blurred one as to ink, and a very sleazy one as to paper," that is "so metaphysically and insufferably entitled as this:—'Chronometricals & Horologicals'" (207). He characterizes the content as "a very fanciful and mystical, rather than philosophical Lecture, from which, I confess, that I myself can derive no conclusion which permanently satisfies those peculiar motions in my soul, to which that Lecture seems more particularly addressed. For to me it seems more the excellently illustrated re-statement of a problem, than the solution of the problem itself" (210). Ambiguous about the intrinsic worth of the "sleazy rag," the narrator is also indeterminate about its effect on Pierre (which effect is, after all, presumably the reason for including it in the narrative). Did Pierre comprehend the first impact of the pamphlet's new ideas on his beliefs? "It will be observed, that neither points of the above speculations do we, in set terms, attribute to Pierre in connection with the rag pamphlet. Possibly both [principles] might be applicable; possibly neither." Did it affect what he did? When, if ever, did he understand and apply it? The answers are indefinite, but the narrator decides to include the text and the episode in the account,

> foreseeing, too, that Pierre may not in the end be entirely uninfluenced in his conduct by the torn pamphlet, when afterwards perhaps by other means he shall come to understand it; or, peradventure, come to know that he, in the first place, did—seeing too that the author thereof came to be made known to him by reputation, and though Pierre never spoke to him, yet exerted a surprising sorcery upon his spirit by the mere distant glimpse of his countenance. (209–210)

Plinlimmon himself is an ambiguity, a philosopher who is never observed writing, who would decline the gift of books in favor of liquor, a man neither happy nor unhappy—self-contented, nonbenevolent, inscrutable. Pierre's "mere distant glimpse" shows "that remarkable face of repose,—repose neither divine nor human, nor any thing made up of either or both—but a repose separate and apart—a repose of a face by

itself. One adequate look at that face conveyed to most philosophical ob-
servers a notion of something not before included in their scheme of the
Universe" (291). Plinlimmon remains an enigma to all—characters, narrator, and readers,—the appropriate source for a blasphemous lecture that
begins "I hold that all our so-called wisdom is . . . but provisional" and
that disappears from the story as magically as it came.

Melville destroys all general knowledge in *Pierre* and all hope of knowing. His strategy of presentation is to use oblique means—disclaimers,
indefinite symbols, narrator uncertainty or duplicity, novelistic fakery, and
so forth—and throw open the whole question of narrative authority. *Pierre*
itself thus is a kind of rag pamphlet Melville tries to slip between the
linings of our overcoat.

The Confidence-Man: His Masquerade (1857) takes us even farther down
the road of destructivist narration. The novel assembles on the riverboat
Fidèle a Whitmanesque cross-section of American types, and it presents a
number of encounters among them, of which the predominant surface
theme is confidence, probity, trust, but the connotative undercurrent is all
ambiguity, duplicity, and manipulative intent. At the center of this epi-
sodic tale is a man (or is it a series of men?) of questionable identity,
whose motivation seems to be to profit from the credulity of fellow pas-
sengers. Unlike the narrator of *Pierre*, the narrator of this tale gives us no
help interpreting the passing scene. Additionally, while some elements of
that passing scene are presumably happening as we watch, others are
overheard and quoted by the narrator, offered second- or even thirdhand.
The indeterminacy is thus multiple: not only are the identities and/or
motives of a number of these characters dubious, but the words, sentiments, and events of the stories they tell might be entirely spurious, fabricated with insidious intent. The "Cosmopolitan" who tells the tale of the
gentleman-madman Charlemont ultimately admits he made up the story
simply to "amuse" his listener. The novel's narrator, anticipating the charge
that his book is unrealistic, makes the claim, both devastating and dis-
arming, that "it is with fiction as with religion: it should present another
world, and yet one to which we feel the tie" (158).

In creating the world of this novel, then, Melville pushed the boundaries of indeterminateness well beyond those in *Pierre*. Indeed, no other
English-language novel before the twentieth century resolves so little of
what it poses. *The Confidence-Man* is not utter epistemological and ethical
nihilism, though. It presents characters who are too knowing to be deceived and characters too principled to countenance charlatanism; the tenor
of the novel too implies that veracity and integrity in human dealings

matter, however rare and beleaguered they might be in the contemporary world. Still, the novel stands as a casebook on credulity and a striking criticism of the idealistic American brand of faith-in-nature and faith-in-fellowman. And its means is the destabilization of the knowledge on which faith is based.

4 Emily Dickinson and the Destruction of the Language of Knowledge

. . . you, woman, masculine
in singlemindedness
for whom the word was more
than a symptom—

a condition of being.
Till the air buzzing with spoiled language
sang in your ears
of Perjury. . . .
—from Adrienne Rich, "E"

The higher knowledge failed Dickinson too, and a good number of her works imply the falsity of consensus on the higher questions, the falsity even of the terms by which the questions had been put. In the matters she seems to have felt the most deeply—faith, love, mortality—her experience simply and candidly belied the knowledge of her day. "The poems of Emily Dickinson," said Richard Wilbur, voicing an important insight of twentieth-century criticism, "are a continual appeal to experience, motivated by an arrogant passion for the truth," and "her chief truthfulness lay in her insistence on discovering the facts of her inner experience."[1] Similarly, Allen Tate pointed out that Dickinson's work, like all great poetry, "probes the deficiencies of a tradition."[2] Belatedly, and as part of the rejection of our culture's simple sexist myth of Emily Dickinson, "experience" and "candor" have come to be seen as governing elements in her work, as they are in the work of Whitman and Melville.

Dickinson used her poetry for a variety of purposes, and in a variety of states of mind,* and our new myth sees the real Dickinson more in the searching, wit-guided, mind-bending meditations—and that is (pretty exclusively) where the destruction of knowledge occurs. In these poems

---

*Richard Sewall's *The Life of Emily Dickinson* (Farrar, Straus & Giroux, 1974) demonstrates her close familiarity with all the standard reading of her day—not just Shakespeare and the Bible, but Ik Marvell's *Reveries,* Longfellow's *Kavanaugh,* and even the likes of the poems in the *Springfield Republican* (see vol. 2, 668–705, and appendix 4, 742–750); his study shows how a good deal of the shallowly sentimental literature of her day affected her imagination, at times even producing direct, sincere borrowings and imitations. Her relationship to such literature was as complex and varied as were her states of mind or her relationships with the persons to or about whom she wrote her poems.

she is committed, in a very knowing way (unlike Whitman and Melville), to the mediation of language between self and reality and to methods of indirection. She was not given to leaping out beyond thought and language and human limitation to grasp for some new, direct connection to the absolute, nor driven to forays of madness, blasphemy, and overt chicanery to force the truth out of things. There is real anguish in those of her poems that express the lack of a direct and certain relationship to God —resignation is one aspect of her acceptance of mediation and indirection —but there is also an underlying faith in language to do what can be done and an irrepressible enthusiasm for her own verbal virtuosity. As she once wrote in a letter to Joseph Lyman: "We used to think, Joseph, when I was an unsifted girl and you so scholarly that words were cheap and weak. Now I don't know of anything so mighty. There are [those] to which I lift my hat when I see them sitting princelike among their peers on the page. Sometimes I write one, and look at his outlines till he glows as no sapphire."[3]

Her great problem as a thinker and her great challenge as a creative artist came from the fact that the words, imagery, figures, and symbols available to her had definite and conventional significations that tended toward social confinement and artistic and intellectual stultification. The language of religion tended toward hollow or unwitting affirmation and societal sanctimoniousness; the language of nature veered toward prettiness and pap; the language of human relations trapped one (especially a female one!) in a sentimentalized, tyrannical scheme of stratification. Worse still, language tended toward absolutism, the common significations of words and the ordinary statements and sayings becoming frozen truths, forever blocking the possibility of new and different insight that might be more experientially valid. Thus the knowledge Dickinson needed to destroy was the knowledge implicit in language.

Her solution was to turn language back on itself—to use words in unexpected senses, to fracture the forms of conventional saying, to broaden the possibilities of ambiguity—and thus to weaken the tyranny of knowledge over experience. Take, for example, the following poem:

Doom is the House without the Door—
'Tis entered from the Sun—
And then the Ladder's thrown away,
Because Escape—is done—

'Tis varied by the Dream
Of what they do outside—

Where Squirrels play—and Berries die—
And Hemlocks—bow—to God—[4]

When we reach the last line we feel ourselves in familiar territory, despite the strangeness of some of the foregoing imagery—of course, it's a nature-declares-the-glory-of-God sort of lyric, an old friend. "Because Escape—is done—" can reassure us in a familiar way too, with death as the end of all our travail, of all the things that need escaping from, death as the final rest and comfort. The poem cites the familiar reassurances, but doesn't rest there; it employs them ambiguously, perhaps ironically, in a new context of insight. The hemlocks, for example, bowing anthropomorphically apparently signify acceptance, acquiescence, worship. But even if we pass over the undeveloped question of tree volition (may we wonder whence comes this arboreal capacity to acquiesce and worship?), we still are faced with the question of what in the poem is being acquiesced to. That isn't terribly clear, but some of its possibilities are more disquieting than otherwise.

The poem's own little two-stanza, universe model is a two-part system involving the realms of "Doom" and "what they do outside." Characterizing Doom as "the House without the Door," the poem's speaker forgoes all reference to the Christian concept of afterlife; death is represented by a negation. "House" denotes "abode," but unlike "home" is a word of neutral or ambiguous tone; here, in connection with "Doom," it is chilling and melodramatic. Doorlessness suggests noncommunicability, confinement away from the outside, and finality. As poetic figures go, this one is generalized (not concrete and vivid), ambiguous (not precisely interpretable), and utterly phenomenalistic (not at all assertive of anything beyond human perception of phenomena). The metaphors used to represent the entry into the Doom-house seem to me bizarrely unconventional and ultimately irreduceable by symbol-interpretation. The fact that the entry to Doom seems to involve some climbing, (some effort, maybe even volition?) is a strangeness. The uncertainty of its direction deepens the strangeness and increases the ambiguities, as do the figurative possibilities of the ladder and its peremptory disposal. Does one enter *from* the sun in the sense of the sun being a way station on a longer climb, or in the sense of the climb's being *away from* the sun? Is the ladder a variant of Jacob's ladder, suggesting (perhaps ironically) a vision of the approach of the kingdom of God by a climb to or through the sun, or is it a direct route down to the grave? The ladder's explicitly being thrown away suggests the uniqueness of an individual's own life- (or death-) climb, but for what purpose? Dickinson's very original twisting of these very conventional symbols certainly leaves her readers without the customary bearings in this poem, although I seriously doubt that an effect of interpretive confusion was a part of her objective; that the askance bizarreness of her imagination sometimes outran her ability to communicate, I am more ready to believe. "Because Escape—is done" in the context of these subtly ambiguous and off-putting elements reads ambiguously too—does it suggest the satisfaction of a safe haven or the despair of a final and hopeless imprisonment? The punctuating of the line, the dash producing a prolongation of the effect(s) of "Escape," reinforces the complex and unique quality of that word choice. Life has then been a process of escaping? death is an escape? escape is a burden? a hope?—such is the ambiguity that dash draws out, while it emphasizes the absoluteness of a condition-without-escape.

"What they do outside," the other realm, is seen only as "Dream," and we are not given grounds for deciding whether "Dream" is a dream in the sense of an insubstantiality, of a remote and possibly unreliable vision, or of a hopeful aspiration. "What *they* do" emphasizes the indefinite otherness of the creatures outside the house of Doom; the self seems to be alone in a featureless house with the only dream of life being a dream of others outside. The life outside is not vividly described, only named, but its nouns,—"Squirrels," "Berries," and "Hemlocks," certainly (I won't try to decide about "God")—are the only nouns in the poem capable of being construed nonmetaphorically. Here we have our only direct and denotative concreteness, the events being inconsequential, everyday nature events, without mind, soul, destiny, or special significance. With, however, death. The nature events are like human events, but without the uncertainty and the sense of (possible or actual) loss. The Hemlocks are thus bowing in the context of their own cosmic insignificance, behaving in the only way they were made to behave (just as Squirrels play and Berries die) and, in the process, gesturing worshipful acquiescence to a system of arbitrary mortality, in which humans can only climb to an "Escape" which, whatever else it might be imagined to offer, gives assurance only of permanent separation from the phenomenal world. The dashes internally punctuating the line, like the one that snagged the reassurance in line four, give reflective space for doubt and irony; as the line shifts from image to metaphor, its simplicity of tone dissipates, the ambiguity and doubt flood in.

The poem offers uncertainties, then, instead of conventional clear understandings and positive reassurance, and its tone is genuinely indeterminate (earnest or ingenuously coy or bitterly sardonic, depending, really, on the interpretive propensities of the reader), a perfect artifact by the artist who advises "Tell all the truth, but tell it slant."[5]

Standard wisdom plays an important part in Dickinson's "slant" technique of truth-telling, as she re-employs, re-defines, and even perverts conventional ideas, images, and words to confront the inadequacy of knowledge with the depth and complexity of experience:

> I shall know why—when Time is over—
> And I have ceased to wonder why—
> Christ will explain each separate anguish
> In the fair schoolroom of the sky—
>
> He will tell me what "Peter" promised—
> And I—for wonder at his woe—
> I shall forget the drop of Anguish
> That scalds me now—that scalds me now![6]

The reassurance of conventional wisdom saturates this poem until the repetition of "that scalds me now" in the last line. The speaker is *not* reconciled to her experience by the Christian promise, we suddenly realize. The repetition and its vehemency echo back through the poem, profoundly qualifying all of the preceding wisdom, and we realize that Dickinson has all along been presenting it very subtly in a very complex way. There is a note of sarcasm in her speaker's learning "why" only after she has ceased to wonder, a note of childish reassurance about the expectation of an explanation of "each separate anguish," a note of satire about the scheme of things that belittles the sky into a "fair schoolroom," and a note of impatience with the pedantry that will tell her the old lesson of "what 'Peter' promised." She is being treated like a schoolgirl by this knowledge system, and it will not serve. The idea of *anguish* comes through the poem most clearly—the poem's profoundest subject, in fact—the experiential element so deep and strong that it can only be defined in contrast to the terms of the tenets of wisdom and faith that fail to explain or reconcile it. The word *anguish* is thus placed in crucial positions at the end of the third lines of both stanzas, lowercased in the first stanza, the subject there of a recitation on the (ordinary?) vicissitudes of life, but capitalized, made insistent, in the second stanza and juxtaposed with Christ's lowercased "woe" at the end of the preceding line. Slantwise, doubts about the Christian promise exist only in the overtones and innuendos, the only approach to blasphemy being a single typographical juxtaposition. Dickinson's way of destroying knowledge was to set it in a new context that would reveal its shortcoming, to surprise it with a flash of askance light that came directly from experience.

What it is that lies behind or beyond experience, that unifies and justifies the experiential world, Dickinson's poems do not determine. It is not that she disbelieved in the existence of a higher scheme, but rather that she just doubted that we do (or even can) know anything about it. She brought into American poetry what Melville brought into its fiction: the keenest sense heretofore of the difference between the events in our experience and the symbols and categories and biases by which we conceptualize them. Both writers were committed to blocking off naively reflexive perception such as Emerson's, both tried to find a true boundary between the self and the nonself, and both invented in their own terms their own imaginative phenomenalism:

> Four Trees—upon a solitary Acre—
> Without Design
> Or Order, or Apparent Action—
> Maintain—
>
> The Sun—upon a Morning meets them—
> The Wind—
> No nearer Neighbor—have they—
> But God—
>
> The Acre gives them—Place—
> They—Him—Attention of Passer by—
> Of Shadow, or of Squirrel, haply—
> Or Boy—
>
> What Deed is Theirs unto the General Nature—
> What Plan
> They severally—retard—or further—
> Unknown—[7]

Carefully, scrupulously, in this poem Dickinson avoids any imputations of order to the scene, any projections of purpose. The poem focuses not on the trees themselves (they aren't at all specifically described), but on their lack of any expression of inherent purpose; the only significance they can have is such as an observer can read into them; from our human perspective the poem seems to say that these suppositions about observable relationships are all the knowledge we can legitimately have. With this outlook one could mix comfortably with Wittgenstein and Wallace Stevens, yet here it is in the work of a contemporary of Longfellow and Thoreau.

In many poems Dickinson played back and forth over the boundary between the perceived object and the projective perceiver, toying with personification and supposition yet keeping distinct the otherness of the world:

> Apparently with no surprise
> To any happy Flower
> The Frost beheads it at its play—
> In accidental power—
> The blonde Assassin passes on—
> The Sun proceeds unmoved
> To measure off another Day
> For an Approving God.[8]

The nature of the world we experience is better apprehended, she shows, through an understanding of the projective responses that do not apply. The technique of personification of Flower and Frost, Sun and God makes especially pointed the message that human standards of significance and morality do not apply to natural processes. Personify them (as we are so wont to do) and still, if we watch them accurately, they behave utterly contrary to what we would humanly expect. However a human observer might feel about that fact (in this poem there is an interesting complex of possible feelings), that fact remains, and its recognition is an indispensable step in knowing. Dickinson's technique of backspin personification—of using personification to destroy personification—is worth an additional moment's consideration in the larger context of nineteenth-century knowledge destruction. Bizarrely ingenious like Melville's backspin morality novel *Pierre*, it is a case of the writer's grappling for epistemological leverage without the benefit of science or philosophy or anything extraliterary, with only the resources of the decadent literary language and form themselves.

Playing back and forth over the boundary between life and death, as Dickinson's poems so often and so strikingly do, is another special characteristic closely related to her personal phenomenalism.* What kind of experience would it be to inhabit a realm where human categories don't prevail? Beyond knowledge and perception and even feeling, in a realm

*Sharon Cameron sees the destruction of this particular boundary in Dickinson's poems as one of her most important techniques in her struggle against "temporal finitude." See *Lyric Time: Dickinson and the Limits of Genre* (Johns Hopkins University Press, 1979), 92.

where "I could not see to see,"—where one is in "the Atom's Tomb—
Merry and Nought, and gay, and numb"?[9] Only the starkest negations,
the most hypothetical of metaphors can say, but the saying brings us up
against our radically circumscribed and fallible human nature.

Dickinson is amazingly imaginative in hypothesizing lyric perspectives from which human limitations can be freshly discovered. Her poem
can come from the viewpoint of a corpse or a queen, a saint or a soldier, a
bird or a bee, a ship or a gun, or even an abstraction. It can be located
anywhere or nowhere, and focus on an eternal universal or a momentary
triviality. She often uses bizarre viewpoint to put a strain on the ordinary
modes of thought:

> Funny—to be a Century
> And see the People—going by—
> I—should die of the Oddity—
> But then—I'm not so staid—as He—
>
> He keeps His Secrets safely—very—
> Were He to tell—extremely sorry
> This Bashful Globe of Ours would be—
> So dainty of Publicity—[10]

Here again we see the playful anthropomorphism, the self-aware self-
projection that precisely knows the limits of that game. How would the
world look to our very human speaker from the viewpoint of a century?
Its time frame, of course, is different, and that makes *all* the difference for
a mortal. The speaker "should die of the Oddity," a statement couched in
quaint and ambiguous diction that can signify (at the mild end of the
range of possibilities) that the curiousness of the experience should be an
embarrassing strain on her composure or (at the severe end) that it should
be unsurvivably intolerable, the disorientation and the experience of "the
People—going by." (And it is ironic, if we cogitate on the situation, that
she should die if she were a century watching people go by, since her fate
being a person watching the century go by is exactly the same.) The male,
capitalized century is godlike in his exemption from quick extinction, and
"staid" (imperturbable, and stayed?) beyond human capacity of imitation;
here we have another of Dickinson's open, blank, negation-like symbols
of whatever is beyond mortal experience. In relation to "His Secrets" (the
first of which is probably the stark and absolute perception of human
mortality), the by-going world is "Bashful . . . /So dainty of Publicity"
(unwilling—even at great cost—to have its temporality revealed). The

surface tone of genteel euphemism here is another instance of Dickinson turning the spoiled language back on itself: the kind of words with which the world shields itself from its uncomfortable truths are just the kind to represent it in that dainty escapist mode. Thus a pleasantly coy understatement teeters on the edge of a seething sarcasm about the language —and attitude—of conventional wisdom.

Purely coincidentally, it is interesting to ponder one of the stories told about the young Albert Einstein who, the story goes, imagining what the universe would look like to one traveling along with a light beam at the speed of light, was led into the frame of thought in which he was later to develop the theory of relativity. Dickinson, rejecting her culture's arbitrary perspective (as Einstein was later to reject science's prevailing mechanism) and able to imagine herself in forms like a century seeing the people go by, also understood the essential relativity of all knowing:

> The Robin's my Criterion for Tune—
> Because I grow—where Robins do—
> But, were I Cuckoo born—
> I'd swear by him—The ode familiar—rules the Noon. . . .
> Without the Snow's Tableau
> Winter, were lie—to me—
> Because I see—New Englandly—
> The Queen, discerns like me—
> Provincially—[11]

The exploration of the full significance of the inescapable provinciality of discerning—her relativity—occupied a considerable portion of her imaginative effort and technical ingenuity. This aspect of her work has come to be better understood and appreciated under the scrutiny of recent critics whose approaches are markedly post-relativity. Charles Anderson has stressed the way that phenomenalistic rather than absolutistic perception was her mode, transient processes rather than fixed forms were her subject, and "matter always interested her less than energy."[12] Robert Weisbuch has studied the indeterminate, semi-analogical, situational matrices of her poems.[13] Sharon Cameron has studied her techniques of expressing relativistic time, relating them to the concepts of mortality inherent in Dickinson's works and in the lyric genre itself.[14] The relativistic bent even extended to Richard Benson Sewall's approach in his biography of Dickinson, in which he attempted to reveal her in her own world by offering separate chapters on the individual persons and cultural forces with which she had been connected.[15]

In the representation of the self Dickinson's poetry is especially provocative. The self is relative to its experiences, feelings, and moods in her poems, and not at all definable in fixed and simple terms. Furthermore, the experiences, feelings, and moods are only obliquely, indirectly, transiently knowable, not simple and accurately identifiable entities like crayons in a box. Her explorations of self and states of soul, in preserving experiential authenticity, generated new metaphor systems, new language—and generated them out of the old, worn language of devotion, of romance, of tragedy. Thus, not even words have standard, absolute natures, but are malleable, renewable in the context of individual experience that envisions, for example, the feeling of coming upon a snake as "a tighter breathing/And Zero at the Bone—,"[16] or represents the feeling of partially recovering from the loss of someone very precious in these terms:

> I got so I could take his name—
> Without—Tremendous gain—
> That Stop-sensation—on my Soul—
> And Thunder—in the room—[17]

The psychophysiological sensations of sudden shock are what she is describing, but she uses language in which ordinary words—"tighter," "Zero," and "gain"—are transposed from the vocabularies of different sorts of activities, coinages like "Stop-sensation" recombine old words into new nouns, and perspective reversal of a noun like "Thunder" can designate a physiological sensation by naming the external event that customarily produces it.

With the old knowledge of self and soul destroyed, diverted, or at least consigned to the pale of agnosticism, what kind of self-representations can an individualist make, relying only on experience, imagination, and linguistic virtuosity? Probably forced and provocative, at times brilliant and at times melodramatic or just plain incomprehensible. Dickinson had no more hope of a consensus than Melville had in his mad maunderings:

> The Soul has Bandaged moments—
> When too appalled to stir—
> She feels some ghastly Fright come up
> And stop to look at her—
>
> Salute her—with long fingers—
> Caress her freezing hair—
> Sip, Goblin, from the very lips
> The Lover—hovered—o'er—

Unworthy, that a thought so mean
Accost a Theme—so—fair—

The soul has moments of Escape—
When bursting all the doors—
She dances like a Bomb, abroad,
And swings upon the Hours,

As do the Bee—delirious borne—
Long Dungeoned from his Rose—
Touch Liberty—then know no more,
But Noon, and Paradise—

The Soul's retaken moments—
When, Felon led along,
With shackles on the plumed feet,
And staples, in the Song,

The Horror welcomes her, again,
These, are not brayed of Tongue—[18]

Like her other great Gothic introspections, "I felt a Funeral, in my Brain,"
"I heard a Fly buzz—when I died," and "It was not Death, for I stood
up," this poem offers no broad perspective from which the emotional
problem can be resolved. We are utterly *in* a situation (like a pit with a
pendulum) with no hope for rescue but with an extraordinary courage
about facing out the appalling truth. There are no direct names of things,
so we need to work at understanding through a screen of metaphor and
indirection. And the rules of the quest seem to favor the bizarre: the truth
is more likely to be revealed in unexpected departures from customary
language, figure, and thought—by surprise.* The Soul with Bandaged
moments is a figure that clearly shows the characteristics of this kind of
imaginative analysis. "Bandaged" is an unexpected word, a transposition
from the physico-medical realm. It has a complex effect, much of which is
brilliant in indicating the characteristics of an emotion too actual to be
nameable; it suggests something muffled, comforted, isolated, constrained,
numb—the mitigation of some awful hurt underneath. But visually it is
ridiculous—picture a soul in a bandaged moment and just try to think
some serious thought about it. So we must try to take the figure as a
purely verbal-emotional conception and ignore the distracting overtones

*The main theme of Charles Anderson's *Emily Dickinson's Poetry: Stairway of Surprise*
(Holt, Rinehart & Winston, 1960).

of poetry forcing the unexpected. The ghastly Fright is an unnameable ambiguous something, visibly personified as a Gothic haunt; its relationship to the soul seems to be that of a captor to a captive, a torturer to a paralyzed and helpless victim. The sexual overtones of this encounter between a soul and its worst fear are unmistakable: the Fright-Goblin is male and vile and invasive, sadistic in the subtle but unmistakable gestures of his power and intent, while the soul is female, frozen with fright —someone who has (or formerly had?) a lover not in any way present or possibly present to reprieve her. One possible reading of the poem is that the loss of her lover is itself the soul's wound, its ghastly Fright, although there is no internal reason in the poem for the lover to be any less metaphoric than the Fright. A post-Freudian reading might see the lover and Goblin as one and the same, a Dr. Jekyll and Mr. Hyde whose darker, sexual aspect chills and persecutes her, although this reading must assume the naive, dreamlike relationship of the poet to her poem such as is a frequent requisite of Freudian interpretations. But whether the poem is translatable into a lost-love story, a parable of mood-possession, or a fable of frigidity, its insight with respect to the quasi-sexual compulsion/repulsion ambivalence toward one's own depression is original and provocative. And especially interesting in terms of technique is the way Dickinson suggests and then eludes the theme of sexual defilement, with the Goblin using the lips the lover (only?) "hovered—o'er," and then shifting the poem to an unpictorial, depersonalized, general-summary mode in a lighter tone (out of an English madrigal rather than a Gothic horror story?) that it "unworthy" was "that a *thought* so mean/Accost a *Theme*—so—fair."

The soul's moments of Escape are as extreme as its Bandaged moments, "bursting," dancing, swinging—mindlessly, instinctually, "delirious borne," like a bee released from confinement on a summer noon. The simile-bee is no longer "Dungeoned" from his rose: the term is another example of transposed vocabulary (and of noun transmuted into verb), and it serves well to echo the poem's first pseudo-scene and to establish the idea that deprivation of some instinctual love-object is imprisonment. The soul dancing "like a Bomb" is another of Dickinson's forced and purely verbal conceptions, functioning admirably to indicate both the extremity of release and the incipient danger of such a release, but at the same time making a grotesquely silly picture.

The impossibility of any permanent freedom from Fright, any prolongation of paradise, is indicated by "The Soul's retaken moments." The Soul returns to its dungeon, to the Horror to which it belongs, now like a "Felon," as if its natural and proper state were Bandaged, and as if it felt guilt about the moments of Escape. Birdlike in captivity, however, its "plumed feet" shackled and its Song "stapled" (in another dramatic transposition of vocabulary), it seems to be a thing that ought naturally to fly free and sing. The ambivalent oughts are part of the poem's experiential insight: both the depression and the release seem both right and wrong.

The soul has no choice, however, and is delivered over to the Horror, who in an understatement that tellingly implies a sardonic courtliness, "welcomes her, again." Such inevitable moments, says the teller harshly, as if pronouncing an indictment against all happy and reassuring poetry about human emotions, "are not brayed of Tongue." "Brayed" is a coarse and unexpected word here, suggesting that the experience of being retaken by the Horror could only be celebrated in an animalistic antisong.

This fable-poem describes a hopeless emotional ritual: since the soul *has* all these kinds of moments, there is the implication of serial repetition, with, as I said earlier, no perspective from which the situation could be resolved, no way off the wheel. The insights are harsh and, though they are highly melodramatized through the Gothic and Romantic imagery, we feel that because they "ring true," because they are unexpected in the connections they make, and because their portent is not reflexively, egocentrically reassuring, they are experientially authentic. Dickinson somehow makes profound analysis and disturbing new insight out of trite imagery, commonplace words and meters, and a forced verbal virtuosity.

Her technique is founded upon strategic disorientations—of perspective, of tone, of figurative reference, of diction, of grammar, of image, of wisdom. Critic Charles Anderson sees her approaching language like "an explorer in new lands," a "wit," a "word-juggler"; he sees her adopting many Shakespearian linguistic techniques (shades of Melville), such as the reference back to the etymology and root meanings of words, the substitution of simple concrete terms for abstract ones and vice versa, the juxtaposition of words from different connotative spheres, the abrupt change from one level of discourse to another, and the rearrangement of word order. "Within the context of the individual poems," he says, "old and new symbols are maneuvered by the language of surprise so as to illuminate the two profoundest themes that challenged her poetic powers."[19] Cheryl Walker relates Dickinson's paradoxes, doublings, and reversals of expectations to a characteristically probing "structural progression from the real to the surreal";[20] and Sharon Cameron sees Dickinson deliberately courting ambiguity and inconclusion in a battle against time's finitude, using such elements as broken syntax, negations, blank or indistinct metaphors, suggestions of "presences" which are indefinable, the "description of those temporal moments in a given [indefinable] experience that chart its boundaries," and multiple, dialectical or paradoxical representation of things.[21] Certainly the particular poems and techniques for which Dickinson has recently come to be appreciated are those in which she inverted or distorted or destroyed the culturally sanctioned beliefs of her day. She was willing to accept the risks—"much madness is divinest Sense—/To a discerning Eye, —" she wrote, "Much Sense—the starkest Madness, —"[22] and with her inner experience as her guide and her individualistic poetic imagination as her vehicle, she invented a personal path out beyond the knowledge limitations of her time.

II   Science and the Knowledge of Knowing

American writers of the twentieth century, then, inherited a tradition in attitudes toward knowledge and knowing that was at its farthest reaches radically skeptical, anti-authoritarian, and individualistic to the point of anarchy. The destructivist tendency was far from being a predominant characteristic of the style of our national letters (at the beginning of the century Dickinson's work was sparsely and somewhat distortedly known, Melville was a little-read author of sea stories, and Whitman and Emerson were generally viewed as great optimists of democracy), but the interaction of American experience and individual genius was producing destructivist stances of considerable power and originality. Mark Twain and Henry Adams would represent two more of them.

As the twentieth century developed, the game would be profoundly changed, mainly through the new science and new insight into the processes of thought that made up science. America was entering into an age of epistemology, and a much wider range of writers and thinkers would be unsettled in their views of perception, conceptualization, and representation—and unsettled in some very characteristic ways.

In the nineteenth and twentieth centuries science itself was proving to be a kind of knowledge-destroying system, countervailing not only conventionally held beliefs about the physical world but also conventionally employed categories and techniques of knowing—even some of its own most fundamental categories and techniques. Unlike the idiosyncratic approaches of Melville and Dickinson, nineteenth-century science operated by rejecting and counteracting individual, personal bias in knowing; it developed a discipline of systematic objectivity, relying increasingly on quantification, empirical verification, and the canons of inductive logic to remove the vagaries of individual fantasy and fallibility from the knowing process. Out of the nineteenth century's diversity of scientific methods, of techniques and theories, of worldviews and philosophical preconceptions, there grew the knowledge myth that knowing was a matter of free, systematic, empirical investigation within the parameters of a logical discipline. That came to be the idea of knowledge that united scientists of such diverse approaches, visions, and preconceptions as Lamarck, Darwin, and Mendel, as Carnot, Kelvin, and Liebig.

Scientific method developed gradually throughout the nineteenth century and so did the understanding of its nature and potential. As the culture's thinkers and creative writers were gradually coming to terms with science's persuasive vision, with its rapidly increasing power over the physical world, and with the integrity of its method, that method itself was changing and taking on different aspects. Taking as a baseline the views of naive, nineteenth-century realists who conceived of their results as the literal description of the Laws of Nature, we can see a revolution in basic epistemological assumptions, gradual at first, then sudden after the turn of the century with the Einsteinian revolution in physics.

The Einsteinian perspective brought with it the idea that knowledge is an artifact, that the insights that make up our understanding of the natural world are not simple discoveries but (at least partially) inventions of the human mind hypothetically projected onto the physical world. The passing of the earlier naive realism altered the problem of knowledge quite essentially; the new science thus put the creative writer in a nonabsolute, indeterminate, humanly defined universe after all. And longstanding culturally sanctioned concepts of perception and mind and knowledge stood firmly no more.

Likewise the longstanding and presumably unimpeachable vision of the universe as a rationalistically orderly, fundamentally material, inherently and ultimately knowable mechanism had been irreparably undermined. There would henceforth be a new vision of space and of time, of matter and of cause. Its promulgation would have an undeniable effect on the literary culture, and part of that effect would come through science's demonstration of the possibility and promise of the destruction of knowledge.

In the two chapters that follow it is my intent to show some of the motifs of the new scientific epistemology which are most clearly relatable to the literature of the early twentieth century. There are, of course, movements and figures and concepts important to modern epistemology that I must omit to maintain the larger focus of my book.

5   Scientists and Their Knowledge

■ Reflexiveness and "Objectivity"

Emerson's rhodora disappears in the web of its author's self-projections, just as William Cullen Bryant's well-known waterfowl flies a course precharted by its author, feeling only what its author would feel about the "abyss of heaven," the "boundless sky." For most nature poets in the earlier nineteenth century, being "attuned to nature" meant nearly its opposite: the trick was to write a poem that to a large extent attuned nature to you. In purely epistemological terms the result was decorative tautology, whatever the fineness of sentiment, psychological insight, or felicity of expression.

Nineteenth-century science offered an alternative to simple reflexiveness in its unremitting dedication to the ideal of pure objectivity. Later we shall have to qualify our sense of that term's significance, but the formation of the periodic table of the elements by Dimitri Mendeleyev in 1869 gives a good example of how nineteenth-century science achieved understanding of the nonhuman universe by methods which at least mitigated reflexiveness. Mendeleyev's table (or one of its more current versions) is familiar to anyone who has sat in a chemistry classroom, appreciated the way the bland uniformity of the room's decor was varied by the multicolored chart on the wall, and marveled at the intricate near-symmetry it signifies. Its import is that the elements of our physical universe, if we arrange them in the order of their atomic numbers in periods of eight, show not only an amazingly regular arithmetical progression, but a likewise remarkable periodic similarity of properties such as valence, melting point, and salt solubility. The relationships are chemically and mathematically based, and unrelatable to any a priori human relevance.

The old Aristotelian system of elements—earth, air, fire and water—was clearly a human-centered system, since hot and cold, wet and dry, solid, liquid, and gas are primary (sensory!) factors in human experience, and perception of them is immediately related to our welfare and our species' survival. But scientists long since had come to think of elements in terms of subtler, less species-oriented properties; thus Mendeleyev accomplished his arrangement of all the known elements nonmetaphorically, relying only on the concept of absolute physical atoms with fixed atomic weights and unvarying chemical properties and on the clear intimation of rational order. He didn't do it out of the blue, since many other knowledgeable and accomplished chemists had been hypothesizing various arrangments of the elements—based, for example, on triadic relationships, on regular exact multiples of the weight of hydrogen (assuming hydrogen as a kind of "primary matter"), and even on a recurrent eightfold increment of atomic weights. In his superbly cogent account of the discovery of the periodic law, Don C. Rawson concludes that "in each case the intrigue of numbers led these investigators to seek more precise and aesthetically satisfying relationships than their data could support." Mendeleyev's genius, in Rawson's view, was an ability to compare not just similar but dissimilar groups of elements and to see not only relationships within the groups but analogues of those relationships between groups.[1]

Mendeleyev's first draft of what was to become the system's definitive statement seems to have been a sudden insight, scrawled "on the back of a letter to Mendeleyev from A. I. Khodnev, secretary of the Free Economic Society in St. Petersburg, inquiring about Mendeleyev's preparations to inspect some cheese-processing plants for the society. The letter is dated 17 February, 1869,"[2] and the same day Mendeleyev sent a draft of the whole scheme to the printer. (The fate of the cheese-processing plants is unknown.)

There were gaps in his system, but Mendeleyev boldly insisted they were undiscovered elements. Quite specifically he foretold their natures as well as their existences: there must exist a metal, he claimed, "occupying the place immediately below aluminum, having atomic weight about 68, bearing the same relation to that metal that zinc does to magnesium, forming an oxide, R_2O_3, being a stronger base than alumina, forming a salt resembling alum, and having a specific gravity about 6."[3] The discovery of gallium in 1875, with atomic weight of 69 and specific gravity of 5.9 confirmed his prophesy and validated his system; the later discoveries of scandium and germanium did likewise. His system worked; as he himself would later point out: "The confirmation of a law is possible only by deducing consequences from it, which would be impossible and unexpected without it, and by justifying those consequences by experimental proof."[4]

Free of the anthropomorphic and teleological elements that made "discoveries" such as Emerson's or Bryant's so simply reflexive, Mendeleyev's law constituted knowledge that could lead to the discovery of elements that were in nature but were not in any other way anticipatable. Human knowledge of nature could more readily expand, and not merely reconceive and reflect and repeat.

■ The Mechanistic Worldview and Its Demise

Despite splendid accomplishments such as Mendeleyev's in approaching objectivity, nineteenth-century science remained manifestly anthropocentric. As later philosophers of science would point out, the governing categories of a great deal of nineteenth-century science were categories of mechanics, growing out of the necessities of human survival in the realm of physical objects and forces, and out of Western culture's amazingly burgeoning technological prowess. The objectivity of nineteenth-century science retrospectively appears to have been a peculiarly human objectivity, related to peculiarly human needs and sensory capacities—and (as total system) to traditional patterns of human rationality as well. Thus the self-absentness achieved by nineteenth-century science left substantial but largely unrecognized residues of species-specific and culture-specific determinants.

For most scientists throughout most of the nineteenth century the universe was a mechanical, mathematical, simply physical system. It was made of material atoms moved about by forces according to deterministic laws. Gravitation was the force of mutual attraction of bodies across space; space was uniform emptiness, the absolute location of bodies and events; time was a universal, equable flow; heat was the agitation of material molecules, and so forth. Even biological and psychological phenomena were characteristically described in categories of magnetism, thermodynamics, and such. The methods of nineteenth-century science were heavily dependent on the methods of mechanics, with its ways of identifying and quantifying physical entities and events and of tracing simple causal chains. In the spirit of naive realism, the laws and categories of science seemed absolute, grounded in the bedrock of empirical fact, as eternally reliable as repeatable sense perception. This was the sort of science that came to be mythologized in the minds of the literary naturalists; the problem was not that it was false but that it was much more limited, tentative, reflexive, and earth-bound than its practitioners and advocates could know.

The progress of physics in the first half of the twentieth century not only radically changed the laws and principles of the seemingly absolute structure that was nineteenth-century mechanism, but also utterly supplanted the categories and assumptions that underlay them. The work of Einstein, Lorentz, Eddington, Bohr, Heisenberg, and De Broglie (among others) constituted a revolution in physics that left little of the old knowledge unaffected. Einstein's special theory of relativity (1905) challenged the basic mechanistic categories of space, time, and motion; in the new physics there would be no absolute frame of reference. Space isn't merely space—that vacant linear container of things and events—because what had always been thought of as space was really partly time too: the universe spread out around us at this moment never really existed as a simultaneous universe from any other point in spacetime. Some of those lights in the night sky took a million years to get to us and others only a few minutes; from another point in the universe those relationships would be different, the dying star we see long dead, perhaps. Simultaneity is no more than a characteristic of a particular perspective, and space and time are separable only by an arbitrary intellectual act. Furthermore, in the new physics the classical (and still rather prevalent commonsensical) distinction between matter and space disappears in the concept of the field, just as do the concepts of mass and energy. In Einstein's words, "Matter which we perceive is merely nothing but a great concentration of energy in very small regions. We may therefore regard matter as being constituted by the regions of space in which the field is extremely intense."[5] In this new conception gravitation is no longer a force but a geometrical property of a field; atoms of matter are no longer the solid basic units of a fundamentally material universe but are intricate systems of electromagnetic charges and wavelike vibrations. And in the very microphysical depths of those atom systems the behavior of the individual particle is, with respect to any possibility of our knowing both its position and its velocity, indeterminate.

As imposing a concept as the mechanistic universe was, as pervasive, absolute, and self-evident as it seemed, it did not survive—as a general picture, at least—the onset of relativity and quantum mechanics. This is not to say that some of its particular concepts and modes of thinking do not still prevail in scientific and popular thought, or that specific theories of the classical period—like Mendeleyev's periodic table—haven't been fully accommodated into the new structure. Many of the habits and the real accomplishments of the age of mechanism are still indeed with us, but our understanding of the whole theoretical framework in which they exist can no longer be the naive construction it used to be.

■ Twentieth-Century Scientists' Vision of Scientific Knowing

Twentieth-century scientists themselves had a great deal to do with the radical revision in our understanding of the nature of physical knowledge and with our increasing preoccupation with method. They frequently contributed directly to the growing consensus that in science—or more specifically, in physics—empirical observation was innately biased and relative and theoretical generalization was inescapably symbolic and hypothetical. Physicist Percy Bridgman, for example, giving much credit to Einstein for revising the basis of physical thought, insisted that scientific concepts had to be linked to specific procedures to have any real meaning:

> In general, we mean by any concept nothing more than a set of operations; *the concept is synonymous with the corresponding set of operations.* If the concept is physical, as of length, the operations are actual physical operations, namely, those by which length is measured; or if the concept is mental, as of mathematical continuity, the operations are mental operations, namely those by which we determine whether a given aggregate of magnitudes is continuous.[6]

Einstein himself often argued that the old atomistic-mechanistic view was played out, that its theories, formed according to physical phenomena of the middle realm of volumes and velocities, were not consistently borne out on the micro and macro levels. He had a simple but highly influential epistemology, based on his own scientific work:

> The belief in an external world independent of the perceiving subject is the basis of all natural science. Since, however, sense perception only gives information of this external world or of "physical reality" indirectly, we can only grasp the latter by speculative means. It follows from this that our notions of physical reality can never be final. We must always be ready to change these notions—that is to say, the axiomatic substructure of physics—in order to do justice to perceived facts in the most logically perfect way.

Indirect, speculative, and tentative though it may essentially be, our understanding of nature can, Einstein thought, be reliably based on experience and on mathematics:

> Our experience hitherto justifies us in believing that nature is the realisation of the simplest conceivable mathematical ideas. I am convinced that we can discover by means of purely mathematical constructions the concepts and the laws connecting them with each

other, which furnish the key to the understanding of natural phenomena. Experience may suggest the appropriate mathematical concepts, but they most certainly cannot be deduced from it. Experience remains, of course, the sole criterion of the physical utility of a mathematical construction. But the creative principle resides in mathematics.[7]

The development of quantum mechanics constituted one of the century's greatest challenges to the customary assumptions of scientific thought and even to the new orthodoxy in theories of knowing. For if the quantum of action were the indivisible unit that the latest "mathematical construction," quantum theory, discovered it to be; if the individual quantum indeed were indeterminable in location-and-velocity, unlike all other physical entities; and if the principles of its behavior were random, discontinuous, and only statistically consistent and describable, then the fundamental process of the universe seemed out-of-keeping with our whole approach to knowledge. The identity of an elementary particle, its causal connection to other particles and events, and even our discreteness from it would be concepts that were conventional, subjective, and highly fallible. According to Niels Bohr,

> we have gradually reached a complete understanding of the intimate connection between the renunciation of causality in the quantum-mechanical description and the limitation with regard to the possibility of distinguishing between phenomena and their observation, which is conditioned by the indivisibility of the quantum of action. The recognition of this situation implies an essential change in our attitude towards the principle of causality as well as towards the concept of observation. . . .
>
> The epistemological problem under discussion may be characterized briefly as follows: For describing our mental activity, we require, on one hand, an objectively given content to be placed in opposition to a perceiving subject, while, on the other hand, as is already implied in such an assertion, no sharp separation between object and subject can be maintained, since the perceiving subject also belongs to our mental content. From these circumstances follows not only the relative meaning of every concept, or rather of every word, the meaning depending upon our arbitrary choice of view point, but also that we must, in general, be prepared to accept the fact that a complete elucidation of one and the same object may require diverse points of view which defy a unique description.[8]

Einstein disagreed with the ultimate implication of this theory—"I cannot but confess that I attach only a transitory importance to [Bohr's] interpretation. I still believe in the possibility of a model of reality—that is to say, of a theory which represents things themselves and not merely the probability of their occurrence—"[9] but it was evident that by the mid-1920s quantum theory had given a new depth to the realization of the relativity of our knowing.

6   Science and the Epistemologists

Even before the great age of scientific mechanism, classical epistemologists such as Berkeley, Hume, and Kant had raised questions that seriously impugned the system of knowing that mechanism would employ. The doubts raised by these philosophers suggested that our concepts and even our perceptions could not help but be at least partially subjectively determined. Yet they had no more than slight impact on science and on the culture at large. Whether their lack of impact was because epistemology was a field of more dispute than consensus or because their insights were too complex and too far outside the framework of commonsense discourse is problematical. What is certain is that naive realism was working very well for nineteenth-century scientists, and science has always had a strong and essential bias against gratuitous complication. It took the revelation by scientists themselves that naive realism produced fallible science to bring the epistemological issue into the light: for example Darwin showing the term *species* to be a mental construct rather than a real entity (and one that could *limit* our knowledge of the living world) or Einstein demonstrating that the Newtonian framework for the universe had gaps and contradictions and that a superior alternative hypothesis could be proposed.

The doubts and cavils of the classical epistemologists were made newly relevant by the new science. (Hume was a culture-hero after all.) Thus the challenge for a philosopher of knowledge of the early twentieth century would be an immense one: to integrate this array of doubts, limits, and deconstructions that was the epistemological heritage with experience on the one hand and with science on the other. Somewhat ironically, the new philosophical accommodations often involved provocative new destructions.

■ Early Twentieth-Century Philosophical Models
of Knowing: Analytical Philosophies

The infusion of twentieth-century science changed the focus, the techniques, and even the language of philosophy. If we take the philosophy of John Dewey as our entry point to the analytical branch of scientific philosophies we can see this clearly, as well as confronting a number of issues —experience, abstraction, rationality, subjectivity—that were very much on the minds of novelists and poets of the period. Dewey was one of the most insistent advocates of new scientific views, arguing in dozens of books and essays for the destruction of traditional, abstractly idealistic, and rationalistic philosophical approaches, and for the creation of an approach that was empirical, pragmatic, and based on the only credible foundation for thought—experience. In his view experience was accessible mainly by means of science. Science's methods and criteria needed to be applied to all circumstances of knowing, Dewey insisted. "All knowledge is experimental," he said in the 1916 introduction to his *Essays in Experimental Logic*.[1] Presumably "subjective" elements of experience should not be disregarded but rather formulated in ways that are experimentally testable. "Instrumentalism" is what he called his approach, and he defined it as "an attempt to constitute a precise logical theory of concepts, of judgments and inferences in their various forms, by considering primarily how thought functions in the experimental determinations of future consequences."[2]

His concept of truth as pragmatical and functional (following C. S. Peirce and William James), along with his emphases on experimentation, logic, and the role of reason not as absolute but as "reconstructive or mediative" mark Dewey's approach as a harbinger of a new epistemology, although his sense of scientific thought processes is distinctly less sophisticated than Einstein's or Bohr's. Fundamental to his purposes, certainly, is his effort to destroy the old dualists' sense of the mind as "something purely 'subjective,' a peculiar kind of existence which lives, moves, and has its being in a realm different from things to be known," and the thing to be known as "a fixed, ready-made thing which has no organic connections with the origin, purpose, and growth of the attempt to know it, some kind of *Ding-an-sich* or absolute, extra-empirical 'Reality.'"[3]

The development of analytical philosophy was, of course, one of the most significant features of twentieth-century philosophy, and it coincides quite closely, as we shall see, with the development in literature of a preoccupation with language, its semantic possibilities, and its relation to perspective. Analytical philosophy focuses attention on the study of concepts, their language and their interrelationships, and is a movement dedicated to bringing the strictest sort of scientific and logical criteria to bear on philosophical discourse. Such philosophical analysis begins, naturally, in an attitude of extreme skepticism about previous philosophies and an attempt to systematically expunge all metaphysical concepts and approaches from the domain of knowledge. Analytical philosophers focus on the nature of meaning rather than the meaning of nature; their ideal is to reduce knowledge to what is logically certain.

Bertrand Russell was one of the pioneers of analytical philosophy and one of its most renowned and notorious advocates. His concept of the world and its makeup changed or modulated in the course of his long career—we might find him presenting himself as more or less a dualist one time and as more or less a phenomenalist the next—but his sense of how thought is to be carried on and how knowledge is to be arrived at marks him as one of the new style of thinkers. A theoretical mathematician, he brought the special insights of mathematics to the business of knowing: a special sense of the role of symbolism in rational thought and a special propensity to explore and represent reality in terms of relationships.

Russell was first of all a doubter: "I think on the whole that the sort of method adopted by Descartes is right: that you should set to work to doubt things and retain only what you cannot doubt because of its clearness and distinctness."[4] But Descartes' purely rational sense of clearness and distinctness had no appeal for Russell, who was second of all an empiricist. His empiricism, like Dewey's, was grounded in experience rather than in the abstract "matter" of the pre-Einsteinian physicists: as he pointed out in 1915,

> instead of supposing, as we naturally do when we start from an uncritical acceptance of the apparent dicta of physics, that *matter* is what is "really real" in the physical world, and that the immediate objects of sense are mere phantasms, we must regard matter as a logical construction, of which the constituents will be just such evanescent particulars as may, when an observer happens to be present, become data of sense to that observer.[5]

The shift from a philosophy of knowledge based on *reality* to one based on *experience* involves, Russell shows, an acknowledgment of variant perspectives: "The system consisting of all views of the universe perceived and unperceived, I shall call the system of 'perspectives'; I shall confine the expression 'private worlds' to such views of the universe as are actually perceived. Thus a 'private world' is a perceived 'perspective'; but there may be any number of unperceived perspectives."[6] It was like the shift in narrative technique from Howells and Dreiser on one hand to Dos Passos and Faulkner on the other, this shift in focus from reality to experience and its perspectives and "private worlds."

However rife with possibilities for the imagination these ideas were, Russell developed them purely in the direction of logical analysis. Conceiving of the world as being constituted of *sensibilia* (the elementary sense data of the "private worlds" and the potential elementary sense data of the perspectives), or what he at a later stage characterized as "event-particles," he attempted to construct a logical hierarchy of atoms and molecules of fact. In time the monistic basis of this system came to seem undeniable to him, and the distinctions between subject and object, between sensation and sense datum faded—as they previously had for Mach and William James—into artificial, metaphysically tinged, and ultimately unnecessary suppositions. Russell's universe of knowing thus bore a distinct similarity to the physical universe described by Einstein and Bohr: elementary event-particles existing in a spacetime continuum, perceivable only in an act which is itself part of the system of particles.

But Russell's forays into reality-charting remained only forays for him, often introduced in terms that emphasized their hypothetical nature: "I suggest the following as an outline of a possible structure of the world; it is no more than an outline, and is not offered as more than possible."[7] His more earnest efforts were dedicated not to relating experience back to the factors that caused or affected it, but to relating concepts and theories back to the experiences upon which they could be based. "Whenever possible," he stated, "substitute constructions out of known entities for inferences to unknown entities."[8] Russell's program was termed *Constructionism*, and in Morris Weitz's view it functioned principally as a justification for science, since "this substitution of empirical for unempirical symbols means, of course, that scientific symbols are defined in sensory terms, which validates the claim of (natural) science that it is empirical." Russell felt that in the larger realm of thought the constructionist ought to examine all propositions for their closeness to experience, and to establish a "hierarchy of dubitables" in which the system of thought would be based on the most reliable (or least unreliable) propositions.[9]

Analytical philosophy led quite naturally into the analysis of language and its role in the shaping of knowledge. As Russell pointed out, "the influence of language on philosophy has, I believe, been profound and almost unrecognized. If we are not to be misled by this influence, it is necessary to become conscious of it, and to ask ourselves deliberately how far it is legitimate."[10] Vocabulary precipitated one set of problems, especially by way of our overriding tendency to believe in the unity and actuality of the things words named. Russell also thought that our faith in our words made us liable to miss crucial individual differences in phenomena we customarily designated by the same general term; likewise it led us to reify abstractions and generally impelled our thought "towards a kind of platonic pluralism of things and ideas." Syntax brought another set of problems: the "subject-predicate logic" he decried, and the "substance-attribute (noun-modifier) metaphysic."[11] The languages of mathematics and symbolic logic could, he thought, be useful tools in the analysis of philosophical propositions. They would be our best hope for controlling the corrupting influences of language on thought.

D. F. Pears has characterized Russell as "the philosopher who gave empiricism an adequate logical framework."[12] He certainly was the philosopher who made numerous Americans aware of the logical and linguistic aspects of knowing, for he was a popularizer as well as a philosopher, and his lucid and urbane style made him a mentor in the new scientific views and attitudes for many Americans not in the thought professions. His widely read books and essays offered American culture a coherent approach and a new vocabulary for the destruction of metaphysical concepts and thought patterns.

His followers and colleagues in the analytical movement had a somewhat different sort of impact. They generally wrote as professional thinkers and for professional thinkers, and they attempted to establish purer, stricter, and more circumscribed systems of thought. For example, whereas Russell valued the activity of philosophy precisely because it dealt in unanswerable questions and uncertain concepts,[13] the Vienna school of analytical philosophers (the likes of Ludwig Wittgenstein, Moritz Schlick, and Rudolph Carnap) classified questions and concepts not amenable to empirical verification or logical proof as meaningless. "*The logic of science takes the place of the inextricable tangle of problems which is known as philosophy,*" Carnap asserted,[14] following Wittgenstein's dictum that

> The right method in philosophy would be this. To say nothing except what can be said, i.e. the propositions of natural science, i.e. something that has nothing to do with philosophy: and then always, when someone else wished to say something metaphysical, to demonstrate

to him that he had given no meaning to certain signs in his propositions. This method would be unsatisfying to the other—he would
not have the feeling that we were teaching him philosophy—but it
would be the only strictly correct method.[15]

Carnap's program for the reconstruction of knowledge is typical of
the Vienna school. Knowledge is to be strictly scientific, profoundly dependent on mathematics and physics; it is to be constructional, all of its
concepts hierarchically and logically related to what is given in experience
and universally verifiable; and it is to be experiential, its basic, atomic
elements being elementary "total impressions" ("the total impression is
primary, while sensations and particular feelings, etc., are only the result
of an abstracting analysis").[16] Knowledge is *only* what can be so formulated, Carnap insisted; other insights commonly referred to as knowledge
simply are not:

> Unquestionably, there are phenomena of faith, religious and other-
> wise, and of intuition; they play an important role, not only for prac-
> tical life, but also for cognition. Moreover, it can be admitted that, in
> these phenomena, somehow something is "grasped," but this
> figurative expression should not lead to the assumption that knowl-
> edge is gained through these phenomena. What is gained is a certain
> attitude, a certain psychological state, which, under certain circum-
> stances, can indeed be favorable for obtaining certain insights. Knowl-
> edge, however, can be present only when we designate and formu-
> late, when a statement is rendered in words or other signs.[17]

Carnap's scrutiny of language, most notably in *The Logical Syntax of
Language* (German ed., 1934; English, 1937), goes much farther than Russell's had, both in attempting to clarify and purify language to make it
more accurately reflective of logical relationships and in developing correspondences between syntax, logic, and empirical relationship.

Of special interest from a literary standpoint is his analysis (written
in the mid-1920s) of our capacity to know and conceptually represent
another person. "Construction" on the "heteropsychological level" is what
he calls it, and his two main points about it could give confirmation to the
approaches of many a fiction writer working in the twenties and thirties.
For one thing he traces our knowledge of other persons down to our own
experiences: *"the entire experience sequence of the other person consists of nothing but a rearrangement of my own experiences and their constituents."*[18] For
another thing he insists on our representing the clear empirical details

about the other person and avoiding inferential and theoretical accretions. "The heteropsychological with all its characteristics depends upon the recognition of the corresponding physical occurrence," he states, continuing with a cautionary example about what we do and don't know about another person, "A," who is acting in such a way as to seem joyful:

> By saying "A is joyful" and not merely "A shows facial expressions of such and such a form," I express that I have a representation of a feeling of joy, although a feeling of joy in the autopsychological sense, since I cannot know any other. However, to assume that by using the psychological instead of the physical language, that is to say, by using the expression "joy" instead of "facial expressions of such and such a form," we express a fact which goes beyond the physical state of affairs, is to confuse the theoretical content of the statement with an accompanying representation.[19]

This sort of strict logical analysis of interpersonal knowledge seems to share some theoretical premises with the fictional approaches of Hemingway, Dos Passos, William Carlos Williams, and other writers who try to develop techniques to demarcate and respect the boundaries between another person and one's own projections.

No poet or fiction writer could work within the sanctions and strictures of analytical philosophy—he or she would have too deep a belief in what he or she was doing to be satisfied with a personal vision of truth that was second to science's or with the operation of an imagination second to logic—but there is no question that there are certain specific areas of common assumption and concern. The disbelief in abstractions, the belief in the primacy of experience (especially the "total impression"), the desire to discriminate clearly between empirical event and interpretation, the sensitivity to language and the techniques of making meaning—all these are significantly mutual.

■ Early Twentieth-Century Models of Knowing:
Process Philosophies

The epistemological philosophy that developed the view of both reality and knowing as *process* went farther than any other in repudiating preconceptions about how we know. Its principal formulators were Henri Bergson, William James, and, a decade or so later, Alfred North Whitehead; it is in some ways directly antithetical to the analytical philosophies, and it is the epistemological view with the greatest and most direct influence on twentieth-century American literature. Beginning in psychology rather than mathematics or empirical physics, the process philosophers cast doubt on more aspects of knowing than the analytical philosophers had; and in impugning all traditional notions of mind, and especially those of intellect, they opened many new avenues of possibility for writers. Ordinary notions of time and of experience, of perception and of reflexiveness, of individual perspective and of language would no longer be the same. These philosophers influenced some writers directly and some indirectly, gave a new slant to the destruction of knowledge, and contributed importantly to the culture-wide preoccupation with epistemology.

William James's position in American culture is formidable, unchallengeable. In Harold Stearns's 1922 anthology *Civilization in the United States* (noted for containing a number of very negative views of its subject) James is recognized by anthropologist Robert H. Lowie as "the solitary example of an American pre-eminent in a branch of science who at the same time succeeded in deeply affecting the cultural life of a whole generation." And philosophical expert Harold Chapman Brown claimed that "if James has drawn to himself the greatest reading public of all American philosophers, it is because in him each man can find the sanction for himself. Without dogmatism or pedantry, James is the voice of all human experiences."[20] James's colleague Bergson was a prominent French philosopher not without an American following of his own. Bergson and James read each other's books with great interest, exchanged ideas, and worked for the acceptance of each other's thought. So many of their ideas were mutually arrived at, borrowed, or amended on advice from the other that questions of priority are intricate and unsuitable for sorting out here.

Their revision of knowledge began in revolt against the regnant rationalistic theory of mind, which they both regarded as reductionist and out-of-keeping with our actual mental experience. Bergson's first assault came in *Time and Free Will* in 1888, in which he claimed that because we mistakenly identify our *experience* of time with our *concept* of time, we reason our way into a spurious determinism. He wanted us to unlearn the mechanistic rationalism that pictures time as a homogeneous succession of instants and pictures conscious states as discrete entities like physical bodies in space. His remedy was to have us discover the *durée réelle* that is the primary datum of our experience:

> Below homogeneous duration, which is the extensive symbol of true
> duration, a close psychological analysis distinguishes a duration whose

heterogeneous moments permeate one another; below the numerical multiplicity of conscious states, a qualitative multiplicity; below the self with well-defined states, a self in which *succeeding each other* means *melting into one another* and forming an organic whole.[21]

James made a major assault, independent of Bergson's, with *Principles of Psychology* in 1890. For him the inhibiting body of knowledge was not so much a dominant philosophical view of spatialized time as it was the dominant psychological view of atomized mind, but he came out at the same place as Bergson.

> Most books start with sensations, as the simplest mental facts, and proceed synthetically, constructing each higher stage from those below it. But this is abandoning the empirical method of investigation. No one ever had a simple sensation by itself. Consciousness, from our natal day, is of a teeming multiplicity of objects and relations, and what we call simple sensations are results of discriminative attention, pushed often to a very high degree.

James too insisted that our primary experience was not of a succession of discrete mental entities, but of a complex, ever-changing whole:

> Consciousness, then, does not appear to itself chopped up in bits. Such words as "chain" or "train" do not describe it fitly as it presents itself in the first instance. It is nothing jointed; it flows. A "river" or a "stream" are the metaphors by which it is most naturally described. *In talking of it hereafter, let us call it the stream of thought, of consciousness, or of subjective life.*[22]

Thus, in rejecting conventional concepts of mind and mental experience and trying to rediscover a preconceptual mental life, these two philosophers proposed an idea (and coined a term) of vast import and applicability in the understanding of modern narrative fiction.

At the core of both men's destruction of the conventional means of knowledge acquisition is their concept of the intellect and its role. Bergson developed his theory in *Creative Evolution* (1908; Arthur Mitchell's English American edition, 1911) in an evolutionary biological perspective that

> shows us in the faculty of understanding an appendage of the faculty of acting, a more and more precise, more and more complex and supple adaptation of the consciousness of living beings to the conditions of existence that are made for them. Hence should result this

consequence that our intellect, in the narrow sense of the word, is intended to secure the perfect fitting of our body to its environment, to represent the relations of external things among themselves—in short, to think matter. Such will indeed be one of the conclusions of the present essay. We shall see that the human intellect feels at home among inanimate objects, more especially among solids, where our action finds its fulcrum and our industry its tools; that our concepts have been formed on the model of solids; that our logic is, pre-eminently, the logic of solids.[23]

The intellect conceives of the world in terms of hard objects, spatial relations, and static states, Bergson thought, and tends to obscure our perception of change, life, and novelty. Further, as the distinguished Bergson scholar Milič Čapek points out,

> One of the central, doubtless most controversial, but also most interesting, theses of his epistemology is that the sensory elements of our macroscopic experience are subtly and insidiously present even on the highest level of logical and mathematical abstraction. This is the meaning of his claim that our logic is the "logic of solid bodies" and that the operations of conceptual thought, at least in its classical form, betray the influence of our macroscopic perception of solid bodies as well as our technique by which these bodies are manipulated.[24]

Bergson stands at an opposite pole from the analytical philosophers in this respect, setting little stock in the ability of logical and mathematical intellection to put us clear of reflexiveness in our knowing. He sees intellection in general as rooted in our particular evolutionary situation and as introducing baseless and distorting elements into our consideration of phenomena of life and change. Bergson's epistemology was formed in direct reaction to the mechanistic thought and the naive realism that so pervaded science and philosophy in his early years. One of his main purposes was to bring intellect down from its widely reputed status as sole and absolute guide to reality and establish for it a real though radically limited legitimacy. "An intellect bent upon the act to be performed and the reaction to follow, feeling its object so as to get its mobile impression at every instant, is an intellect that touches something of the absolute," he says, and goes on to assert that "Intellectual knowledge, in so far as it relates to a certain aspect of inert matter, ought . . . to give us a faithful imprint of it, having been stereotyped on this particular object. It becomes relative only if it claims, such as it is, to present to us life."[25] Such was the nature of Bergson's anti-intellectualism.

James similarly saw the intellect as having a useful but limited function in the whole realm of human mental activity. In *A Pluralistic Universe*, the published version of his 1908 Hibbert lectures, he stressed intellect's use solely "to guide us in the practical adaptation of our expectancies and activities." He surveyed the way philosophers such as Hegel, Bradley, and Royce used intellectual logic, and swore that "For my own part, I have finally found myself compelled to *give up the logic*, fairly, squarely, and irrevocably. It has an imperishable use in human life, but that use is not to make us theoretically acquainted with the essential nature of reality. . . . Reality, life, experience, concreteness, immediacy, use what word you will, exceeds our logic, overflows and surrounds it." He claimed that historically

> intellectualism in the vicious sense began when Socrates and Plato taught that what a thing really is, is told us by its *definition*. Ever since Socrates we have been taught that reality consists of essences, not of appearances, and that the essences of things are known whenever we know their definitions. So first we identify a thing with a concept and then we identify the concept with a definition, and only then, inasmuch as the thing *is* whatever the definition expresses, are we sure of apprehending the real essence of it or the full truth about it.
>
> It is but the old story, of a useful practice first becoming a method, then a habit, and finally a tyranny that defeats the end it was used for.

He especially endorsed Bergson's critique of intellectualism: "In my opinion he has killed intellectualism definitively and without hope of recovery."[26]

James insisted that *experience* is prior to and more inclusive than any intellectual concepts or categories and that we, as thinkers dedicated to reliable empirical methods, need to begin our investigations there. His notion of experience is certainly different than Dewey's; in his 1912 (posthumous) collection *Essays in Radical Empiricism* "pure experience" is the term by which he designates "the immediate flux of life which furnishes the material to our later reflection with its conceptual categories," and "experience in its immediacy," he insists, "is perfectly fluent."[27] He had been maintaining that about mind and experience from the beginning: in *Principles of Psychology* he had identified "five important characters in thought" which established the individual relativity and the fluency of mental experience and the abstractive, selective nature of perception.[28]

For James knowledge was inescapably subjective—even in the most personal sense (and such a realization could warm the heart of any poet or novelist, since it put the seal of validity on even the most individual feelings and utterances). For one thing all our perceptions are tinged (*at least* tinged) by memory. James felt we need to recognize that although "sensations are the stable rock, the *terminus a quo* and the *terminus ad quem* of thought," still *"pure sensations can only be realized in the earliest days of life. They are all but impossible to adults with memories and stores of associations acquired."*[29] This means that in the process of perception "any quality of a thing which affects our sense-organs does also more than that: it arouses processes in the hemispheres which are due to the organization of [the brain] by past experiences, and the result of which in consciousness are commonly described as ideas which the sensation suggests."[30]

For another thing our emotions affect all we know. James's Radical Empiricism recognized a valid place for emotion in the activity of knowing: since feelings and tones were integral to experience, they must provide access to reality if any experience did. Only an intellectualist would try to separate experience artificially and arbitrarily into "subjective" and "objective" elements and deny or belittle the validity of emotion. Even experiences characterizable as religious or mystic were not and should not be excludable. James urged, described, and carefully qualified their legitimacy in the face of mechanistic science in *The Varieties of Religious Experience* in 1902, and in a 1910 essay, "A Suggestion about Mysticism," he proposed "that states of mystical intuition may be only very sudden and great extensions of the ordinary 'field of consciousness.'"[31] He admitted that his own "direct personal experience" with such phenomena affected his understanding of them. I might note here that James's epistemological viewpoint is quite vulnerable to charges of being unscientific and idiosyncratic, and his critics often make them.

Bergson's topography of the mind was somewhat more schematic than James's, involving the division of mental capacities into the categories of instinct and intuition as well as of the partially discredited intellect. Instinct he saw as bearing the imprint of life, as intellect bore the imprint of matter. "Instinct is sympathy," the most direct connection between life and ourselves; unfortunately it is only transitory, immediate, and incapable of providing understanding of the world. It remained for intuition to link life and understanding: "It is to the very inwardness of life that *intuition* leads us—by intuition I mean instinct that has become disinterested, self-conscious, capable of reflecting upon its object and of enlarging it indefinitely."[32] (His choice of terms was unfortunate: to many of his readers "intuition" carried its vernacular signification of a passive faculty of feeling and fancy, whereas Bergson repeatedly had to insist that he was using the term to designate a strenuously critical though nonrationalistic sort of reflection.) Perception, even for the most sensitive of intuitions, could never be pure, and knowledge was never absolute, although great possibilities for understanding could be realized through the integration of the three basic functions: "Intelligence remains the luminous nucleus around which instinct, even enlarged and purified into intuition, forms only a vague nebulosity. But, in default of knowledge properly so called, reserved to pure intelligence, intuition may enable us to grasp what it is that intelligence fails to give us, and indicate the means of supplementing it." "Suppose these other forms of consciousness brought together and amalgamated with intellect," he projects, "would not the result be a consciousness as wide as life?"[33]

Bergson's schematization was a vulnerable one, but it, like James's concepts (themselves no model of precision), put forward and influentially sanctioned the idea that reality had aspects that were approachable only by the nonrational capacities of the mind. Intuition, introspection, empathy, and imagination here emerge from the realm of the classical epistemologists' secondary and tertiary qualities.

Not surprisingly, the pioneering process philosophers had the highest regard for aesthetic creation and appreciation. They saw the act of artistic imagination as the act of fullest understanding. In *The Creative Mind* Bergson envisioned it as an act of disinterested empathy: "When [artists] look at a thing, they see it for itself, and not for themselves. . . . It is therefore a much more direct vision of reality that we find in the different arts; and it is because the artist is less intent on utilizing his perception that he perceives a greater number of things."[34] In *Creative Evolution* he used the act of artistic imagination as the very paradigm of the kind of act a thinker needs to perform in order to understand life:

> Our eye perceives the features of the living being, merely as assembled, not as mutually organized. The intention of life, the simple movement that runs through the lines, that binds them together and gives them significance, escapes it. This intention is just what the artist tries to regain, in placing himself back within the object by a kind of sympathy, in breaking down, by an effort of intuition, the barrier that space puts up between him and his model. It is true that this aesthetic intuition, like external perception, only attains the indi-

vidual. But we can conceive an inquiry turned in the same direction as art, which would take life *in general* for its object, just as physical science, in following to the end the direction pointed out by external perception, prolongs the individual facts into general laws.[35]

James takes even farther the idea of the imaginative empathy necessary to understand our world. We are unable to know even a single concrete thing, in view of the multiplicity of intellectual perspectives in which we can place it.

> Our intellectual handling of it is a retrospective patchwork, a post-mortem dissection, and can follow any order we find most expedient. We can make the thing seem self-contradictory whenever we wish to. But place yourself at the point of view of the thing's interior *doing*, and all these back-looking and conflicting conceptions lie harmoniously in your hand. Get at the expanding centre of a human character, the *élan vital* of a man, as Bergson calls it, by living sympathy, and at a stroke you see how it makes those who see it from without interpret it in such diverse ways.[36]

In the light of the process philosophers' emphasis on the personal aspects and dimensions of knowing, their theory of perception bears interestingly on the problem of the reflexiveness of knowledge, and it helped to prepare the way for the self-aware and intentional reflexiveness in the works of Stein, Stevens, Williams, and Dos Passos. For Bergson and James, since it is a delusion to pretend that any rationalistic ways of knowing are free of personal, cultural, and biological bias, one ought to strive for a self-projection that is self-aware, imaginative, wholly intentional, and especially sensitive to details unlike oneself and one's expectations. Since whatever one does, one can only project oneself into the object of knowing, best to do it consciously. As James puts it,

> Our own bodily position, attitude, condition, is one of the things of which *some* awareness, however inattentive, invariably accompanies the knowledge of whatever else we know. We think; and as we think we feel our bodily selves as the seat of the thinking. If the thinking be *our* thinking, it must be suffused through all its parts with that peculiar warmth and intimacy that make it come as ours. . . . *Whatever* the content of the ego may be, it is habitually felt *with* everything else by us humans, and must form a *liaison* between all the things of which we become successively aware.[37]

Thus, whereas the scientists and analytical philosophers tried to control reflexiveness by rigorously excluding the self of the knower from the technique of knowing, from the structure and even to some extent the very purview of knowledge, the process philosophers committed themselves fully and enthusiastically to the self as the only legitimate access to the world outside the self.

The essence of the self was an homogeneous process; in James's terms "within each personal consciousness thought is always changing. . . . Within each personal consciousness thought is sensibly continuous."[38] The self's truest, least-mediated experience was process, the self itself was process, and furthermore the world outside the self was process; sequentially, this is how the ideas of both Bergson and James grew, beginning with a psychological insight into the divisionless flux of experience and culminating in a metaphysical vision of universal process. In the words of our contemporary, Milič Čapek, "Just as Bergson's 'true duration,' originally purely psychological, became finally a 'creative evolution' on the cosmical scale, James's final affirmation of 'the everlasting coming of novelty into being' was but an extended vision of his 'stream of consciousness.'"[39]

Reality's indivisible contextuality, its everywhere-mutual interinvolvement, was as important a feature as its flux. James gives this vivid analysis in his *Principles of Psychology*:

> Into the awareness of the thunder itself the awareness of the previous silence creeps and continues; for what we hear when the thunder crashes is not thunder *pure*, but thunder-breaking-upon-silence-and-contrasting-with-it. Our feeling of the same objective thunder, coming in this way, is quite different from what it would be were the thunder a continuation of previous thunder. The thunder itself we believe to abolish and exclude the silence; but the *feeling* of the thunder is also a feeling of the silence as just gone.[40]

And later in his *A Pluralistic Universe* he explains that "inside of the minimal pulses of experience, is realized that very inner complexity which the transcendentalists say only the absolute can genuinely possess. The gist of the matter is always the same—something ever goes indissolubly with something else. You cannot separate the same from its other, except by abandoning the real altogether and taking to the conceptual system."[41] Experience's structure is reality's structure for these philosophers, and rational intellection is something different, far more specialized. Novelty, multiple simultaneous interrelationships, and continuous divisionless

change are all fundamental aspects of reality virtually inaccessible to knowledge as it was then constituted. Thus the process philosophers' efforts to
reconstitute it. They recognized language as a crucial shaper and inhibitor
of knowing, and although, unlike some of the poets and novelists who
also had this insight, they wrote in standard language and conventional
expository form, they pointed out some of the ways language retarded
knowing. As James said after the above-quoted thunder passage, "here,
again, language works against our perception of the truth."[42] He and Bergson saw a fundamental, unavoidable incompatability between experience
and language. True experience—fluid, complex, contextually and tempo-
rally interpenetrative, inescapably individual—could be represented only
imperfectly in words and only through a struggle with the conventions,
the propensities, and the very nature of language.

As James considered the situation in some detail in several parts of
Principles of Psychology, he saw that one serious problem was language's
featuring the "substantive" parts of the stream of consciousness at the
expense of the "transitive" parts; language draws attention to things, qualities, assertions, and resolutions and denies attention to the subtle texture
of relationships, transitions, and intervals that are equally authentic elements of experience. "We ought to say a feeling of *and*, a feeling of *if*, a
feeling of *but*, and a feeling of *by*, quite as readily as we say a feeling of
blue or a feeling of *cold*. Yet we do not: so inveterate has our habit become
of recognizing the existence of the substansive parts alone, that language
almost refuses to lend itself to any other use."[43] Additionally, language
misrepresents reality's contextuality: in its essential function of designating objects and thoughts, it simplifies to the point of distortion the experience it purports to represent: "We name our thoughts simply, each
after its thing, as if each knew its own thing and nothing else. What each
really knows is clearly the thing it is named for, with dimly perhaps a
thousand other things. It ought to be named after all of them, but it never
is."

James even lamented the fact that language carried its own quite spurious test of meaning: "if words do belong to the same vocabulary, and if
the grammatical structure is correct, sentences with absolutely no meaning may be uttered in good faith and pass unchallenged." "The birds filled
the tree-tops with their morning song, making the air moist, cool, and
pleasant,"[44] is an example of journalistic prose he recalls as a statement
that makes only linguistic sense.

Bergson too, in the seminal work of his career, *Time and Free Will*, examines the problem of language in some detail, concluding that "there is no

common measure between mind and language."* "We instinctively tend to solidify our impressions," he says, "in order to express them in language": "Hence we confuse the feeling itself, which is in a perpetual state of becoming, with its permanent external object, and especially with the word which expresses this object. . . . Our constantly changing impressions, wrapping themselves around the external object which is their cause, take on its definite outlines and its immobility" (130). The linguistic representation of our "simple sensations" presents an even more critical problem,

> for sensations and tastes seem to me to be *objects* as soon as I isolate and name them, and in the human soul there are only *processes*. What I ought to say is that every sensation is altered by repetition, and that if it does not seem to me to change from day to day, it is because I perceive it through the object which is its cause, through the word which translated it. This influence of language on sensation is deeper than is usually thought. (131)

Thus language loses the essential uniqueness of each experience, as well as falsifying the essential character of experience itself. It loses human individuality and authenticity as well:

> A violent love or a deep melancholy takes possession of our soul: here we feel a thousand different elements which dissolve into and permeate one another without any precise outlines, without the least tendency to externalize themselves in relation to one another; hence their originality. We distort them as soon as we distinguish a numerical multiplicity in their confused mass. . . . A moment ago each of them was borrowing an indefinable colour from its surroundings: now we have it colourless, and ready to accept a name. . . . By separating these moments from each other, by spreading out time in space, we have caused this feeling to lose its life and its colour. Hence, we are now standing before our own shadow: we believe that we have analysed our feeling, while we have really replaced it by a juxtaposition of lifeless states which can be translated into words, each of which constitutes the common element, the impersonal residue, of the impressions felt in a given case by the whole of society. (132–33)

Bergson saw our linguistic predicament as inevitable and insurmountable:

---

*Trans. F. L. Pogson (Harper & Row, 1960), 164–165. Parenthetical page numbers in this discussion refer to this volume.

In short, the word with well-defined outlines, the rough and ready word, which stores up the stable, common, and consequently impersonal element in the impressions of mankind, overwhelms or at least covers over the delicate and fugitive impressions of our individual consciousness. To maintain the struggle on equal terms, the latter ought to express themselves in precise words; but these words, as soon as they were formed, would turn against the sensation which gave birth to them, and, invented to show that the sensation is unstable, they would impose on it their own stability. (132)

Given the high regard the process philosophers had for the artistic imagination as well as their sensitivity to the relation of mind to language, it was inevitable that they would recognize the role of the creative writer as especially important. Bergson, for example, gave explicit recognition to the novelist, on two occasions designating him as the hero in the noble but ultimately hopeless struggle to unite language and experience. The novelist has insight and craft that can narrow the unbridgeable rift, and even his inevitable failure to conquer it can bring us the advantage of a more vivid recognition of our situation. I quote the two passages at length:

We estimate the talent of a novelist by the power with which he lifts out of the common domain, to which language had thus brought them down, feelings and ideas to which he strives to restore, by adding detail to detail, their original and living individuality. But just as we can go on inserting points between two positions of a moving body without ever filling up the space traversed, in the same way, by the mere fact that we associate states with states and that these states are set side by side instead of permeating one another, we fail to translate completely what our soul experiences. (164)

Now, if some bold novelist, tearing aside the cleverly woven curtain of our conventional ego, shows us under [the] appearance of logic a fundamental absurdity, under [the] juxtaposition of simple states an infinite permeation of a thousand different impressions which have already ceased to exist the instant they are named, we commend him for having known us better than we knew ourselves. This is not the case, however, and the very fact that he spreads out our feeling in a homogeneous time, and expresses its elements by words, shows us that he in his turn is only offering us its shadow: but he has arranged this shadow in such a way as to make us suspect the extraordinary and illogical nature of the object which projects it; he has made us reflect by giving outward expression to something of that contradiction, that interpenetration, which is the very essence of the elements expressed. Encouraged by him, we have put aside for an instant the veil which we interposed beween our consciousness and ourselves. He has brought us back into our own presence. (133–134)

Even a heroic effort with an inevitably imperfect language must fail, however; more immediate and presentational means are needed. As Bergson suggested in an essay in *The Creative Mind*, "The moment we reach the spiritual world, the image, if it merely seeks to suggest, may give us the direct vision, while the abstract term, which is spatial in origin and which claims to express, most frequently leaves us in metaphor."[45]

Thus Bergson and James are literally and strictly anti-intellectualist thinkers, although not at all in the popular style that would link intellect with learned nonsense, impracticality, and snooty pride. Their assault on intellectuality is an assault on the stultifying patterns of knowledge and knowledge acquisition that especially sprouted with mechanistic science and naive realism. Their alternative epistemology resisted radical objectivization and depersonalization and sanctioned a more personal and spontaneous system of learning. "Trust experience," they in effect say, "instead of the mental constructs of conventional mechanism and all other forms of conventional knowledge." Consequently, their legacy has been sanction, latitude, and inspiration for writers and artists eager to discover and follow the dictates of their individual imaginations. Their philosophical legacy has been more ambiguous, although that needn't concern us here.

Alfred North Whitehead developed an influential philosophy of process too, following by a few years the thought of Bergson and James. Already a distinguished mathematician-logician when he turned his attention to the question of our knowledge of nature, he developed, in a series of books written in the teens and twenties, an epistemological system that was broader, more intricate, and more specifically oriented toward the new physics than was Bergson's or James's. In representing the problematical relationship between mind and nature, Whitehead strove to discover and express distinctions that were both especially precise and absolutely comprehensive. The vocabulary of the English language was, however, inadequate to represent these distinctions in the way that he realized them, so he coined and reformed and adapted words into what seemed (and for the most part has tended to remain) a kind of personal jargon. He assaults the "bifurcation of nature" inherent in conventional attempts at knowledge and urges the analysis of the relations perceived in experience according to their "extension," their "cogredience," and their "ingression." Because of his specialized vocabulary, Whitehead's influence on writers of literature is far more likely to have come through intermediate channels than James's or Bergson's.

Like those thinkers Whitehead developed a holistic, experience-centered concept of knowing; he opposed the "bifurcation of nature" into mutually alien realms of experience and scientific description, just as he opposed all other manifestations of the abstractive scientific outlook. Subject and object are inseparably linked in "events," the basic (though interconnected) whole units of experience; thus "events" include emotion as well as motion, they need to be known from the inside as well as from the outside, and "presentational immediacy" is as important a mode of perceiving them as is "causal efficacy." "Events" are characterized by their internal organic interdependency, and what we identify as objects, locations, and happenings are simplified abstractions of complex actual contexts.[46]

Correlatively and of some significance to twentieth-century literature, Whitehead developed a conception of the identity of a person as an essentially temporal and contingent quality. "The 'man in his whole life history' is an abstraction compared to the 'man in one . . . moment,'" he states.[47] And in keeping with many novelists' concerns with point of view and authorial perspective, he stressed not only the relativity of knowing's perspectives, but the legitimacy of individual emotion in its operation, saying "Feeling is the agent which reduces the universe to its perspective for fact."[48]

■ Conclusions: The New Ordinary Universe and How to Know It

American writers in the first half of the twentieth century thus had an intricate, unsettling, and yet stimulating heritage of notions of knowledge and knowing. Nothing like a dominant new knowing paradigm emerged; no regnant phenomenalism, scientism, positivism, new realism, or the like was ushered in on the flurry of doubt, imagination, and analysis. Some old concepts and habits were dead, and new possibilities, fueled by every sort of radical inquisitiveness, abounded. In this milieu knowing was no mere capacity or function; it was a challenge and an adventure.

Science was at the epicenter of the disturbance. In the nineteenth century, through the work of scores of ingenious and dedicated individuals, each pursuing his or her own investigation, science had simply dispensed with knowledge and approaches that were unscientific or that grew to be obsolete. Traditional humanistically and theoretically based conceptions were simply of no particular use in investigating physical nature, and they could be left wholly out of account for that purpose. When the venerable Euclidian and Newtonian concepts of rational structure led to contradictions and dead ends, they were demoted from universal to local applicability. When the naive realism that had been a motivating faith of much early nineteenth-century science became a limitation on physical supposition, it was even more unceremoniously relegated.

The cultural effects of this continuous revolution in the content and mode of knowing had to have been enormous. In its throes, for example, physicists in effect put the physical universe beyond the reach of common sense and ordinary perception. Even to be able to conceive of the universe science describes—matter that is not material but concentrated energy field; gravitation that is not attractive force but space curvature; fundamental particles that are not particles at all but transient vibration patterns, and ambiguous in their fundamentalness at that—required a good deal of abstractive imagination and ability to suppress the patterns and pathways of practical, everyday thought. In the words of philosopher of science Milič Čapek,

> Today it is obvious that the objective substrate of physical phenomena cannot be described in imaginative [physically pictoral] terms; all sensory qualities are basically on the same phenomenal level, which is a result of interaction of our conscious organism and the transphenomenal physical processes. The transphenomenal level itself seems to be thus forever inaccessible both to our perception and to our imagination; it can be neither perceived nor imagined. Abstract mathematical constructs seem to be today the only way, not to reach, but to *represent* the structure of the transphenomenal plane.[49]

The words of scientific popularizer J. W. N. Sullivan are blunter and more sweeping: "The workings of nature, as we have come to know them during the present century, are so unlike our ordinary experience that we can not picture them at all."[50]

In this context we seem to need new, radically uncustomary mental powers. And the simple yearning for direct connection with a real thing-in-itself seems doomed. The science-precipitated age of epistemology has produced a multitude of new insights about knowing, but none of them promises directness or finality. The rash of questions they introduced about perception is by itself enough to make an absurdist out of an empiricist. The questions involved (for one thinker or another) every conceivable element, event, or relationship in the perceiving transaction: a perceiver who was a complex and fallible self, shaped by his or her psychological, cultural, physical, and even evolutionary history; a complex set of impressions, complexly related to that perceiving self; a complex and unascertainable set of relationships between the perceiver's impressions and external entities and events; and a dubious and problematical external reality. Cognitive psychology, evolutionary biology, atomic physics, physiology, optics, semantics—the effect of every careful scrutiny of elements involved in human perception has been to introduce new levels of uncertainty and relativity. Not inconceivably an unsophisticated viewer of this phenomenon—or a viewer for whom surety was a primary importance —might conclude that everything is indeterminate, that intellect is inherently unreliable, that the mind doesn't even know what it knows.

The emerging epistemological awareness had put all speculation about nonobservable ultimates on dubious ground. Many advocates of scientific thought advocated the destruction of all concepts and approaches that could be characterized as "metaphysical." Certainly there was a widespread awareness of the way in which metaphysical ideas could bias thought, determine perception, and limit inquiry.

Critical awareness had also grown in regard to the somewhat subtler problem of reflexiveness. By the mid-nineteenth century scientific modes of thought stood in clear contrast to simple anthropomorphism, self-projection, and personification, in the way that Mendeleyev's methods clearly differed from Emerson's. In other ways the less obvious biases of species, culture, and convention still imbued the new approaches, right down to their very mathematics. But the awareness had been raised—there was a suspicion in the air that any and all knowing might be reflexive, and the doubters and scrutinizers of the early twentieth century were (collectively, at least) thorough, ingenious, and relentless in searching out knowledge's fallibility. The theory of relativity gave a vivid sense of what it was to be earthbound as an observer of the physical universe; contemporary epistemology extended that sense to all other kinds of knowing. One could try to come to terms with that reflexiveness either subjectively, through exploring and avowing it at its most individual level (like James and Bergson), or objectively, through universalizing and depersonalizing the terms and pathways of thought (like Russell and Wittgenstein).

Reflexiveness could be mitigated methodologically—science had established that—and in the early twentieth century new ideas about method abounded. In one (not all) of their directions, a kind of scientization of thought occurred, bringing a new understanding, veneration, and imitation of scientific method: of hypothetization, mathematization, verification, and the like. Analytical imagination shaped by coherent discipline was the ideal inherent in science, and it had a good deal of appeal for defining the activity in other fields as well. The new knowledge myth would stress method: the best results of investigation came from a strict attention to the means of investigation and representation.

Outside the strict domains of science, though, investigation was through language, and representation *was* language, and so language, its nature, and its true (and untrue) capacities became the subjects of sophisticated scrutiny in the early twentieth century, a scrutiny that incidentally completed the destruction of naive realism. Language ensconced most of the metaphysical and reflexive tendencies of thought, so purism became one prominent motif of the age of epistemology. Vocabulary was especially problematical, but syntax too needed screening to detect elements of bias and presupposition and implicit interpretation. The possibility of imaginative liberation became another prominent motif, however. Recognizing the artificial, imagination-born nature of all words and sentence structures, and recognizing it in juxtaposition to the inexpressive or multiply ambiguous otherness of the external world, and to the often wordless, asyntactical stream of our own impressions, constituted a disturbing new awareness; but with awareness came freedom, and with freedom, power.

The new speculation represented knowing as open, diverse, and specially disciplined, and its product as an artifact—created, hypothetical, and revisable. Understood rightly, science worked that way, and science had vindicated its way by producing results that were vastly practical and sometimes unimaginable. The age of epistemology destroyed the idea that knowing was simply a matter of generalizing or verifying empirical perceptions. It was that in addition to imagining, hypothesizing, de-hypothesizing, playing, encoding, picturing, de-picturing, and all the functions the human intelligence and/or intuition could perform. In our day, Gerald Holton, reviewing all of Einstein's writings in an essay, "On Trying to Understand Scientific Genius," decides that "the key words are *Bild* and *Spiel*."[51] In their day Bergson and Einstein and others insisted that a key element in knowing is aesthetic perception, or as American philosopher Clarence Irving Lewis put it, "the nearest approach to pure givenness is doubtless the esthetic experience. . . . There is such a thing as direct *appreciation* of the given, and such immediate apprehension of the *quality* of what is presented must figure in all empirical cognition"[52] [emphasis mine].

A whole new concept of creativity is implied in the new age's diverse epistemological insights. Science and the investigative styles of its greatest practitioners induced it, and it became an influential model for creativity in other fields as well—in literature for one, in which the free play of imagination and the destruction of conventional concepts and forms are especially appealing.

But what of the metaphysical picture of the universe implied in all this new knowledge of knowing? Wasn't that also likely to be profoundly influential on the imaginations of writers? Early twentieth-century science presented a picture in transition—transition from a mechanistic universe of absolute forces and matter to a relativistic universe of space-time and indeterminate particles. The older view pictured humankind in a condition of helplessness and insignificance, in a philosophical predicament like that depicted in the old determinism and the much older fatalism; the new view pictured humankind more in a condition of open and humanly defined possibility, in a predicament such as the emerging existentialism would define. The American imagination in the early twentieth century stood, then, at the point of confluence and conflict of two conceptions of nature, the import of both of which was that the universe was impersonal and devoid of humane values. The first literary experiments we shall examine in the subsequent section are those exploring this most basic antireflexive hypothesis: imagine that the universe doesn't give a damn about humankind or any human individual.

But let me add a William Jamesian caveat about this whole study before we go on: a culture is no simple, monolithic thing—it is multifariousness itself, and its inconsistencies and discontinuities are as real and as important as the neatest and most convincing coherencies we can imagine. Thus, while we will be able to trace some revealing connections and analogues between the endeavor of a number of literary artists and the insights and practices of the age of epistemology, this by no means implies that we are witnessing the advent of a new, uniform mind-set, culture-wide and simultaneously present. There is, for one thing, a great deal of activity going in other directions. For another, there is a factor of cultural lag in the assimilation of scientific ideas into literature. There is a gap in basic comprehension as well. None of the literary works we will be examining shows a clear, balanced, and disinterested understanding of Bergson or Einstein or any other thinker or theorist. This is almost necessarily the case, however, since the literary artist has his or her own vision to shape, and someone else's vision is likely to be only a means to that end.

All we can assert generally is this: with the basis of science and epistemology altering so radically, literature would alter too, in some similar and analogous ways. Literature had been on its own path of innovative evolution, from the days of Melville and Dickinson, through Conrad, Henry James, Yeats, and Joyce; and the age of epistemology, with its far-reaching destruction of knowledge and its creation of new approaches to knowing, combining with this evolution, exposed to the imaginations of writers a deep vein of new possibilities.

III Realisms in a Relativistic World

There were two main variants of American realism, the literary and the philosophical. Curiously, they had no connection with each other: Edwin Bissell Holt would seem to have had no knowledge of William Dean Howells, just as Theodore Dreiser probably knew nothing of Arthur O. Lovejoy. Both variants shared, however, a fundamental impulse to penetrate the veil of concepts and impressions and judgments and to base art and knowledge on a nonanthropomorphized, objective reality. The self-characterized realists were dedicated to the destruction of many received ideas, techniques, and styles, and yet they had faith in an objective absolute, and, in most cases, in the power of language and mind to approach that absolute authoritatively. They were part of the destruction of knowledge, but only to a point, and it was that point that marked the beginning of their own destruction in the history of thought.

Both variants of realism maintained some fairly obvious things: there really is a world out there beyond our mental vision of it, it is independent of our knowing, and it is itself the surest guide and most appropriate focal point of our thought and art. Their problems came when they attempted to construct a rationale for doing and thinking what in fact almost everybody did and thought. In a way it seems absurd that reality in its everyday sense should have to have an "ism" dedicated to its support. But then again, the travail of the realisms shows the extent to which knowledge and common experience had diverged.

Philosophical realism was first and foremost an attack on the idealism that dominated American academic philosophy around the turn of
the century. In formulations such as those of American Josiah Royce and
Englishman F. H. Bradley, idealistic philosophies were subtle and formidable epistemological visions, and for philosophers to challenge them in
their own arena and try to defend the objective reality those visions denied was an exacting undertaking. Literary realism was a far simpler matter, although differently focused. Its exponents were first and foremost
reacting against the artificiality, sentimentality, and easy moralism of popular literature of the day, against "idealism" in the everyday sense. They
could simply (even naively) insist that literature must face reality and tell
the truth instead of romantic lies. Their "reality" was far simpler than that
of the philosophers, but their underlying task, unlike that of the philosophers, involved social as much as intellectual reform. They aimed to break
down the complacent genteel attitudes that pervaded American society.
Their cause indeed involved them with philosophical matters but, in a
sense, only contingently.

Science played into the hands of the realists and then out of them
again. The ultimate reality of the external world was relatively easy to
justify in the context of the nineteenth century's absolute, measurable
universe of material atoms and causal forces. But then relativity theory
and quantum mechanics, in prohibiting the assumption that our concepts
can directly represent absolute external states, made the game a whole lot
chancier—not in the sense that the realisms were erroneous, but in the
sense that they were obsolete in the new realm of hypothetical physics
and language-as-artifact. The problems addressed by the realists were not
so much solved, as the saying goes, as outgrown.

The universe as conceived of by realistic writers was hard and fast
and causally nonhuman. Looked at without the coloring of anthropomor-

phic sentiment or genteel idealism, it seemed bleakly, even stringently alien. Stephen Crane and Robert Frost demonstrate two literary versions of coping in that universe: ways of facing that nonhuman, realist's reality squarely while carefully measuring human needs and human perceptions in relation to it. These writers' works are a part of the destruction of the naively reflexive, naively absolutistic knowledge of the turn of the century, but not part of the indeterminate universe or the knowledge anarchy of those who would later attempt to deny all systems of explanation and comprehension.

7   Literary and Philosophical Realisms: Uncertain Paths Toward Certainty

■ Literary Realism

Manifestoes by literary realists were ordinarily quite forthright about which aspects of literature and thought needed to be destroyed. Frank Norris's comes with the longest roll of thunder: "The People have a right to the Truth as they have a right to life, liberty and the pursuit of happiness. It is *not* right that they be exploited and deceived with false views of life, false characters, false sentiment, false morality, false history, false philosophy, false emotions, false heroism, false notions of self-sacrifice, false views of religion, of duty, of conduct and of manners."[1] However hackneyed and anticlimactic his rhetoric, Norris's sentiments are strong and sincere, and what he is calling for is a revolution not only in literary taste but in basic social understandings and behavior. Literature was vitally important for the realists; they felt that a human being's intrinsic potential is negated by shallow, complacent, class-serving literary visions. The realists' campaign for social and psychological *candor* always had elements of social reform- ism, of the drive to reorient perceptions to oppose those delusions that distract and misrepresent, exploit and stifle. The presence of latent re- formist motifs complicates and sometimes even confuses works of some of the principal realists. For example, in some of Norris's own works, or those of Jack London or Theodore Dreiser, the reformism will out despite the distraction or contradiction it offers to a context otherwise shaped by themes of strict objectivism, mechanistic fatalism, or of the personal force of the superior individual. Whatever the focus of a particular book, a kind of social consciousness was intrinsic to literary realism, and thematic con- sistency was not. Nor, as we shall see, was epistemological sophistication.

William Dean Howells was the subtlest, most literate of realism's the- orists, and he saw the new candor as the defining characteristic of a major new movement in literary history. Just a century ago Romance had fought against "effete classicism," he observes, and "Romance then sought, as

realism seeks now, to widen the bounds of sympathy, to level every barrier against aesthetic freedom, to escape from the paralysis of tradition. It
exhausted itself in this impulse; and it remained for realism to assert that
fidelity to experience and probability of motive are essential conditions of
a great imaginative literature."[2]

"Fidelity to experience and probability of motive" would involve the
inclusion of subject matter and motivation not customarily included in
the canons of contemporarily popular literature. Henceforth the parameters of gentility would not determine the limitations of literature. In characterizing the attitude of "the true realist," Howells says, "In life he finds
nothing insignificant; all tells for destiny and character; nothing that God
has made is contemptible. He cannot look upon human life and declare
this thing or that thing unworthy of notice, any more than the scientist
can declare a fact of the material world beneath the dignity of his inquiry."[3]

Howells understood that the attempt to have a reality-directed literature meant controlling the reflexiveness of the presentation. The habit of
anthropomorphism, of conceiving and viewing every element of experience in the light of one's values and judgments, tended to block that
access to reality. The realist needed to let reality come across with a minimum of intermediation. English critic Arthur McDowell put it most directly:
"the realistic thinker, like the realistic artist, is not anthropomorphic, but
the reverse. . . . Realism is a philosophy of self-effacement rather than of
self-assertion."[4] The minds-off approach would presumably involve no
diminution of the moral impact of literature: the loss in moral guidance
would be more than compensated by the gain in moral insight.

In terms of fictional technique, opening literature to experience implied a controlling point of view that could produce and justify a wider
frame of reference and a wider range of subjects and details. The standard
moral and aesthetic judgments would have to be kept in abeyance while
the possibilities of experience were reexplored: like the scientist, Howells
noted, the writer could not overlook a fact. And yet literary creation was
for him no mere matter of accumulating observations: "When realism becomes false to itself, when it heaps up facts merely, and maps life instead
of picturing it, realism will perish too. Every true realist instinctively knows
this, and it is perhaps the reason why he is careful of every fact, and feels
himself bound to express or to indicate its meaning at the risk of over-
moralizing."[5] The objective method of the scientist united with the underlying sense of purpose of the broadened, enlightened, realistic writer
—this is the sort of balance Howells wanted the realist to have in his point
of view. In Howells's formulation it is the judgment of the individual writer

and not the method that controls the reflexiveness, degree, and type of moral mediation. In theoretical terms it is difficult to see how the realist's point-of-view problem could be solved any more securely, yet this particular accommodation left the window open for the great deal of moralizing, slanting, pontificating, loading, foreshadowing, symbolizing, fortune-telling, and self-deceiving that spatters American realistic narrative. At the hands of Dreiser, Norris, and the rest, presumably realistic point of view often became technically no different than sentimentalist point of view. Only the message of the moralizing had been revolutionized.

The realists had a program for the techniques of representation too, again quasi-scientific and again semi-successful. It was first of all another attempt to put candor in the place of manipulative intermediation. The realist's job, said Howells, was "to break the images of false gods and misshapen heroes, to take away the poor silly toys that many grown people would still like to play with."[6] Thus, romanticized characters, heightened predicaments, rigged plots, and endings brimming with reassurance and poetic justice would need to be dumped in the interest of things as they are. The dumping posed no problems at all, given any measure of stylistic sensitivity, but really connecting to things as they are did. Howells didn't seem to perceive any difficulty, although he often seemed to be groping to find authentic terms to say what that connection would be like: "No author is an authority except in those moments when he held his ear close to Nature's lips and caught her very accent,"[7] he urged, clinging to a hackneyed and hapless romantic metaphor. In another attempt he asked his readers to imagine a scientist examining a grasshopper and accosted by a self-satisfied pedant who urges him to put aside the dull real-world grasshopper and attend to a grasshopper "evolved at considerable pains and expense out of the grasshopper in general, . . . made up of wire and card-board, very prettily painted in a conventional tint, . . . and perfectly indestructible." "I hope the time is coming," Howells goes on, "when not only the artist but the common, average man . . . will reject the ideal grasshopper wherever he finds it, in science, in literature, in art, because it is not 'simple, natural, and honest,' because it is not like a real grasshopper."[8]

Significantly, even Howells's forced figurativeness carried the message that science had the approach that realism needed. Howells himself knew little science and referred to it infrequently, but what he understood as the characteristics of its approach and outlook—objectivity, meticulous analysis, and unmitigated empiricism—he held in the highest esteem. His fellow realists tended to go all the way to naturalism. More attuned

than he to specific scientific (and pseudo-scientific) findings and generalizations, many of them felt that the way to attain closeness to nature was
to read experience in the light of these most persuasive natural truths.
Writers who built such explanations into their works paid the price in
terms of the quick obsolescence of some of their presumedly eternal
insights: Norris using features of Joseph LeConte's Christian evolution-
ism and Cesare Lombroso's psychophysiology of the criminal, London
using the sociobiological ideas of Herbert Spencer, and Dreiser using the
chemopsychological theories of Jacques Loeb, Elmer Gates, and numerous others. It all turned out to be partial or bogus wisdom, and it flavors
American literary naturalism with an essential and enduring quaintness.[9]

But even the attempt to reform the procedures of literary representation by adopting Howells's more general sense of science's objectivity,
analytical bent, and empiricism offered long-range problems unforeseen
by the realists. The science they so admired and emulated was the simplistic, absolutistic science of the nineteenth century. It was characterized
by an attitude of naive realism, an attitude that assumed that our mental
constructs can be accurate and absolute representations of objective reality. That attitude, as we have seen, had been undermined in nineteenth-
century thought and literature, and it was not to survive the revolution in
scientific epistemology; yet here were these writers, Howells and the others, saying that what one needed to do was simply shun belletristic approaches and depict reality directly. The lesson in relativism of Melville's
whale was certainly lost on the student of grasshoppers.

The realists' idea of language involved a belief in its potential trans-
parency, and that belief was a decisive factor in their movement's perish-
ability. They seemed to operate under the naive (and commonsense!) assumption that properly chosen words can indeed represent reality directly
and absolutely. What they didn't foresee was that while the language in
their works could indeed effectively destroy conventional misconceptions
about human experience, representing reality directly was an entirely different order of endeavor. Even their most carefully chosen words and
structures inevitably brought along elements of attitude and ignorance, of
both cultural and individual determination that, unbeknown to them, determined their picture before the paint was on the canvas. There really is
no absolute language and no truly objective language made up of words
that people actually use, but the realists went on as if there were.

They had some elements of a sophisticated theory of language, however, and although it was to some extent only implicit, it was far from
negligible in the history of American literature. Not even spokesman How-

ells said much on the subject of language, but his critical writings contain occasional attacks on the artificiality, the sentimental manipulativeness, and the class-pretentiousness of the language of contemporary literature. "If we bother ourselves to write what the critics imagine to be 'English,' we shall be priggish and artificial, and still more so if we make our Americans talk 'English,'" he states. Another time he asserts, of the style of a great writer (like Mark Twain): "It has a thing to say, and it says it in the word that may be the first or second, or third choice, but will not be the instrument of the most fastidious ear, the most delicate and exacting sense, though it will be the word that surely and strongly conveys intention from the author's mind to the reader's." Thus Howells advised that prose should be guided by the ideals of truth and communicability rather than those of elegance or tradition. "What is unpretentious and what is true is always beautiful and good, and nothing else is so."[10]

Directness and colloquialness were prime virtues in the realistic philosophy of language, and in these categories we observe even more clearly Howells's underlying philosophy of American democracy. Twain is praised for his "singleminded use of words . . . to express the plain, straight meaning their common acceptance has given them with no regard to their structural significance or their philological implications." The underlying premises are clear—that language changes, and that the writer should find it among the people who use it: "It has always been supposed by grammarians and purists that a language can be kept as they find it; but languages, while they live, are perpetually changing. God apparently meant them for the common people—whom Lincoln believed God liked because he made so many of them; and the common people will use them freely as they use other gifts of God." "Let fiction," he says on another occasion, ". . . not put on fine literary airs; let it speak the dialect, the language, that most Americans know—the language of unaffected people everywhere." When fiction's characters speak, Howells asserts, "I should like to hear them speak true American, with all the varying Tennesseean, Philadelphian, Bostonian, and New York accents."[11]

Along with this conscious attempt to establish as the language of realistic fiction the common, ordinary language of the American people, there was in the practice of realistic narrative a movement toward literalness. The realists' preference for literalness over conventional figurativeness is logically and inevitably part of their general program. They could see, on the one hand, that conventional literature specialized in the production of metaphors and symbols that served as vehicles for conventional preconceptions and simple reflexiveness, as shortcuts in perception and representation and judgment. On the other hand, literal enumeration of details very much seemed to be in keeping with the empirical, inductive style of contemporary science. It was the attempt to bring their language more in line with the reality underlying their experience that led the realists to describe so carefully the literal details of a neighborhood, say, or a room, a streetcar, or a snowstorm, and to present those details as the truth itself—not as symbolic of something that was somehow higher or more significant. The literalist tendency was, of course, not consistent in the works of the realists. Nothing actually was, not even (or, especially not) the tendency to use a common and colloquial prose style. Norris, Sinclair, and Dreiser are at times as artily metaphorical or symbolical as Poe or Hawthorne, just as most of the realists were occasionally as unrealistic in their word debauches as they were in their metaphor frenzies.

The new, sophisticated epistemologies of the early twentieth century were to take the ground out from under literary realism. The realists' dream of putting fiction firmly on the track to absolute truth was impossible to realize, and their naïveté about perception and knowing, reinforced by the naive realism of the nineteenth-century science they so admired, led their movement and significant parts of their works to early obsolescence. Yet new intracultural relationships were established here between literature, one of the oldest forms of knowing, and science, the newest and increasingly most influential. Quite subtly the mode and pattern of the scientist's creativity were becoming influential in the writers' conceptions of how they themselves created new insight; and in several ways, some not subtle at all, the view of the world presented by science was entering into the created worlds of the fiction writers. For certain we would get a new literature when a sophisticated, nonabsolutistic science prevailed and destroyed realism's knowledge.

As theory, literary realism had no fallback position whatever. As performance, especially in the aspects of its movement toward a direct and common language, a literalistic, documentary mode of representation, and a much broadened range of subject matter, it became an indelible part of subsequent literatures. Hemingway and Pound, Williams and Dos Passos (among others) would later develop self-aware and consciously disciplined versions of these characteristics within their literary visions.

■ Philosophical Realism

The basic impulse that was so strong in the minds of the theorists of literary realism in the 1890s and early 1900s—to affirm and lock in on reality itself, bypassing or strictly minimizing conceptual intermediation

—moved a number of American philosophers in the teens and early twenties as well. The philosophers' efforts were somewhat, though only somewhat, more intellectually sophisticated than those of the fiction writers. The history of their attempt is especially revealing as a cultural phenomenon, even beyond the impact they had on later writers and the analogies their ideas provide. These men intended to promote a collective position that was unanimous and irrefutable, yet they wound up in schism and verbal entanglement; rather than final consensus, they got inadvertent relativism. And ironically, their most direct and rational (and dogmatic) attempts to fix verbally and conceptually on the reality we all know so well often leave us with the feeling that we're watching spacemen trying to make contact with an alien planet. Their efforts unintentionally bring to a focus this critical question in the history of human knowing: is it at all in the capacity of language to establish the existence and nature of an independent, external, only peripherally linguistic world?

The names of the philosophical realists are not at all well known today beyond the bounds of philosophy departments—at least they are not known for their accomplishments as realists. Ralph Barton Perry is probably better known as the biographer of William James, A. O. Lovejoy as the author of *The Great Chain of Being*, and George Santayana as "the last Puritan," the author of a book on philosophical poets, and a commentator on American society. The others—Edwin B. Holt, Walter T. Marvin, W. P. Montague, Walter B. Pitkin, E. G. Spaulding, Durant Drake, James Bissett Pratt, Arthur K. Rogers, Roy Wood Sellars, C. A. Strong, and Evander B. McGilvary—have importance for this movement, but were themselves hardly carried to fame by it. The movement is best preserved in a pair of credo-anthologies—*The New Realism*, by Holt and others, published in 1912, and the revisionist *Essays in Critical Realism*, published by Drake and others in 1920—although a goodly number of individual books and articles surround these works. The movement was a complex and intricate affair; my coverage of it here will necessarily be simplified and highly selective and will treat the debate only as far as the early 1920s.

The essence of the realists' program was an affirmation of the reality and independence of existence: in Drake's words, "All who thus believe that existence is far wider than experience—that objects exist in or for themselves, apart from our experiencing them—are properly to be called realists."[12] That basic belief was directly aimed against the idealisms that dominated American philosophy in their day, as their manifestoes, like this one by W. P. Montague, both implied and stated outright:

1. Realism holds that things known may continue to exist unaltered when they are not known, or that things may pass in and out of the cognitive relation without prejudice to their reality, or that the existence of a thing is not correlated with or dependent upon the fact that anybody experiences it, perceives it, conceives it, or is in any way aware of it.

2. Realism is opposed to subjectivism or epistemological idealism which denies that things can exist apart from an experience of them, or independently of the cognitive relation.[13]

A. O. Lovejoy offers the best, most homely examples of the way that the processes of nature do not stop when we stop noticing them: picture a man building a coal fire in his fireplace, leaving the room, and returning later, he asks. Or to affirm that we share perceptions that are based on real objects, imagine a hundred men from different places all going to Geneva for a convention.[14]

The realists were trying to affirm some sort of epistemological position that would give new philosophical credibility to the everyday world and our commonsense perceptions and understandings of it. Thus Lovejoy urged belief in "the simplest, most intelligent hypothesis that can be offered in explanation of what is in fact perceived";[15] Montague argued that perception and understanding were properly based in that prephilosophical "primordial common sense . . . " that believes the "independent world can be directly presented in consciousness";[16] and Santayana propounded a doctrine of "animal faith" that stressed the naturalness and inevitability of our accepting the reality of our experience as it occurs to us, since our very capacity to experience originates in that nature.[17]

Their affirmation of commonsense perception was a way of attacking another problem, largely inexplicit in their writings: that of the conceptual gap dismayingly widening between scientific reality and everyday experience. Perhaps a newfound trust in the evidence of our senses, cutting through the subjectivism and conceptual red tape of idealistic epistemology, would incorporate and legitimize science's direct empiricism as well. They would have to step carefully around contemporary physics, and its tendency to work from imaginative hypotheses, and avoid the knotty question of the relationship of mathematics to the world, but the realists yearned to prove that the universe was all one universe, comprehensible and authentically present in ordinary perception—a universe neither schizoid nor entirely mental.

But if the philosophical realists' Charybdis was universal mentalism, their Scylla was the very sort of naive realism the literary realists banked on. The philosophers well knew that naive realism, or "direct realism" as some of them called it, was an epistemologically untenable proposition. They were walking a very narrow wire, though, especially because of their commitment to commonsense perception. Montague, for example, makes this attempt to define naive realism as outside the pale of new realism:

> The theory of naive realism is the most primitive of . . . theories [of knowing]. It conceives of objects as directly presented to consciousness and being precisely what they appear to be. Nothing intervenes between the knower and the world external to him. . . . There is in this naive view a complete disregard of the personal equation and of the elaborate mechanism underlying sense perception. In a world in which there was no such thing as error, this theory of the knowledge relation would remain unchallenged; but with the discovery of error and illusion comes perplexity.[18]

The realists' principal challenge thus came to be accounting for error in a system in which perceptions were perceptions of actualities. Interestingly, every step away from naive realism took them further away from uniformity, concord, and even comprehensibility. Each philosopher wound up elaborating his own epistemological (and ultimately metaphysical) system, and as the implications, complications, and ad hoc adjustments to each system multiplied, realism—a philosophy intended to bring directness, absoluteness, and surety back into American thought—fragmented and controverted itself into utter relativity.

Let the philosophy of W. P. Montague represent a kind of baseline realism; it's of the earlier, new realism variety, though it's neither the simplest nor most radical realism. Error for Montague was the interruption of the mind's direct apprehension of an object by some element in the mind itself or in the intervening medium. He analyzed the process of perception in terms of an "epistemological triangle" of object, cerebral state, and perceived object. He conceived of their relationship in terms of a metaphor from energetics:

> The physical objects send forth waves of energy in various directions and of various kinds, but all in some measure characteristic of the objects from which they proceed. These energies impinge upon the organism, and the sensory end-organs and the nerve fibers then transmit to the brain the kinds of energy to which they are severally ad-

justed or attuned. The final effect is the resultant of these sensory energies modified by the reaction of the brain.[19]

The role consciousness played in the process of perception was basically "relational," or selective, rather than "constitutive," or creative in Montague's scheme. Perceptibility was really a quality of existent objects, and those objects were actually, physically/energetically present to the knower.[20] Thus error in our conception of things occurred either through a physiologically based misperception or a cerebrally based intervention.[21]

The new realism was a basically monistic movement: that is, its exponents believed that in true perception the perceived object really was present in the perceiver's mind, and Montague's allowance for the mind's effect in shaping the idea of the object, at least in the case of erroneous perception, was something of a softening of the strict monist's position. Some of his confreres, like Holt and Perry, tried more strictly to conceive of the mind's apprehensions as purely direct, and of errors and illusions as being as much an authentic part of the self-presenting universe as actual objects and states.[22] In Holt's words, "Consciousness, whenever localized at all in space, is *not* in the skull but is 'out there' precisely wherever it appears to be." Or in the most sweeping terms, "The universe is not all real; but the universe all is." Yet Holt still would allow that dreams and illusions could give one the same vividness as outside stimulation, since "the nervous system, even when not stimulated from without, is able to generate within itself nerve-currents of those frequencies whose density factor is the same as in ordinary peripheral stimulation."[23]

The distinctions developed by the practitioners of monistic new realism got subtler and semantically chancier than this, but for our purposes such was the basic outlook of the movement which, according to philosophy historian W. H. Werkmeister, "predominated and gave color to the whole range of philosophical discussion from about 1907 to 1914." Werkmeister explains the next phase, marked by the publication of *Essays in Critical Realism*, in these terms: "It is the high-water mark in the floodstream of American realism. [Yet] a few years after its publication the critical realists are sharply and hopelessly divided into two major camps, and metaphysical doctrines rather than problems of knowledge stand in the foreground of realistic debate."[24]

For the critical realists, outside reality was every bit as independent and determining and ultimate as it was for the new realists, but they could not feel that it was in any true sense directly present to our minds. The difference was focused on the concept of the data of consciousness:

whatever the world's nature might be, it was not immediately but medi-
ately present to our minds. Drake attempts an explanation in a footnote in
his introductory essay in *Essays in Critical Realism*:

> The question whether we should or should not make . . . [a] dis-
> tinction between what is "given" (the "datum") and the character of
> the mental existent which is the vehicle of the givenness, is the one
> question in our inquiry upon which we have not been able fully to
> agree. This appears, however, to be a question as to terms, not a dis-
> agreement as to the existential situation in knowledge. . . .
>
> We agree that what is "given" is what is grasped in knowledge,
> what is contemplated, the starting-point for discourse; and that what
> we thus contemplate (are aware of) is, in the case of perception, some-
> thing outward, *apparently* the very physical object itself. This outer
> existent, however, is not literally grasped, as the neo-realists sup-
> pose; only its *what*, its essence or character, is grasped. . . .
>
> Our difference of opinion consists in a divergent use of the terms
> "given," "datum," etc. Some of us speak of as "given" only those
> traits that are traits of the mental existent of the moment—traits, that
> is, that have actual, literal, psychological existence. The rest of us
> include in the term the traits apprehended as belonging to the object
> through the attitude, or reaction, of the organism.[25]

As we have seen, not even the new realists themselves could stick with
the proposition that the objects of our perception were real objects directly apprehended. The critical realists, in beginning by assuming that
reality is dual, that perception is never direct, opened the knowing process to an enormous variety of possible analyses, however. They were
exploring familiar territory suddenly grown strange, each armed only with
his own arsenal of standard words and relationship concepts; the presumptively definitive account each brought back differed from the others
in far more than just "terms." Together their accounts baffle consensus,
just as individually some of them baffle clear comprehension.

For Drake it was a matter of "outer objects" coming together with
"mental states" that "make us suppose certain quality-groups to exist about
us." Attending to the outer objects, we "live and move in the presence of
what are, in a sense, hybrid objects—existences really there, but clothed,
in our mind's eye, with the qualities which our mental states put into
them." Drake characterizes this as "a logical, essential, virtual grasp of
objects."[26] Sellars theorizes that "an appearance is a datum, correlated
causally with the object of perception," and, recognizing that "the per-

ceptual experience is thick and shot full of meanings and relationships,"[27] pronounces that "it is *as though* we were directly aware of a thing."[28] For Santayana our consciousness "translates natural relations into synthetic and ideal symbols by which things are interpreted with reference to the interests of consciousness itself."[29]

The realists' nomenclatures provide a great variety of terms for the ultimate atoms of experience, what for the monistic Montague had been "events" or "elemental particulars." From Drake we get "quality-groups," "hybrid objects," and "character complexes" and from Sellars "thing-experiences." Pratt focuses on "perceptual images" and "quality groups" too. Strong and Santayana favor the (tradition-laden) term "essences." The precise measure of external-to-internal constituents varies in each of these atoms, of course—they are not mere synonyms—but en masse their effect on an observer is to introduce a strong sense of relativity into what was meant in each case to be a definitive, absolute diagnosis. There seems to be a real indeterminacy in the nature of the "given."

There is a real indeterminacy in the mental processing of that given, too. Several of the critical realists were sensitive to forces such as were shaping modernist and cubist art and experimental and destructionist literature. The concepts that challenged representational and pictorial realisms—considerations of perspective and representational medium —were the factors that spurred the modifications and adaptations of philosophical realism. Perry had identified what he called the "egocentric predicament," the factor that made it inconceivable that one could understand the specific distortions in the knowing process, since it was impossible to know anything by any other means. Santayana, taking a radically skeptical point of departure for his realism, insisted that "Discourse is a language, not a mirror. The images in sense are parts of discourse, not parts of nature: they are the babble of our innocent organs under the stimulus of things." For him the human perspective "has a material station and accidental point of view, and a fevered preference for one alternative issue over another."[30] Sellars strove pseudoscientifically toward his point that consciousness is "personally toned" and "synthetic," "a function of the total stress relations of that node or focus in the universe usually denominated the psychophysical organism. . . . This focus or ganglion and its complexity are the product of evolution and must not be looked upon as either psychical or merely physical."[31] Without even becoming psychological (as he might well have done too) the realist implied the mind was a kind of derivative, intricately accumulated adaptive device unlikely to have definitive access to reality.

But even if it could be freed from its innate reflexiveness and the limitations of its origins and its place in the scheme of things, human consciousness would still be radically limited by the very space and time that constituted its existence. Several of the realists were sensitive to the implications of perspective: Strong, for example, points out that "Out of . . . [the] principle of the diminution of apparent size with distance arises the whole element of *perspective* in visual perception. . . . Perspective represents a distortion of real things, which fails to strike us as in glaring contrast with their proper constitution only because we are so familiar with it." There is an obvious perspective factor in time too, he goes on. "The distance of objects from us involves a difference in the time it takes them to produce impressions on us"; he offers as an example our perception of the flash and roar of a distant gun's firing. Thus it is evident, he adds, "that the physical thing cannot be identified with the datum as such."[32]

The farther critical realism went in its elaborations of epistemology the more phenomenalistic it became and the more its prime tenet, the absolute existence and sensory accessibility of the external world, came to seem like a matter of sheer faith. By the light of critical-realistic analyses, it seemed that the thing-in-itself occurred to us in a cascade of perceptual and conceptual possibilities, ranging from raw sense experience to mathematical physics to wild hallucination. Our processing of that cacophony necessarily involved careful and highly disciplined selection. It was a far cry from new realism, which in its monistic versions had no credible theory of error; critical realism could explain error in so many ways that the existence of knowledge of any kind became an improbability.

Finally, then, reading realists' theories for the seeds of the destruction of realism (doing our own job of selecting and comparing), we can see that the indeterminacy inherent in their ideas of the atoms of experience and the relativity inherent in their conception of the human mind and its perceptual situation undermined any hope of an ultimate vision of what was real and how we might access it. But the realists' problems were not only conceptual but semantic. With few exceptions they seemed to regard language as a simple and transparent medium, as did the literary realists. And ironically, the language most of them wrote was beset by vagueness and banality at the same time that it was being trusted to represent the subtleties of reality with perfect fidelity.

One crucial aspect of the realists' reality that raises semantic questions is its concept of entityhood. The aforementioned categories of "elemental particulars," "quality-groups," and "essences" seem likely examples of confused if not outright misplaced concreteness, and Holt, for one, shows a good deal of naïveté about the relationship between words and existent realities when he sets down his first principles:

1. The entities (objects, facts, etc.) under study in logic, mathematics, and the physical sciences are not mental in any usual or proper meaning of the word "mental."
2. The being and nature of these entities are in no sense conditioned by their being known.
3. The degree of unity, consistency, or connection subsisting among entities is a matter to be empirically ascertained.[33]

We don't even need the vagueness of that "etc." to alert us to the fact that the real, independent entities of this real, independent world, since they're what's "under study in logic, mathematics, and the physical sciences," are likely to correspond awfully closely to our own concocted and habitual verbal and mathematical categories.

Concepts are reified and verbal distinctions grow into actual dimensions of the universe in the language of some of the realists. Strong, for example, (on the very page on which he makes the aforequoted statement about perspective) expounds the idea that if our apprehension of color is real, then science's vision of "oscillations of the luminiferous ether" cannot be, and vice versa; his thinking is being dominated by his sense of the either-or alternatives of his verbal options. Sellars gives birth to a whole new universe in awkwardly attempting to be so very precise in his verbal discriminations:

> Affirmation never arises apart from some datum, perceptual or ideational. Thus, in perception, objects are clothed in spatial form and distinguished by position. In critical knowledge the intuitional setting is removed, and the element of position becomes a preliminary bit of knowledge valuable for the selection of the object intended. This minimum must be annexed to every specific knowledge claim. It answers the question: What object are you thinking of? If you cannot tell what object you are thinking of, it is meaningless to tell what exactly you are thinking in regard to it.[34]

Objects "clothed" in "spatial form" and "distinguished" by "position" are crucially imprecise, difficult to conceive of, and disturbingly like a metaphor of well-dressed professors. Sellars' suggestion of the removal of "the intuitional setting" would seem to mean the separating out of the personal, relative frame of the perception, but when we are left with the "position" determining "the selection of the object intended," the process seems more Tralfamadorian than earthly — "intended" by whom? or what? And with the "annexation" to a "knowledge claim" of some "minimum" (of spatial position?), we experience a whole new set of entities that leave us indeed wondering whether under such conditions *anybody* could ever know what object they're thinking of.

I would exempt Lovejoy and certainly Santayana from the charge, but most of the realists are imprecise and dull writers with awkward or pedestrian vocabularies, boringly obvious repertoires of illustrations, and no senses of humor or irony. Naive and generally untalented in their linguistic habits and assumptions, they are still overconfident in their attempts to characterize the perceivable world. As Drake boasts, "We have found it entirely possible to isolate the problem of knowledge; and we believe that its solution lies along the lines that we here have indicated."[35] Yet too many of their effusions come out disappointingly flat or, like this sally from Holt, foolish: "Now for realism by no means everything is real; and I grant that the name realism tends to confuse persons who have not followed the history of the term. For the gist of realism is not to insist that everything is real, far from it, but to insist that everything that is, is and is as it is."[36] Gertrude Stein never said it any better in wordplay *intended* to destroy conventional meaning.

Finally, it seems as though realism should have been the philosophy of ordinary people in the realm of commerce, science, finance, politics, technology, and so forth, whose activities were transforming the society and making the more recondite philosophies increasingly inconsequential. The pioneering cultural historian Vernon Parrington took the line that realism was quite characteristically born out of the industrialized, mechanized society, and William Henry Werkmeister reaffirms this judgment, quoting Holt to the effect that previous metaphysical speculation would now come to look like decorative romanticism, "a marble temple shining on a hill."[37] Yet realism did not endure. However socioculturally appropriate it might have seemed, it was virtually ignored by the American public outside the preserves of philosophy; it was bypassed by contemporary physics and that discipline's special epistemology, neither of which did the realists seem equipped to understand; it was picked apart by critics (another story which could be told if there were time and reason to do so); it was fragmented by schism, by the inability of its practitioners to derive a definitive vision; and finally (hopeless from the start) it was self-doomed in its attempt to channel traditional metaphysical impulses through language and conceptual systems which had come to be recognized as essentially, unignorably relativistic.

In several ways philosophical realism pointed toward developments in twentieth-century literature. In its critiques of naive realism it certainly at least anticipated the way that twentieth-century writers would become much cagier about the proposition of capturing reality directly, the way Howells thought he could do. William Carlos Williams would stress the necessity of artistic and empathetic imagination in realizing the otherness of the other, for example. In its elaboration of the concept of perspective, realism reinforced an increasingly important notion, especially psychologically, in literature from Stephen Crane and Frost to Stevens and Faulkner. And in its vision of experience as being comprised of elemental, atomic particulars it coincided with very different experiments being done by Stein and Dos Passos in fragmentation and reorganization of the flux of life and language.

But it is the surety of the realists that haunts us—the confidence shown, for example, in this pronouncement by Pratt, "That we can make these various independent entities the objects of our own thought, and by reasoning upon our experiences can come to conclusions about them which are true and which deserve the name of knowledge."[38] But what entities? How independent, and how objects of our thought? What sort of reasoning? What exactly is an experience? Realism finally seems an equation with no fixed quantities.

8 Stephen Crane and Robert Frost: Nonreflexive Perception and Dehumanized Universe

■ Stephen Crane and the Tragicomedy of Human Perception

Stephen Crane began his career as a realist—he referred to himself as such and was proud of his connections with Howells and Hamlin Garland and the help he got from them. He had their realist's sense of the world as external, sure, causal, and nonanthropomorphic and of language as a reliable medium. But he was a literary realist with a difference, one who rejected the assumption that external reality was surely accessible by the human mind. Recent Crane scholars have ingeniously and exhaustively explored that fact; an eminent example is James Nagel, who emphasizes "the epistemological nature of Crane's narrative methods" and shows how in his work "isolation, delusion, cognitive restrictions, apprehensional difficulties, fantasies, and fears all qualify and restrict the potential for knowledge."[1] The epistemological view of Crane has actually diverted discussion of him from the streambeds of naturalism into those of modernism, with the result that our canon now includes Stephen Crane, the early modernist. In terms of the present study we can picture Crane's performance as standing midway between the reflexiveness and naive realism of much nineteenth-century writing and the relativism and radical destructionism of the most innovative twentieth-century writing.

Only in a very few of his works does Crane develop epistemological themes, but those works are the ones that have come to be regarded as his classics. Their passages of explicit knowledge analysis are the ones always quoted in studies of Crane's thought and art. Crane seems to have done his best writing on epistemological themes, and I think there is excellent reason for that. Crane was first of all (even before he was an epistemologist, a realist, an impressionist, or any other -ist) a very affect-oriented writer. In his works he seems to be trying—at times even straining—to produce emotions in his readers, at maximum strength per page. The episodes of war and confrontation and narrow escape; the images of death, disfigurement, and dire poverty; the tones of irony, grimness, and fatality: these are only a few of the characteristic ways Crane's fictions grab our emotions. There is also a general feeling of awe, fear, and wonder; Crane seems to want to haunt us with a sense of inexplicability, whether it be evoked by the irony of human desires and fates, the sudden epiphany of manliness (instinctual, reactive, or calculated), or the pathos of ignorance and helplessness. The challenge to him as a writer, then, he being a young man in an age of sentimental art, was to create strong effects while avoiding the routines of stock melodrama and sentimentality. He was not entirely successful at that: for example, the heavy-handed and improbable symbolism of the cash register in "The Blue Hotel" and the child in "Death and the Child," who asks the battle-frightened correspondent "Are you a man?"; the heavy slanting of *Maggie*; the stock moralism of *George's Mother*, the pasteboard romance of *Active Service*; and so forth. Constantly under pressure to produce, Crane never decisively outdistanced melodrama.

The epistemological theme was a salvation of sorts. Here was a way to induce awe and wonder in a narrative without using hackneyed or obvious kinetic means. Coincidentally, it was a way of broaching large-scale philosophical issues without overt philosophizing. If a protagonist could have only very limited and partial knowledge about his or her actual circumstances, there would be a great deal that was mysterious and uncontrollable about his or her immediate fate. And if a collection of such severely limited insights were all the knowledge that humankind was capable of, our social, terrestrial, and cosmic situations would certainly be sufficiently dire and dramatic. The lack of absolute understanding is, in certain of Crane's works, a universal, generic human quality; an abiding, haunting fallibility of the human condition; a kind of secular original sin. And it does bring with it a legitimate and challenging sense of wonder, evoked in vivid images of a treacherously indeterminable reflexiveness and a universe utterly unconcerned about the fate or the understanding of any person. The theme of distorted perception, already highly developed in the fictions of Poe and Hawthorne, was brought by Crane fully into the realm of the normal—was made, in fact, into an inescapable human characteristic.

Crane was another of the American knowledge destroyers who based his vision on an absolute reverence for experience. He was locked in an extended argument—fundamentally the realist's argument—with his society, and especially with its gentility, sentimentality, idealism, and complacency. His works seem calculated to open his readers' eyes to the brutalization of life in the slums, to the hollowness of wartime heroism, to the destructiveness of social self-righteousness, to the dangers of cultural myths and their believers, to the revelation that the universe doesn't love us. H. G. Wells's English perspective is especially revealing: in 1900 he saw Crane as defined by "the expression in literary art of certain enormous repudiations. . . . It is as if the racial thought and tradition had been razed from his mind and its site ploughed and salted."[2] Crane had been practicing "enormous repudiations" right along, throwing off his family's religious and social philosophies and even his own education. Retrospectively he wrote,

> Not that I disliked books, but the cut-and-dried curriculum of the college did not appeal to me. Humanity was a much more interesting study. When I ought to have been at recitations I was studying faces on the streets, and when I ought to have been studying my next day's lessons I was watching the trains roll in and out of the Central Station. So, you see, I had, first of all, to recover from college.

Experience was one prime ingredient of Crane's reconstruction of knowledge, and candor was the other: "I understand that a man is born into the world with his own pair of eyes, and he is not at all responsible for his vision—he is merely responsible for his quality of personal honesty."[3]

Crane's program of telling the truth about experience involved him from the outset in maximally utilizing his vivid sense of the reflexiveness of human mentality. His most indelible works feature a realism that specifically focuses on perception and interpretive understanding: what is so carefully realized is the inescapable pervasiveness of a personal viewpoint. It is a realism not of events but of apprehensions—apprehensions in both senses (anxious expectations and conceptualized perceptions) which are in various ways brought up against suprapersonal actuality to yield a lesson in human self-absorption and littleness. Scholar Henry Cady speaks of Crane being a part of a "shift . . . toward an increasingly psychological realism";[4] Gordon O. Taylor similarly, in his valuable study of "fictive psychology" in the period 1870–1900, shows how increasingly (presumably with Crane in the vanguard) "the development of narrative as well as the shaping of fictive issues depends on . . . [the mind's] response to environmental stimuli."[5] In Crane's own day Edward Garnett had characterized him as a literary "impressionist," and more recent scholars like Rodney O. Rogers and James Nagle have expanded on this idea, linking Crane's implicit aesthetic to the impressionist movement in painting and stressing his "emphasis . . . on psychological reality, on a concern for the human receptor of sensory experience rather than external reality itself."[6]

Crane's realism of apprehensions gives us plenty of affect. It serves as *internal* melodrama that is at the same time characterization and thematic figuration of the limitedness of human understanding. Take *The Red Badge of Courage* as an extended case in point. Reading through it, we share Henry Fleming's often hair-raising apprehensions, viewing from the third person but immersed seven-eighths or more in his impressions. His earliest premonitions, although infected with an obviously self-centered, immature romanticism that is his own and weighted down with the narrator's heavy-handed irony, still envelope us in a universe of will-he-won't-he personal achievement and heroic possibility: "In visions, he had seen himself in many struggles. He had imagined peoples secure in the shadow of his eagle-eyed prowess. . . . His busy mind had drawn for him large pictures, extravagant in color, lurid with breathless deeds."[7] His subsequent apprehensions all carry us along a nearly-claustrophobic path of inner destabilization: his animistic images of columns of soldiers like "two serpents crawling from the cavern of the night," the campfires that made "weird and satanic effects"; his anticipations of going to look at "war, the red animal—war, the blood-swollen god" and expecting to hear "a thousand-tongued fear that would babble at his back, and cause him to flee"; his preoccupation with trying "to mathematically prove to himself that he would not run from a battle"; and his morbid fascination with the first corpse he comes upon.

Henry's expectations—and they are nearly the boundaries of the world the reader witnesses—are in a state of conflict when the battle actually begins (Henry, the singular eagle-eyed hero, already made abject by these monsters of his imagining). What the battle offers is largely unforeseen. Its experiences are different, other: Henry feels a "subtle battle brotherhood," "a blistering sweat," a "red rage," and there is "a singular absence of heroic poses" in the din of the clanging steel ramrods. The smoke and noise are more than he could have expected, and his perceptions are more fragmentary, the minutiae of his experiences more random and compelling than he could have been ready for. When he actually does run, it seems a blindly impulsive act, the feeling of horror having overwhelmed all categories, all reason, all perception, all volition.

He thus enters a new mental state in which his senses seem preternaturally sensitive to the nightmarish images actually surrounding him, while his mind forces every thought and impression in the direction of self-justification. His interpretations of his world—of nature, of the behind-the-lines chaos, of his own motives and situation—come in shifting patterns of wild surmise, spurred by his ego's ferocious need for justification.

Nature, for example, first hostilely impedes him, and it seems to him "he could not conciliate the forest"; but then again a quiet landscape "gave him assurance," and nature seems "a woman with a deep aversion to tragedy"; further along, the squirrel that shies from his casually thrown projectile demonstrates to him nature's law of self-preservation; still further, in the chapel-like clearing, all his interpretive categories are overwhelmed by his discovery of a staring corpse and he retreats in panic, "pursued by a sight of the black ants swarming greedily upon the gray face and venturing horribly near to the eyes."* When the silence of the wood is suddenly broken by "a tremendous clangor of sounds," again "his mind fled in all directions," all his rationalizations erased.

All the while Henry is behind the lines and experiencing the destruction of his whole system of understanding and justification—while he is encountering Jim Conklin, the tattered man, and others, and all the accidental and direct references to cowardice that he feels so personally—we are kept aware of a reality outside Henry's apprehension. We pick up snatches of conversation and reaction from other soldiers and references to real roads, fields, and trees and to a real (and unpersonified) battle going on at some little distance. Henry's attempted definitions of life and nature, of his comrades and himself, of the army and the world—manifestations of a generically shallow human consciousness trying desperately not to face its dark night of the soul—finally play themselves out. His accidental blow on the head produces a still deeper disorientation. Back within his regiment (with the help of the cheery soldier—another reminder of a different sort of life going on) he can focus on action rather than thought and thereby reintegrate his personality.

In the latter phases of the novel Henry's experiences come with much less mental mediation than had been the case earlier. By focusing his attention in the realm of immediate needs and duties, he perceives more clearly and acts more purposefully. Henry's interpretation of the world is nowhere near definitive, even at the end of the novel after he feels confirmed in his manhood. He merely understands and comports himself better because he does less (and *needs* less) interpreting, previsioning, and rationalizing in this particular context. His cycles of misconception, disintegration, and self-justification will likely continue, but for the time

---

The Red Badge of Courage, ed. Fredson Bowers (University Press of Virginia, 1975), 48. The manuscript version of the novel, published in an edition by Henry Binder (W. W. Norton, 1979) includes a good deal more of this casting about than does the original published version, especially philosophical casting. This does make Henry's fallibility more evident, although for my taste the novel's structure and pace are better without it.

being he has achieved a limited freedom from certain fears and immaturities. The manhood he feels he has attained is as illusory, ironic, or spurious as it is regarded by most scholar-critics, but as a token of a genuine physical performance and as a symbol for a local and temporary mental victory, it supplies plausible enough closure for the novel. Henry's personal orientation toward battle has changed, although the generic human limitations of his self-confined understanding have not.

In a great deal of his writing Crane's stock-in-trade fictional situation is (like that of Melville's early works) one in which reality is brought up against an individual's expectations and previsions and in which drama and insight come out of the clash of mental image and actuality. Not only *The Red Badge*, but "The Blue Hotel," "The Bride Comes to Yellow Sky," "Death and the Child," and a number of other works feature the motif prominently. The often-quoted wayfarer poem offers a version that perhaps more apparently than the stories reveals a tone of grim satisfaction in the discovery of human shortsightedness:

> The wayfarer
> Perceiving the pathway to truth
> Was struck with astonishment.
> It was thickly grown with weeds.
> "Ha," he said,
> "I see that none has passed here
> "In a long time."
> Later he saw that each weed
> Was a singular knife.
> "Well," he mumbled at last,
> "Doubtless there are other roads."[8]

Crane's centerpiece epistemological drama is "The Open Boat." The men in the boat—adrift, imperiled, and denied the possibility of "other roads"—explore the intricacies of human reflexiveness as though their lives depended on it, as indeed to some extent they do. An important feature of their inquiry is its shared, mutual aspect. The men even help each other in measuring, if not in bridging, the tragic distance between hope and actuality:

> The cook had said: "There's a house of refuge just north of the Mosquito Inlet Light, and as soon as they see us, they'll come off in their boat and pick us up."
> "As soon as who see us?" said the correspondent.

"The crew," said the cook.

"Houses of refuge don't have crews," said the correspondent. "As I understand them, they are only places where clothes and grub are stored for the benefit of shipwrecked people. They don't carry crews."

"Oh, yes, they do," said the cook.

"No, they don't," said the correspondent.

"Well, we're not there yet, anyhow," said the oiler, in the stern.

"Well," said the cook, "perhaps it's not a house of refuge that I'm thinking of as being near Mosquito Inlet Light. Perhaps it's a life-saving station."

"We're not there yet," said the oiler, in the stern.[9]

They need to realize, without distorting visions or anticipations, the reality of their special situation, and an essential step is to come to know in the deepest sense the precise relation between their (personal, relativistic, survival-obsessed) selves, their senses, and external actuality. Just after the oiler and the correspondent curse the cook for mentioning pie and ham sandwiches, the men have impressed upon them the simple bleakness of the world they then inhabit:

> As darkness settled finally, the shine of the light, lifting from the sea in the south, changed to full gold. On the northern horizon a new light appeared, a small bluish gleam on the edge of the waters. These two lights were the furniture of the world. Otherwise there was nothing but waves.[10]

Another epistemologically oriented writer, Wallace Stevens, would, in "The Idea of Order at Key West" over three decades later, have a similar insight about the relation of the world to human needs and senses. The mood is radically different, but the experience and its import are not:

> . . . tell why the glassy lights,
> The lights in the fishing boats at anchor there,
> As the night descended, tilting in the air,
> Mastered the night and portioned out the sea,
> Fixing emblazoned zones and fiery poles,
> Arranging, deepening, enchanting night.[11]

For the men in the open boat, though, the discovery of the dimensions of their reflexiveness is a dismaying experience, revealing in the process the ultimate, uncaring otherness of the rest of the universe. From the waves themselves, from the birds that bob about unconcernedly, unsinkably, on top of those waves, and from the shark that skims by just beneath the surface, the message is one of random, unintentional malice. The universe is simply going about its business, and the fate of the men really doesn't matter more than a jot in its scheme. All assumptions, all expectations, all bets about fate and nature's agency are off, and the men are left with no justification but a lonely and futile cri de coeur and an answer from nature that establishes unforgettably the chasm between hope and fulfillment, between reflexiveness and otherness:

> "Yes, but I love myself."
> A high cold star on a winter's night is the word he feels that she says to him. Thereafter he knows the pathos of his situation.[12]

What makes "The Open Boat" different from most of Crane's other epistemological stories is the fact that the characters themselves come to know the pervasiveness of their egocentrism: "When it came night, the white waves paced to and fro in the moonlight, and the wind brought the sound of the great sea's voice to the men on shore, and they felt that they could then be interpreters."[13] Thus their epiphanic experience goes farther than Henry Fleming's had, not only overcoming their customary egocentric categories of understanding, but leaving them with a much broader recognition that a human being is a very small thing, that the human mind is a limited, relative, self-centered organ, and that the sea in its incomprehensible vastness is utterly alien to human concerns.

Crane's underlying realism is evident in this and other stories in the fact that whatever delusions and misperceptions the characters progress through, there is still an abiding force of things-as-they-are that confronts them, whether in the form of the sea, a battlefield, a blizzard, or a social order. J. C. Levenson quite correctly observes of Crane that "he did not relinquish the common-sense idea of objective reality" and identifies that reality as fundamental in his stories, in which character growth "does not simply come from within. The encounter with reality has made a crucial difference."[14] Reality often proves unknowable from a particular—or from *any* particular—human point of reference, however. Like some of the philosophical realists we observed in chapter seven and unlike the other literary realists, Crane combines a metaphysical faith in realism with relativistic, agnostic epistemology.

Finding a voice in which to embody his particular sense of things was not one of Crane's distinguished accomplishments. His prose is inconsistent, full of forced effects, and, compared with Conrad's, say, or Twain's, it shows a relative paucity of original means. Scholar

Frank Bergon offers a useful diagnosis of how Crane's prose works at its best:

> Through immediately rendered impressions, Crane's style draws the reader into a scene, but that same style, through explicit statement or incongruous images or shifts in diction, forces the reader to consider the presented reality from a detached and often contradictory point of view. . . . [Thus] the reader is forced to organize his impressions and judge them according to two or more frames of reference."[15]

In the mode of "immediately rendered impressions" Crane's writing is often superb: vividly detailed, with a subtle awareness of the linguistic tags and formulae in which people experience, explain, and reflect. He was proud of his intent and ability to write this way; as he once said in a letter: "Preaching is fatal to art in literature. I try to give readers a slice out of life; and if there is any moral or lesson in it, I do not try to point it out. I let the reader find it for himself."[16] Writing journalism offered Crane special opportunities for serving slices out of life, as we can see in this excerpt from a feature, "Heard on the Street Election Night," which, entirely in auditory images, "covers" the public reaction to a Tammany Hall defeat:

> "Down in Fourteenth Street,
> "Hear that mournful sound;
> "All the Indians are a-weeping,
> "Davie's in the cold, cold ground."
>
> ———
>
> "If Tammany wins this time, we might as well all quit the town and go to Camden. If we don't beat 'em now, we're a lot of duffers and we're only fit to stuff mattresses with."
>
> ———
>
> "Say, hear 'em yell 'Goff.' Popular? I guess yes."
>
> ———
>
> "He won't, hey? You just wait, me boy. If Hill can't carry this State at any time in any year, I'll make you a present of the Brooklyn Bridge, and paint it a deep purple with gold stripes, all by myself."[17]

Crane could hear and represent experience in a fashion that even T. S. Eliot could probably admire, that anticipated Pound's imagism, Williams's literalism, and Dos Passos's documentary devices.

But in his fiction, Crane seemed committed to a fuller, more explicit presentation, and especially when he worked through a detached point of view, his language shows a lack of empathetic imagination and a susceptibility to authorial posturing and forced elegance. Take, for example, a moment from *Maggie* in which Maggie is appealing to Pete, who has seduced her and is now upset by the way she is endangering the decorum required by his bartender's job:

> "Why, Pete! yehs tol' me—"
> Pete's glance expressed profound irritation. His countenance reddened with the anger of a man whose respectability is being threatened.
> "Say, yehs makes me tired. See? What d'hell do yeh wanna tag aroun' atter me fer?"[18]

It is precisely the juxtaposition of the two frames of reference that calls attention to their mutual inadequacy. In the presence of the orthographically forced street slang, the interpretive interjection sounds supercilious. Its diction is coyly weighty, and it reverberates with stock irony and moralism. (It sounds like upper-class sarcasm, and not very mature upper-class sarcasm at that.) Inherent in the diction is a subtext of authorial superiority, and the classism of that subtext tends to undermine the story's more intentional and explicit compassion for Maggie.

Maggie presents an extreme (and, I would assert, an apprentice) version of Crane's prose, but the tendency to use artily literary language in attaining complementarity of viewpoints is a predominant characteristic of all his work. Gordon O. Taylor shrewdly observes of a characteristic passage in *The Red Badge* that "the abstractly moral and concretely psychological aspects of Crane's concern . . . remain in somewhat uneasy balance, as the archaic elements in the technique of this passage imply."[19] Chester Wolford (*The Anger of Stephen Crane*, 1983) makes the interesting suggestion that a good deal of Crane's compositional style derives from his fascination with the epic, its modes and its satiric possibilities. That fascination, we might feel, is a source of much of Crane's forced elegance and overwriting. Even so, he seems to be using a two-stringed lute, to be short on options, if his only alternative to vernacular is inflated writing, regardless of his subject.

Caught between the need to produce rapidly and the desire to affect his audience deeply, Crane was susceptible to melodrama and moralism, and his life was cut short before he was able to develop a varied, broad originality. But he was able to give us fictional moments of terrific clarity and intensity and to develop a psychological, epistemologically sophisticated realism, exploring the tragicomedy of human reflexiveness and the alienness of a universe devoid of our self-projections.

■ Robert Frost and the Ordinary Person's Guide to Modern Knowing

Robert Frost, although far from being an innovator in theories of perception or knowledge or in literary technique, was nevertheless one of the
earliest and most insistent of American authors in presenting the new
conception of a neutral or nonreflexive universe. What was a stunning
discovery for Stephen Crane—that the universe was an "other" having
no stake or interest in the outcome of human affairs—was an everyday,
commonsense understanding for Frost, albeit one that, when you contemplated it, told you a lot about yourself and your place, as human being
and individual, in the scheme of things. Again and again his poems examine the difference, the separateness of the human self and the things
of nature. Conservative though he is in so many ways, he is a modernist
and a knowledge destroyer in relation to the traditional reflexive basis of
nature poetry. Rejecting both the moral presence that Wordsworth and
Arnold could imagine speaking to them in the landscape, and the didactic correspondences Thoreau and Emerson could realize, Frost could conceive of a surrounding universe as "A blanker whiteness of benighted
snows/With no expression, nothing to express."*

Frost's destruction of knowledge takes place only in a limited way,
within the confines of orderly poetic form, a language that is standard
and predominantly rational, and a realist's sense of the world and humanity's place in it.** In this regard it is worthwhile to consider him the
way James Cox introduced him in his anthology of criticism in 1963: "he
was writing poetry," Cox said, "before modern literature had really begun
to happen."[20] It was 1894 when Frost published his first poem, he was
thirty-nine when he published *A Boy's Will* in 1913, and he was then, and
he continued to be, steeped in the poetry of the past. Richard Poirer has
noted that "poetry and nature are fused in Frost's consciousness without
being identical" and that the modes and even attitudes of some of his
poems seem to follow from his "experiments with certain poetic styles" of
the nineteenth century.[21] (His devotion to Palgrave's *Golden Treasury*—from
1906 on, really—is well known.) Frost's collected works reveal a deep
strain of conventionality, and their besetting hazard is banality, rather than

*"Desert Places," *The Poetry of Robert Frost*, ed. Edward Connery Lathem (Holt, Rinehart
& Winston, 1969), 296. Parenthetical page numbers in the discussion of Frost refer to
this volume.

**As Dennis Donaghue points out, "Frost communicates through one resource. He has
it, and he expects his reader to have it—a sense of 'the way things are.'" *Connoisseurs of
Chaos* (Macmillan, 1965), 165.

the incomprehensibility and sheer grotesqueness that imperil the works of Melville and Dickinson.

Many of his best poems focus on humankind in the nonreflexive universe. His images of man-made objects amidst natural desolation represent the situation powerfully: in "The Wood-Pile" it was a cord of maple, "cut and split/And piled—and measured, four by four by eight," that had years ago been abandoned

> far from a useful fireplace
> To warm the frozen swamp as best it could
> With the slow smokeless burning of decay.
> (101–102)

In "The Black Cottage" it is a cottage, once the scene of dignified domesticity and undeserved misfortune, now weathering and overgrown, its doorsteps so neglected that "The warping boards pull out their own old nails/ With none to tread and put them in their place" (56). And in "The Need of Being Versed in Country Things" it is an old farm homestead, surrounded by birds and lilacs, but burnt-out and forsaken so that "Now the chimney was all of the house that stood,/ Like a pistil after the petals go" (241). These are symbols of human hope and purpose stranded and overwhelmed in the processes and purposes of nature.

When his poems juxtapose persons and nature, we more than likely get situations like those in "Stopping by Woods on a Snowy Evening," "Desert Places," or "An Old Man's Winter Night," of an individual awed into muteness by the vastness and otherness of nature:

> One aged man—one man—can't keep a house,
> A farm, a countryside, or if he can,
> It's thus he does it of a winter night.
> (108)

The old man is vacant and bewildered, finally going to sleep while "All out of doors looked darkly in at him," the trees roared and cracked in the wind, and the moon *kept* "his snow upon the roof/His icicles along the wall." Any human "keeping" or knowing or even belonging in such a universe is ironic. And when the speakers in Frost's poems try to make connections with the larger universe, we see that the cosmos is just as alien as the earth. In "On Looking Up by Chance at the Constellations" we learn from the speaker that the heavens feel no obligation to fulfill our human needs, that their placid program and time frame are not on a scale of anything we can experience:

We may as well go patiently on with our life,
And look elsewhere than to stars and moon and sun
For the shocks and changes we need to keep us sane.
(268)

And in "Stars" the speaker imagistically identifies the stars' total disengagement from human affairs, as he sees shining above us

. . . with neither love nor hate,
   Those stars like some snow-white
Minerva's snow-white marble eyes
   Without the gift of sight.
(9)

Still, human beings have a deep and inescapable need to be loved, respected, or at the very least acknowledged by the universe they inhabit, Frost feels. Much of his poetry focuses on persons yearning for and searching for that reciprocity, or on their anticipating and projecting it whether nature ever responds or not. Frost's poetry candidly anatomizes the reflexive impulse that produced Emerson's "The Rhodora" and a great preponderance of nineteenth-century nature poetry and, judging it by experience, by what really happens, finds it just a human foible.

The Most of It
He thought he kept the universe alone;
For all the voice in answer he could wake
Was but the mocking echo of his own
From some tree-hidden cliff across the lake.
Some morning from the boulder-broken beach
He would cry out on life, that what it wants
Is not its own love back in copy speech,
But counter-love, original response.
And nothing ever came of what he cried
Unless it was the embodiment that crashed
In the cliff's talus on the other side,
And then in the far-distant water splashed,
But after a time allowed for it to swim,
Instead of proving human when it neared
And someone else additional to him,
As a great buck it powerfully appeared,
Pushing the crumpled water up ahead,
And landed pouring like a waterfall,

> And stumbled through the rocks with horny tread,
> And forced the underbrush—and that was all.
> (338)

Here again Frost exposes the illusion of the human "keeping" of what won't be kept: a universe vast and impersonal and monumentally, magnificently *other*. The man is not simple—he wanted more than sound reflexivity, "copy speech." He wanted "original response," some sign of recognition out of the depths of things, and he seems to have wanted it enought to have "cried" repeatedly (on a stronger impulse than "called" would have represented), although "nothing ever came of what he cried." "Unless it was the embodiment . . . ," the narrator suggests, himself wiser than the protagonist, knowing the outcome, the disparity between hope and fulfillment, and using a word, "embodiment," that conveys both indistinctness and the sorts of higher expectations that might have been occupying the protagonist's mind. The protagonist's human expectation of a human sort of response to his cry unsuits him (and us) for the nonhuman nonresponse that actually occurs—just a buck crossing the lake and pushing into the underbrush. The narrator's language here creates an interestingly complex tone: there is strangeness ("pushing the crumpled water up ahead,/And landed pouring like a waterfall"), strangeness and magnificence too; there is also a strong suggestion of sexuality ("it powerfully appeared," "stumbled . . . with horny tread,/And forced the underbrush"); and there is also a comic tone (to have one's cry of longing raise only a great buck on the prowl is to get a funny comeuppance, especially when it is colored by those sexual connotations).

Frost saw all efforts at interpreting and knowing as beset by the reflexive habit of mind. This is especially apparent in poems in which people try to understand animal behavior (and vice versa). The speaker in "To a Moth Seen in Winter," catching a surprisingly out-of-season moth on his bare hand, discovers the impossibility of imbuing it with his own prudent rationality:

> You must be made more simply wise than I
> To know the hand I stretch impulsively
> Across the gulf of well-nigh everything
> May reach to you, but cannot touch your fate.

And he realizes that

> . . . what I pity in you is something human,
> The old incurable untimeliness,

Only begetter of all ills that are.
(356–357)

Similarly the little bird in "The Wood-Pile" will keep his distance from the anthropomorphic projections of its observer, "And say no word to tell me who he was/ Who was so foolish as to think what he thought" (101). It seems to be the first stage of wisdom to forgo projecting one's expectations and values into the creatures and processes around one. Confronted by so humanly sad a sight as an abandoned home, it is difficult to realize that the birds are only going about their own birdy business, with no reference to human fates or feelings, but that is what one must do: "One had to be versed in country things/ Not to believe the phoebes wept."[22]

For intellectual knowledge, on the other hand, Frost seemed to have no patience; the mere suggestion of it seemed to shift him into the mode of opinionated doggerel, as in "To a Thinker":

You call this thinking, but it's walking,
Not even that, it's only rocking,
Or weaving like a stabled horse:
From force to matter and back to force,
From form to content and back to form,
From norm to crazy and back to norm.
(325)

With some glee he characterizes humankind's whole philosophical endeavor as a kind of children's game in the two-line poem "The Secret Sits": "We dance round in a ring and suppose,/ But the Secret sits in the middle and knows" (362).

About science and its way of knowing Frost was radically ambivalent, his attitude depending, probably, on whether he was at the moment seeing science as an imaginative endeavor like his own or a curb, dogmatic or technological, on his freedom of thought. "Even in an atom there's more space than matter," he writes, metaphorically justifying, with some relish, the period of isolation in his early development, —"The matter in the universe gets together in a few terribly isolated points and sizzles."[23] In an interview for *The Detroit News*, headlined "Science Can't Dishearten Poets, Says Robert Frost," (1925) Frost admitted, according to the reporter, that although science did indeed tend to debunk the great myths and legends and demystify the world, "Think of the great abysses opened up by our study of the atom. Think of the strange and unaccountable actions of the hurrying winds experienced by our travelers of the skies. Think of the marvels of marine life lately brought to us by the explorers of the distant oceans, each more wonderfully wrought than ever mermaid or water sprite of which the poets dreamed."[24]

Still, science was one of his favorite whipping boys (along with collectivism, modernism, liberalism and the New Deal, all of which seemed to be connected in his mind). Our age, he says in his introduction to E. A. Robinson's posthumously published *King Jasper* (1935), may come to be known as one that "ran wild in the quest of new ways to be new. . . . Science put it into our heads that there must be new ways to be new. Those tried were largely by subtraction—elimination."[25] In his view science entailed reductionism—the oversimplification of complex experience and the diminishment of humankind to Darwinistic dimensions—and this tendency he abhorred. The Darwinian paradigm fascinated him in its application to the experiential facts of the natural world: of the tumult of butterflies around a milk-weed pod he says,

> But waste was the essence of the scheme.
> And all the good they did for man or god
> To all those flowers they passionately trod
> Was leave as their posterity one pod
> With an inheritance of restless dream.
> . . . [T]he reason why so much
> Should come to nothing must be fairly faced.[26]

Yet when applied to human beings, the paradigm is pernicious:

> Our worship, humor, conscientiousness
> Went long since to the dogs under the table.
> And served us right for having instituted
> Downward comparisons. . . .[27]

What Frost perceived as science's tendencies toward reductionism, dogmatism, novelty obsession, and technological amorality led to his simple polemical rejection of it:

> Sarcastic Science, she would like to know,
> In her complacent ministry of fear,
> How we propose to get away from here
> When she has made things so we have to go
> Or be wiped out. . . .[28]

A strong influence of William James on Frost's thinking is urged by Lawrance Thompson in his Frost biography. Thompson shows Frost repeatedly referring to his admiration for James—"My greatest inspiration, when I was a student, was a man whose classes I never attended," he had liked to say; and Thompson establishes that Frost took a course at Harvard that studied James's *Psychology* and later, himself then a teacher of future teachers, assigned James's *Talks to Teachers on Psychology* and *Psychology, Briefer Course* as texts. Thompson suggests numerous ways in which James's ideas may have affected Frost's poetry and philosophical outlook. The poem "Design," for example, he links to the Jamesian critique of teleological explanations of events in our experience.[29] Richard Poirer agrees with Thompson: Frost's dispensing with philosophical absolutes seems typically Jamesian, as do his ideas that "truth is *made*" and that a belief can create its own confirmation. According to Poirer, "Frost is a poet without pieties" who tried to steer his own course in what James called "the right channel" between too much and too little belief.[30]

Frost's whole attitude toward knowing is fairly and playfully represented by his poem, "For Once then, Something." His sense of the reflexive quality of the human mind, the primacy of experience and the indeterminacy of any ultimate structure beneath it are pictorally imagined here, and the whole poem brims with Frost's casual disregard of intellect and its disciplines and his sense of his own independent uniqueness.

> Others taunt me with having knelt at well-curbs
> Always wrong to the light, so never seeing
> Deeper down in the well than where the water
> Gives me back in a shining surface picture
> Me myself in the summer heaven, godlike,
> Looking out of a wreath of fern and cloud puffs.
> *Once*, when trying with chin against a well-curb,
> I discerned, as I thought, beyond the picture,
> Through the picture, a something white, uncertain,
> Something more of the depths—and then I lost it.
> Water came to rebuke the too clear water.
> One drop fell from a fern, and lo, a ripple
> Shook whatever it was lay there at bottom,
> Blurred it, blotted it out. What was that whiteness?
> Truth? A pebble of quartz? For once, then, something.
> (225)

Finally neither humanist nor naturalist, Frost took an attitude toward humankind and nature best characterized as one of respect for each and appreciation of their separateness. He shows no desire for humankind to prevail over nature; in contradiction to so much of the self-congratulatory progress-propaganda of his time, he often voices or implies an advocacy of unorganized, unutilizable nature, as in his poem "Unharvested" in which his speaker, coming upon an apple tree that had dropped all its fruit on the ground, says a little prayer, to nobody in particular, for entropy:

> May something go always unharvested!
> May much stay out of our stated plan,
> Apples or something forgotten and left,
> So smelling their sweetness would be no theft.
> (305)

Throughout his lifelong struggle for intelligibility and form, he believed in and appreciated the chaos against which he strove. As he says in a 1935 letter to *The Amherst Student*,

> The background is hugeness and confusion shading away from where we stand into black and utter chaos; and against the background any small man-made figure of order and concentration. What pleasanter than that this should be so? Unless we are novelists or economists we don't worry about this confusion; we look out on it with an instrument or tackle it to reduce it. It is partly because we are afraid it might prove too much for us and our blend of democratic-republican-socialist-communist-anarchist party. But it is more because we like it, we were born to it, born used to it and have practical reasons for wanting it there. To me any little form I assert upon it is velvet, as the saying is, and to be considered for how much more it is than nothing. If I were a Platonist I should have to consider it, I suppose, for how much less it is than everything.[31]

But although he deplores the idea of a wholly known and human-dominated world, still he does not advocate nature's domination of human affairs. The messages nature sends (or *seems* to send) to people are expressive of its own processes and purposes and often run athwart or counter to human needs and objectives. The speaker in "A Leaf-Treader" justifiably ignores the falling leaves' invitation to mortality: "But it was no reason I had to go because they had to go" (298). And the speaker in "Reluctance," standing in the crusted snow in the dead fields, still realizes a counter-yearning, directionless but firmly human:

Ah, when to the heart of man
   Was it ever less than a treason
To go with the drift of things,
   To yield with a grace to reason,
And bow and accept the end
   Of a love or a season?
(30)

In their most finely attuned moments, nature and humankind are presented as independent entities, both homage-worthy in their separateness. When, in "Two Look at Two," a buck and doe, calm and poised, look at two human lovers across a wall on the mountain side, "Two had seen two, whichever side you spoke from," and objectively that was all—although the magnificence of the moment is translated by the human participants into the reflexive feeling that "the earth in one unlooked-for favor/ Had made them certain earth returned their love" (230). "Stopping by Woods on a Snowy Evening" expresses this same kind of appreciation of the mutual otherness of human being and nature, although starkly without the reflexive translation of the experience.

Frost developed several techniques for representing this sense of the separateness of nature and humankind. The extent of his technical innovation is modest, and intentionally so. He was especially committed to clear communication ("Better say correspondence is all. Mind must convince mind"),[32] and his theory of poetic creativity was resolutely casual (poets "stick to nothing deliberately, but let what will stick to them like burrs where they walk in the fields").[33] Among the modernists and destroyers of knowledge Frost is a nonchalant individualist trying modest tricks of empathy and anti-empathy, of language, cadence, and metaphor, in an attempt to stay in that middling "right channel."

One of the ways his poems avoid asserting more than would actually have been observable is through a variety of little hedging qualifiers. Richard Poirier has noted how often his poems use such devices as "disclaimers embedded in assertions ('For once, then, something')" and "evasive tactics in the use of words like 'almost' and 'somehow,' of 'unless' and especially 'as if' ('As if the earth in one unlooked-for favor. . .')."[34] Frost is especially keen both at catching human perception as it is about to become self-projection, and at clarifying, with the slightest nudge of one of those little qualifiers, the distinction between natural event and human interpretation. The stars congregate overhead on a wintry night "*As if* with keenness for our fate" (9; my emphasis); and the lonely walker in

"Come In," hearing the last thrush song in a darkening wood, interprets it, before pulling back from his projection as

> *Almost like* a call to come in
> To the dark and lament.

> But no, I was out for stars:
> I would not come in.
> I meant not even if asked,
> And I hadn't been.
> (334; my emphasis)

Frost plays at reflexive perception too, humorously or ironically attributing human characteristics to, say, the horse in "Stopping by Woods," who "gives his harness bells a shake/To ask if there is some mistake," or the ant colony in "Departmental," who act out a kind of "The Death of the Worker Ant" as a parody of collectivism. Only occasionally in his early poetry does he slip into the conventionally poetic mode of personification and lose that line between human and natural concerns: as with the "bewildered butterfly" in "The Tuft of Flowers," "Seeking with memories grown dim o'er night/Some resting flower of yesterday's delight" (22); or the singing bird of "The Oven Bird," "The question that he frames in all but words/ Is what to make of a diminished thing" (120). In the poetry of his middle and late career—*West Running Brook* and after—the instances of naive and conventionally reflexive figures of speech are more abundant (see "Acceptance," "Once by the Pacific," "Lodged," "Bereft," "Sand Dunes," "The Birthplace," and so forth). For whatever reason he thus strayed from the distinctiveness of his original perception.

His sense of metaphor lies at the root of both the strengths and weaknesses of his approach to poetic knowing. He seems all along to have had the idea that all knowing is really metaphoric: as he articulated the idea in a 1931 address on the subject of education, "unless you are at home in the metaphor, unless you have had your proper poetical education in the metaphor, you are not safe anywhere. Because you are not at ease with figurative values: you don't know the metaphor in its strength and its weakness. You don't know how far you may expect to ride it and when it may break down with you. You are not safe in science; you are not safe in history."[35] He knew at that point about science's figurativeness: he introduced to that same audience some of the "charming mixed metaphors" of contemporary physics—those of the indeterminacy principle, the definition of objects as events, and the curvature of space: "'In the neighborhood of matter space is something like curved.' Isn't that a good one! It seems to me that it is simply and utterly charming—to say that space is something like curved in the neighborhood of matter. 'Something like.'"[36] Such an awareness can, of course, keep a writer from being taken in by the culture's widely prevalent and persuasive tendency to perceive things anthropomorphically or absolutistically. Frost here seems to have been on the modernist side of that dialectic. But his conviction, stated in a 1946 preface, that "Poetry is simply made of metaphor. . . . Every poem is a new metaphor inside or it is nothing"[37] may well relate to his practice in many of the poems of his middle and later years, of forcing the utterance toward an applied metaphor, to make certain that what "begins in delight" indeed unfailingly "ends in wisdom," whatever the expense of arbitrariness or pedantry.*

Frost had a philosophy of poetic language that tended to draw his poems in the direction of the particular, the limited, and the quasi-dramatic, emphasizing their relative, human locus. Like so many American writers he was preoccupied with narrowing the gap between experience and its literary representation, and he saw that this involved more than the use of regional lore and locutions. It involved, first of all, a specific locus in time and space and human experience—a poem for Frost was that group of words that occurred to someone as he or she was in the midst of experiencing or reflecting about experiencing something. Secondly it involved the use of the cadence patterns of actual speech.** Frost called the first technique making it "dramatic" and the second giving it "the sound of sense." "Everything written," he wrote in the Preface to his play *A Way Out*, "is as good as it is dramatic. It need not declare itself in form, but it is drama or nothing." The lyric poem was perhaps a special case, but its potential was high if it were "heard as sung or spoken by a person in a scene—in character, in a setting." But however interesting local point of view could make a piece, it was the sentences that could give it authenticity:

> A dramatic necessity goes deep into the nature of the sentence. Sentences are not different enough to hold the attention unless they are

---

*According to his explanation in "The Figure a Poem Makes," a poem ideally follows a course of discovery "unforeseen" yet "predestined from the first image of the original mood"; it "inclines to the impulse," and "it begins in delight and ends in wisdom" (*Selected Prose*, 18).

**Elaine Barry points out Frost's "central idea of the importance of the speaking voice" in theoretical statements he made throughout his career (*Robert Frost on Writing* [Rutgers University Press, 1973], 10; see Barry's discussion, 10–15.)

dramatic. No ingenuity of varying structure will do. All that can save them is the speaking tone of voice somehow entangled in the words and fastened to the page for the ear of the imagination. That is all that can save poetry from sing-song, all that can save prose from itself.[38]

"The sound of sense" was an idea in which Frost seems to have put a great deal of stock, developing it frequently in lectures and letters to friends and to professional critics whose interest he was trying to involve in his poetry.* It is an attractive idea, especially in the context of the destruction of knowledge, because it denies both the fixity of the meanings of words and the measurability of poetic meter and it makes the sound of the spoken sentence, the experienced utterance, the most crucial determinant of context. "A sentence is a sound in itself on which other sounds called words may be strung,"[39] he hypothesizes, calling this sentence sound "the abstract vitality of our speech . . . pure sound—pure form" and advising that "the best place to get the abstract sound of sense is from voices behind a door that cuts off the words."[40] "The grammatical sentence is merely accessory to the other and chiefly valuable as furnishing a clue to the other,"[41] he claims. His enthusiasm for the concept led him in the mid-teens to elaborate it in ways that seem almost as much religious as literary: in one letter he attributes his revival of interest in people, after a long period of isolation, to his fascination with their vernacular sentence sounds.[42] Several other times he indicates a belief that there are a limited number of archetypal sentence sounds and that a writer endows his work with their power if he can sense and utilize them. ("Just so many sentence sounds belong to man as just so many vocal runs belong to one kind of bird. We come into the world with them and create none of them. . . . We summon them from Heaven knows where under excitement with the audile [audial] imagination."[43] "They are always there—living in the cave of the mouth. They are real cave things: they were before words were. They are as definitely things as any image of sight. The most creative imagination is only their summoner."[44]) As his way of breaking the forms of convention and putting himself in touch with human actuality and what he conceived of as its archetypal forms, therefore, Frost strove for "the sound of sense."

Judging from his poems, however, his success was intermittent and even his striving was sporadic. We can feel what seems to be "the sound

---

*See *Selected Letters*, pp. 79–81, 102, 107–108, 110–113, 140–141, 158–160, 191–192, with editor Lawrance Thompson's introductions to the recipients and explanations of Frost's intentions in writing, for example, in the letter to W. J. Braithwaite on 157–158.

of sense" most frequently in the dramatic and situational poems of his early and midcareer, in poems like "Home Burial," "A Servant to Servants," "The Death of the Hired Man," and "The Census-Taker." Frost's "ear" for how somebody would say or think something at a certain moment could at times be excellent: witness the statement by the Frenchman Baptiste at the end of the poem "The Axe-Helve" where, contemplating the axe-helve he has crafted—"Erect, but not without its waves, as when/ The snake stood up for evil in the Garden"—he says "See how she's cock her head!" (188). But such inspiration was rare (as Frost certainly knew), and given his belief that you had to take a poem as it came, without much revision, his cadences all too frequently fall back on the jog-trot of a conventional rhythm-rhyme pattern when the oracle in the cave of the mouth wasn't coming across quickly enough. Nobody ever talked like this, except at a Frostean poetry-reading:

> *Misgiving*
> All crying "We will go with you, O Wind!"
> The foliage follow him, leaf and stem;
> But a sleep oppresses them as they go,
> And they end by bidding him stay with them. . . .
>
> I only hope that when I am free
> As they are free to go in quest
> Of the knowledge beyond the bounds of life
> It may not seem better to me to rest.
> (236)

Frost was a poet restrictive of his imagination and technical resources, who, especially later in his career, wrote a good many poems that were not only flatly uninspired but untrue to his own best insights about poetry and the world. However, in those numerous poems of his that do come across clear and true, he kept his epistemology straight and brought more twentieth-century people into contact with twentieth-century knowledge of the world than any other poet.

IV   The Revolution in Visual Arts

The most spectacular displays of knowledge destruction occurred in the twentieth-century visual arts. Here the revisions and re-revisions in ideas of perception and representation were mercurial, blatantly radical, and widely publicized. And there is no question that the artists themselves and their apologists considered their work as fundamentally epistemological. Writer Alexandre Mercereau, influential in introducing cubism to eastern Europe, put it straightforwardly in his 1914 "Introduction to an Exhibition in Prague": "Our artists ardently desire to achieve an integral truth as opposed to an apparent reality. In harmony with the innovations of science, today's art seeks to discover ultimate laws more profound than those of yesterday.[1]" Cubist painter Juan Gris explained somewhat more retrospectively (in 1925) how this new style of painting represented quite a different knowledge relationship to the physical world than that implied by his forerunners, the impressionists:

> By way of natural reaction against the fugitive elements employed by the Impressionists, painters felt the need to discover less un-stable elements in the objects to be represented. And they chose that category of elements which remains in the mind through ap-prehension and is not continually changing. For the momentary effects of light they substituted, for example, what they believed to be the local colours of objects. For the visual appearance of a

form they substituted what they believed to be the actual quality of this form.[2]

German expressionist painter Max Beckmann put his epistemological concerns more personally and directly: "The stronger my determination grows to grasp the unutterable things of this world, the deeper and more powerful the emotion burning inside me about our existence, the tighter I keep my mouth shut and the harder I try to capture the terrible, thrilling monster of life's vitality and to confine it, to beat it down and to strangle it with crystal-clear, razor-sharp lines and planes."[3] With those being the fundamental objectives of so many artists, it is no wonder that Hugo Ball, German writer and prominent dadaist, would recall that "It might seem as if philosophy had been taken over by the artists; as if the new impulses were coming from them; as if they were the prophets of the rebirth."[4]

Western society was in turmoil, and the artists' efforts to interpret it or to order (or disorder) it came from deeply felt responses. The effects of the world war, for example, were powerful. Expressionist painter Franz Marc, serving in the German army, felt much the way John Dos Passos felt serving with the allied ambulance corps (see pp. 313–314, below):

> Out here, anxious and expectant, our heads filled with orders, riding and marching without rest, sleeping a couple of hours at a time like a bear—it's impossible to think. We just experience things, simply and directly; and our consciousness wavers between two questions: is this absurd soldiering a dream? or are our occasional memories of home a dream? Right now it seems that both are fantasy rather than fact.

Marc had great hopes that "the great war will also put an end to many things which the twentieth century mistakenly preserved, including the pseudo-art which Germans up to now have good naturedly tolerated."[5] Marc himself was not to survive that war, and many of those modernist artists in Germany who did survive experienced in the thirties a politically impelled resurgence of the "pseudo-art" and an attack on their experiments in cubism and dadaism as, in Adolf Hitler's own words, "the morbid excrescences of insane and degenerate men."[6] They thereafter had the choice of exile or silence. The political situation in Russia was as bad, once the great liberating promise of the revolution had Stalinized into the standardization of art along the lines of "socialist realism."

Not only was rapid and radical change through sociopolitical upheaval and scientific and technological revolution a condition of the artists' world, but the "look" of their world was changing radically too, with the rampant urbanization and commercialization of Western culture. And so, naturally, were the means of focusing, of promulgating, of interpreting that "look." Italian futurist painter Giacomo Balla was one of those enthused about the burgeoning visual environment:

> Any store in a modern town, with its elegant windows all displaying useful and pleasing objects, is much more aesthetically enjoyable than all those passéist exhibitions which have been so lauded everywhere. An electric iron, its white steel gleaming clean as a whistle, delights the eye more than a nude statuette, stuck on a pedestal hideously tinted for the occasion. A typewriter is *more architectural* than all those building projects which win prizes at academies and competitions.[7]

The rapid development of photography in the early years of the twentieth century provides the most significant example of how new means of purveying the "look" of the age could change the game for artists. Both a technique of representation and an artistic medium in itself, photography posed special problems and offered special opportunities. Indeed, as one critic pointed out in 1905, "One might say it has entered the art-world as has radium the physical world; there is something decidedly uncanny about it, and we really don't know where we stand."[8] Where the pictorial, principally representative artist stood was the most precarious. "Imitation by itself may, if one likes, be an art, but one that photography may easily bring to perfection," as French critic Maurice Reynal pointed out in a 1912 preface to a cubist catalog. (It was part of his claim that the most original and important twentieth-century artists needed to be like the "large number of intrepid scientists, who have devoted themselves to extraordinary scientific researches the mere starting-points of which have made nonsense of accepted views and vulgar sensibility.")[9] Other technologies were likewise, though perhaps not as conspicuously, making a shambles of conventional visual aesthetics: motion pictures, new optics, new materials.

But whether analyzed according to sociopolitical or aesthetical-epistemological or any number of other hyphenated matrices, the conditions of the twentieth century conduced to enormous complexity of potential insight. The best formula I have seen for the situation is a retrospective one of artist Robert Motherwell: *"as long as modern society remains what it is, and man's insight into it and himself increases, the distance between the objects in the world and an enlightened mind will lengthen."*[10] In the art and the aesthetics of the early twentieth century the attempts to bridge or structure or explore that distance were legion. Today, over half a century later, their variety, individuality, and ingenuity still seem amazing. The categories, the "movements," the "isms" by which the individual artists are customarily described are approximate and even distorting, but surveying their array can indicate the wide epistemological range opened by modernist art, provided we keep in mind the deeper levels of real individual variety our categories belie. Some of the "isms" were concocted by artists themselves or by promoters closely associated with them, while others originated with contemporary critics or later scholars. Having an "ism" (or at least designating one) seems to have been the thing to do, and there came to be "isms" of every kind, based on every conceivable aspect of perception and representation.

In relation to an object or a natural form to be represented, there were "isms" by which artists sacrificed the conventional, single-perspective, visual aspect to an exploration of an object's spatiality or its potential to be viewed from a number of perspectives (cubism); to its kinetic aspects and its motion-over-time (futurism); to its formal qualities as abstractly expressed in basic geometrical configurations (de Stijl); or to the forms created by the intersection of light rays reflected by it (rayonnism). Other "isms" would project a formally exact, idealized representation of the object (precisionism); present us with the object itself as its own representation (dada); or even deny that art involves physical objects at all (abstract expressionism, suprematism).

Some "isms" venerated rationality, making it the essence of their art (Bauhaus, purism, de Stijl), while others aimed at its complete overthrow (dada, surrealism, expressionism). Some "isms" immersed in subjectivity, avidly exploring moods and dreams (surrealism), attempting nearly direct depiction of inner emotions (expressionism), or striving to attain some intuitive spirituality (Blaue Reiter, suprematism); others denied that inner states or subjective individuality had anything to do with art at all (de Stijl, Bauhaus). With respect to artistic techniques too, there were "isms" with every sort of theoretical allegiance: to line or shape, volume or surface, color or blank canvas, geometry or spontaneity, perspective or ray. Collectively, the artists and their movements also managed to take every kind of position on science, on the issue of the machine in modern life and art, and on the question of the social relevance of art (to what extent should art be aimed at improving the human condition? And how?).

The variety of modernist approaches to the visual arts is staggering, but a common denominator of nearly all of them is the destruction of conventions, of forms and perspectives, even of the regnant ideas of art's nature and function. Art historian John Golding characterizes the discontinuity as far more radical than the traditional "succession of different schools, different styles, different pictorial idioms" that makes up the history of earlier Western art: "None of these has so altered the principles, so shaken the foundations of Western painting as did cubism. Indeed, from a visual point of view it is easier to bridge the three hundred and fifty years separating Impressionism from the High Renaissance than it is to bridge the fifty years that lie between Impressionism and Cubism."[11] What Golding maintains about cubism can be said for almost any of the other twentieth-century "isms" as well.

The destruction of visual forms and perspectives was not really an indigenous impulse in America, though. At the turn of the century the American artistic avant-garde was largely fighting the battles of realism and impressionism against academic classicism and romanticism. The modernist revolution was imported from Europe. Its conduits were a number of American artists eager for liberation and inspiration and a number of appreciators and promoters anxious to free American art of its provinciality.

The beginning of the modernization of American art is ordinarily dated from the notorious Armory Show of 1913. That show, the inspired project of a small group of progressive-minded artists in the Association of American Painters and Sculptors, presented to a large American audience for the first time the work of Matisse, Derain, Picasso, Braque, Duchamp, Picabia, Delaunay, Léger, Kandinsky, and other modernists, in the context of the art of nineteenth-century masters such as Goya, Ingres, Corot, and the impressionists. The show was heavily attended and widely controversial, and the attacks of critics provided modernistically inclined Americans with clear senses of mission and comradeship.

A number of American artists had exposed themselves to the European scene even before the Armory Show: specific influences are risky to claim, but painters such as Lionel Feininger, Arthur Dove, John Marin, Marsden Hartley, and Joseph Stella had experienced European modernism and were experimenting with their own abstractionism, expressionism, and radical pictorial effects.

Photographer Alfred Stieglitz had been a campaigner, and a very effective one, for acceptance of the new, the radical, and the stimulating in art for several years before the Armory Show. He had founded photosecession (on the models of the German and Viennese Secession movements) because, according to William Innes Homer in *Alfred Stieglitz and the American Avant-Garde*, "For Stieglitz to fight honestly for his beliefs required the act of secession, separation from the 'fetters of conventionalism, tradition and provincialism' which dominated most American photography."* Stieglitz's main concern was photography's artistic legitimacy, and in that interest the magazine he founded and ran, *Camera Work*, interleaved photographs and discussions of photographic art with reproductions of paintings and drawings and discussions of visual aesthetics and modern movements in art. Although not thoroughly modernist, *Camera Work* brought its readers the whole contemporary artistic scene, even featuring such literary landmarks as Gertrude Stein's verbal-cubist portraits of Matisse and Picasso (her first literary works to be published in a periodical) and an excerpt from Wassily Kandinsky's widely influential work, *On the Spiritual in Art*.

Stieglitz also ran a New York gallery, "291," now legendary for the stimulation and support it gave American artists (and even some writers,

---

*(New York Graphic Society, 1977), 28–29. The influence of the Stieglitz circle is well covered in Homer's book and in Bram Dijkstra, *The Hieroglyphics of a New Speech* (Princeton University Press, 1969).

including William Carlos Williams and Wallace Stevens). Stieglitz's purpose was as pure as it was fervent; in Homer's words again, "he . . . wanted to establish at 291 a community of artists and critics whose interaction would generate new discoveries and new statements in the arts." By 1913, "291 . . . had become a center for avant-garde art unequaled anywhere else in the world."[12] Its look and its significance are described this way in Lloyd Goodrich's *The Decade of the Armory Show*, with a quote from a member of the Stieglitz circle, Marsden Hartley:

> Stieglitz's gallery was small, in a shabby building with a creaking elevator, but as Hartley said, "It was probably the largest small room of its kind in the world." The list of Stieglitz "firsts" is still impressive: among others, the first exhibitions in America of Matisse, Rousseau, Cezanne, Picasso, Picabia, Brancusi, and African Negro sculpture. But Stieglitz also believed passionately in the future of American art, and specifically in certain young modernists. He was the first to give one-man shows to Maurer, Marin, Hartley, Dove, Carles, Bleumner, Nadelman, O'Keeffe and Macdonald-Wright.[13]

Stieglitz's 291 group included many prominent American painters and practically all the important American photographers, from Gertrude Kasebier and Alvin Langdon Coburn to Edward Steichen and Paul Strand. The 291 spirit affected them all.

Another very significant group of artists, writers, and miscellaneous modernists came together in the New York salon of the Walter Conrad Arensbergs. Arensberg was wealthy, hospitable, adventuresome, and fascinated by artistic experimentation. He did some modernist writing himself, and he made his apartment the scene of nightly (sometimes around-the-clock) gatherings. The Arensberg group functioned in the years 1915–1921, after 291 and the Armory Show had had their impact. The group was more involved than Stieglitz's with a single artistic movement —dada—and it was decidedly more dedicated to partying. Two of the most notable French modernist painters and campaigners for experimentation, Marcel Duchamp and Francis Picabia, frequented the Arensbergs' (Duchamp in fact lived there for a time), and the American avant-garde was immeasurably stimulated by their presence. European artists Jean Crotti and Albert Gleizes, modernist musician Edgar Varèse, dancer Isadora Duncan, American artists Charles Sheeler, Joseph Stella, Man Ray, and Stuart Davis, writers Mina Loy, Alfred Kreymborg, Amy Lowell, and William Carlos Williams, political controversialist Max Eastman, and dada personalities Arthur Cravan and Baroness Elsa von Freytag-Loringhoven, and a good many others were Arensberg salon habitués.*

Americans abroad were supplying much of the inspiration (and publicity) for the visual revolution. Ezra Pound in England allied himself with painter-writer Wyndham Lewis and sculptor Henri Gaudier-Brzeska in the vigorous promotion of their movement, vorticism—most notably (and noisily) in their periodical, *Blast*. Gertrude Stein and her brother Leo were early discoverers of modern painting, principally cubism, and they made their Paris domicile a combination salon and gallery. At home to a great number of European painters (Picasso, Braque, Matisse, Picabia and others), art critics, musicians, and writers, as well as to visiting American artists and writers, they provided invaluable stimulation, support, and education in modernism for their guests. Indeed, in William Homer's estimation, "Had Gertrude and Leo Stein not been Americans, hospitable to their compatriots, the course of modern American art would have been far different."[14] Of modern American literature too, we might add.

*For good coverage of the Arensberg circle, see Rudolph E. Kuenzli, *New York Dada* (Willis Locker & Owens, 1986), William Marling, *William Carlos Williams and Painters* (Ohio University Press, [c. 1982]), and Dickran Tashjian, *Skyscraper Primitives* (Wesleyan University Press, 1975).

Partly out of the stimulation of the Stein coterie in Paris, Mabel Dodge (later Luhan) established a salon in New York in the early teens, intermingling artists and unionists, psychoanalysts and clergymen, writers and political radicals. The booming Bohemian quarter of New York, Greenwich Village, also had several groups that contributed a great deal to the cross-stimulation of writers and artists. Although they were generally radically modernist, they tended to be somewhat less involved with new-vogue European painters than were the uptown salons, and more dominated by literary, theatrical, and political concerns.

There were new studios too. Gertrude Vanderbilt Whitney opened the Whitney Studio in 1914 (she had quite possibly been the backer of the older Madison Gallery "that offered free exhibitions to little-known progressive American artists" in the early teens.[15] Stieglitz colleague Marius de Zayas opened the Modern Gallery, and there were openings of a number of others in the wake of 291 and the Armory Show;[16] the new art soon had its outlets in and around New York, at least.

Many of the revolutionary changes in the visual arts and their aesthetics were based on the same sorts of epistemological insights that were troubling and inspiring the scientists of the period and, of course, the writers as well. As the writers conceived the issues, and as they looked around for ideas and support, they quite naturally found the art more congenial—more engaging and more accessible—than the science. Thus the influence of the visual arts is more direct in this respect than that of the sciences.

The writers' personal associations tended this way too. Stein early abandoned her scientific career and collected modern art and artists, her friendships with Picasso, Braque, Matisse and the others putting her at the center of cubism and related movements in contemporary art. Pound was the promulgator (and a number of times the subject) of modern art.

Hemingway developed a gallery habit under Stein's tutelage in Paris. Stevens used the New York art world as a stimulating alternative to the domain of fire insurance; he knew the Stieglitz operation, visited with Arensberg, met Duchamp, and so forth. Williams likewise cherished his weekends in New York away from New Jersey doctoring; a habitué of 291, the Arensbergs', and the Village, he was also a personal friend of American painters Charles Demuth and Marsden Hartley and of painter-photographer Charles Sheeler. Stein and Williams had tried to be painters in their apprentice years, as had Dos Passos. Dos Passos had contacts with artists in Paris (hanging out with writers and theater people who associated with and introduced him to Léger and Goncharova) and in the Village. Dos Passos also had a deep interest in film and its artistic possibilities, making a pilgrimage to Eisenstein a prominent objective of his trip to Russia. Thus the modern art scene was very much present to these American writers, a potential source of models, analogies, and inspiration for their most venturesome work.

9 The Artistic Process and the Wider Event

■ The Destructions

Each of the movements of modernist visual art had its own particular program of destruction of what the new artists saw as art's culturally sanctioned norms and conventions, and individual artists often had intense personal interests, antipathies, and viewpoints that carried them beyond the program of a particular movement, so that the tide of convention destroying was as various as it was pervasive. Artists repudiated (among numerous other things) what they saw as art's inhibition of their individuality, its supercilious social role, its obliviousness of the technological-industrial world, and (most especially for our purposes) its obsolescence in terms of the new epistemological insights.

The attacks had as a common basis the realization that conventional pictorial representation narrowed and simplified the whole perceptual event—excluding as it did differing perspectives, the individuality and the motives of the seer, the multiple characteristics of the object, and to a large extent the determining effects of the social, religious, and artistic contexts. Modernist artists variously attempted to focus artistic attention on these aspects of the wider event that were conventionally ignored. The time-honored tradition of concealing the stage machinery yielded to the new impulse to encompass the wider event.

The cubists were the first to force the issue. Picasso and Georges Braque painted their way into a new epistemology and left it to others to rationalize and explain the destructions. The pictures they were doing in the 1900s and early teens—for example *Les Demoiselles d'Avignon* or *Ma Jolie, Still Life with Violin and Pitcher* or *Le Portugais*—were patent assaults on all standard ways of knowing and representing physical objects. They reconstructed the physical world according to radical insights about volume and point of view and destroyed shape and perspective and recognizability in the process. In a 1911 article art critic and cubist apologist

Roger Allard cited the destructionist "shared ideal" of the new "*group*": "*To react with violence against the notation of the instant, the insidious anecdotalism and all the other surrogates that pass under the name of impressionism.*"[1] Cubist painter Jean Metzinger in 1910 likewise endorsed "the abandonment of the burdensome inheritance of dogma; the displacing, again and again, of the poles of habit; the lyrical negation of axioms; the clever mixing, again and again, of the successive and the simultaneous."[2]

The futurists drew similar conclusions by working in the opposite direction, beginning with principles and then producing the art to go with them. As Marjorie Perloff recently pointed out, there was a "manifesto fever that swept across Europe in the years preceding the First World War," with the futurists in the vanguard, producing over fifty manifestos by 1915 and fine-honing the manifesto as a literary genre in itself.[3] A 1910 manifesto, signed by Umberto Boccioni, Carlo Carra, Luigi Russolo, Giacomo Balla, and Gino Severini, declares, for example: "We will fight with all our might the fanatical, senseless and snobbish religion of the past, a religion encouraged by the vicious existence of museums. We rebel against that spineless worshipping of old canvases, old statues and old bric-a-brac, against everything which is filthy and worm-ridden and corroded by time." They vow to "destroy the cult of the past, the obsession with the ancients, pedantry and academic formalism," and to "support and glory in our day-to-day world, a world which is going to be continually and splendidly transformed by victorious Science." They want their art to express "the tangible miracles of contemporary life—the iron network of speedy communications which envelops the earth, the transatlantic liners, the dreadnoughts, those marvellous flights which furrow our skies, the profound courage of our submarine navigators and the spasmodic struggle to conquer the unknown."[4] A manifesto by Carlo Carra details some of the necessary destructions, including "the extremely vulgar perspectives of *trompe-l'oeil*. . . . The concept of colour harmonies. . . . Contemplative idealism, which I have defined as a *sentimental mimicry of apparent nature*. . . . [and] All anecdote and detail."[5] Even the parameters of art and literature and music were under attack: other futurists urged "The chaotic, unaesthetic and heedless mixing of all the arts already in existence and of all those which are and will be created by the inexhaustible will for renewal which futurism will be able to infuse into mankind."[6] "Our art will probably be accused of tormented and decadent cerebralism," a manifesto by the original five concludes, "But we shall merely answer that we are, on the contrary, the primitives of a new sensitiveness, multiplied hundredfold, and that our art is intoxicated with spontaneity and power."[7]

Abstract expressionism was less organized, less programmatic than futurism, although in its individual forms no less destructivist. In his influential theoretical study, *The Art of Spiritual Harmony* (*Über das Geistige in der Kunst*, 1912), Wassily Kandinsky voiced this reservation about that same science that the futurists were worshipping as the source of progress and prophesy: people might ask, he suggests, "'If the science of the day before yesterday is rejected by the people of yesterday, and that of yesterday by us of to-day, is it not possible that what we call science now will be rejected by the men of to-morrow?' And the bravest of them answer 'It is possible.'"[8] The deepest significances were neither transient nor traditional, these expressionists felt, and their pictures in the early teens—Kandinsky's several "Improvisations," or Franz Marc's *Tyrol*, for example—often tended toward total abstraction. As painter Ludwig Meidner put it, "Henceforth we will no longer follow deadly reason, the old church dogmas, a political goal or a current fad—rather we shall create a spiritual, transcendental realm on our canvases out of primeval depths of feeling; out of elemental, immediate visions; yes, right out of our own spiritual being."[9] Kandinsky put a great deal of emphasis on artistic freedom—freedom to use any forms or materials or means of expression —since one of the most revealing "marks of a great spiritual epoch" was "a great *freedom*, which appears limitless to some," but which "makes the *Spirit* audible." People might see the results of such freedom as anarchy; they might "wrongly envision a purposeless subversion and chaos." "But," he goes on, "anarchism actually signifies planning and order, though not by external force or coercion but by an intuition of the *Good*. Here too there are limits, but these must be defined as *inner* limits which replace external ones. And these limits are steadily being extended. In this way freedom grows and creates that open road which leads to the Spirit."[10]

It was the dadaists who produced the most fervent, most thoroughgoing, and most notorious attempts to break the molds of knowledge, art, and reality. They named their movement after a word chosen randomly out of a dictionary (a "dada" is a toy horse), and they insisted that dada was basically an attitude or a state of mind—as Tristan Tzara puts it, "you may be gay, sad, afflicted, joyous, melancholy or Dada." Apparently, to be dada was to be gaily nihilistic about any form of art or order. The movement thrived on bizarre parties, wildly antiorganized multimedia performances, or any occasion (like innocently respectable art exhibitions) that could be subverted to antagonize the artistic community, the bourgeoisie, the establishment, or anybody who happened to be watching. Bafflement and blasphemy, chaos and controversy, deconstruction and dismay—these were their goals. But they regarded their obstreperous play as a serious form of cultural revolution: modern society was a decadent, hypocritical, inhumane affair, and the dada state of mind was both consequent to and antidote for that condition. As Tzara claimed,

> The beginnings of Dada were not the beginnings of an art, but of a disgust. Disgust with the magnificence of philosophers who for 3000 years have been explaining everything to us (what for?), disgust with the pretensions of these artists-God's-representatives-on-earth, disgust . . . with the false prophets who are nothing but a front for the interests of money, pride disease, disgust with the lieutenants of a mercantile art made to order according to a few infantile laws, disgust with the divorce of good and evil, the beautiful and the ugly. . . . Disgust finally with the Jesuitical dialectic which can explain everything and fill people's minds with oblique and obtuse ideas.[11]

German dadaist disgust was particularly political: by its lights German militarism, extreme nationalism, and manipulation of the population through art seemed dangerously decadent. Dadaist Richard Huelsenbeck declared, for example, that "the Dadaist considers it necessary to come out against art, because he has seen through its fraud as a moral safety valve. . . . The Germans are masters of dissembling, they are unquestionably the magicians (in the vaudeville sense) among nations, in every moment of their life they conjure up a culture, a spirit, a superiority which they can hold as a shield in front of their endangered bellies."[12] Similarly, George Grosz felt compelled to react against artistic smokescreens—"the vaporous tendencies of the so-called sacred art which reflected upon cubes and gothic structures while the marshals were painting with blood."[13]

It was human rationality that led humankind into its plight, the dadaists felt, so it seemed the job of irrationality to work a redemption. As Jean Arp put it,

> The Renaissance bumptiously exalted human reason. Modern times with their science and technology have turned man into a megalomaniac. The atrocious chaos of our era is the consequence of that overrating of reason. [Thus, he later recalled,] Dada wished to destroy the reasonable frauds of men and recover the natural, unreasonable order. Dada wished to replace the logical nonsense of the men of today with an illogical nonsense.[14]

Dadaist art is extremely various, ranging from George Grosz's caustic cartoonish caricatures to Francis Picabia's meticulously drawn spark plug

(*Portrait D'une Jeune Fille Americaine Dans l'Etat de Nudité*) to Marcel Duchamp's Mona Lisa with a moustache drawn on, but its common denominator is an attack on art as it was known in Western culture. Much of the
dadaist subversion of art is witty, like Man Ray's construction "Object to
Be Destroyed," a metronome with a picture of a staring eye paper-clipped
to its pendulum; and much of it is enigmatic—intentionally and primarily designed to scramble the perceptual categories of the viewer—like
Duchamp's wooden birdcage of sugar cubes (carved out of marble!) entitled *Why Not Sneeze Rrose Selavy?* Duchamp's "ready-mades" challenged
the idea of art most profoundly. The standard men's room porcelain urinal he entered in the exhibition of the Society of Independent Artists in
1917 (designated *Fountain*, by R. Mutt) was the most notorious of them,
but there were also, on other occasions, a bottle rack, a snowshovel, and a
bicycle wheel mounted upside down on a high stool. The special sanctified
status of the art object was thus exploded, along with the customary criteria of artistic taste. And the artist's absolute autonomy was triumphant:
whatever he said was a work of art *was* a work of art, norms and standards be damned.

The relative brevity of dada's flourishing points up an interesting aspect of the relation of artistic movements and destruction in the twentieth
century. Kandinsky (among others) acknowledged the need not only for
destruction but for *continual* destruction of cultural and artistic forms:

> All evolution, i.e., internal growth and external culture, becomes a
> matter of breaking down barriers.
> Barriers destroy freedom and prevent new revelations of the spirit.
> Barriers are constantly being built up out of the new values which
> have overthrown the old.[15]

With dadaism, however, where the destruction itself was the heart of
the style, it is surprising to see the transformation of the barrier-break-
ing into the new barrier. Duchamp in 1962 had to express dismay at
what had happened to his pure and outrageous gestures: "When I discovered ready-mades I thought to discourage aesthetics. In neo-dada
they have taken my ready-mades and found aesthetic beauty in them.
I threw the bottle-rack and the urinal into their faces as a challenge and
now they admire them for their aesthetic beauty." Commentator Jack
Flam points out the irony: "Dada, which had started out as anti-art, had
been incorporated into the artistic mainstream and had become, among
other things, an artistic stance."[16] The phenomenon holds true in literature as well, as we can see in the reframing of twenties destructionism

in so many prominent works of the sixties: anti-style becomes style, anti-art art.

■ The New Role of the Object

Whatever its future as art, destructionism was enormously successful in establishing an atmosphere of liberation. The art world of the early twentieth century became a riot of experimentation, much of it along epistemological lines. The object itself and the way that it looks were no longer presumptive givens nor were they inevitably central interests for the artists. As artists strove for ways to access the wider perceptual event, their works often in effect put the emphasis on modes of perception, methods of representation, and the artistic processes themselves. Objects were denatured, deconstructed, contorted, and displaced, while artists explored any and every conceivable aspect of their relationship to them. The new art avidly experimented with the object's great variety of real and potential visual aspects; its formal qualities; its iconic possibilities; its growth or decay, motion or process; its capacities to evoke or reflect or symbolize or block subjective responses; its political, social or subconscious significances. Concurrently, new techniques and new pictorial (and antipictorial) languages were being developed, sometimes themselves the virtual (or actual) objects of the presentations.

At one extreme many artists were experimenting with literalism and with highly object-oriented art, attempting representations that might either reveal the independent otherness of the object, discover connections between the object's formal elements and human sensibility, or in some other way stimulate sophisticated scrutiny of human intermediation in the artistic process. The ultimate object-oriented art is of course the readymade: it says to us simply "I am what I am; I represent myself." A little less far out on the same objectivist road are Rayographs, cameraless photographs produced by Man Ray (at first in a casual, chance gesture) by placing miscellaneous objects on an unexposed sheet of photographic paper and turning on the light. The objects "photographed" themselves, producing an abstraction made up of silhouette and gradations of near-silhouette. Such were some artists' experiments with the capacity of the object to affect our senses in and practically by itself.

"Straight photography" would seem to be another noninterventionist form of art, defined by its practitioners among the American photographers as the production of clear representations using untampered cameras and nonmanipulative processing techniques. Its images were lifelike and virtually conceivable as the object's own self-representation: Stieglitz colleague Mexican painter Marius De Zayas insisted that Stieglitz, "through photography, has shown us, as far as it is possible, the objectivity of the outer world."[17] But the significances of the images of Straight Photography were more than mere slice-of-life. The photographers themselves felt and said this. Stieglitz's famous picture, *The Steerage*, a masterpiece of literal representation, was conceived, he said, when he saw "A round straw hat, the funnel leaning left, the stairway leaning right, the white drawbridge with its railings made of circular chains—white suspenders crossing on the back of a man in the steerage below, round shapes of iron machinery, a mast cutting into the sky, making a triangular shape. . . . I saw a picture of shapes and underlying that the feeling I had about life."[18] One important direction in which Straight Photography grew in the twenties and thirties was toward increasing abstraction. Stieglitz protégé Paul Strand in his pictures of bowls and of porch shadows, Edward Steichen's *Wheelbarrow and Flower Pots*, Edward Weston's *Nude* (1925), and Stieglitz's own cloud pictures, his "Equivalents," all quite impressively show how each photographer's "picture of shapes" can relate to an underlying "feeling I had about life." In Strand's words, "It is in the organization of this objectivity that the photographer's point of view toward Life enters in, and where a formal conception born of the emotions, the intellect, or of both, is as inevitably necessary for him, before an exposure is made, as for the painter, before he puts brush to canvas."[19]

The precisionist movement in American painting—principally involving some artists of the Stieglitz group, such as Charles Sheeler and Charles Demuth—operated similarly, though they seemed dedicated to discovering formal and societal, rather than personal, values. They strove for an extreme in literalism well beyond that of American realists like Sloan and Glackens—for a kind of superrealism or architectural trompe-l'oeil. The paintings in that mode, like Sheeler's *Upper Deck*, a complex composition of rooftop machinery, feature an amazing clarity of detail and architectural line that is practically photographic. Yet closer examination reveals that the verisimilitude is stark, formal, idealized. As critic Martin L. Friedman says, "in the precisionist paintings of skyscrapers, bridges, factories, and docks, all traces of damage or decay disappeared, specific architectural details were vastly simplified, and these forms were recast as the proud symbols of technological splendor." Of their technique, he states, "the pictures are brought to an icily defined and flawless finish, with virtually no evidence of the brush strokes or the trials and hesitations of arriving at the finished stage."[20] In a manner of speaking object became form in the precisionist paintings; it was photographic realism (at least in Sheeler's case), dominated by the artist's sense of pure composition. Knowing was the rationalizing, the purifying of actuality.

Another innovation in the literalistic representation of objects was the use by several cubist painters of fragments of literalism in their paintings and collages. Picasso's *Still Life with Violin and Fruit* (1913), for example, is a two-dimensional cubist composition that features virtually every conceivable form of representation on the literal-to-figurative scale: the violin is figured partly in scraps of barely suggestive sketch, partly in vivid three-dimensional drawing, partly in shape outline and cutouts, and partly in trompe-l'oeil wood-grain painting. The fruit is trompe-l'oeil painting on white scraps layered over real newspaper. Likewise, Braque's *Le Courrier* (1913) presents some of its details in barely sketched ideographic form, some in trompe-l'oeil patterning, and some in the actual presence of pieces of newspaper. One effect of such radical and aggressive mixture of media and forms, of course, is to parody representational art and to call attention to the artistic process in all its artificiality. (Picasso once said, "art has always been art and not nature. And from the point of view of art there are no concrete or abstract forms, but only forms which are more or less convincing lies."[21]) In respect to the pasted-in object —the fragment of ready-made—the mixing of levels of figurativeness creates a double framework of significance. Art historian Marjorie Perloff offers this explanation, from a manifesto of the group *Mu*, in her discussion of the significance of collage: "Each cited element breaks the continuity or the linearity of the discourse and leads necessarily to a double reading: that of the fragment perceived in relation to its text of origin; that of the same fragment as incorporated into a new whole, a different totality."[22] As is the case with the full-scale ready-made, the object is denatured, given a new significance, but it is still itself, bringing along some of its original context as aura. Representing the wider perceptual event becomes in this case a matter of varying and contrasting contexts. As we shall see, the collage technique has literary analogs in Stein's word assemblages and Dos Passos's infusions of bits of actual pop song and newspaper story.

Departures from literalism were of course legion, but the first and most influential were those of the cubists. Styles of cubism changed rapidly, and artists like Picasso, Gris, and Picabia were restless and incessant inventors, like explorers anxious not to let any new territory go undiscovered (or be discovered first by somebody else), so that cubism is best described not as a coherent program but as a set of tendencies, varied and even disparate. Although its origins seem to have been purely painterly (Picasso insisted that this was so), a good deal of it was in keeping with the emerging views of space, time, and events as relativistic and with the new idea of there being any number of possible geometries. And the epistemological questions—how could we know an object and how represent it—were, at least by implication, among its central concerns.

Art dealer Daniel-Henry Kahnweiler, friend and promoter of the cubist painters from the beginning, wrote that the cubists were solving the problem of the essential conflict between representation and structure in new ways that respected spatial structure more than surface appearance. "Cubism," he said, "brings the forms of the physical world as close as possible to their underlying basic forms. Through connection with these basic forms, upon which all visual and tactile perception is based, cubism provides the clearest elucidation and foundation of all forms."[23] Picasso's famous portrait of Kahnweiler (1910) is a complete reconstruction of the subject in geometric fragments—cubes and cylinders, triangles and trapezoids—of varied depths and tones and densities. The details of a head—a hairline, the bridge of a nose, an ear, and a moustache—are schematically suggested in an upper-right-center portion of the canvas that stands out in the density of its volumes and the sharpness of its lines. But for those scant details and the title Picasso gave the picture, it is like a vision of houses and rooftops on a distant hillside, if it is like anything at all.

The next stage in the cubist style would present volumeless, two-dimensional compositions (no "cubes" at all!) and stress the relationships between objects: their shapes, tones, patterns, and various perspectives intermixed and overlayered. Picasso's *Still Life with a Bottle of Maraschino* (1914) and Juan Gris's *The Watch* (1912) and *The Washstand* (1912) are examples of this kind of redefinition of the object. The cubist artist was engaging in a very special kind of abstraction, one that called attention to the fact of the artist's extremely individual intervention yet suggested very little about the artist's own personality. Art historian Guy Habasque suggests the way that Picasso, for example, arrived at his conceptions:

> his new method was to penetrate, by an act of intuition, into the essence of the object and thus to discover its basic characteristics, those that conditioned its very being, and lacking which it would not be what it is. And the next step . . . was to integrate them into a single image, constituting as it were the pictorial essence of the object. The resulting picture would thus contain, potentially, all possible individuations of the object . . . , the essential entity.[24]

Later in this book we shall see Wallace Stevens striving toward a similar sort of abstract essence and Gertrude Stein using this same method in composing her "portraits."*

There were of course other movements in modern art that reinterpreted the object in terms of some salient quality or from some variant perspective. Henri Matisse attempted to concentrate on the element of light in order to expand the boundaries of space, realizing in the perfect moment of vision "the light of the spirit" and "a cosmic space."[25] Russian artists Mikhail Larionov and Natalya Goncharova started the rayonnist movement, based on a perception of "the collisions and couplings of rays *between* objects, . . . the ceaseless and intense drama of the rays that constitute the unity of all things."[26]

The Italian futurists developed a thoroughgoing aesthetic based on the concept of motion. "What we want to do is to show the living object in its dynamic growth," declared Boccioni; and Anton Bragaglia, the founder of "photodynamism," put it that *We seek the interior essence of things: pure movement; and we prefer to see everything in motion*, since as things are dematerialized in motion they become idealized, while still retaining, deep down, a strong skeleton of truth." Boccioni cited Bergson's theories denying the divisibility of motion and the conceptualizing of matter into "autonomous bodies with absolutely defined contours" and produced such paintings as *The Forces of a Street* (1911) and *Charge of Lancers* (1915) using multiple and overlayered images, long diagonals, acute angles, and such to signify motion. "A running horse has not four legs, but twenty, and their movements are triangular," a 1910 manifesto had insisted. Analogous to several of the writers we shall be considering—Stein, Aiken, Stevens, Williams, and Dos Passos—the futurists had a yearning to depict what they referred to as "the simultaneousness of the ambient": the miscellaneous welter of unconnected details and events that make up any given experience in the fullness of its context.[27]

The incessant drive to get new insight from the object led to ever greater degrees of abstraction, especially in the works of the Netherlands group "de Stijl" and the abstract expressionists. De Stijlist Piet Mondrian developed a purely geometric style, using straight lines and rectangles and primary colors in an effort to represent the unity and balance that he felt underlay the phenomenal world. "The peculiarities of form and natural color evoke subjective feelings that obscure the pure truth,"[28] he main-

---

*See below, pp. 197–99 and 260–265. Coincidentally enough, I worked out my analysis of Stein's "portrait" method in purely literary terms, before finding ideas such as Habasque's.

tained. Expressionist Wassily Kandinsky felt that "in each manifestation [of art] is the seed of a striving toward the abstract, the non-material,"[29] and, intuiting a system of correspondences between specific colors and forms and specific "spiritual values," he in time worked himself free from all objective reference in his painting. The deeper motive he strove to realize in his work was not (as with Mondrian) the formal structure of the world but "inner need" (about which more later). In both cases, however, the material objects of this world were things to be passed beyond or through to some more ultimate realm. We shall see the same sort of quasi-religious quest carried on in language and literary discourse by Wallace Stevens, who poses the whole question himself: is that realm of nether-most abstraction a real ultimate or a projection of inner need?

At the farthest extreme from literalism, the work of Robert Delaunay and Kasimir Malevich (among others) achieved the complete disappear-ance of the object from the work of art. Delaunay's purely abstract compo-sitions were designated "Orphic Cubism" by his friend, writer Guillaume Apollinaire: "*Orphic Cubism* . . . is the art of painting new structures with elements which have not been borrowed from the visual sphere, but have been created entirely by the artist himself, and been endowed by him with fullness of reality. . . . This is pure art."[30] Delaunay's *Disk* (1912) is simply a set of concentric circles, divided horizontally and vertically, with the resulting quarter rings painted in different colors. The colors are stra-tegically, semiscientifically juxtaposed to vary in forwardness and inten-sity so that (according to Delaunay's theory) they "vibrate" dynamically for the viewer. Malevich, less technical and more doctrinaire, concocted "suprematism," an attempt at an utterly contentless art. "The essential content of Suprematism," he asserted, "is the totality of non-objective, natural excitations without any goal or purpose. . . . The intrinsic idea of art is non-objectivity." In his works, such as *Suprematist Painting* (a huge cross, off-center and off-balance, made by a thick red vertical rectangle intersecting a black horizontal one on a plain white canvas), he strove for the "supremacy of pure sensation."[31] What "pure sensation" he was after might be indicated by his recollection of the response one of his early suprematist works elicited: "In the year 1913 in my desperate struggle to free art from the ballast of the objective world I fled to the form of the Square and exhibited a picture which was nothing more or less than a black square upon a white background. The critics moaned and with them the public: 'Everything we loved is lost: We are in a desert. . . . Before us stands a black square on a white ground.'"[32]

■ The Reflexive Self

Many twentieth-century artists were vividly aware of the element of self-projection that was essentially and inescapably part of any act of perception, and much of their rejection of earlier art was a rejection of its naïveté regarding that issue. They used their reflexiveness-awareness in a great variety of ways, often negatively by avoiding or attacking sentimentality or rationality, by negating the assumptions of realism or of perspective technique, or by undermining illusionism. And they used it positively too, to explore, to express, to liberate the self, and to attempt to see the self in the context of the widest parameters of the event of seeing. Sophistication was of the essence; epistemological naïveté was no longer viable.

As was the case with their contemporaries the analytical and the process philosophers, modernist artists had two basic approaches for attempting to manage reflexiveness: avoid it, or embrace it as an essential part of the perceptual event. But can reflexiveness really be avoided? Dadaist accidental art might offer one sort of answer—the accidental breakage-in-transit of Duchamp's monumental *Large Glass* ("The Bride Stripped Bare by her Bachelors, Even"), for example, produced a work Duchamp didn't quite intend but came to swear by. *Intentional* avoidance of reflexiveness is theoretically impossible, of course—a contradiction in terms—although a number of artists have struggled toward that goal. Theodore van Doesburg, speaking for the group de Stijl, advocates "suppressing arbitrary subjective elements in the expressional means. . . . We reject all subjective choice of forms and are preparing to use objective, universal, formative means."[33] The de Stijlists and others of that strict formalist bent (the purists, the elementarists) aspired to the suppression of personality (insofar as possible) and the reliance on geometric forms, mathematical relationships, primary colors, and logical laws and systems of construction. Like Mendeleyev, they were attempting to discover the Logic of Nature, although their choices of elements, geometries, and rationales still had an inherently human, culturally determined character. In literature too we shall see an analogous epistemological motive: in, for example, Ernest Hemingway's striving to eliminate self-involved and culture-bound conceptions and build works of art out of primary, universal elements (although the ultimacy he was trying to realize was principally emotional rather than logical).

A great many artists embraced the personal, reflexive element—often reveling in it, in fact—and they found a great many ways to do so. Henri Matisse, for example, having reconstituted space in color and figure in ideogram, celebrated the fact that with the advent of photography, "descriptive painting had become useless," and the way had been cleared for his painting to be "a translation of feelings."[34] Along the same line, the relativity the cubists discovered was personal as well as spatial. According to cubists Albert Gleizes and Jean Metzinger, "There are as many images of an object as there are eyes which look at it; there are as many essential images of it as there are minds which comprehend it."[35] Georges Braque likewise felt that it was a translation of feelings that lay behind his transmutation of the nude in his *Grand Nu* (1908) into an ensemble of repeated and overlayered curves, with head, face, and arms only schematically suggested:

> I couldn't portray a woman in all her natural loveliness. . . . I haven't the skill. No one has. I must, therefore, create a new sort of beauty, the beauty that appears to me in terms of volume, of line, of mass, of weight, and through that beauty interpret my subjective impression. Nature is a mere pretext for a decorative composition, plus sentiment. It suggests emotion, and I translate that emotion into art. I want to expose the Absolute, and not merely the factitious woman.[36]

Somehow, that "Absolute" is accessed through the "subjective impression," the "sentiment," the "emotion"—as if the painting can thereby become not just *an* expression, but a universal expression.

The futurists also had this sense that subjective response was an essential part of the reality of an event or object. Their concept of "the simultaneousness of the ambient" had the same monistic bent as the philosophies of Bergson or Whitehead, and it developed in the dimension of time what the cubists had done in space. Here this sense is expressed by Belgian futurist Mac Delmarle:

> Simultaneity of the aspects of particular objects, including the human figure, is not enough for us. We want the simultaneity of the many sensations which converge to form our emotion.
>
> This emotion, derived from a spectacle and capable of generating works of art, is formed by the contributions of all our senses; this is the only true simultaneity in the real meaning of the word.[37]

"We thus create a sort of emotive ambience," one of the futurists' joint manifestoes states, "seeking by intuition the sympathies and the links which exist between the exterior (concrete) scene and the interior (abstract) emotion." "We thus arrive at what we call the *painting of states of mind*."[38]

The two movements that brought the painting of states of mind to the highest level of complexity and richness were surrealism and expressionism. Both encouraged the breaking of barriers between intuition and expression, between innermost self and artistic product. They followed the dadaists in their quest for nonintermediation. As Tristan Tzara had put it, "What we want now is spontaneity. Not because it is better or more beautiful than anything else. But because everything that issues freely from ourselves, without the intervention of speculative ideas, represents us. . . . The Beautiful and the True in art do not exist; what interests me is the intensity of a personality transposed directly, clearly into the work."[39] The surrealists developed a wildly mixed visual language that ranged (at times even within a single painting) from organic-form cubism to trompe-l'oeil, drawing imagery from dream and alchemy and the Freudian unconscious. The expressionists varied even more widely, from realism to mysticism, sarcasm, or nightmare—even to forms that were utterly imaginatively abstract. In the art of both movements the artist's self—conscious or subconscious—was generally the main point of reference: the source of imagery and form, of psyche and judgment.

The surrealists' theorist-in-residence, writer André Breton, urged artists to develop a grasp of the wider event through "automatism" and, invoking the newest authority on self-searching, claimed that true surrealism had to

> encompass the whole psychophysical field (in which the field of consciousness constitutes only a very small segment). Freud has demonstrated that at these unfathomable depths there reigns the absence of contradiction, the relaxation of emotional tensions due to repression, a lack of the sense of time, and the replacement of external reality by a psychic reality obeying the pleasure principle alone. Automatism leads us in a straight line to this region.[40]

That automatism was likely to take the artist not only into the exploration of self but the exploration of psychosis as well was a possibility both recognized and appreciated by several of the surrealists. Salvador Dali eagerly anticipated being able "to systematize confusion thanks to a paranoic and active process of thought, and so assist in discrediting completely the world of reality." He strove to develop "a spontaneous method of irrational knowledge based upon the critical-interpretive association of delirious phenomena."[41]

Surrealism was a spontaneousness not of technique but of imagination. Surrealist works were very carefully painted, the imagery ordinarily being clear and precise, with all the spontaneity being expressed in the

strangeness of the locale, the metamorphosis of the objects, and the am-
biguousness of the symbolism. Inez Hedges's valuable study of dadaist
and surrealist literature and film studies the extent to which the people in
these movements were fascinated with mystical analogies, with systems
of esoterica like alchemy that were founded on concepts of transformation, metamorphosis, and correspondence. As Hedges explains, "the surrealist enterprise defined itself as the search for a new language that would
be in direct communication with the unconscious."[42]

Take, for example, Max Ernst's painting *Oedipus Rex* (1922). It is a
dreamlike non sequitur, presenting us with three fingers and a thumb
protruding through a very small rectangular window in a brick wall. The
fingers and thumb fill the window opening and hold a walnut, barely
split open, pierced by an arrow; one finger and the thumb are also im-
paled (bloodlessly) on an unidentifiable hooked device that is strung like
a bow. The device is wider than the window and would seem not to be
removable from the thumb and finger. There are two heads of what look
like birds (although one has a pair of horns) sticking up through a hole in
an outdoor platform. A form like a picket fence partially enwraps one
bird's head, the pickets pointing toward its eye, and a piece of string or
wire loops around the other bird's horns and disappears skyward. In a
distant, otherwise empty sky, a hot-air balloon is hovering (escaping?).

What we can say of this picture would hold for most surrealist paintings. The conglomeration of images is visually very potent and inexplica-
bly disturbing. It touches some deep chords that put us in mind of our
own dreams, in the present instance suggesting confinement and freedom, entrapment and menace. The symbol system is too esoteric or too
personal (or both) to be readable by an uninitiated viewer, but this is no
problem for the artist dedicated to maximizing reflexiveness by exploring
the dreams and myths and symbols of the subconscious. Surreality is
reality of the most personal, least rational kind. In Breton's words, "I
believe in the future transmutation of those two seemingly contradictory
states, dream and reality, into a sort of absolute reality, of surreality, so to
speak."[43]

Artistic expressionism can consist of anything from the distortion of
the image of a person, object, or scene, as in works of Beckmann, Kirchner, and Schiele, to the projection of a whole world of imagined color and
form, as in works of Klee, Marc, and Kandinsky. In any case the projection of some inner feeling or vision is the dominating factor in the artistic
process. As Ernst Ludwig Kirchner put it in speaking for the Dresden
expressionist group Die Brücke, "We claim as our own everyone who re-

produces directly and without falsification whatever it is that drives him to create."[44] The whatever-it-is-that-drives-the-artist-to-create might be a matter of political or moral opinion that dictates the distortions of figures and forms or it might be a matter of pure visual imagination that generates a realization of its own potentials for form and rhythm, color and relationship.

Max Beckmann's *The Night* (1918) is a nightmare vision of murder and cruelty, with a very high level of distortion of form in the cause of moral outrage. The seven figures are cartoonish grotesques, oversized for the size of the room and extreme in their gestures. The two victims are stiff, their legs spread and straight and angular: the man facing us has an expression of extreme strangulation; the woman has bared back and buttocks, and with wrists tied angularly over her head her fingers twist in a gesture of agony. The tormentors are a varied group: one a rough-looking laborer, another a pop-eyed, pipe-smoking businessman, and another a small woman with a sadistic stare. The artist has opted for vividness rather than subtlety and for message rather than verisimilitude in the technique, his outrage shaping the figures, the composition, the tone.

Wassily Kandinsky's painting *With the Black Arch* (1912) is wholly non-objective, although it is as vivid in execution as Beckmann's. On a whitish background that suggests the reshaping of the frame into something perhaps septagonal, Kandinsky presents us with three large forms, nongeometric and somewhat lumpish, predominantly blue, red, and brown respectively, each the habitat of various color areas (gradations of white, yellow, and brown), as well as of lines, straight and slightly curved, some crossing and some parallel, principally in black. The black arch of the title occupies much of the upper half of the canvas, an uneven inverted "V" that overlies the red and the brown shapes but not the blue. Two smaller shapes also float in the clouded swirl of the background: a red spot upper left and a much quieter brown and yellow near-rectangle upper right. Not unsurprisingly, words fail to give any but the vaguest sense of what the abstract expressionist painting looks like. The sense of motion, stabilized by the arch; the sense of space, shallow but complex and not quite consistent in its planes; the sense of size and of the painting's insistence: these are all viewer impressions of a piece of work that is really utterly untranslatable. And Kandinsky's own aesthetic theories—of warm and cold lines and angles and colors, of their "inner sound," and of the significances of the point, the line, and the plane—help the interpreter not at all. Perhaps only Kandinsky can see those characteristics (or that allegory?) in such a work. Abstract expressionism can be beautifully imaginative, though hardly specifically communicative.

Herbert Read offers this explanation of how Kandinsky worked, of how an artist could compose an expression of an inner feeling that was totally nonreferential:

> Kandinsky maintained that the supreme work of art is a highly conscious construction determined by the patient elaboration of plastic forms to correspond to a slowly "realized" inner feeling. The forms might have an arbitrary beginning—a scribble, an improvisation of line and color; but these forms are then modified or manipulated, teased and tested, until they correspond to an even more clearly realized inner feeling—the feeling is realized as the forms achieve a correspondence—can be realized only if the artist succeeds in so disposing the forms that they express the feeling.[45]

In either type of expressionism the artist clearly recognized the factor of self-realization in the work. Like a great many other modern artists who were no longer epistemologically naive, the expressionists were certainly under no illusions about their own role in creating their own perceptions.

Finally, in viewing modernist art as a complex collective phenomenon, we can see that accuracy of representation had become for these artists not a mandate, but merely another option. They took on the task of depicting the wider event—not just the object as seen from this perspective at this time, but the object as seeable, the act of seeing, the artistic process, the history of art, the social context, the seer him- or herself, and even the very substance of the paint or stone or celluloid that is the art's "medium." They substituted a sophisticated, often conscious epistemology for an unconscious, conventionalized one. Like physicists in the age of relativity, artists in the age of relativistic epistemology had many new considerations to take into account if they were to function as its seers.

Their art explored and redefined the boundaries of knowing, and in so doing subjected its viewers to "difficult art" of a very special kind—a kind that accustoms its viewers to imaginative uncertainty, to unresolvable ambiguity, to the potential legitimacy of radically differing constructs and perspectives. The artists-in-words we shall next consider developed in the same period a similar sense of the wider event.

V   The American Writer in the Age of Epistemology

We turn now to a consideration of some of the twentieth-century writers who took especially destructive stances toward the knowledge and knowledge acquisition of their day. These are writers who had a special yearning for authenticity, for contact with the actual, and who felt that since customary approaches were highly fallible or downright misleading, radical approaches were called for. There were many others, artists and intellectuals, who shared the near-revolutionary fervor in the early twentieth century. Harold Stearns, for example, in his monumental and often bitterly negativistic *Civilization in the United States: An Inquiry by Thirty Americans* (1922), unleashes this tirade as part of his introduction:

> The most moving and pathetic fact in the social life of America to-day is emotional and aesthetic starvation, of which the mania for petty regulation, the driving, regimentating, and drilling, the secret society and its grotesque regalia, the firm grasp on the unessentials of material organization of our pleasures and gaieties are all eloquent stigmata. We have no heritages or traditions to which to cling except those that have already withered in our hands and turned to dust. One can feel the whole industrial and economic situation as so maladjusted to the primary and simple needs of men and women that the futility of a rationalistic attack on these infantilisms of compensation becomes obvious. There must be an entirely new deal of the cards.[1]

The destructionist writers shared such an attitude (if not—very often —the garbled and overwrought terminology). Often implicitly and in their own inimitably diverse ways, they rejected the status quo of American culture, attempting to foster a mind revolution beginning in art and lan- guage that might reach to social organization, economics and politics, or daily life. A new literature seemed called for—one that had the potential of initiating a whole new consciousness.

Considered collectively, the destructionist writers were sensitive to a great variety of radical influences: artistic, political, literary, scientific—from positivism to dada, from James Joyce to Einstein, from Picasso to Lenin to Freud. Most relevant to our purposes, they learned to take new stand- points regarding perception and representation, with special awareness of reflexiveness in knowing, of the arbitrariness and artifactuality of lan- guage, of the confining nature of all the certified truths of life and litera- ture. Like the scientists and visual artists of their day, they were fascinated with methodology: discovery through process was their hope and faith, whether the process be the strictest of disciplines or a riot of unfettered imaginings. And originality—discovering their own world in their own individual linguistic way—was their most fervent ambition. The motley of verbal visions they thus loosed on the world is like an extravagant circus—not only in its bizarre color and diversity, but in its quality too, with some acts extremely ingenious and accomplished, others strained and pointless. The new range of possibilities they introduced into litera- ture is still providing ideas and material and inspiration for writers.

They explored points of view that were extremes of authorial disen- gagement and extremes of engagement; they experimented with new va- rieties of self-representation; they discovered unanticipated modes of self- reflexiveness. They structured literary works in a variety of new ways, from representing the flux of experience to representing its atomicity. They focused variously and radically on different elements of the literary work: on the image, the impression, the experienced event, the event's emotional impact, the locution or slogan, and even on the word or its implied semantic framework. They explored minimal means for producing precise effects, and maximal means for overwhelming all categories of relevance, for foregrounding everything. They pushed the limits of language, experimenting with syntax and antisyntax, with literalism, with abstraction, and with the pure objectivism of literature as words on a page. They concocted new representations of time—as process, as stasis, as recursion —and new versions of identity—in process, in milieu, in lingo.

Whatever the extremes and vagaries of their individual approaches, they all seem agreed on the ultimate indescribability of reality; on the uselessness of rationalistic and conventional approaches to understanding; on the indelible individuality of experience; and on the necessity for uncompromising candor and originality. By no stretch of the imagination, though, are they always playing epistemological hardball. Sometimes they're just *playing*, cavorting, self-demonstrating. But then play can destroy the veneer of official certification on conventional concepts as well as anything.

10 Gertrude Stein and the Splendid Century

No writer did more in the business of knowledge destruction than Gertrude Stein (1874–1946). She flatly annulled the wisdom of the ages (people of earlier times saw things quite differently, she said). She abandoned conventional literary forms or she skewed them completely to suit her own predilections. She even spurned the standard and established uses of language, trying to forge new connections between the written word, artistic form, and psychological process. In her own world—cross-cultural, radically modernistic, and shaped by her certainty of her own genius—she attempted a knowledge revolution of unprecedented scope. And she did it for reasons of epistemology.

On the face of it her program—for so she described it in the self-explanatory mode of her middle career—should have had more effect. Her audience was never large and enthusiastic, though, and posterity, while not really relegating her work to neglect, has not embraced it as the great achievement it presents itself as being. Her reputation hasn't shared the fates of Melville's or Dickinson's, and there are some good reasons for her bad luck, I think, quite evident to anyone who has tried to read right through, say, *The Making of Americans*, *The Geographical History of America*, or *Stanzas in Meditation* in a concentrated and attentive way.

In her education she followed her own predilections and they led her directly into preoccupations of the twentieth century. They involved her early in science—psychology and medicine—then, later, in modernistic art, although we might suspect in both cases that she was more attuned to fascinating and challenging persons than to any particular fields. "The important person in Gertrude Stein's Radcliffe life was William James," her alter ego points out in *The Autobiography of Alice B. Toklas*.[1] Stein biographers have revealed her at that stage as an individualistic and enthusiastic undergraduate with a good deal of gusto for laboratory experiments in psychology, a competence in coauthoring psychology journal articles, and a deep admiration for James and his way of thinking and doing. Her subsequent adventure in medical school was intended to be her first step on the way to becoming a psychologist like James, although his inspiration as a role model seems to have declined at the same rate that her monumental indifference to chemistry and physiology mounted, and in time she (very wisely) abandoned that path. Her brother Leo was another strong influence, and he led her in the direction of Europe and contemporary art. With Leo she established a home in Paris, and through Leo she got a start in appreciating and collecting paintings and meeting artists. Together they discovered Pablo Picasso (they were among the very earliest to do so). Gertrude's understanding of Picasso was deeper and longer-lasting than Leo's, though, and in Picasso she found another genius-colleague to stimulate her imagination. She was no painter herself, and she would have made a poor psychologist-philosopher (she *did* make a poor psychologist-philosopher in some of her writings!), but she was greatly inspired by her connection with these unique and talented people.

Gertrude Stein characterized her own twentieth century as "splendid," defining it mainly in terms of the nineteenth-century characteristics it negated, especially "reasonableness":

> So the twentieth century is . . . a time when everything cracks, where everything is destroyed, everything isolates itself, it is a more splendid thing than a period where everything follows itself. So then the twentieth century is a splendid period, not a reasonable one in the scientific sense, but splendid. . . . [It] is a century which sees the earth as no one has ever seen it, the earth has a splendor that it never has had, and as everything destroys itself in the twentieth century and nothing continues, so then the twentieth century has a splendor which is its own.[2]

It needs noting that the century's wars and political and social turmoil were not what Stein had in mind when she appreciated its splendor. She lived in France most of the time during both world wars, and by all accounts demonstrated considerable compassion, generosity, grace, and courage. But her imaginative identification was not with the sociopolitical, and her opinions in that realm were few and simple—part nineteenth-century conservatism and part fervent antipaternalism, whether the political father be Hitler, Stalin, or Roosevelt. The social upheavals of the day provided no more than a distracting backdrop to Stein's fascination with the developing new possibilities for perception, mind-play, and artistic creation. Her identification was with the revolution in the visual arts (for example, the "splendid century" quotation is from her 1938 book on Picasso) and with her own writing and what it did.

Gertrude Stein actually had no characteristic experimental style and no consistent philosophy of composition.* After the period of her most extreme experimentation, she became a prolific explainer of her works and their intentions, but from these accounts it is easy to overestimate the coherence of her aims and development. Stein scholar Richard Bridgman sounds an appropriate note of caution: "Gertrude Stein did argue persuasively on occasion for her innovative practices, but in doing so she gave her career a symmetry and certitude that it never possessed. The greater part of Gertrude Stein's writing was improvisational."[3] She improvised purposes and aims and justifications as well as words and structures. Like those of any basically improvisational artist, her productions are of an uneven quality. Stein continually keeps her critics in that awkward state of uncertainty as to whether a given passage is a new kind of difficult perceptiveness or just a misplaced riff. What she got from the splendid century was not an aesthetic program, a philosophical viewpoint, or a writing style or set of standards, but an enormous range of possibilities and an indomitable sense of personal artistic freedom.

Freedom and possibility were born in destruction for Stein, the destruction of certified knowledge and standard usage. Certainty was a fiction and a bore: "It is only in history government, propaganda that it is of any importance if anybody is right about anything. Science well they never are right about anything not right enough so that science cannot go on enjoying itself as if it is interesting, which it is."[4] Knowledge was personal or it was nothing: "One cannot come back too often to the question what is knowledge and to the answer knowledge is what one knows."[5] And "what one knows" is dependent on perception, itself an act channeled and conditioned by personal and cultural factors: "what is seen depends upon how everybody is doing everything."[6] It is not difficult to find the influence of James implicit in this attitude toward fixity and finality, this insistence on the fluidity and subjectivity of truth. Nor is it difficult to find throughout Stein's work echoes of the continental modernists —Cézanne, Picasso, Matisse, Apollinaire—and their lessons on the transience of perception and the arbitrariness of representation. Habituated perception simply was not seeing, just as knowledge of certified reality

*Marjorie Perloff argues effectively against simplistic categorizations of Stein's style and bravely designs a sixfold typology in Bruce Kellner, ed., *A Gertrude Stein Companion* (Greenwood, 1988), 96–108.

was not knowing, and James and the modernists helped Stein gain leverage against these clichés of the mind. But although philosophers and artists gave her insights and inspiration, she waged her own headstrong and highly individualistic campaign. Critic Norman Weinstein insists on this point: "Gertrude Stein, although a woman intensely aware of the intellectual life about her, was nonetheless her own woman. With a single-mindedness bordering on preposterous megalomania she stubbornly kept writing according to her most singular program."[7]

Gertrude Stein's fundamental act of knowledge destruction, the one from which all her experimental writing followed, was basically linguistic, a set of tricks and routines that grew along with the intuition that language is an artificial, conventionalized system of arbitrary symbols. In our postmodernist age that realization no longer seems so radical, but for a writer at the time of the First World War to challenge the virtually universal assumption that language was purely a medium for the representation of reality was a drastic departure. If language were conceived of in these uncustomary terms, the whole epistemic relationship between a person, the reality she experienced, and the words she used was altered. In *Tender Buttons* (1914), for example, we find this passage:

> EATING
>
> It was a shame it was a shame to stare to stare and double and relieve relieve be cut up show as by the elevation of it and out out more in the steady where the come and on and the all the shed and that.
>
> It was a garden and belows belows straight. It was a pea, a pea pour it in its not a succession, not it a simple, not it a so election, election with.
>
> SALAD
>
> It is a winning cake.
>
> SAUCE
>
> What is bay labored what is all be section, what is no much. Sauce sam in.
>
> SALMON
>
> It was a peculiar bin a bin fond in beside.[8]

I know of no connection between Gertrude Stein and Edward Sapir, one of the pioneers in the field of linguistics, but it seems to me that they share the same essential awareness of language as an artifact: as Sapir says in his classic work, *Language* (published seven years after *Tender Buttons*), "the essence of language consists in the assigning of conventional, voluntarily articulated, sounds, or of their equivalents, to the diverse elements of experience."[9] "Sam in"—"salmon": it was the idea of the arbitrariness of the relation of linguistic sign and experiential referent, of word and thing and person selecting the word that underlay Stein's whole little literary revolution.

In the realization of that arbitrariness she may well have been drawing on the inspirations of her painter friends and William James. The cubists' visual epistemology certainly involved the knowledge that paint was paint.* In her midcareer, theorizing in the essay "What Are Masterpieces and Why Are There So Few of Them," she recalls that "In writing about painting I said that a picture exists for and in itself and the painter has to use objects landscapes and people as a way the only way that he is able to get the picture to exist."[10] William James's specific influence is also likely here—for one thing, in his keen and insistent sense of the disjunction between language and experience, the way that language is able to represent the stream of consciousness only fitfully and distortedly; for another thing, in his clear admonitions against believing that words always represented actual and fixed entities and that syntactical relationships expressed real relationships (see p. 91, above).

In Stein's context, then, language was only language, not a mirror of reality. Furthermore, if a writer were to possess herself of all the freedom entailed in that realization, she needed to wage a very diverse and concentrated war against accepting language's characteristics as the parameters of her thought and its conventional function and usages as definitive of reality. And this is what she does in her most radical writing, attacking especially the conventions of literary form and the standard devices of coherence—syntax, logic, time sequence, and so forth—by which a piece of writing customarily made meaning. The words are intact (actually the startling shifts and juxtapositions give them some new aspects), but the continuity, message, and form are systematically, perhaps painstakingly, denied. For example, take this selection from the beginning of *IIIIIIIIII.* in *Geography and Plays*:

IIIIIIIII.

INCLINE.
Clinch, melody, hurry, spoon, special, dumb, cake, forrester. Fine, cane, carpet, incline, spread, gate, light, labor.

---

*See the extensive discussion of this connection in Jayne L. Walker, *The Making of a Modernist* (University of Massachusetts Press, 1985).

BANKING.

Coffee, cough, glass, spoon, white, singing. Choose, selection, visible, lightning, garden, conversation, ink, spending, light space, morning, celebration, invisible, reception, hour, glass, curving, summons, sparkle, suffering the minisection, sanctioning the widening, less than the wireless, more certain. All the change. Any counselling non consuming and split splendor.

Forward and a rapidity and no resemblance no more utterly. Safe light, more safes no more safe for the separation.

M----n H---.

A cook. A cook can see. Pointedly in uniform, exertion in a medium. A cook can see.

Clark which is awful, clark which is shameful, clark and order.

A pin is a plump point and pecking and combined and more much more is in fine.

Rats is, rats is oaken. Robber. Height, age, miles, plaster, pedal, more order.

Bake, a barn has cause and more late oat-cake specially.[11]

Literary form is broken down in the very title of the piece; is it ten first-person pronouns with a period (could it be a sentence?!), like a repetitious and unpronounceable self-assertion, or is it a string of Roman numeral ones, a longhand designation of the tenth section of a work that doesn't have a preceeding nine, or is it simply an eye-stopping shape on the page? Whether to take it as language, numeral, or shape is indeterminable; the very convention of titling and its (customarily very predictable) function in initiating a certain kind of transaction between writer and reader is here utterly overthrown. Then logic gets the same treatment. None of the section titles has a discernible general-to-particular relationship with the material within its section. "INCLINE" does not incline, although it repeats that word in the midst of what seems to be a carefully randomized list. "BANKING" does not bank, although it contains "spending," "change," and "safes" along with a miscellany of other words. And the designation "M----n H---" looks like it might be a disguised name (an actual personal reference?), although what is subsumed under that heading focuses only in caprice. Nothing is ever explained. Things are listed, predicated, modified, sometimes almost described, but never clarified, developed, or interpreted. One of Stein's biographers, Elizabeth Sprigge, made the suggestion: "description is for her explanation."[12]

No sense of continuity or development emerges as we read the sections; they go, as "BANKING" (perhaps only coincidentally) tells us, "Forward and a rapidity and no resemblance no more utterly." Likewise we find none of the symbolism or motivic repetition we would expect from writing ordered along psychological lines, either conscious or unconscious. The randomization, the continuity-avoidance is exemplary and, I suspect, very carefully studied.* It is difficult·to avoid continuity and significance on so many levels at once.

Conventions of grammar are violated in Stein's creation of new word relationships based on sound, cadence, anomalous juxtaposition, and meaning shift. In "INCLINE" the two sentences are only two word-sets, but they are balanced at eight words apiece. In "BANKING" "Coffee" phonetically modulates into "cough," then perhaps brings along "glass" and "spoon" associationally, though "white" and "singing" break the connection of sound, association, and even part of speech. It would seem that one of the main purposes of connection of any kind is to be surprised and left broken. Even surprising and breaking can be done with artful cadence though, as with "curving, summons, sparkle, suffering the minisection, sanctioning the widening, less than the wireless, more certain." Similarly sound or word repetition (a factor of continuity) is often used as the vehicle for changes in meaning or function (a factor of discontinuity), as in "Safe light, more safes no more safe for the separation," or "Clark which is awful, clark which is shameful, clark and order." Such shards of patterning glint in the hundreds and hundreds of pages of *Tender Buttons*, *Geography and Plays*, *Portraits and Plays*, *Bee Time Vine* and others, but the dominating presence in Stein's innovative works is that which has been broken—logic, syntax, continuity, meaning (in every ordinary sense), and literary convention.**

*Some time after the completion of this chapter, I came across Ulla Dydo's "Reading the Hand Writing: The Manuscripts of Gertrude Stein" (in Bruce Kellner, ed., *A Gertrude Stein Companion*, 84–95), a cogent study of Stein's writing habits as evidenced in her manuscripts. Dydo's account effectively discourages attempts to read Stein's innovative writing as implied or allegorical autobiography. According to her, Stein "often begins literally with descriptions of what she sees, including [her companion, Alice] Toklas. Very quickly these become elements of description, no longer elements of Toklas. By the time they are seen formally, they are elements of composition, and writing has begun" (88). Dydo concludes, "what Stein meant to leave for posterity was her literature —self-contained, disembodied words in movement, without clues or keys to the world. As she said over and over, she wrote literature, not references. It is the construction, not the references, that creates her art and her meaning" (95).

**Interestingly, scholar of aesthetics John D. Erickson points out that such techniques

Stein took a special interest in the breaking of narrative patterning. In *The Making of Americans* (written 1906–1908) she jettisoned the chronicle-novel's customary narrative voice and conventions of characterization, presenting the narrative as at least in part the story of her own creation of it; and the characters as representatives of a universal human typology of her own concoction. The well-known *Melanctha* (1909) has some of the look of a conventional piece of fiction of that day, but its innovations are substantial and crucial to that work's character. Turn-of-the-century fiction, especially that dealing with the common people, would ordinarily show a difference in the language between the narrator and the characters, notably in the levels of diction and the categories of understanding. In *Melanctha* the lingo of the characters defines the language limits of the entire work. Furthermore, *Melanctha* forgoes the usual past-tense narration for what Stein later called a "prolonged present," studded with present and past-present participles and auxiliary "becoming" and "being" constructions. The work focuses analytically on the characters' subtly shifting readings of their own and each others' motives, and in doing so it moves the narrative along almost like an oratorio, with long analytical arias and confrontational duets by the characters, connected by the narrator's summary-recitatives.

Stein's experiments with narrative had from the beginning tended to subordinate the representation of "story" in terms of development or succession, in emphasizing static states of being. When in the 1930s she turned theorist of narrative (especially in four lectures collected as *Narration* [1935]) she was ready to forgo the literary representation of the passage of time entirely. Her "Portraits," "Geographies," and eerily static "Plays" exemplify this dissociation of word stream and the external world's transience. Here is how she explains her idea. The *narrative* aspect of narrative prose comes solely from the way sentences follow one another and become paragraphs: "the creating of sentences that were self-existing and following one after the other made of anything a continuous thing which is paragraphing and so a narrative that is a narrative of anything."[13] Formerly, Stein asserts, narrative was built around the idea that one could make a "progressive telling of things that were progressively happening. . . .But now we have changed all that we really have. We really now

and objectives were characteristics of "the Dada poem" as it was produced by Picabia, Arp, Tzara, and others in the late teens. He defines it by its "destruction of temporal and spatial sequences . . . [and of] referentiality." See *Dada: Performance, Poetry, Art* (Twayne, 1984), 88, 134(note 21).

do not really know that anything is progressively happening and as knowledge is what you know and as now we do not know that anything is
progressively happening where are we then in narrative writing."[14]
"Knowledge is not succession but an immediate existing," she claims.
Thus, "the narrative of to-day is not a narrative of succession as all the
writing for a good many hundreds of years has been." Now the key to
narrative is "not being a successive thing but being something existing."[15]

(Stein broke her rules to write in the older way the autobiographies
that made her famous. *The Autobiography of Alice B. Toklas* and *Everybody's
Autobiography* have chronological frameworks, and they "cover," in pretty
customary ways, specific intervals of time in Stein's life. Yet there are associational leaps and juxtapositions which defy any connection—associational, logical, or chronological—even in these books.)

What Stein outside of her autobiographies saw as the breakdown of
knowledge sequence, of the capacity to recall and verbalize the flux of
experience, involved the very negation of memory, identity, and time in
literature. In her view literature brought into focus a basic epistemological
predicament: memory is a fading, unreliable thing; time past can only be
distortedly, artificially present in our minds; and our own identities exist
only as phantasms in this unreal realm. Whether or not these insights
came to her from intellectual sources, she conceived of them in vividly
experiential terms:

> It is a funny thing about addresses where you live. When you live
> there you know it so well that it is like identity a thing that is so much
> a thing that it could not ever be any other thing and then you live
> somewhere else and years later, the address that was so much an
> address that it was a name like your name and you said it as if it was
> not an address but something that was living and then years after
> you do not know what the address was and when you say it it is not a
> name any more but something you cannot remember. That is what
> makes your identity not a thing that exists but something you do or
> do not remember.[16]

The key criterion for literature was its purity: truly great works simply did
not falsify experience by mixing in that unreal realm. Here is how she
puts it in "What Are Masterpieces and Why Are There So Few of Them":

> the master-piece has nothing to do with human nature or with iden-
> tity, it has to do with the human mind and the entity that is with a
> thing in itself and not in relation. The moment it is in relation it is

common knowledge and anybody can feel and know it and it is not a master-piece.

And so then why are there so few of them. There are so few of them because mostly people live in identity and memory that is when they think. They know they are they because their little dog knows them, and so they are not an entity but an identity. And being so memory is necessary to make them exist and so they cannot create master-pieces. . . .

It is not extremely difficult not to have identity but it is extremely difficult the knowing not having identity. One might say it is impossible but that it is not impossible is proved by the existence of master-pieces which are just that. They are knowing that there is no identity and producing while identity is not.

That is what a master-piece is.[17]

Another of Stein's assaults on the assured, the conventional, and the certified—and the last point I plan to consider in this extended ledger of her repudiations—is her assault on emotion in literature. The reader of her most innovative works (like the above-quoted passages from *Tender Buttons* and *IIIIIIIIII.*) experiences wit and surprise along with multileveled deconstruction, but no identification or compassion, no pity or fear. There is no evidence that the author is either expressing or depicting any feelings (other than linguistic relish) in the work and no indications that she means to elicit any in the reader. Whatever the real motivation behind this emotionlessness—William H. Gass in 1970 argued that it was a strategy of concealment of feelings too personal and too unacceptable socially (some of them being lesbian),[18] though there are other plausible explanations—Stein explicitly made emotionlessness part of a revision of the very premises of literature. Emotion in literature involved triteness, self-projection, distortion, and fakery, and its antidote was purity, discipline, and exactitude. As she says in *The Autobiography of Alice B. Toklas,*

> Gertrude Stein, in her work, has always been possessed by the intellectual passion for exactitude in the description of inner and outer reality. She has produced a simplification by this concentration, and as a result the destruction of associational emotion in poetry and prose. She knows that beauty, music, decoration, the result of emotion should never be the cause, even events should not be the cause of emotion nor should they be the material of poetry and prose. Nor should emotion itself be the cause of poetry or prose. They should consist of an exact reproduction of either an outer or an inner reality.[19]

Here then are the instructions that come with the Gertrude Stein knowledge destroying kit:

1. Recognize that literature's representations of objects, people, and events are arbitrary illusions, constructed out of language, itself an artifact.

2. Assume that your literary heritage is hopelessly conventionalized, mired in artificial, trite, and incredible assumptions.

3. Be a radical phenomenalist (at least for long stretches at a time). Refuse to acknowledge logical, causal, or even sequential relationships or nonobservables like essences and identities.

4. Avoid imputing self-reflexive qualities to your subject, especially associational emotion, sentiment, meaning, or memory.

There is good reason for this closing-down of cultural traditions and mental propensities, but what it induces as a state of mind for creating might seem disturbingly like amnesia compounded by anesthesia. Could any specific literary gains come of such a state?

Judging by Stein's own radical literary productions, masterpieces could not. Despite her fascination with masterpiece production, the awesome indeterminacy of writing without conventions could not, as it turned out, be monumentally shaped by her out of routines inspired by or adapted from modern painting or psychological theory, or even out of her own indomitable linguistic ingenuity. Instead of masterpieces, in this vein she gave us a panoply of strange and original approaches and techniques, twists of viewpoint and turns of word or phrase. New insights about language, literary representation, and the intricate relationship of ourselves to the outside world are what we gain, along with considerable enjoyment of wordplay and mind-bending. The inchoateness, the radical exclusions, and the long-run strain on our attention we simply must learn to tolerate.

For Stein, wordplay was a pleasurable, wittily entertaining, socially oriented activity of the very deepest seriousness. "I like anything that a word can do," she said, "and words do do all they do and then they can do what they never do do."[20] Like the nineteenth-century destroyers of rational constructs and conventional meanings, she sought new sources of power within the word itself. Like Dickinson on words—"I don't know of anything so mighty. . . . Sometimes I write one, and look at his outlines till he glows as no sapphire" (p. 52, above),—or like Whitman —"*Names* are magic,—One word can pour such a flood through the soul" (p. 21, above), she initiated her reconstruction of knowing at that atomic level where the forces of the elements of writing reside: "I found myself plunged into a vortex of words, burning words, cleansing words, liberating words, feeling words, and the words were all ours, and it was enough that we held them in our hands to play with them; whatever you can play with is yours, and this was the beginning of knowing."[21]

She was atomistic in her approach, concentrating on the separateness of each individual word (or phrase or saying), isolating it semantically with abrupt changes of subject, tone, syntax, or viewpoint. Semantic discontinuity within a framework of apparent grammatical continuity could, she believed, isolate words, locutions, turns of phrase or catches of conversation in ways that would release their individual power. Stein's achievement with individual words was what other writers tended to value most about her work. Sherwood Anderson (after quoting his brother's reaction to *Tender Buttons*—"It gives words an oddly new intimate flavor and at the same time makes familiar words seem almost like strangers, doesn't it") characterized her work as "a rebuilding, an entire new recasting of life, in the city of words."[22] According to William Carlos Williams, "Stein has systematically gone smashing every connotation that words have ever had, in order to get them back clean," and "the words, in writing, she discloses, transcend everything."[23] Suppose we take a passage —the concluding part of section I of *Pink Melon Joy*—to scrutinize for examples of the twofold atomic nature of this writing: the separateness and the power of its basic particles.

Come in. 1

Splashes splashes of jelly splashes of jelly. 2

Weather. 3

Whether he was presented. 4
I meant to stay. 5

Easy or blocks 6
Do not be held by the enemy. 7
All the time. 8

Now line or them. 9

That's an established belt or tooth. Really not. I 10
didn't mean to bellow. I won't be a table. I regret it. I 11
shall be very likely to be walking. I shall introduce myself 12
fairly. I do mind it. 13

Not again.   14

I do say not again.   15

I mean to be heavy.   16

It stands up against as much as it stands up for. That's   17
what I object to. I don't want to be unflattering to us but I   18
think it has been entirely forgotten.   19

Furs.   20

Perhaps you will. Then she wrote a very warm letter and   21
sent these furs.   22

Shall ill.   23

I don't like it and in neglecting cherishing songs I am   24
so pleased with all and by settling chalk. I am satisfied.   25
We are neglected immensely. Not resting.   26

Shall it be continuous the liberty of sobriety. The dear   27
thing. Little tremors. I ask the question.   28

With a wide piano.   29

Come.   30

Neglecting cherishing says shall I mistake pleases. In   31
mistakes there is a salutary secretion. What. I said it.   32

Now and then.   33

War is Saturday and let us have peace.   34

Peace is refreshing, let us bear let us be or not by that   35
mine.   36

Mended.   37

Now I come to stay away.   38

Answer.   39

I shook a darling.   40

Not eating Oh it was so timely.   41

Why should pitchers be triumphant. Does it proclaim that   42
eleven, eleven, eleven, come across, speak it, satisfy a man,   43
be neat, leave off oxes, shine flies, call spoken shouting   44
call it back call it by little dotted voices and do be sweet,   45
do be sweet, remember the accoutrement. No I will not pay   46
away.   47

What a system in voices, what a system in voices.   48

I met a regular believe me it is not for the pleasure in   49
it that I do it. I met a regular army. I was not certain of   50

that, I was not certain of paper. I knew I was safe. And so   51
he was. Shall I believe it.   52
    I can't help mentioning that I was earnest. In that   53
way there was a reason. I can destroy wetter wetter soaps.   54
I can destroy wetter soaps.   55
    I do.   56
    I do not.   57
    Leave it in there for me.   58
    Leave it in an especial place. Do not make that face.   59
Show it by the indication. I do mean to spell. I am. Believe   60
me.[24]   61

If we conceive of individual words and phrases as each carrying its own particular frame of reference, its own aura of implied meanings and conventional usages (probably what Williams meant by *connotation* in that foregoing quotation), we can see that Stein's atomic method works by assaulting those frames. Most obviously there is the stark semantic incongruity of "an established belt or tooth" (10), "War is Saturday" (34), "I shook a darling" (40), or "little dotted voices" (45), in which there is the collision of incompatable (or very nearly incompatable) frames. There are also unusual epithets and predications which, while not quite incongruous, put strain on the frames: "cherishing songs" (24), "a salutary secretion" (32), "a system in voices" (48), and "I can destroy wetter soaps" (55), for example.

The number and variety of changes in this writing are truly remarkable. Topics change kaleidoscopically, sometimes word-by-word: "I ask the question./ With a wide piano./ Come./ Neglecting cherishing says shall I mistake pleases" (28–31). In a quick and casual count I find seventy-five changes of basic topic in these sixty-one lines of *Pink Melon Joy*; the exact number is indeterminable, but the changes are profuse, each one thwarting the customary expectations built up in a reader by one frame ("Weather" [3]) by its juxtaposition to the next ("Whether he was presented" [4]). Compounding that kind of discontinuity, Stein's statements will often shift in syntax ("Peace is refreshing, let us bear let us be or not by that mine" [35–36]) or in voice or point of view ("In mistakes there is a salutary secretion. What. I said it" [31–32] or "I knew I was safe. And so he was" [51–52]). There is nothing either casual or automatic about the discontinuity in this writing.

The words or sayings caught in the changes often reveal new dimensions of themselves. For instance, "call spoken shouting call it back" (44–45) intermingles the different senses of "call" satirically and deconstructs the locution *to call something back*. Likewise "Now I come to stay away" (38) confronts the locution *to come to some decision or predicament* with the absurdity of another meaning of "come to." Words are often ambiguous in their syntactical function and consequently indeterminate in their frames. Take, for example, line 31, "Neglecting cherishing says shall I mistake pleases." Perhaps we can decide what "neglecting cherishing" is (here detached from the "songs" it was connected to in line 24), but when that verbal becomes the nominative of the verb "says" our frame is broken; likewise "shall I mistake pleases" hangs up both *mistake* and *pleases* between noun and verb functions and thwarts any attempt to salvage rationality, although the sentence still suggests the psychological insight that by taking a neglectful or apathetic attitude toward another person, one might well misunderstand that person's attempts to please—and the moral insight, through the words *shall I*, that that misunderstanding is a matter of one's choice.

But instances of the familiar sorts of literary meaning are rare in this Steinian mode, and the analytically minded reader will soon discover that most ordinary processes and techniques of interpretation are fruitless. Are any parts of this passage ironic? There's no way to know, since the incessant fragmentation of reference-frames leaves us with no norms by which to discern tone. Likewise, there are no norms for determining the degrees of figurativeness of the statements. Is the "settling chalk" of line 25 some kind of metaphor? Are we to conceive of "I met a regular. . . . / I met a regular army" (49–50) literally, figuratively, or only as a play on *regular* as noun and adjective and *army* as noun but perhaps also adjective in an incomplete construction? The indeterminacy of figurativeness at times provides humor rather than just uncertainty, especially in the literal interpretation of figurative locutions, as in "Then she wrote a *very warm letter* and sent these furs" (21–22) or "It *stands up against* as much as *it stands up for*" (17).

So far in our analysis the advantages of this atomic style of writing are principally linguistic. *Pink Melon Joy* seems to be a kind of casebook in semantic fragmentation and wordplay, implying an audience fascinated with language. That is certainly enough for a book to be, and the fact that its technique can be related to pictorial cubism and a kind of modernistic psychology-of-the-passing-present-moment gives the scholarly minded even more to appreciate (and Stein certainly meant her work to be appreciated that way). The knowledge destroyers of the premodernist age gave us a representation of life too, though—of living and needing and suffering as well as of knowing and saying. How exclusive are the peculiar obsessions of the age of epistemology in the minds of its writers? In *Pink Melon Joy* there are more references to interpersonal interactions than there are to any other realm of activity. Many of these references are standard pleasantries or simple functional remarks ("Come in" [1], "I meant to stay" [5], "I shall introduce myself fairly" [12–13], "the dear thing" [27], "Leave it in there for me" [58]). But a surprising number express or imply some sort of social disharmony ("I didn't mean to bellow" [10–11], "I won't be a table" [11], "that's what I object to" [17–18], "We are neglected immensely" [26], "No I will not pay away" [46–47], "Do not make that face" [59]). It is surprising that such linguistic gaiety could be expressive of so much dissatisfaction and conflict, and we might be inclined to view this positive-negative balance as another attempt at a semantic stymie, like the direct and inconclusive opposition of "I do" and "I do not" of lines 56 and 57, except for the fact of the noticeable number of frames that involve the subject of warfare ("Do not be held by the enemy" [7], "War is Saturday" [34], "Peace is refreshing" [35], "I met a regular army" [50], "I can destroy wetter soaps" [55]). These warfare references (not at all usual in Stein's innovative writing) are indeed less concrete than the details of domesticity the selection uses ("jelly" [2], "table" [11], "piano" [29], "pitchers" [42], "flies" [44], and so forth), but they do serve to accentuate the social disharmony motif.

There is no coherent symbolism here, though, no pattern of allegory or theme that will unify the details and make them more than themselves. Their sum is simply the conglomeration of the incompatible individual frames. *Pink Melon Joy* is one of many of Stein's works that is a piece of literature about language, a picture of the peculiar ways we say things and conceive of things verbally. Some of its frame-fragments are revealing or diverting, as are some of its juxtapositions and sequences. Still, some are vacuous or redundant, like cubist filler for a writer with a word quota. Stein's omni-deconstructive approach strikes some genuine sparks, but in terms of the works it produced, a remark made by my wife Barbara seems to fit best: the sum of the parts is greater than the whole.

Some of Stein's works do more than others to hook their atomic fragments into sequences or progressions of sound, suggestion, or repetition. Sometimes while she is de-signifying words and destroying through parody any sense of writing's rational arrangement and systematic progression, she can produce a passage of extraordinary musicality, as in the opening segment of "Jean Cocteau":

Needs be needs be needs be near.
Needs be needs be needs be.
This is where they have their land astray.
   Two say.
This is where they have their land astray
Two say.
Needs be needs be needs be
Needs be needs be needs be near.
   Second time.
It may be nearer than two say.
Near be near be near be
Needs be needs be needs be
Needs be needs be needs be near.
He was a little while away.
Needs be nearer than two say.
Needs be needs be needs be needs be.
Needs be needs be needs be near.
He was away a little while.
   And two say.
He was away a little while
He was away a little while
   And two say.
             Part two.
Part two and part one
Part two and part two
Part two and part two
Part two and part one.
He was near to where they have their land astray.
He was near to where they have two say.
Part two and near one. Part one and near one.
Part two and two say.
Part one and part two and two say.[25]

There is a new construct here, witty in its permutations, engaging in its harmonies, and compelling in its rhythms. It communicates by subrational means: the nearly explicit holiday from logic is confirmed both by the nonsensicalness of words pounded by repetition into an alien objecthood and by the infectiousness of the rhythm, reaching us at levels like those of chant, litany, and hypnosis. Of course all poetry and even some prose attempts to use rhythm and repetition to affect readers on the subrational level, but what Stein has brought into American literature is the aggressive and uncompromising antirationality of which these techniques became a part. Her literary cubist acquaintance Artaud and the dadaists had gone as far in French writing, and Kandinsky's aesthetic had pointed the way to discovering the spiritual properties of words through their repetition,* but in English not even Poe was a precedent for this kind of immersion in the subrational.

Oddly enough, she set no stock in this aspect of her work. As her Alice-persona instructs us, "it has been so often said that the appeal of her work is to the ear and to the subconscious. Actually it is her eyes and mind that are active and important and concerned in choosing."[26]

Still we can hear and feel as well as see and think the complex antimessages of many passages, such as this one from *Tender Buttons*, in which the word-artist celebrates (mocks? justifies? deconstructs?) her own act of creation and its product:

ORANGE IN
   Go lack go lack use to her.
   Cocoa and clear soup and oranges and oat-meal.
   Whist bottom whist close, whist clothes, woodling.
   Cocoa and clear soup and oranges and oat-meal.
   Pain soup, suppose it is question, suppose it is butter, real is, real is only, only excreate, only excreate a no since.
   A no, a no since, a no since when, a no since when since, a no since when since a no since when since, a no since, a no since when since, a no since, a no, a no since a no since, a no since, a no since.[27]

"Real is" is "only excreate," materializing out of "pain soup," "butter," "question," and "suppose" (lovely recipe) and actually excreated into a resonant thrumming of "when" and "no since" (or know since? know sense? no sense? nonsense? nuisance?). Thus, as "no," "since," and "when" lose their conventional meanings and begin to glow with new possibili-

*This connection between Stein and Kandinsky had been noted as early as 1914 by Alexander S. Kaun, who referred to this passage of Kandinsky's *Concerning the Spiritual*: "The apt use of a word (in its poetical sense), its repetition, twice, three times, or even more frequently . . . will not only tend to intensify the internal structure but also bring out unsuspected spiritual properties in the word itself. Further, frequent repetition of a word (a favorite game of children, forgotten in later life) deprives the word of its external reference. Similarly, the symbolic reference of a designated object tends to be forgotten and only the sound is retained." See Gail Levin's discussion of this Kandinsky-Stein-Kaun link in "Wassily Kandinsky and the American Literary Avant-Garde," *Criticism* 21 (1979), 347.

ties, some of the deepest aesthetic and epistemological questions are implanted—not posed or explained or answered—by a rhythmic verbal vortex occurring between the oranges of the previous section and the salad dressing of the section to follow.

Stein's work lives and dies by abstraction—abstraction of some original and curious kinds. The relationship between her words and a world outside her own mind is a problematical one. Stein insisted in her lecture-circuit self-explications that each of her works, including *Tender Buttons* and the portraits, was a precise depiction of something, some special essence of a person or a thing. In *The Autobiography of Alice B. Toklas* she reveals herself as focusing her writing on "the insides of people, their character and what went on inside them," and "the rhythm of the visible world,"[28] as well as caring a great deal for the exactitude of depiction. Her explicit accounts of her aesthetic offer no particular support for my foregoing analysis in terms of repetition to the point of nonsense, infectious rhythms, and subrational implantation. But so curious is her idea of literary representation by midcareer that a reader coming to the works she was producing then has little else to go by. It had been quite clear what was being represented in *Three Lives* and also in *The Making of Americans*, despite that book's more intricate inclusiveness, but for her extreme linguistic abstractions we have only her word that they have any subject at all. Separate the titles of the portraits from the portraits themselves, scramble them, and they could only be matched up again—if at all—with a great deal of highly personal knowledge. *Tender Buttons* so scrambled would ultimately be impossible to rearrange—for example, how to decide how the passage I just quoted is a representation of "Orange In." What kind of depiction of things is this, then? Edmund Wilson, in a chapter generally quite appreciative of Stein, finds her opaque abstractionism a dead end: "We see the ripples expanding in her consciousness, but we are no longer supplied with any clew as to what kind of object has sunk there."[29]

Let us turn to her own descriptions of her intentions, then, for some clues as to what those ripples mean and why she's sunk whatever it is in precisely this way.

First of all—and we probably intuited this ourselves—her approach is circumlocutional: "I too felt in me the need of making it be a thing that could be named without using its name. After all one had known its name anything's name for so long, and so the name was not new but the thing being alive was always new."[30] (Oddly enough, she credits Whitman with changing the form of poetry—"he wanted really wanted to express the thing and not call it by its name"[31]—although how she finds this quality in Whitman remains a mystery.) If it is timeworn and dull to name or describe a thing directly, it is exciting, she felt, to explore the words that associated themselves with it in one's own mind: "And the thing that excited me so very much at that time and still does is that the words or words that make what I looked at be itself were always words that to me very exactly related themselves to that thing the thing at which I was looking, but as often as not had as I say nothing whatever to do with what any words would do that described that thing."[32] The process she describes is a personal and subjective one—a scientist would classify it as an unrepeatable experiment—and its product is not only unique but —and this is the most radical premise of her theory, the most radical position a writer can take—uncommunicable. In effect she rejects the idea of any sort of transpersonal knowledge. Knowing begins and ends within a person, and the only authentic wellspring of insight is one's own immediate everyday experience. Thornton Wilder quoted Stein as saying in conversation:

> Now what we know is formed in our head by thousands of small occasions in the daily life. . . . I mean what we really know, like our assurance about how we know anything, and what we know about the validity of the sentiments, and things like that. . . . Now if we write, we write; and these things we know flow down our arm and come out on the page. . . . Now, of course, there is no audience at that moment. . . . At that moment you are totally alone at this recognition of what you know. And of that thing which you have written you are the first and last audience. This thing which you have written is bought by other people and read by them. It goes through their eyes into their heads and they say they agree with it. But, of course, they cannot agree with it. The things they know have been built up by thousands of small occasions which are different from yours. They *say* they agree with you; what they mean is that they are aware that your pages have the vitality of a thing which sounds to them like someone else's knowing; it is consistent to its own world of what one person has really known.[33]

Immediate personal experience had been for Emily Dickinson too the ultimate reference point, the source of her insights and the standard by which she judged all ideas and sentiments. But Stein's version of writing directly out of experience, besides being much narrower in its range of feelings and utterly devoid of self-doubt, totally gives up the attempt to render a comprehensible subject. As she says in elucidating her portrait of George Hugnet, "It really does not make any difference who George Hugnet was or what he did or what I said, all that was necessary was that there was something completely contained within itself and being contained within itself was moving."[34]

Wendy Steiner points out in her book on Stein's portraiture how Stein, even from the days of her psychology study, "must have been aware that an aspect of the personality that seemed spontaneous and 'creative' expressed itself in repetitions. . . . Stein at first thought of repetition, or 'insistence' as she preferred to call it, as the prime means by which people expressed their inner being."[35] In representing people, then, Stein tried to feel the other's inner insistence, as she said, "in hearing and saying the things he hears and says when he is hearing and saying them," and to put down on paper her own word-stream reaction to that: "I must find out what is moving inside them that makes them them, and I must find out how I by the thing moving excitedly inside me can make a portrait of them."[36]

All depiction is abstraction, of course, but Stein's depiction of people —and of objects or places by the same essential method—is abstraction to the fourth power, filtered through her own consciousness as perception, verbalization of perception, observation of that verbalization, and verbalization of that observation. She is vividly and very appreciatively aware of this complex processing, identifying the abstraction she's describing as "the successive moment of my containing within me the existence of that other one achieved by talking and listening inside in me and and inside in that one."[37]

Strangely enough, this perceptual hall of mirrors within the writer's self gives a version of "the successive moment of my containing within me" that is objectified. There's no sense of self-depiction or self-projection in this writing. The reflexiveness problem is solved in this systematization of subjectivities, and Stein knows it:

> I am I not any longer when I see.
> This sentence is at the bottom of all creative activity. It is just the exact opposite of I am I because my little dog knows me.[38]

What we get, then, in Stein's most innovative works is abstractions of perceived verbalized abstractions, incomprehensible to us in any ordinary way, but still disciplined by their author to exclude self-depiction as scrupulously as they exclude direct description and semantic coherence. Yet if the presentation of her personality is minimalized in these works, her purely personal frame of reference engulfs them. Her selectivity and sense of focus, the imagery and lingo of her "thousands of small occasions," the people she knows and does or doesn't admire, the connotations she feels in particular words, the social and conversational rituals of her own circles, and so forth are the be-all and end-all of the literature. And she insists on the absoluteness of her role as creator—Henry James *was* a general, George Washington *was* a novelist.[39] In the act of reading we must give over all criteria of truth, meaning, and relevance and enjoy the verbalized play of her imagination over her own abstract perceptions or we have nothing but willful and inaccurate buffoonery.

Her principal subject thus is not the person or thing that the title names, that initiated her seeing and saying, but the play of the imagination over, under, around, and through it. The themes of her depictions are not exclusively ideas like "Pablo is a domineering presence," or "Jacques is a dreamer," but shadows of them, intermixed with ideas like "this is how perceptions are initiated and grow," "this is how a creator-perceiver relates to her verbal medium," and "this is how an imagination moves." It is a literature of recondite essences and processive picturing, each work implying the story of its own creation.

LIPCHITZ

Like and like likely and likely likely and	1
likely like and like.	2
He had a dream. He dreamed he heard a pheasant	3
calling and very likely a pheasant was calling.	4
To whom went.	5
He had a dream he dreamed he heard a pheasant	6
calling and most likely a pheasant was calling.	7
In time.	8
This and twenty and forty-two makes every time a	9
hundred and two thirty.	10
Any time two and too say.	11
When I knew him first he was looking looking	12
through the glass and the chicken. When I knew him	13
then he was looking looking at the looking at the	14
looking. When I knew him then he was so tenderly	15
then standing. When I knew him then he was then	16
after then to then by then and when I knew him then	17
he was then we then and then for then. When I knew	18

him then he was for then by then as then so then to	19
then in then and so.	20

He never needs to know. 21

He never needs he never seeds but so so can 22
they sink settle and rise and apprise and tries. 23
Can at length be long. No indeed and a song. A 24
song of so much so. 25

When I know him I look at him for him and I 26
look at him for him and I look at him for him when I 27
know him. 28

I like you very much.[40] 29

Whatever there is of Lipchitz that is recognizable by anyone but him and Stein crystallizes around two scenes from the past—like still snapshots—one of Lipchitz dreaming he heard a pheasant calling (3–4, 6–7) and the other of Lipchitz "looking looking through the glass and the chicken," "tenderly then standing" (12–20). The verbal formulation of each of these stills generates a series of improvisations in which it is the qualities of the words themselves that determine their direction. The first time around we get the mirror repetition of "a pheasant was calling" (nice cadence), spinning off into the locution "calling to whom" and the stopper "went" (5). "A pheasant was calling" is represented as being both dreamed and likely real, which implants some ideas about the subject's world of reality and imagination, especially through the mirror repetition of the words. The second time around, the repetition "a pheasant was calling" spins off into "In time" (8), which in its irreducible ambiguity (in the whole context of temporality? at just the necessary moment?) both suggests a problematical sense of time in art and a sense of the shifting frames of syntax. And that shifting goes on, especially through the way time shifts from "in time" (8) to "every time" (9) and "Any time" (11), with each occurrence of *time* having a different meaning and implied syntactical frame. The frame shifting of *time* is doubled (appropriately enough) by the interwoven shifting of *two* from "forty-two" (9) to "a hundred and two thirty" ([10], a different kind of two) and then to "Any time *two* and *too* say" (11).

The second verbalized snapshot from the past is specified as happening "When I knew him first" ([12], implying yet another *time*), and it begins by representing an intensified state of his *looking* (the word itself is haunting, and it has several connotations appropriate for the artist-subject).

He is looking not only "through the glass and the chicken" ([13] is that a figure of speech or a bit of absurdity?) but even "looking looking at the looking at the looking" (14–15)—intense and multiply aware. This passage shifts to an extended set of variations on the words *when* and *then* from the locution "*When* I knew him *then*" (13–14)—truly words to conjure with. They remain only generically evocative, however, and as their repetitions get more frequent (16–20), the cadence transfers the emphasis to the prepositions ("*for* then *by* then *as* then"); not only do those prepositions make an interestingly patterned cadence, but each of them changes the semantic frame of *then* (19–20).

The words themselves lead in the verbal dance that is *Lipchitz*, and it is very often the minor words, the purely functional words, the words we usually don't pay any primary attention to that steal the show. The portrait's opening line blitzes us with variations on *like* and *likely*, all semantically ambiguous until *likely* turns up in an utterly inconspicuous functional role in "He dreamed he heard a pheasant calling and very *likely* a pheasant was calling" (3–4). And after the assault of *then* and the prepositions, we get a euphonious passage (20–25) which might indeed be self-characterized as "A song of so much so." As William James had said, "we ought to say a feeling of *and*, a feeling of *if*, a feeling of *but*, a feeling of *by*" (see p. 91, above); in some of the writings of his former pupil his idea of putting the emphasis on the *transitive* elements of language rather than just the *substantive* parts came to a strange and insistent sort of realization.*

In Stein's student days James had been teaching that writers and thinkers needed to understand that their experience was a flux, artificially frozen by language and thought patterns, and Stein seems to have tried to represent both the flux and the artificiality in her innovative writings. It is interesting to discern what moves and what stands still in her works. In the *Lipchitz* it is two still snapshots—two attempts to represent the subject's recondite essence—and a closing statement about continuing relationship, with an unusually clear and direct personal compliment (25–29, the last of the *likes* begun in line 1) that stand still, while the imagination of the writer moves restlessly and spontaneously, seemingly determined merely to allow no coherence and to follow the lead of the words, especially the transitive words. The end product is a record of the process of its own creation, putting us in touch with Stein's verbal impulses as she

---

*The linking of Stein's grammatical practices and James's psycholinguistic theories was first made by Ronald Bartlett Levinson in "Gertrude Stein, William James, and Grammar," *American Journal of Psychology*, 54 (January 1941), 124–128.

was feeling them. Whatever revelations about Lipchitz are represented in the dreaming, the looking, the *then*, and the *so*—some transient and word-born insights about his relation to perception, imagination, time, and reality do come across—glimmer only fitfully in the author's stream of imagination.

Gertrude Stein thus reverses literature's conventional time relationships: instead of a moving subject observed from some still point in time (Silas Lapham's adventures recounted omnisciently from some indefinite but final temporal perspective; Marlow's account of Lord Jim's career, unfolding slowly for his friends on the veranda in a kind of hiatus in time, itself observed from an even stiller time), she gives us a still subject observed from a moving point in time. In describing the process by which she created the innovative works of her mature period she emphasized the factors of spontaneity and serendipity:

> Now if we write, we write; and these things we know flow down our arm and come out on the page. The moment before we wrote them we did not really know we knew them; if they are in our head in the shape of words then that is all wrong and they will come out dead; but if we did not know we knew them until the moment of writing, then they come to us with a shock of surprise. That is the Moment of Recognition. Like God on the Seventh Day we look at it and say it is good.[41]

Thus the spontaneity and serendipity themselves come to be subjects of the work, both partaking of and representing its process of creation.

At least since *Melanctha* (1909) Stein had been manifestly concerned with the representation of time. Her "Composition as Explanation" set forth the idea of a "prolonged present" that she had been trying to convey in that work, and critics were quick to relate that idea to the work's unusual vocabulary and syntax. Michael J. Hoffman, for example, cited the insistent use of present participles and the vocabulary of process in *Melanctha*, amplified in *The Making of Americans* in substitutions such as *middle living* for *middle age*.[42] But such stylistic practices are still focused solely on the process-quality of the work's subject. A changeover happens in *The Making of Americans*, and Hoffman noted this too, in the way that Stein interspersed in that work explicit commentary about her own process of writing; as he quotes her,

> Alfred Hersland then, to be certain of the being in him, was of the resisting kind of them in men and women and now then I will wait again and soon then I will be full up with him, I am now then not

completely full up with him. . . . I will be waiting and then I will be full up with all the being in him, that is certain, and so then now a little again once more then I am waiting waiting to be filled up full completely with him with all the being ever in him.[43]

In passages such as this the time of the work's creation began to be part of the work's subject. From *Tender Buttons* onward, then, Stein managed to represent this sense of time implicitly rather than explicitly, in the very nature of the word-stream rather than in explanations to herself and/or her reader. And time of creation probably seemed to her more convincingly represented by its own real tracks and traces than by discussions or explanations of it.

Stein often showed an interest in tying in her innovative works to some framework of broader significance than the immediate tracks of her imagination, and these broader frameworks involved essentially static constructs. An ambitious system of classification of human types had been a prominent factor in *The Making of Americans* (an example is the statement in the preceding quotation about Alfred Hersland being "of the resisting kind of them in men and women"), but she seems to have found this system to be untenable by the time she wrote *Tender Buttons* and the portraits. Stein scholar Jayne L. Walker makes the interesting suggestion that it was recollection of William James's ideas that freed Stein of the thralls of typological essences—such Jamesian ideas, Walker says, as his regarding "all conceptions as 'teleological instruments' created by the human mind, for its own ends, to impose order on what he called the 'concrete chaos' of immediate sensory experience."* Certainly Stein made no further efforts to find rationalistic frameworks for her stream of imagination. Henceforward she would try to maintain the particularities of verbalization as the ultimate semantic reference points of her writing and look to painterly constructs for broader frameworks that were nonsemantic. In this new phase "she was concerned with the unique and came closer to those painters for whom a thing exists only as the moment of vision," as Gertrude Sprigge points out.[44]

Literary genre was one aspect of her works that Stein learned to manipulate to give them frameworks that did not rationalize their content. Borrowing from the painters their designations *portrait* and *landscape*, she was able to focus her and her reader's attention on the fact that a given work did indeed have a still and essential center, without sacrificing any

---

The Making of a Modernist, 104. Walker also has an excellent discussion, based on Stein's notebooks, of the sources and origins of her typological thinking, 47–49.

of the uniqueness of the subject or the "moment of vision." She used the terms *geography* and *prayer* similarly and even attempted to redefine the designations *play* and *opera* along the same lines. Another painterly solution to the problem of framework was Stein's use of the concept of "composition"; in 1946 recalling its origins in her work, this is how it looked to her:

> Everything I have done has been influenced by Flaubert and Cézanne, and this gave me a new feeling about composition. Up to that time composition had consisted of a central idea, to which everything else was an accompaniment and separate but was not an end in itself, and Cézanne conceived the idea that in composition one thing was as important as another thing. Each part is as important as the whole, and that impressed me enormously, and it impressed me so much that I began to write *Three Lives* under this influence and this idea of composition.[45]

Her new idea of "composition" here was "one thing was as important as another thing." In her Picasso study (published in 1939) it was "each thing was as important as any other thing," and she regarded that concept as linked to the whole spirit of the times because "really the composition of this war, 1914–1918, was not the composition of all previous wars, the composition was not a composition in which there was one man in the centre surrounded by a lot of other men but a composition that had neither a beginning nor an end, a composition of which one corner was as important as another corner, in fact the composition of cubism."[46] Thus to her mind the artists had interpreted—really to some extent anticipated —"how everybody is doing everything"[47] in the splendid century.

Stein felt her contribution was to pioneer the bringing of the new composition into literature. Literary composition, thus conceived, involved the foregrounding of everything within the framework. Stein critic Randa Dubnick follows William Barrett's diagnosis of modern literature's "cubist" tendencies, and she appropriately describes the aesthetics of Stein's portraits in these terms: "These portraits reflect this new composition. . . . [E]ach individual moment becomes important in itself. Each sentence is important, and no one sentence carries climactic meaning as in the traditional narrative. Instead, each sentence carries equal weight, emphasis, and information."[48] Stein's spontaneous wordplay, conceived of spatially by herself and her interpreters, becomes an assemblage of equivalent details, an atomic collage, a still picture of imagination's passage.

Composition as explanation fascinated Stein (as her essay bearing that title demonstrates): if explanation—a specifically discursive activity, customarily structured by logic and chronology—would henceforth be a presentational matter of assemblage and arrangement, mind and culture would be revolutionized. The literary artist had a special problem with the new order, however: how to adapt the linear nature of language to this essentially presentational ideal of composition:

> The time in the composition is a thing that is very troublesome. If the time in the composition is very troublesome it is because there must even if there is no time at all in the composition there must be time in the composition which is in its quality of distribution and equilibration. . . . [T]his is what is now troubling every one the time in the composition is now a part of distribution and equilibration. . . . [T]here must be time that is distributed and equilibrated.[49]

Thus Stein's view of reality, mind, and art at the time of her most innovative writing takes on the aspect of an extended and unresolved debate between Heraclitus and Parmenides. The fluxlike elements—the existence-in-the-world of her subject, the spontaneous play of her verbalizing imagination, and the inescapable linearity of language—are interleaved with the fixities—her intuition of her subject's essence, the atomic absoluteness of individual words, and the spatialization of each work as a "composition" and a representation within a basically static genre.

"Einstein was the creative philosophic mind of the century, and I have been the creative literary mind of the century,"[50] Stein avowed, and we can see many ways in which it is so. The very intricate, intentional, and original way in which she probed the processes of perception and representation not only revealed the new epistemology to her readers but gave them firsthand experience of it. Still, the visions she gave us are multiply abstract, manifoldly intellectualized things that suggest that the great and vivid world itself can be lost in an excess of epistemological insight. The self-centeredness of her innovative work is another of its drawbacks. The things that don't interest her personally—even large twentieth-century things like political revolution, rampant militarism, social upheaval, economic change, technological progress, religious crisis, and incipient feminism—play no direct part in her works and have no role in her revision of modern consciousness. Stein's revolt was not quite like that of the dadaists, whose work hers resembles in many respects.*

*Norman Weinstein, *Gertrude Stein and the Literature of Modern Consciousness* (Frederick Ungar, 1970), 104–108, presents a good comparison of Stein and the dadaists.

Theirs was in many cases a revolt that grew out of the conviction that the wars and injustices of the twentieth century were the effects of a perverted civilization, a civilization which badly needed to be put back in touch, by art, with its fundamentally human emotional nature. Stein's revolution is far more narrowly based, on her own predominantly epistemological passions and proclivities. Her literary revolution undeniably inclines, subliminally and substantially, toward infrapolitical revolution, but the monuments of her art, expressions such as they were of her powerful, impersonal self-centeredness, would remain more eccentric than central to her splendid century.

11 Ezra Pound and Ernest Hemingway: The Discipline of Destruction

■ Ezra Pound: "A Few Don'ts"

Although he himself was a knowledge destroyer only in a limited and selective way, Ezra Pound (1885–1972) was a primary agent in the transmission of destruction-related motifs to a great array of American modernists. As a critic, his specific targets were a number of venerated figures in the English tradition (Milton and Wordsworth especially) as well as romanticism, realism, impressionism, idealism, symbolism, sentimentalism, and—most especially—the complacent insularity of almost all American poetry. Pound did advocate tradition, however—or, more precisely, some certain traditions like the Provençal French, the medieval/renaissance Italian, or the early Chinese that he felt provided the most effective antidote to contemporary vacuousness—and this conservatism separates him from the true knowledge destroyers like Melville and the thoroughgoing modernists like Stein. But it was not his specific repudiations or his traditionalism (or even, I would assert, his poetry) that sparked his followers so much as the literary theory he brought them. Coleridge and Arnold did not speak to them but Ezra Pound did, bringing them into a realm of theory that related their techniques and practices to the twentieth-century world. Pound denied that poetry was what was in the trite and imitative American literary magazines and insisted that it was a powerful confluence of senses and matter and language and knowing and image and breathing and essence and soul and the fundamental energy of the universe. His ideas—however consistent, however original—gave poetry stimulation, a new rationale, a new sense of mission; out of their impulse even William Carlos Williams turned theorist, Louis Zukofsky and Charles Olsen invented their -isms. And poets today still quote Pound's pronouncements and call him the father of their art.

Pound's theorizing is a miscellaneous, individualistic matter, following the bent of his often eccentric antagonisms and enthusiasms.* Along with his veneration for the practices of the troubadours and the ancient Greeks, there was his admiration for the critical minds of several of his contemporaries like Ford Madox Ford and Rémy de Gourmont and his sense of shared principles with literary philosopher T. E. Hulme (who was introducing Bergson into English literary theory). Further off the beaten track were his espousal of Ernest Fenollosa's *The Chinese Written Character as a Medium for Poetry*, with its curious mixture of nouveau-orientalism and scientism, his friendship with the volatile young French sculptor Henri Gaudier-Brzeska, and his collaboration with modernist painter/writer Wyndham Lewis. Like Gertrude Stein, Pound came to conceive of literary creativity in terms of creativity in the visual or plastic arts (for example, trying to discover how a writer could, like a stone sculptor, "cut direct," without working from preliminary models).[1] Unlike Stein he derived a significant part of his patterning of the literary act from science: "What the analytical geometer does for space and form, the poet does for the states of consciousness. . . . As the abstract mathematician is to science so is the poet to the world's consciousness. Neither has direct contact with the many, neither of them is superhuman or arrives at his utility through occult and inexplicable ways. Both are scientifically demonstrable."[2]

Discipline is the cornerstone of Pound's aesthetic. Significantly, it was in "A Few Don'ts" (in *Poetry*, 1913) that he set the tone of his campaign. There he urged aspiring writers to take as a model the discipline of the scientist in conforming to the ideals of factual accuracy and parsimony ("consider the way of the scientists rather than the way of an advertising agent for a new soap!").[3] In other contexts he would evoke literary tradition, but characteristically with the intent of urging his "Don'ts," invoking, for example, the discipline of an ancient Greek in telling the thing directly and forcefully ("Objective—no slither; direct—no excessive use of adjectives, no metaphors that won't permit examination. It's straight talk, straight as the Greek!").[4] Pound fiercely and repeatedly attacked

*The eclecticism of Pound's approach has been a bonanza for scholars of various orientations—and some very good scholars at that. For Ford Madox Ford's influence on Pound, see Herbert N. Schneidau, *Ezra Pound: The Image and the Real* (Louisiana State University Press, 1969); for Rémy De Gourmont's, see Richard Sieburth, *Instigations* (Harvard University Press, 1978); for T. E. Hulme's see Noel Stock, *The Life of Ezra Pound* (Random House, 1970); for that of a number of philosophers and aestheticians, see Sanford Schwartz, *The Matrix of Modernism* (Princeton University Press, 1985); for Pound's connection with art, see Harriet Zinnes, ed., *Ezra Pound and the Visual Arts* (New Directions, 1980); and for his connection to science see Ian F. A. Bell, *Critic as Scientist* (Methuen, 1981).

artificiality, periphrasis, self-indulgence, and decorative effects in the literature of the contemporary establishment. The well-known proclamation of the principles of imagism—concocted by Pound, H. D., and Richard Aldington—elevated the antislither campaign to the level of a program (and, in time, an institution):

1. Direct treatment of the "thing" whether subjective or objective.
2. To use absolutely no word that does not contribute to the presentation.
3. As regarding rhythm: to compose in the sequence of the musical phrase, not in sequence of a metronome.[5]

Poetry "must be *as well written as prose,*" Pound was fond of saying, "as simple as de Maupassant's best prose, and as hard as Stendhal's." It must have "precision," "objectivity," concreteness, and a natural actuality— "nothing—nothing that you couldn't, in some circumstance, in the stress of some emotion, actually say."[6]

There is a premium placed on candor in this ideal of composition and that quality presumably gives the writer's work its enduring value: "The serious artist is scientific in that he presents the image of his desire, of his hate, of his indifference as precisely that, as precisely the image of his own desire, hate or indifference. The more precise his record the more lasting and unassailable his work of art."[7] Ultimately, the writer's technical discipline is a moral thing—"I believe in technique as the test of a man's sincerity," he said, specifying its destructive and regenerative use "in the trampling down of every convention that impedes or obscures . . . the precise rendering of the impulse."[8]

The effect Pound had on modern literature in terms only of this category of the self-discipline of technique was immense. As Eliot said, "Pound's great contribution to the work of other poets (if they choose to accept what he offers) is his insistence upon the immensity of the amount of *conscious* labour to be performed by the poet."[9] Yeats admitted to a very personal rejuvenation (apropos of a conversation with Pound): "He is full of the middle ages and helps me to get back to the definite and concrete away from modern abstractions. To talk over a poem with him is like getting you to put a sentence into dialect. All becomes clear and natural."[10] And as for the best of them all in the "trampling down of every convention that impedes or obscures . . . the precise rendering of the impulse," Ernest Hemingway, one can concoct a fair facsimile of his literary theory simply by taking Pound's ideas of artistic discipline and changing the term "slither" to "bullshit."

To Pound a disciplined art liberated, it instigated discovery, and it necessarily began with the destruction of conventional thought and representation: "the function of an art is to strengthen the perceptive faculties and free them from encumbrance, such encumbrances, for instance, as set moods, set ideas, conventions."[11] Abstraction was a primary encumbrance—"Go in fear of abstractions," Pound counseled in "A Few Don'ts."[12] Cliché was another and so were the standard little techniques of poetry that aimed at symmetry or prettiness or the easy fulfillment of stock expectations rather than aiming at truth:

> I should like to break up *cliche*, to disintegrate these magnetised groups that stand between the reader of poetry and the drive of it, to escape from lines composed of two very nearly equal sections, each containing a noun and each noun decorously attended by a carefully selected epithet gleaned, apparently, from Shakespeare, Pope, or Horace. For it is not until poetry lives again "close to the thing" that it will be a vital part of contemporary life.[13]

Logic and grammar were other encumbrances. Pound could see that scientists in the twentieth century had other quite valuable ways of relating phenomena, and he lamented, "As far as writing goes we are laggards, I mean in relation to scientists; we still cling to modes of expression and verbal arrangements sprung from, and limited by, scholastic logic. . . . We no longer think or need to think in terms of monolinear logic, the sentence structure, subject, predicate, object, etc."[14] Looking at Pound's aesthetic in more culturally comprehensive terms, scholar Sanford Schwartz, in locating the philosophical and aesthetic coordinates of what he calls "the matrix of modernism" proposes the idea that one of Pound's (and the period's) deepest motives is the struggle against "imposed order," or "coercive uniformity"—conceptual and political as well as aesthetic.[15]

Behind Pound's specific destructions there seems to be a presupposition that we need a fresh understanding of what we are and where we stand in relation to our universe. In this vein his epistemology is agnostic, relativistic. "Our consciousness is utterly ignorant of the nature of the innate essence," he says. "For instance: a man may be hit by a bullet and not know its composition, nor the cause of its having been fired, nor its direction, nor that it is a bullet."[16] In a dark time it is the (self-disciplined) poet who has the best perspective: "As the poet was, in ages of faith, the founder and emendor of all religions, so, in ages of doubt, is he the final agnostic; that which the philosopher presents as truth, the poet presents as that which appears as truth to a certain sort of mind under certain conditions."[17]

Pound squarely faced the characteristic predicament of the writer in the Age of Epistemology—no use trying to capture the thing itself with your words, since your act of perception is an indissoluble part of it. Pound used the recognition of this predicament to move beyond realism to a richer realm: "An 'Image' is that which presents an intellectual and emotional complex in an instant of time," he said in the early pronouncement that would become one of his most famous.[18] In his next phase he insisted that "Vorticism is a legitimate expression of life," because "the vorticist is expressing his complex consciousness . . . instinct and intellect together."[19] If this sounds Bergsonian (except for the catchword "vorticism"), perhaps it is; Pound had earlier been exposed to Hulme's explanation of Bergson's concept of the image.[20] But whatever its genealogy, this concept of the writer's relationship to world, self, and expression got into a number of literary imaginations via Pound.

Another way in which Pound's aesthetic was on the cutting edge of modernism (and, again, had a distinctively Bergsonian character) was in its emphasis on dynamism, on process. Even his earliest writings show a clear sense that reality is process and that literature, if it is to touch the real, needs to represent reality's flow; in the preface to his 1910 book, *The Spirit of Romance*, he launched the following admittedly "florid and metaphorical" comparison:

> Art or an art is not unlike a river, in that it is perturbed at times by the quality of the river bed, but is in a way independent of that bed. The color of the water depends upon the substance of the bed and banks immediate and preceding. Stationary objects are reflected, but the quality of motion is of the river. The scientist is concerned with all of these things, the artist with that which flows.[21]

(William James's idea of the "stream of consciousness" had been published thirty-one years earlier, and Joyce's *Portrait* two years earlier, but in 1910 the idea was still quite novel in American literature.) Conventional thought, with the fixity of its ideas, was boring and unreal to a mind attuned to reality's dynamism. In the following passage Pound in 1919 brings this criterion sharply to bear on the unlikely subject of translations of Aeschylus; note the destruction of Browning's idea of thought, the modernist touch of the scientific analogy, and the traditionalist's assumption that Aeschylus too felt the dynamism of things, since his drama manifests it so effectively:

> "Thought" as Browning understood it—"ideas" as the term is current, are poor two-dimensional stuff, a scant, scratch covering. "Damn

ideas, anyhow." An idea is only an imperfect induction from fact.

The solid, the "last atom of force verging off into the first atom of matter" is the force, the emotion, the objective sight of the poet. In the *Agamemnon* it is the whole rush of the action, the whole wildness of Kassandra's continual shrieking, the flash of the beacon fires burning unstinted wood, the outburst of . . . "Troy is the Greeks'."[22]

Pound seems to have felt the energetics metaphor to be essential in the explanation of the dynamic process. "The vortex is the point of maximum energy," he asserted, and developed *vortex* (much the same way Herbert Spencer developed *force*) as an actual element in mechanics, energetics, aesthetics, history, human psychology, and so forth:*

> All experience rushes into this vortex. All the energized past, all the past that is living and worthy to live. ALL MOMENTUM, which is the past bearing upon us, RACE, RACE-MEMORY, instinct charging the PLACID, NON-ENERGIZED FUTURE.
>
> The DESIGN of the future in the grip of the human vortex. All the past that is vital, all the past that is capable of living into the future, is pregnant in the vortex, NOW.[23]

Vorticism—Pound himself took credit for coining the term, although admittedly he worked out its characteristics with Lewis and Gaudier-Brzeska. Pound was thinking pan-artistically, pan-culturally in leaving imagism behind and concocting vorticism, but he still believed in the image as the "primary pigment" of poetry. Perhaps concerned that *image* as previously defined might signify something static, he redefined it along more dynamic lines: "The image is not an idea. It is a radiant node or cluster; it is what I can, and must perforce, call a VORTEX, from which, and through which, and into which, ideas are constantly rushing."[24]

By editing and publishing Ernest Fenollosa's *The Chinese Written Character as a Medium for Poetry*, Pound was further promulgating the notion of dynamism, since Fenollosa's book represented poetry as primarily capable of "getting back to the fundamental reality of *time*" in its structure of representation. Since reality is all process and interconnection, Fenollosa asserted, the language of poetry needs to be able to represent "*the transference of power*" rather than fixed things with fixed qualities in static states or passive conditions. The "Chinese transitive sentence," which Fenollosa used as an ideal norm, "brings language close to *things*, and in its strong

---

*For the philosophical and scientific backgrounds of the vortex idea, see Bell, *Critic as Scientist*, 14–15.

reliance upon verbs it erects all speech into a kind of dramatic poetry."[25]

Fenollosa's analysis of the relationship between reality, the poet, and the language of poetry worked its way into Pound's imagination, although it never became as dominant a concern as the Image or the Vortex. From the beginning of his career Pound had been concerned with aligning poetry and reality as exactly as possible: "Poetry is a sort of inspired mathematics, which gives us equations, not for abstract figures, triangles, spheres, and the like, but equations for the human emotions."[26] Fenollosa's work showed him by what linguistic techniques such equations could be derived. In addition, Fenollosa's ideas strongly reinforced Pound's feeling that knowledge of different languages was essential to a writer's sense of the possibilities of "certain mechanisms of communication and registration."[27]

Pound never really had Gertrude Stein's sense of the almost total arbitrariness of language. The influence of Fenollosa's theory that metaphors and linguistic structures were based in nature would certainly obscure such a possibility.* Nonetheless, Pound occasionally recognized some of language's nonreferential aspects and saw them as opportunities for literary use. In "How to Read" (1928) he listed as one of the characteristics of language, *Logopoeia*:

> Logopoeia, "the dance of the intellect among words", that is to say, it employs words not only for their direct meaning, but it takes count in a special way of habits of usage, of the context we *expect* to find with the word, its usual concomitants, of its known acceptances, and of ironical play. . . .
>
> *Logopoeia* does not translate; though the attitude of mind it expresses may pass through a paraphrase.[28]

Pound also at times could use words or quotations as objects, language *as* language, as several of his critics have maintained. Ian F. A. Bell, for example, basing his views on ideas put forth by Richard Sieburth, cites the *Cantos'* practice of

---

*Michael F. Harper expands on this point and relates it to what he sees as the failure of Pound's Cantos: "It is Fenollosa's epistemology that is flawed, and the same epistemology is responsible for the *Cantos*. Pound believed that reality was accessible to 'direct' examination, that the significance or essence of any part of that reality was there to be perceived. Language, too, was transparent; . . . the serious artist . . . could render his own language transparent to all. These beliefs, and the fact that they are mistaken, explain so much that is at first puzzling about Pound. ("The Revolution of the Word," in Daniel Hoffman, ed., *Ezra Pound and William Carlos Williams* [University of Pennsylvania Press, 1984], 102–103.)

incorporating whole chunks of quotations from primary sources as part of its insistence on its own objectivity, its capacity for the "real," through a materialist poetics. Words themselves are offered in the form of tangible objects as, following Richard Sieburth, "quotation involves shifting the emphasis from language as a means of representation to language as the very object of representation," a shift that involves "a mode not merely of copying or reflecting but of including the real."[29]

In his poetry Pound developed the technique of using shards of the past—images, legends, recorded facts, and quotations—to create an intricate knowledge mosaic that can represent at one and the same time the whole complex of human potential and achievement and the incremental development of the poet's own insight and attitudes. The Cantos, in fact, turn out to be largely *about* the human past so conceived. As early as 1911 Pound wrote a series of articles championing what he referred to as "a 'New Method in Scholarship,' . . . the method of Luminous Detail, a method most vigorously hostile to the prevailing mode of today—that is, the method of multitudinous detail, and to the method of yesterday, the method of sentiment and generalisation."[30] Only four years past graduate school here he was, redoing the syllabus according to the principle that a year later was to be launched as imagism. Eliot and Joyce, of course, were to build their works of the twenties on just this sort of use of the past. Throughout his career Pound's poetry (even more than his historical scholarship) would convey its meanings through the construction of a mosaic out of historical Luminous Details. Here, for example, is a piece of Canto XXXVIII:

> *il duol che sopra Senna*
> *Induce, falseggiando la moneta.*
> > *Paradiso XIX,* 118.

> An' that year Metevsky went over to America del
> > Sud
> (and the Pope's manners were so like Mr. Joyce's,
> got that way in the Vatican, weren't like that before)
> Marconi knelt in the ancient manner
> > like Jimmy Walker sayin' his prayers.
> His Holiness expressed a polite curiousity
> > as to how His Excellency had chased those
> electric shakes through the a'mosphere.

The materials are like stock items, public and personal, out of the past's warehouse, although the varying of the voice (speech inflections and rhythms) and the intuitional logic of the shard-flow are characteristically (vortically) modern.* And frequently the original fragment—the fact or the quotation—is given a new, modern, often ironic tone by the context of its presentation:

> Austria had some Krupp cannon;
> Prussia had some Krupp cannon.
> "The Emperor ('68) is deeply in'erested in yr. catalogue
> and in yr. service to humanity"
> (signed) Leboeuf.[31]

Such linguistically conglomerative techniques are frequently employed by writers in the thirties and later to achieve breadth, a sense of the still-living quality of the past and, simultaneously, a personal, modernist perspective in their works; *U.S.A.* and *Paterson* are important examples.

The extent of Pound's influence is undeterminable, of course, but his theoretical pronouncements—those strange, dogmatic, and heterogeneous surges of revivified traditionalism and avant-garde modernism, with their strong undercurrents from modern science, painting, and sculpture —show up variously in the thought and work of a number of his contemporaries, some of whom cited him as the master, the father, and the promoter of modernism. His thought had the potential to take them out of the literary preconceptions of the preceding generation and into a new-old world of possibility.

■ Ernest Hemingway: The Sequence of Motion and Fact

Ernest Hemingway (1898–1961) was the most famous knowledge destroyer of them all. His Fredrick Henry in the midst of war-ravaged Italy puts it straight in this well-known passage: "Abstract words such as glory, honor, courage, or hallow were obscene beside the concrete names of villages, the numbers of roads, the names of rivers, the numbers of regiments and

---

*Michael F. Harper insists that Pound's poetry should be read as if its images "constitute a natural language" and that their juxtaposition in effect produces Fenollosian ideograms ("The Revolution of the Word," 90, 99). Sanford Schwartz sees "the interaction between past and present" in Pound's work as manifesting "a 'tensional' relationship that mediates between the desire to recover suppressed experience and the desire to project new forms that reshape the world around us" (*The Matrix of Modernism*, 114).

the dates." Ultimately, the world was a world of physical events and emotional sensations, and thought could only be a handicap: "it was not my show anymore and I wished this bloody train would get to Mestre and I would eat and stop thinking. I would have to stop."[32] Hemingway comes at the destruction of knowledge and the re-creation of knowing from a standpoint apart from (and invulnerable to) the intellectual anti-intellectuals. His interpretive paradigms come predominantly from hunting, boxing, bullfighting, and warfare, and his writing techniques are, in the main, carefully and consciously honed techniques of journalism. Yet in terms of the originality and impact of his whole way of seeing things, he certainly prevailed.

Education had never been his strong suit. Unlike most of the knowledge destroyers, he wasn't college-educated, and, as Michael Reynolds points out in *The Young Hemingway*, he began by trying to be a writer of mass-market magazine stories, with a mass-marketer's literary knowledge and taste. Hemingway's discovery of serious American literature, Reynolds claims, came through the tutelage of Sherwood Anderson.[33] And, of course, when Hemingway got to Paris, Gertrude Stein and Ezra Pound, recognizing his talent and appreciating his avidity, continued the job. The Anderson curriculum emphasized the classic Russian novelists and contemporary Americans; Pound's pushed the classic French novelists and the contemporary British; Stein's featured modernist French painters and the writings of her own inimitable self.

That aesthetic education certainly "took." Hemingway carried Tolstoy's books with him on African safari;[34] he claimed to have learned to write from looking at Cézannes at the Jeu de Paume and the Luxembourg on an empty stomach[35] (though Reynolds points out that his "taste in art [then] was and remained rooted in traditional representative painters");[36] and he elevated principles very like Pound's into an exacting writing code.

But it was his own experience and his own sense of things on which he would base his works. "I thought about Tolstoi and about what a great advantage an experience of war was to a writer,"[37] he says, implying, of course, his own "great advantage." His reading, for that of a writer, involved an inordinate number of items that were practical, nonintellectual guides to experience, about fishing and firearms, Spain and Africa, boxing and camping.[38] He was the prime example of what Philip Rahv later termed "the cult of experience,"[39] and he scoured the world for opportunities to test his mettle and feed his art. What he had seen and done, what his reactions had been, defined the perspective and the substance of his art, whatever the effect of tutelage and example.

He had a strong personal antipathy to idealism, sentimentality, and rationalism. The kind of self-deluding vision that was expressed, as he saw it, by convention-bound women or by humanists simply had no place in the real world. It occurs in the optimism of Harry's wife in "The Snows of Kilimanjaro": "'You can't die if you don't give up'"; in the religion of Harold Krebs's mother in "Soldier's Home": "'God has some work for every one to do. . . . There can be no idle hands in His Kingdom'"; and even in the sentiments of his own mother about *The Sun Also Rises*:

> The critics seem to be full of praise for your style and ability to draw word pictures but the decent ones always regret that you should use such great gifts in perpetuating the lives and habits of so degraded a strata of humanity. . . .
>
> What is the matter? Have you ceased to be interested in loyalty, nobility, honor and fineness in life . . . surely you have other words in your vocabulary besides "damn" and "bitch"—Every page fills me with a sick loathing—if I should pick up a book by any other writer with such words in it, I should read no more—but pitch it in the fire.[40]

The fully initiated man answers such conventional idealism and is seconded by the world: Harry with "'Where did you read that? You're such a bloody fool'";[41] Harold with "'I'm not in His Kingdom.' . . . Krebs looked at the bacon fat hardening on his plate";[42] and Hemingway himself with *Men Without Women*, *A Farewell to Arms*, and *Death in the Afternoon*. His rebuttal of genteel idealism is far more patient and more chilling in "A Natural History of the Dead." He begins with a quotation from Mungo Park, who claims to have felt this reassurance from a moss-flower while lost on the African desert: "Can that Being who planted, watered and brought to perfection, in this obscure part of the world, a thing which appears of so small importance, look with unconcern upon the situation and suffering of creatures formed after his own image? Surely not."[43] Hemingway follows, deeply sardonic, in a natural historian's tone, with a graphic description of animals and people killed by disease, accident, warfare, and brutality, closing the piece with a brilliantly conceived episode of conflict at a field hospital between a doctor and an artillery officer over the handling of a soldier with a crushed skull. The two men are driven to physical aggression in their disagreement over how to most humanely treat the hopelessly injured man, who dies during the course of their conflict.

Hemingway's own experience in the First World War was undoubtedly crucial in focusing his destructive vision. As he later represented the situation in *A Farewell to Arms* and a number of short stories, he and his comrades were entrapped in a raging antipersonal chaos and given only empty verbal rationalizations to justify it.

In Hemingway's work civilization's judgments and principles are bankrupt, and civilization itself is only a fading illusion. The motifs of his fiction—the insistent violence and death and depravity—seem especially intended to shake the readers, to break down their complacencies and imperceptivities, and to force them to face the simple, brutal, nihilistic facts of experience. As Robert Penn Warren pointed out so well a number of years ago, the natural world does not sustain human values in Hemingway's vision;[44] more recently Thomas Leitch, in a study of short story aesthetics, stated "Hemingway's wisdom . . . is always worldly wisdom: there is no hidden truth or revelation that makes the world intelligible; given the ultimate resistance of the nonhuman world to individual action, Hemingway can only provide information about that world and our possible responses to it."[45] Thus Hemingway's approach is that of a literary naturalist, with nature or the simple course of events providing the only acceptable intelligibility for experience; and he's a purer naturalist than his predecessors Dreiser, Norris, and London in that he entirely dispensed with the mediation of scientific and pseudoscientific theory. A knowledge destroyer in the fullest sense, he tried to stay free of all fabricated paradigms and of the rationalizing intellect that produced and relied on them.

Hemingway's readers recognize the *Nada* he envisions, the unreality of interpretive ideas and ideals, and they recognize the author as someone who's "been there and seen it all," who'll shock the gentry and speak to the cognoscenti in a language that's all their own, rife with tacit understandings. The Hemingway philosophy is amazing in what it does for his self-image and his fan clubs. Among the characters he has created, the specially elect are those who are tuned in to the *Nada* and deny themselves the conventional shielding from the essential chaos and meaninglessness of things. The Hemingway "code" (as Penn Warren later characterized it) had a great deal to do with knowing and unknowing.

Thematically, the epistemology his works so often teach is one of individual concentration on the concrete impressions—physical and emotional—of the passing present moment. Knowing was personal, individual knowing for Hemingway as it was for Crane, but Hemingway's was come to with more coolness, more literalness, more discipline. And, as a number of his critics have pointed out, with a quality of aestheticism. Tony Tanner, for example, identifies the "exclusive trust in the single perceptual event" as the fundamental factor of knowing in Hemingway's fiction, and he goes on to suggest that the characters' acts of perception are ideally paced, "unhurried," in their concentration on what's actual: "Sensations should not be collapsed together and pressed into generalizations: rather they are to be delicately and carefully separated out and each given their individual contours. (Stein's theories, of course, corroborate and clarify this intention.) Experience should be as little prejudged as possible."[46] "The careful relish of sensation," Warren calls it, and Hugh Kenner ingeniously suggests its connection to Walter Pater's quest to maximize the perfect passing moment, with all the transience and poignancy thereby implied.[47] It is well worth recalling at this point the relationship philosophers Henri Bergson and Clarence Irving Lewis found between aesthetic apprehension and the fullest sort of knowing (see pp. 88, 98, above). In whatever way aesthetic, the peak moment of perception in Hemingway's works is the Moment of Truth; the frame of mind conducive to the fullest degree of self- and situation-awareness is that of a person poised to face a crisis—Manolo sizing up his bull, Robert Jordan surveying the well-guarded bridge, Santiago scanning the eighty-five-day fishless ocean. Theirs are the habits of perception that make for truth and, if carried into everyday life, whether in bistro or big two-hearted river, put one in communion with what is real and important.

For Hemingway the discipline of perception and knowing is part and parcel of the discipline of writing—the "code" is authorial as well as experiential. In writing its first principle is destructionist, an absolute prohibition against the language of betrayal, and this includes fanciness and excess as well as bullshit. Hemingway himself is largely responsible for our idea of the discipline, the ritual quality of his act of writing—here is a version from *A Moveable Feast*, a reminiscence about what he had to put into it in those early days in Paris:

> But sometimes when I was starting a new story and I could not get it going, I would sit in front of the fire and squeeze the peel of the little oranges into the edge of the flame and watch the sputter of blue that they made. I would stand and look out over the roofs of Paris and think "Do not worry. You have always written before and you will write now. All you have to do is write one true sentence. Write the truest sentence that you know." So finally I would write one true sentence, and then go on from there. It was easy then because there was always one true sentence that I knew or had seen or had heard someone say. If I started to write elaborately, or like someone intro-

ducing or presenting something, I found that I could cut that scroll-work or ornament out and throw it away and start with the first true simple declarative sentence I had written.[48]

He vehemently attacked what he saw as undisciplined technique: in *Torrents of Spring* parodying the soft realism and shallow philosophizing of Sherwood Anderson's *Dark Laughter*; in *Death in the Afternoon* flaying the intellectualism of Aldous Huxley ("For a writer to put his own intel-lectual musings, which he might sell for a low price as essays, into the mouths of artificially constructed characters . . . is good economics, per-haps, but does not make literature");[49] also, in the satirical persona of "Dr. Hemingstein, the great psychiatrist," branding neo-mysticism in prose as "erectile writing" ("trees for example look different to a man in that por-tentous state. . . . All objects look different. They are slightly larger, more mysterious, and vaguely blurred").[50] Gertrude Stein's spontaneous writ-ing he found simply a symptom that "she disliked the drudgery of revi-sion and the obligation to make her writing intelligible." *The Making of Americans* "went on endlessly in repetitions that a more conscientious and less lazy writer would have put in the waste basket."[51] He had little tolerance of approaches different from his own, even of writers he re-spected, like Melville, whose knowledge of "actual things . . . is wrapped up in the rhetoric like plums in a pudding."[52]

Ezra Pound was a great deal of help in Hemingway's finding his own plums.* As they colluded in Paris in the early twenties, swapping boxing lessons for help with writing and getting published, Pound had been for some years the elder who had been counseling young writers to "go in fear of abstractions," to be direct, "objective—no slither," to throw off conventions, prettification, and cliché. Hemingway was a sometime jour-nalist and just the sort of young writer Pound had in mind, with a strong (and growing) sense of the craft of serious writing and the feeling that the raw truth he knew was not represented in the run-of-the-mill literature of the day. As he reminisced about Pound in *A Moveable Feast*, "here was the man I liked and trusted the most as a critic then, the man who believed in the *mot juste*—the one and only correct word to use—the man who had taught me to distrust adjectives as I would later learn to distrust certain people in certain situations."[53] It is easy to imagine the force and special sanction Pound must have added to Hemingway's program of distillation,

*Excellent studies of the Pound-Hemingway relationship are Harold M. Hurwitz, "Hem-ingway's Tutor, Ezra Pound," *MFS* 17, no. 4 (Winter 1971), 469–482; and Linda W. Wagner, "*The Sun Also Rises*: One Debt to Imagism," *JNT* 2, no. 2 (May 1972), 88–98.

deletion, and denial in general, but Charles A. Fenton's study of revisions Hemingway made from 1922 to 1924 in one of the vignettes, chapter iii ("Minarets stuck up in the rain . . . ") of *in our time*, shows specifically that Hemingway cut the number of words in half, reduced the number of descriptive adjectives by two-thirds, and shortened the sentences and made almost all of them simple and declarative in changing a journalistic sketch into a literary vignette.[54] The effect of this discipline was not merely to produce conciseness and sharp focus, but, Fenton points out, to minimize the overt shaping of the reader's responses, to cut down the mediation and preinterpretation of the material.

This stringently disciplined prose represents a mind-set very close to that of logical positivism—strictly empirical, scrupulous about the particular accountability of statements, intolerant of metaphysics, and distrustful of metaphor. I don't mean to infer any sort of direct influence of Wittgenstein, Dewey, or Russell, but merely to point out the similarity of attitude toward what had been standard conceptual processes. Hemingway's approach to literature is just such an analytical, radically reformist endeavor.

But its analytical, positivistic qualities hardly explain the power of Hemingway's prose at its best. Warren again offers an excellent lead: in considering what he calls Hemingway's technique of understatement, he identifies it as "stemming from the contrast between the sensitivity and the superimposed discipline."[55] Suppose we consider the following highly disciplined passage from *The Sun Also Rises* and try to determine the sources of its "sensitivity." Brett has admitted to Jake that she is falling in love with Romero, and Jake has arranged for the young bullfighter to join them at their cafe table, at which this scene occurs:

> "You know English well."
> "Yes," he said. "Pretty well, sometimes. But I must not let anybody know. It would be very bad, a torero who speaks English."
> "Why?" asked Brett.
> "It would be bad. The people would not like it. Not yet."
> "Why not?"
> "They would not like it. Bull-fighters are not like that."
> "What are bull-fighters like?"
> He laughed and tipped his hat down over his eyes and changed the angle of his cigar and the expression of his face.
> "Like at the table," he said. I glanced over. He had mimicked exactly the expression of Nacional. He smiled, his face natural again. "No. I must forget English."

"Don't forget it, yet," Brett said.

"No?"

"No."

"All right."

He laughed again.

"I would like a hat like that," Brett said.

"Good. I'll get you one."

"Right. See that you do."

"I will. I'll get you one to-night."

I stood up. Romero rose too.

"Sit down," I said. "I must go and find our friends and bring them here."

He looked at me. It was a final look to ask if it were understood. It was understood all right.

"Sit down," Brett said to him. "You must teach me Spanish."

He sat down and looked at her across the table. I went out. The hard-eyed people at the bull-fighter table watched me go. It was not pleasant. When I came back and looked in the cafe, twenty minutes later, Brett and Romero were gone. The coffee-glasses and our three empty cognac-glasses were on the table. A waiter came with a cloth and picked up the glasses and mopped off the table.[56]

In a very familiar passage in *Death in the Afternoon*, Hemingway describes his narrative strategy in terms of presences and omissions: "If a writer of prose knows enough about what he is writing about he may omit things that he knows and the reader, if the writer is writing truly enough, will have a feeling of those things as strongly as though the writer had stated them. The dignity of movement of an ice-berg is due to only one-eighth of it being above water."[57] Obviously, one of the sources of power in the narrative of Romero, Brett, and Jake is the "presence" of deeply salient factors which are never referred to directly in the scene: Romero's and Brett's growing mutual sexual attraction, Romero's status as a future star in the bullfighting world, the bullfighting world's opposition to his poten-tially damaging affair with such a sensation-seeking outsider, and Jake's complex set of conflicting needs and loyalties—his love for Brett, stymied by his war-wound impotence; his *afición* for bullfighting and his absolute admiration of Romero's skill, undermined by his yearning to do right by Brett; his desire to act always with grace and purpose and integrity, thwarted by the complexity of a situation in which it is impossible not to betray somebody (maybe *everybody*) whatever he does or doesn't do.

This symphony of motives is figured only by the simplest of tones —details that are sparse, almost unremittingly empirical, and yet loaded, despite the apparent inconsequence of most of them. Romero's disparagement of the torero who speaks English is both a warning to Brett and a reaffirmation of his status within his profession and nationality. Yet his laugh, changed cigar angle, and parody of the typical bullfighter signify a willingness to come across in response to her suggestion of potential involvement implicit in the question "What are bull-fighters like?" Romero and Brett signal to each other that they can both play games with loyalties when there is such strong attraction. Brett asks him not to forget English yet, offering no explicit reasons, but advancing the verbal foreplay. When she moves along even further by wishing for a hat like his, his response is clearly in the impetuous, courtly suitor mode, whatever the nationality. Jake's move to leave at that moment shows his understanding and acceptance of the subtext. Romero is willing to stay (or more than willing), and his look asks Jake for confirmation: his class and national manners stipulate certain restraints, certain behaviors in response to a woman attended by another man or to another man's woman unattended, whatever the tenor of the conversation. Here, though, for the first time in this scene Hemingway interprets a detail for us—or rather has Jake interpret it for us—and we know Jake's look has "set" all the understandings in the conversation.

He leaves with Brett's "You must teach me Spanish" ringing in his ears—tritely, maybe even satirically seductive. What the episode and the affair mean to him is figured only in the final image of the removal of their coffee glasses and the three empty cognac glasses and of the waiter's cloth mopping off the table. It's an *image*, though, and not a symbol: we can best understand what it means and how it works by regarding it as something like "that which presents an intellectual and emotional complex in an instant of time"—like Ezra Pound's kind of "image." And, in fact then, why not the clichés about English too, and the cigar angle, the wish for the hat, the hard-eyed look of the people at the bullfighter table —aren't they images in that sense too, the verbal as well as the visual? What we've been reading is a sequential string of these intellectual and emotional complexes, each presented with "direct treatment" and "no word that does not contribute to the presentation"—the closest approximation to narrative imagism that can be imagined.*

---

*For another discussion of imagism's presence in this novel, see the aforementioned Linda W. Wagner, "*The Sun Also Rises*: One Debt to Imagism."

But as we look more closely at Hemingway's ideas of literary representation we see that he's looking for not just *an* image, but *the* image. He explains it in *Death in the Afternoon*: searching for a way to represent a moment he had experienced in which an apprentice bullfighter—"a short, thick-ankled, graceless Basque with a pale face who looked nervous and incompetently fed in a cheap rented suit"—had been gored, he says,

> I tried to remember what it was that seemed just out of my remembering and that was the thing that I had really seen and, finally, remembering all around it, I got it. When he stood up, his face white and dirty and the silk of his breeches opened from waist to knee, it was the dirtiness of the rented breeches, the dirtiness of his slit underwear and the clean, clean, unbearably clean whiteness of the thigh bone that I had seen, and it was that which was important.[58]

That image, once he's located it truly (as he would say), seems the definitive representation of that perceived event, not at all just one of a variety of conceivable representations.

His dream was to capture inside/outside reality in language. In his Foreword to *The Green Hills of Africa*, he avowed this purpose: "The writer has attempted to write an absolutely true book to see whether the shape of a country and the pattern of a month's action can, if truly presented, compete with a work of the imagination." And in 1925 he had written to his father "I am trying in all my stories to get the feeling of the actual life across—not just to depict life—or criticize it—but to actually make it alive."[59] He believed language could do this, that it had potentially that absolute a relation to reality if it could be utilized with enough sensitivity and discipline: "It wasn't by accident that the Gettysburg address was so short. The laws of prose writing are as immutable as those of flight, of mathematics, of physics," he claimed in a letter to Maxwell Perkins.[60] When he praised Ezra Pound in that quote above as "the man who believed in the *mot juste*—the one and only correct word to use," he meant it as a matter not of stylistic felicity but ontological precision. To Bernard Berenson he wrote "There are only certain words which are valid and similies . . . are like defective ammunition."*

The experienced event has an essence, Hemingway seems to feel, which has a single, specific verbal formula. For narrative it can be evoked in a particular verbal sequence:

*"Similie" sic. Quoted from Larry W. Phillips, *Ernest Hemingway on Writing* (Scribner's, 1984), 38. I'm certainly willing to exempt that particular simile from its own judgment.

I was trying to write then and I found the greatest difficulty, aside from knowing truly what you really felt, rather than what you were supposed to feel, and had been taught to feel, was to put down what really happened in action; what the actual things were which produced the emotion that you experienced. . . . [T]he real thing, the sequence of motion and fact which made the emotion and which would be as valid in a year or in ten years or, with luck and if you stated it purely enough, always, was beyond me and I was working very hard to try to get it.[61]

In one sense, then, language is for Hemingway exactly what Howells conceived it to be, absolute in its correspondence to reality. Pound too, when he was specifically inspired by Fenollosa to explore the relationships of phonemes, written symbols, and actual things was working in the same absolutist-realist tradition. Gertrude Stein's sense of language's arbitrariness and Wallace Stevens' sense of its ineluctable subjectivity point in a quite different, more characteristically modernist direction.

In another sense this linguistic realism of Hemingway's has a correlative mystical, prophetic side. Finding the right verbal formula "which would be as valid in a year or in ten years or, with luck and if you stated it purely enough, always" is a quest that would not be foreign to a prophet, priest, or poet of the Bronze Age. The "sequence of motion and fact which made the emotion" is realism's mystical verbal essence. Sometimes the Hemingway persona speaks of the "always" as another, deeper dimension of the writing. In *The Green Hills of Africa* he explains (to one of literature's most convenient straight men) writing's great and deeply satisfying challenge in terms of

"The kind of writing that can be done. How far prose can be carried if any one is serious enough and has luck. There is a fourth and fifth dimension that can be gotten."
"You believe it?"
"I know it."
"And if a writer can get this?"
"Then nothing else matters. It is more important than anything he can do. The chances are, of course, that he will fail. But there is a chance that he succeeds."[62]

Two of Hemingway's special talents helped him in getting the right language to catch and immortalize those particular sequences of motion and fact: his ability to pick up specially significant and self-revealing colloquialisms and his "feel" for the sound and movement of words. Whether directly or indirectly "quoted," his dialogues and monologues could contain wonderfully self-revealing "images" of complex states of affairs, as in the foregoing Brett-Romero-Jake conversation or, in an entirely different idiom, the following passage from "Mr. and Mrs. Elliot"; note the profusion of very accurately caught and sarcastically ensconced genteelisms:

> He was twenty-five years old and had never gone to bed with a woman until he married Mrs. Elliot. He wanted to keep himself pure so that he could bring to his wife the same purity of mind and body that he expected of her. He had been in love with various girls before he kissed Mrs. Elliot and always told them sooner or later that he had led a clean life. Nearly all the girls lost interest in him. He was shocked and really horrified at the way girls would become engaged to and marry men whom they must know had dragged themselves through the gutter. He once tried to warn a girl he knew against a man of whom he had almost proof that he had been a rotter at college and a very unpleasant incident had resulted.[63]

With regard to Hemingway's sense of the "feel" of language, we recognize the influence of Gertrude Stein. He himself long afterwards admitted "She had discovered many truths about rhythms and the uses of words in repetition that were valid and valuable and she talked well about them."[64] To rhythm and repetition we might also add something about the special and particular character of individual words. William Carlos Williams had cited Stein's contribution in "smashing every connotation that words have ever had, in order to get them back clean,"[65] and Hemingway shows a keen sense of how words feel and what they call up after such destruction. Harold M. Hurwitz has suggested the influence of Pound's idea of an "'absolute rhythm . . . which corresponds to the emotion or shade of emotion to be expressed.'"[66] Michael Reynolds, in quoting rhythms and repetitions from Hemingway's pre-Paris journalism, shows, however, that the young writer "already had the hang of it."[67] But however he got or developed it, here is how it reads—colloquialism, connotation, repetition, rhythm, and revelation—in the In Our Time sketch called "Chapter VIII"; two cops have just shot and killed two Hungarians who had broken into a cigar store:

> "Hell, Jimmy," he said, "you oughtn't to have done it. There's liable to be a hell of a lot of trouble."
> "They're crooks, ain't they?" said Boyle. "They're wops, ain't they? Who the hell is going to make trouble?"

> *"That's all right maybe this time," said Drevitts, "but how did you know*
> *they were wops when you bumped them off?"*
> *"Wops," said Boyle, "I can tell wops a mile off."*[68]

The writing game was a game of risks for Hemingway, and the risks were specific to the "code" by which he played. He was not like Stein or Pound or Williams a restless experimenter tending in each new work to break the rules and boundaries of the last; the challenge he set himself in each new work was to come as close as he possibly could to the same essential ideal, to play the very best game he could by the single set of rules he had been coming to recognize ever more clearly since the beginning of his career. If he were to achieve the absoluteness, the universality, the quality of prophecy that was, he deeply felt, the soul of literary accomplishment, his works needed to be absolute in disciplined thought, in empirically focused perception, in minimal signification, and in attentiveness to suggestion and implication.

The risks specific to Hemingway's literary program were garrulity (that he would say too much, either through *needing* to say a great deal or through getting carried away with his own ideas), vacuity (that his portentous prose would in specific passages have no portentous referent but be mere filler or connective), incomprehensibility (that his clues would not constitute a pattern for his readers), and egocentricity (that the experience-essences he felt were not universal or even widely common). The first three could sometimes be simply matters of poor execution in particular circumstances, but all four were to some extent inherent in the endeavor.

The garrulity of *Death in the Afternoon*, the looseness of much of the prose in *A Moveable Feast*, the heavy doses of interpretation in "The Capital of the World," and of explanation in "The Battler," the awkward sententiousness of *The Old Man and the Sea* all witness to the fact that "pure" and "true" writing happened only rarely. Hemingway himself knew this very well, although he acknowledged it infrequently; here in *Death in the Afternoon*, after launching a vividly figurative, shrewdly psychological and philosophical interpretation of the work of a particular Gypsy bullfighter, he gives this disclaimer, acknowledging that only under certain circumstances is the sequence of motion and fact enough: "That is the worst sort of flowery writing, but it is necessary to try to give the feeling, and to some one who has never seen it a simple statement of the method does not convey the feeling. Any one who has seen bullfights can skip such flowerishness and read the facts which are much more difficult to isolate and state."[69]

Vacuity is in some ways an inevitable hazard because the parallel strata of revelation and narration can virtually never be congruent: narrative coherence demands that there be some passages of transition, of connection, of little or no inherent importance. Prose that is starkly economical and densely empirical can often provide at least vivid and sense-awakening impressions when there are apparently no deep and unspoken of factors beneath the surface, and Hemingway's prose is especially effective in that way. Indeed, for many passages in his work, early and late, the comment of Tony Tanner, that "this is Hemingway's wealth: meticulously retained sensations of the scattered munificence of the world,"[70] is entirely on the mark. Sometimes, however, Hemingway's positivistic narration loses its eye-opening vividness in traveling over relatively flat land, and we are left with what seem like the impressions of an epicurean tourist who is none too bright, as in this interlude from a long bus ride in *The Sun Also Rises*:

> As soon as we started out on the road outside of town it was cool. It felt nice riding high up and close under the trees. The bus went quite fast and made a good breeze, and as we went out along the road with the dust powdering the trees and down the hill, we had a fine view, back through the trees, of the town rising up from the bluff above the river. The Basque lying against my knees pointed out the view with the neck of the wine-bottle, and winked at us. He nodded his head.
> "Pretty nice, eh?"
> "These Basques are swell people," Bill said.[71]

Hemingway's novels suffer more from such flatness than do his short stories, the novel being (of course) more subject to attenuation in accommodating the demands of extended continuity. In either form certain kinds of revelation are more effectively represented in the terse, understated style than are others. "Code" prose is especially effective in representing bitchiness, sardonicism, innuendo, anxiety, and fear, and generally far less effective with positive values such as love and courage. This may be true at least in part because the kinds of things that we think of as lying beneath the surface and inspiring pity and fear are negative things.

Hemingway's desire to omit but still imply the sinister factor of his fictional equations gives his *ouvre* a repetitive quality, and the clues his works give are easier to pattern when the works are read in quantity. But even at that there are problems with the comprehensibility of underlying themes. We learn to pick up the hints of impending abortion in "Hills Like White Elephants," of lesbianism in "The Sea Change," of impending suicide in "Out of Season" (although that one, Hemingway's admitted aim, isn't really discernible), of impending death in "The Snows of Kilimanjaro," and of a man's checkered past in "My Old Man." In "A Canary for One" the answer to the puzzle—an impending divorce—turns out to be indecipherable and has to be explicitly stated at the end to be understood at all, and so the reader must think the whole story through again. The technique's success is intermittent—not many fictional situations can be developed in this way. Occasionally, however, as in "The Killers" and more so in "A Clean, Well-Lighted Place," what is omitted remains undeterminable—not merely incompletely figured—and the story takes on a powerful quality of abstraction in its representation of menace.

Hemingway's art has fascinating possibilities in the way that it tests the boundaries of literary aesthetics on two very fundamental fronts: how little literal information is sufficient to positively imply some deeper configuration and which deeper hopes and fears are sufficiently universal to be evocable by such extraordinarily minimal means. Much of his fiction is a wholly serious game played back and forth across those lines and he risks incomprehensibility, total flatness, or the possibility that what he feels are universal species-wide instincts and responses are really only class- or gender-specific. The reader is very much a part of Hemingway's intent, in a way that he/she wasn't for Gertrude Stein. His art is a way of expressing and testing his own very personal, emotional concerns against what his reader can be made to recognize and acknowledge. The responses of "I don't get it" or "I just can't imagine feeling that way" (in my experience relatively frequent from women readers) reflect real losses. But then he knew there would be losses or he wouldn't have played the game.

12　Conrad Aiken and Wallace Stevens: The Mind Watches the Mind Hunting the Real

■ Conrad Aiken: Time and the Decay of Identity

It was one of the characteristics of the age of epistemology that the workings of the mind—in knowing, in perceiving, in representing—became themselves primary subjects of literary exploration. The activity itself was of course nothing new in Western literature, in which we might safely guess that the second poem ever composed was probably about the composition of poetry (and practically every second poem since?), but what *was* new in the 1920s and 1930s was the daunting sense that such exploration had somehow to chart an indefinite void. The newest movements, the cutting edges of the physics, the psychology, the philosophy, and the art of the day had removed the gods and the muses, the anthropomorphized and the reliably objective worlds, the prophetic imagination, and even the simple feeling heart from the process. Henceforth the poetic process would have to be represented out of an uncertain and possibly unstable self in some kind of dubious and metaphoric relation to its own mind and to an outer world that was part indeterminate possibility and part self-projection. Even a tabula rasa would have been a welcome relief, but that wasn't one of the available alternatives.

Conrad Aiken (1889–1973) and Wallace Stevens (1879–1955) were two writers who directly explored in their poetry the new critical awareness of knowing and tried to locate the creative act in the relationship between mind and world—and vice versa. Stevens far more than Aiken, however. Stevens was a businessman who dedicated himself (except during a six- or seven-year period after the publication of his first book) in all his free time and all his imaginative resources to poetry, much of it on this theme. Aiken, on the other hand, was a quintessential man of letters who produced many more books of poetry on many more subjects, as well as stories, novels, autobiography, and reviews. (Aiken had published seven books of poetry by the time Stevens published his first in 1923, and by

1937 when Stevens brought out his second, Aiken had fifteen books of poetry, three novels, a book of stories and a Pulitzer Prize.) Not much of Aiken's work is focused on the problem of the mind and the world, but that which is is his best and most venturesome work, and the work in which he seems to have put the most stock.

Much of Aiken's work seems quite conventional to us today. We see him, in the context of the extremely innovative literary period in which he lived, as highly accomplished in the notable forms and styles—important and influential in his day, but not a writer who much extended the boundaries of possibility in literature. He was a very absorptive writer, though, very conscious of what other writers were doing and likely to adapt their motifs or techniques to his own purposes. (Roy Harvey Pearce, taking an extreme view, classifies him an "influenced" poet: "he has no form or manner which is really his own.")[1] Aiken was in the swim of things—in 1915 he was attacking imagism in three *New Republic* articles; he was a close friend of fellow Harvardian T. S. Eliot ("the Tsetse," he called him); and, as he later recalled, "the 'Others' crowd, under the leadership of Kreymborg and W. C. Williams, also drew me somewhat . . . : the general effect of all this being to teach me flexibility, new colors and tones, a new recklessness with form."[2] The experimentalist thrust of the times certainly must have urged Aiken to new insights and new approaches in his work.

The times' epistemological preoccupation certainly stimulated him. In a 1940 essay, "Back to Poetry," he defined the issue as he had come to see it:

> For surely the basis of *all* poetic activity, its *sine qua non*, its very essence, lies in the individual's ability, and need, to isolate for feeling and contemplation the relation "I: World." That, in fact, is the begin-all-end-all business of the poet's life. It is the most private and precious, as it is also the most primitive, of adventures, the adventure which underlies all others: for until he knows himself, and his twinned worlds, the inner and outer, how can he possibly know the worlds, inner or outer, of another? No: uncorrupted by temporal or social or fashionable or ephemeral distractions and disguises, he must first of all keep steady and intense and pure the essentially *lyric* nature of his relation to his own world and moment. It is unquestionably, but inevitably and rightly, the extreme of individualism; but it is the individualism from which ultimately all other human values are derived.*

*A Reviewer's ABC, ed. & intro. Rufus A. Blanshard (Meridan Books, 1958), 98. Aiken's statement is reminiscent of a similar statement of Whitman's. See above, pp. 22.

In an "adventure" so "private and precious," so "primitive," Aiken could see no help or leverage coming from certified knowledge. Quite the opposite. As a young writer he wrote to his young writer friend T. S. Eliot in standard anti-intellectual terms, brimful of impatience with books and yearning for direct contact with life (his choice of Bergson as archtypical intellectualist is probably not quite as ironic as his addressing these comments to the future author of *The Waste Land* and *Ash Wednesday*):

> Dear Tom: Cheers for you. Not only that you're going to be in Cambridge next year, which is joyful news, but also that you have shunted Bergson down the hill. I struggled with the man last summer, a little in the original, but chiefly in a cheap and unintelligible compendium, and I was irritated with him. It seemed to me that he was not in contact with life: or if he was, in his first premises, he soon lost it in images of light and sound. And I always wax impatient with these withered little spiders who spin endless subtleties out of their own inner consciousness, merely using the external world as attacking-points, or points of suspension. — It has become one of my slogans that truth is not subtle, but simple: simple enough for the comprehension of animal nature! In other language, I would trust a dog or a waiter for philosophy that was healthy before I would trust a Bergson. . . .
>
> I am interested, *myself*, in seeing life straight, myself in relation with it, but why bother seeing that anyone else should see it? What do I care about the other damn fools? Whether they live or die, mentally or physically, cannot matter. So why *write* a philosophy? Why indeed *study* philosophy? Why not instead study life, —and arrive at one's own conclusions, instead of "balancing libraries upon one's poll"?[3]

Years later (writing in his autobiographical study, *Ushant*) he looked back on the example of Eliot in nearly the same terms, saying that "the thing, of course was not to retreat; never to avoid the full weight of awareness, and all that it brought, and above all never . . . never seek refuge from it in the comforting placebos of religious or mystical myth or dogma." Some of the best minds had come to that pass, Aiken acknowledges, "including that best of all, the Tsetse's."[4]

In his works Aiken was clearly a knowledge destroyer, using fables and meditations and even direct didacticism to press the attack. The "Argument" he uses as introduction to the first edition of his philosophical fable *The Pilgrimage of Festus*[5] says of his ingenuous protagonist that "It occurs to him that the possibility of knowledge is itself limited: that knowledge is perhaps so conditioned by the conditions of the knower that it can have little but a relative value." At its direst, as here in the first three stanzas of Prelude V from *Time in the Rock*, the destructive need was no pleasant fable for Aiken; destruction of knowledge was a purification rite that involved a descent into the depths of the human sickness and the deconstruction of all understanding.

> Out of your sickness let your sickness speak—
> the bile must have his way—the blood his froth—
> poison will come to the tongue. Is hell your kingdom?
> you know its privies and its purlieus? keep
> sad record of its filth? Why this is health:
> there is no other, save what angels know.
>
> Ravel the pattern backward, to no pattern:
> reduce the granite downward, to no stone:
> unhinge the rainbow to his sun and rain:
> dissolve the blood to water and to salt:
> is this dishevelment we cannot bear?
> The angel is the one who knows his wings!
>
> You came from darkness, and you now remember
> darkness, terror, windows to a world,
> horror of light, cold hands in violence thrust,
> tyrants diastole and systole.
> O cling to warmth, poor child, and press your mouth
> against the warm all-poisoning side of the world.[6]

Aiken's view of the human condition is not always this bleak, although at no point does he imagine that the question of the relationship between the mind and the world can ever be resolved. Those of his works most focused on the question, the collections of poetic meditations *Preludes for Memnon* and *Time in the Rock*, he subtitles "Preludes to Attitude" and "Preludes to Definition," respectively. Critics have charged that he never gets beyond the "prelude" stage in his works, never gets the philosophical substance realized, the attitude focused, the definition fixed. But it is worth considering that the furthest accomplishment of Aiken's art might be in this very inconclusion, the epistemological paradoxes of his day having produced a creative tension which impelled his insight farther and deeper than mere surety could have taken it. He himself certainly viewed the Preludes this way, as his profoundest, most challenging, most personally definitive, and most unresolved works: as he wrote (in a letter to a friend) of the *Memnon* volume,

> Did I say they were an ending? a beginning? they are both, of course. They represent, *partly* intentionally, a process of adjustment to a new "reality"; the first of them was done at a time when suicide was never long out of my mind; the first third of the book during a period when I was never sober for very long, and many of them written moreover when actually tight; the rest of the book with increasing sobriety and —sanity?—or at least with an increased awareness of the process of reorganization and the necessity for it. Anyway, the book makes a kind of spiritual diary, a history of my reflections and backings and fillings on a good many planes—varying from the intensely and immediately personal to the purely speculative and analytic. Knocking softly on wood, I believe it's my best book, and in my rasher moments I believe it's a knockout. But then I've had those delusions before, so I shall wait and see. . . .[The Preludes] are more directly my own voice and mind, in many senses, than anything done before. They make the rest of my poetry look as if I had always been dodging the essential "What" of aiken. Perhaps ten years from now I'll be saying the same thing of these. Here we go round the mulberry bush. The self-remembering self-devouring self-forgetting continuum, new and old at every point.—I find in my own case that poetry increasingly is of use to me in the recognition of what I have been and am going to be; and therefore is itself a process of becoming. Hence my (abandoned) title "Preludes to Attitude and Definition." But this would be too stiff for the Gen. Reader, so it will probably be Preludes for Memnon.[7]

The self the *Preludes* presents and explores is not quite the very personal self of later American confessional poetry (not like the selves of Robert Lowell and Theodore Roethke), but it isn't quite the fictional, hypothetical, or generic self of Crane and Frost (nor, it would be well to remind ourselves, of the epistemological philosophers) either. The search for "the essential 'What' of aiken" is personalized in some of its details, although the central problem is humankind's epistemological predicament. How can we know ourselves? How indeed can we know anything? Aiken's consideration of the problem introduces a fresh element into American identity- and mutability-poetry: the evanescence of identities and forms:

The chairback will cast a shadow on the white wall,
you can observe its shape, the square of paper
will receive and record the impulse of the pencil
and keep it too till time rubs it out
the seed will arrange as suits it the shape of the earth
to right or left thrusting, and the old clock
goes fast or slow as it rusts or is oiled.
These things or others for your consideration
these changes or others, these records
or others less permanent. Come if you will
to the sea's edge, the beach of hard sand,
notice how the wave designs itself in quick bubbles
the wave's ghost etched in bubbles and then gone,
froth of a suggestion, and then gone.
Notice too the path of the wind in a field of wheat,
the motion indicated. Notice in a mirror
how the lips smile, so little, and for so little while.
Notice how little, and how seldom, you notice
the movement of the eyes in your own face, reflection
of a moment's reflection. What were you thinking
to deliver to the glass this instant of change, what margin
belonged only to the expectation of echo
and was calculated perhaps to that end, what was left
essential or immortal?

              Your hand too,
gloved perhaps, encased, but none the less
already bone, already a skeleton,
sharp as a fingerpost that points to time—
what record does it leave, and where, what paper
does it inscribe with an immortal message?
where, and with what permanence, does it say 'I'?
Perhaps giving itself to the lover's hand
or in a farewell, or in a blow,
or in a theft, which will pay interest.
Perhaps in your own pocket, jingling coins,
or against a woman's breast. Perhaps holding
the pencil dictated by another's thought.
These things do not perplex, these things are simple,—
but what of the heart that wishes to survive change

and cannot, its love lost in confusions and dismay—?
what of the thought dispersed in its own algebras,
hypothesis proved fallacy? what of the will
which finds its aim unworthy? Are these, too, simple?[8]

Bergson would have understood and agreed, and so would Niels Bohr. Every seeming object is actually a process in time. Our experience, minutely scrutinized, gives us no indication of the "essential and immortal"; furthermore, when even the examination of my simple physical self yields no permanent "I," my complex and yearning heart, "lost in confusions and dismay," can only confront me with vaster, deeper bewilderment.

Aiken admits, as narrator of *Ushant,* that the basic idea of that highly stylized autobiographical narrative is an inquiry into the fundamental evanescence of experience and the perspectives taken on it. He had dreamed of doing

> that unattempted project, as of a breaking-down of reality into its so many and so deceptive levels, one under another, one behind another, as if one were peeling off the seven or eight layers of time, and language, and meaning, in a thousand-year-old palimpsest—the personalities and the situations alike altering as the light upon them altered. . . . A drama, yes—but let us admit it, a drama without drama, a story without story, in any sense that the books would admit it to be; unless, as perhaps one should, one could agree that the pursuit of this particular sort of Moby Dick (or should one rather call it a Snark), this subliminal of subliminals in consciousness, the slipperiest of elementals shaping itself again and again for a split second, and then lost, and never, when it thus reappeared (only to vanish) looking quite the same—unless one agreed that this pursuit was possibly the most essential of dramas, the very stuff itself of drama, since that pursuit is the central undeviating concern of every living individual human being.[9]

To represent experience as it was experienced, in other words, one needed to jettison the categories and perspectives of certified knowledge—the fixed identities, the logical interrelationships, and the absoluteness of chronological time—and immerse one's imagination in the infinitely complex and absolutely relativistic sea of process. It is the Romantic's yearning to know and grasp It All, and it does not come out very successfully in *Ushant,* which remains (in my view) a periphrastic, artily written autobiography; but its attitude toward accepted knowledge, liberated consciousness, and universal process characterizes it as an important variety of the modernist writer's radical epistemology.

Not just in its evanescence was the world outside ourselves of no particular help in our search for self and meaning. The quotidian world had the capacity to so dominate and preoccupy the mind that all sense of meaning and purpose might be lost. "One's mind was like this," the protagonist of the story "State of Mind" anguishes, "a puddled sidewalk littered with such odds and ends."[10] Searching for meaning, the mind sticks in the clutter, as here in a segment of the first of the *Preludes for Memnon*:

> Here are the bickerings of the inconsequential,
> The chatterings of the ridiculous, the iterations
> Of the meaningless. Memory, like a juggler,
> Tosses its colored balls into the light, and again
> Receives them into darkness. Here is the absurd,
> Grinning like an idiot, and the omnivorous quotidian,
> Which will have its day. A handful of coins,
> Tickets, items from the news, a soiled handkerchief,
> A letter to be answered, notice of a telephone call,
> The petal of a flower in a volume of Shakespeare,
> The program of a concert. The photograph, too,
> Propped on the mantel, and beneath it a dry rosebud;
> The laundry bill, matches, an ash-tray, Utamaro's
> Pearl-fishers. And the rug, on which are still the crumbs
> Of yesterday's feast.[11]

Evanescent then, distractingly cluttered, and also, Aiken would lament in some lyric moods, ultimately unfathomable in the essence of its process is the world to the mind of the seeker:

> Watch long enough, and you will see the leaf
> Fall from the bough. Without a sound it falls:
> And soundless meets the grass. . . . And so you have
> A bare bough, and a dead leaf in dead grass.
> Something has come and gone. And that is all.
>
> But what were all the tumults in this action?
> What wars of atoms in the twig, what ruins,
> Fiery and disastrous, in the leaf?
> Timeless the tumult was, but gave no sign.
> Only, the leaf fell, and the bough is bare.

This is the world: there is no more than this.
The unseen and disastrous prelude, shaking
The trivial act from the terrific action.
Speak: and the ghosts of change, past and to come,
Throng the brief word. The maelstrom has us all.[12]

That sense of inescapable determinism by incomprehensible processes is
the ultimate anguish for the Romantic. Even our mortality, so markedly
implied in this poem, is merely a sign of our greater helplessness. Observed as nonreflexively, as positivistically as possible, an event in nature
gives us nothing we can regard as meaning. Yet even our utterance teems
with the unknowable tumult behind it (and *us*) all.

Aiken saw no hope of positivistic, nonreflexive perception, strictly
speaking, however. To try to know a thing meant to project one's vision,
one's self onto it and attempt to distinguish echo from reverberation. The
procedure was the same as being sentenced to an eternity of frustration
for one who sought Truth or the Thing-in-Itself:

Surround the things with phrases, and perceptions;
master it with all that muscle gives
of mastery to mind,—all strengths, all graces,
flexes and hardnesses; the hand, the foot;
quick touch of delight, recoil of disgust;
and the deep anguish too, the profound anguish,
which bursts its giddy phrase. Surround the thing
with the whole body's wisdom, the whole body's
cunning; all that the fingers have found out,
the palm touched of smoothness or roughness;
the face felt, of coolness or stillness;
the eye known, of mystery in darkness;
the ear found in silence.

Surround the thing with words, mark the thing out
passionately, with all your gestures become words,
patiently, with all your caution become words,
your body a single phrase—

          And what do you say—?
O simply animal, twisted by simple light—!
do you tell space or time what the thing is?
Or do you tell the 'thing' that it is you![13]

The approach might be anything or everything, even an act of love, sensuous and even sensual, yearning and fully devoted—yet one could elicit no response but an echo.

The basic human problem of unrequited self-projection was further complicated by a powerful individual, personal factor: an ego that envisioned the world in self-justifying terms, that was incapable even of knowing the extent of its own sick self-deception. The protagonist of Aiken's second (not at all inconsiderable) novel, *Great Circle*, suspects this about the only meaning he can distill out of his faithless, alcohol-sodden life: "At what point in your spirited dramatization of yourself did the drama become drama for the sake of drama, and cease to be even so justifiable as a dramatic "projection" can be?" Could it even be true, he goes on, "that consciousness itself was a kind of dishonesty? A false simplification of animal existence?" Introspection is another evanescent thing for Aiken, and this moment passes for his protagonist (satirically enough, in a "genial dissipation of ideas, of which he troubled only to feel the weights and vague directions"), but the utter slippage between reality and understanding had been distinctly felt by character, narrator, and reader alike.[14]

It is in this context that Aiken's interest in Freudian psychology impinges on his epistemology.* He sensed that the (Freudian) ego's pervasive need for self-justification is a need to rationalize (where it cannot manage) its promiscuous libidinal drives and to subconsciously suppress (where it could not bear to admit) the traumatic experiences of its personal past. The protagonist of *Great Circle* is a fully paradigmatic case, struggling as he does to maintain his self-respect despite the havoc his libidinousness wreaks in his relationships, and despite the boyhood secret only partly buried in his subconscious—that his mother had been killed in the course of an adulterous passion. The poems give Freudian glimpses that are more fragmentary than this novel's but along similar lines.

Since Aiken conceived so vivid and various an anatomy of humankind's fallibility, it was only natural that he would sometimes use a comic or a sardonic mode (or a sardonic-comic mode) to represent the futility of man's attempting to comprehend, to adjudge, to attitudinize about the vast and teeming universe. The mode and message remind us of Stephen Crane, although the epistemological backgrounds are more complex:

*"Of course Freud was in everything I did, from 1912 on," he said in an interview for the *Paris Review* in September 1963. (*Writers at Work*, fourth series, ed. George Plimpton [Viking, 1976], 38.)

Thus boasting thus grandiloquent he stood
thus eloquent thus orotund he spoke
thus posing like an acrobat he paused
thus like an actor loosed his syllable
the bright the brief the brave, the seeming certain,
and smirked

   upon that stage of his own making
there in the dirty wings on dirty sawdust
against the trumpets of a vivid world.[15]

Or, in another metaphor, he represents man in his pretentious ineffectuality
as

This biped botanist, this man of eyes,
This microscope with legs, who turns the seasons
Under his lens, one grassblade to another,
Pursuing god from leaf to spore, and seed
To calyx.[16]

The human mind and self seem comically ill-equipped in a natural universe impossibly beyond their ken.

The struggle to know — whether comic or tragic, neither or both — was a standoff for Aiken. The mind defines the world for itself in the only ways it can; the world willy-nilly rules the mind, and there we are. It is symbolism and language that give us whatever understanding we can have of the world, of others, of the self, or the nonself, according to Aiken, and symbolism and language have the insuperable disadvantage of being projections, hypotheses, fables of the would-be knower, and therefore are disavailed at their very source. The gap between symbol and referent is absolute:

Despair, that seeking for the ding-an-sich,
The feeling itself, the round bright dark emotion,
The color, the light, the depth, the feathery swiftness
Of you and the thought of you, I fall and fall
From precipice word to chasm word, and shatter
Heart, brain, and spirit on the maddening fact:
If poetry says it, it must speak with a symbol.

What is a symbol? It is the 'man stoops sharp
To clutch a paper that blows in the wind';
It is the 'bed of crocuses bending in the wind,' the

Light, that 'breaks on the water with waves,' the
Wings that 'achieve in the gust the unexpected.'
These, and less than these, and more than these.
The thought, the ghost of thought, the ghost in a mirror.

Catch a beam in your hands, a beam of light,
One bright golden beam, fledgling of dust,
Hold it a moment, and feel its heart, and feel
Ethereal pulse of light between your fingers:
Then let it escape from you, and find its home
In darkness, mother of light: and this will be
Symbol of symbol, clue to clue, auricle of heart.

The glass breaks, and the liquid is spilled; the string
Snaps, and the music stops; the moving cloud
Covers the sun, and the green field is dark.
These too are symbols: and as far and near
As those; they leave the silver core uneaten;
The golden leaf unplucked; the bitter calyx
Virginal; and the whirling You unknown. [17]

Aiken did little in his work to push back the boundaries of poetic
metaphor or language. Faced with what he saw as their absolute limitation, he explored that limitation thematically in some of his poems and
novels and in his autobiography; unlike Stein or Pound, Cummings or
Faulkner, he invented no new techniques of symbolism, no new linguistic
forms or usages. Rather than assaulting epistemological limitations, he
surveyed and worked within them. He definitely had a flair for the creative use of what would later be termed *ambiguity*, however. The relish he
felt for the suppleness of the language-life connection stands out in several passages, such as this one (from the autobiography) describing his
discovery of that complex suppleness:

The series of shapes and symbols . . . which constituted life, or the
language by which one understood life and thus lived it, had suddenly become apparently inexhaustible, extending and exfoliating in
every direction. Dogs and horses in one world, indeed! But what
about a world of symbols so geometrically and psychologically complex, so shimmering with ambivalences and ambiguities, and alge-
braic extensions or equivocations, that one's dazzled awareness simply hadn't time to take them in, and was on the run, on the gallop,
merely to get a fleeting glimpse of them? The semantic richness in-

volved in merely *being* thus aware, and participating, made him feel as if he were himself the perpetually but logically, if unexpectedly and unpredictably, shifting pattern of prismatic hues and forms under the scrutinizing eye of the kaleidoscope: he was the watching and the watched, and the Law was in both, and alike in both.[18]

Language could represent and suggest some of life's (and self's) rich diversity. This was fundamental to the operation of creative imagination—"language extending consciousness and then consciousness extending language, in circular or spiral ascent." If the writer's highest mandate was "to be as conscious as possible,"[19] language's complex ambiguity was his or her finest tool.

Developing the richest possible consciousness was Aiken's ultimate goal; and the operation of the creative imagination—supported by all the candor about self and world one could muster and by all the complex suggestiveness of image and language—constituted his idea of the most effective approach. The majority of his works don't fit this exacting prescription; many of them bear the signs of a talented writer taking the quick route to finishing another job: conventionalized shortcuts, slapdash construction, simplified causalities and implications. Those of his works with the greatest potential for enriched consciousness are those that plumb the newly discovered depths of epistemology. Like Crane and Frost in his view of the absolute gap between mind and world, he goes farther than they, both in exploring the self-aware reflexiveness of the mind and in discovering the ineluctable evanescence of the things of the world.

■ Wallace Stevens: The Mind, the World, and Abstraction

Wallace Stevens like Aiken accepted as "the begin-all-end-all business of the poet's life" the need "to isolate for feeling and contemplation the relation 'I: World.'" As Stevens put it, "Poetry is the statement of a relation between a man and the world";[20] as his friend and interpreter, Frank Doggett, later said, "he found the central concern of his poetry in the estrangement of the self from a world external to it. Perceiver and thing perceived—this fundamental division of the mere fact of being and knowing was the basis of poems as well as conjectures."[21] Stevens accomplished a great deal more than Aiken as an epistemological poet: his is the greater verbal ingenuity and the better ear for word-music; his imagery and symbolism have greater and less-conventional range than Aiken's; he has a greater and less-conventional variety of lyric approaches; and, most obviously, he simply wrote more in this vein and over a greater part of his career. The two men are not merely coincidentally linked because of their epistemological concerns; there was strong respect between them and mutual support. According to Stevens's daughter Holly, when Stevens's poetic career and inspiration were in a funk after the publication of *Harmonium* (1923), when he wrote virtually no poetry for about six years, Conrad Aiken helped him to get restarted, especially by using his own prestige as Pulitzer Prize winner to promote interest in Stevens in England.[22] According to Stevens scholar Peter Brazeau, Aiken's support was less crucial —Stevens began writing again on his own, though Aiken did "start Stevens thinking about writing his first long poem since 'The Comedian as the Letter C.'"[23] Whichever version is truer, more than twenty years later Stevens was influential in the (successful) nomination of Aiken for a National Book Award.[24]

One of the difficult things about generalizing about Stevens is that his works seem to suggest more unanimity of message, more consistency of approach, and (in a longer run) more logic of development than they actually embody. So much of his work interconnects and overlaps that there is a strong tendency for an interpreter to see Stevens only in terms of either a unified metaphysical and/or epistemological philosophy or of a set of insights that constitute an incremental progression to some ultimate and supermature understanding of things. His later work undoubtedly tends to be more explicitly concerned with epistemology than his earlier, but even having said that, one needs to regard Stevens not as a philosopher but as a poet of many moods, many insights (sometimes mutually inconsistent), many experiments, and quite a few put-ons and bagatelles. The best forewarning comes from J. Hillis Miller, in *Poets of Reality*, when he warns that "For each position and for its antithesis there are fully elaborated poems or parts of poems. It is impossible to find a single systematic theory of poetry and life in Stevens."[25] Here, then, let us look at some of Stevens's salient contributions to the age of epistemology without imagining him a wholly consistent epistemologist.

His mode of representing knowledge and knowing is predominantly what has since come to be designated as deconstructive. Deconstructionist critic Paul Bové claims that Stevens's root insight is that "there is no center," that we inhabit "a world with no firm point of reference."[26] However accurate this is as a characterization of all Stevens, we can certainly see in his work at various times the world represented as unstably changing, part human projection; the human mind represented as category-ridden, self-confined, and partial; cognition as tenuous, relative; and representation itself as hypothetical and arbitrary. The anxieties of the age of epistemology possessed his imagination, and he envisioned poetry at its profoundest as defining and bridging the gap between humankind and the bare possibility of our knowing the reality around us: "poetry becomes and is a transcendent analogue composed of the particulars of reality, created by the poet's sense of the world, that is to say his attitude, as he intervenes and interposes the appearances of that sense."[27]

For Stevens the creation of this "transcendent analogue" was a purely individual act, as was the destruction of knowledge that freed the individual to explore reality's frontier. His revolt against knowledge seems to have come principally from immediate, intuitive sources (as had Whitman's),* although the extreme skepticism of George Santayana probably provided him inspiration and encouragement.** Santayana urged the usefulness of total skepticism, even though that attitude was untenable as a philosophical position: "There are certain motives . . . [he said] which render ultimate scepticism precious to a spiritual mind, as a sanctuary from grosser illusions"; and even a casual thinker could benefit from an approach that "accustoms him to discard the dogma which an introspective critic might be tempted to think self-evident, namely that he himself lives and thinks. That he does so is true; but to establish that truth he must appeal to animal faith."[28]

Stevens has similar insights, although more uncompromisingly anti-intellectual. "Poetry must limit itself in respect to intelligence," he wrote to a friend; "there is a point at which intelligence destroys poetry."[29] In "Notes Toward a Supreme Fiction" he says (addressing another friend):

> You must become an ignorant man again
> And see the sun again with an ignorant eye
> And see it clearly in the idea of it.†

In "Sombre Figuration" he develops the idea of a "man below," superior in that he is not deflected in his knowing by rational logic:

*Diane Wood Middlebrook cites the Whitman-Stevens connection in this regard in *Walt Whitman and Wallace Stevens* (Cornell University Press, 1974), 104.

**Santayana was a professor at Harvard at the time Stevens was in attendance, and the two men exchanged sonnets and indicated a good deal of mutual respect. Stevens's library later contained a number of Santayana's works.

†*The Palm at the End of the Mind*, ed. Holly Stevens (Vintage, 1972), 207. Parenthetical page numbers in the discussion of Stevens refer to this collection.

We have grown weary of the man that thinks.
He thinks and it is not true. The man below
Imagines and it is true, as if he thought
By imagining, anti-logician, quick
With a logic of transforming certitudes.[30]

The figure of the rationalist, in Stevens's various representations, "is variously the contemptible modern and the devotee of inflexible Tradition," as Joseph Riddel points out in his study, *The Clairvoyant Eye* (in which he offers a brief survey of Stevens's rationalists from "The Doctor of Geneva" to Canon Aspirin in "Notes Toward a Supreme Fiction").[31] Perhaps the best-known example is that from the early "Six Significant Landscapes" (1916), the sixth and final section, which provides a nearly didactic conclusion for an otherwise imagistic, quasi-Chinese sequence:

Rationalists, wearing hats,
Think, in square rooms,
Looking at the floor,
Looking at the ceiling.
They confine themselves
To right-angled triangles.
If they tried rhomboids,
Cones, waving lines, ellipses—
As, for example, the ellipse of the half-moon—
Rationalists would wear sombreros.
(17)

Rationality, frequently associated in Stevens's poetry (as in Whitman's) with the indoors, here impresses its arbitrary geometry on the imaginations of its devotees, implicitly blinding them to the sorts of natural outdoor insights discovered in the preceding five "landscapes." The academic cap is the outward symbol of this limitation. Twenty-six years after "Six Significant Landscapes," in "Notes Toward a Supreme Fiction," he says that in our specially lucid moments, like those of the "balances that happen" when a man and a woman love,

We more than awaken, sit on the edge of sleep,
As on an elevation, and behold
The academies like structures in a mist.
(213)

Thus, academic knowing is still the limiting delusion, still alien to the real, to which (more shades of Whitman) we get closer through individual human love.

What is included in the rationalism Stevens wanted to destroy varies, from reasoned philosophy (symbolized by the figure of Descartes in "Notes Toward a Supreme Fiction")* to conventionalized poetic metaphor (as in "Sombre Figuration"):

> The spontaneities of rain or snow
> Surprise the sterile rationalist who sees
> Maidens in bloom, bulls under sea, the lark
> On urns and oak-leaves twisted into rhyme.[32]

Thus, the poet's indispensable escape from rationalism involved not only escaping from his own intellectuality but from the stock poetic symbolism of his cultural heritage as well. In another letter to Hi Simons, Stevens stated, "When a poet makes his imagination the imagination of other people, he does so by making them see the world through his eyes. Most modern activity is the undoing of that very job. The world has been painted; most modern activity is getting rid of the paint to get at the world itself. Powerful integrations of the imagination are difficult to get away from."[33] Stated another way, in terms of his own major project, "the first step toward a supreme fiction would be to get rid of all existing fictions. A thing stands out in clean air better than it does in soot."[34] The protagonist of his poem "The Latest Freed Man" experiences his revelation this way: "Tired of the old descriptions of the world," he comes to understand that nature is prior to doctrine or definition—"It was how the sun came shining into his room:/To be without description of to be." Just so is the man's animal (oxlike) nature prior to any thought or cultural definition—"It was how his freedom came./ It was being without description, being an ox" (165–166). The term "animal faith" again comes to mind here, Santayana's particular expression for the only way we know we exist.

In its broadest aspect Stevens's destruction of knowledge was framed within a set of special insights into our familiar problem of the reflexiveness of knowing. His conception of reflexiveness was rich and complex—not always consistent, but very fervent. Some of its main tenets are: (1) that human self-projection needs to be kept rigorously in check—eliminated wherever possible—if knowing is to take place; (2) that knowing entirely

---

*Stevens himself offered this interpretation in a January 12, 1943, letter to Hi Simons (*Letters of Wallace Stevens*, 433).

without self-projection is unachievable; and (3) that reflexiveness known and controlled, synthesized as imagination, can itself provide a means —probably our only means—to discover the structure of the actual world.

First, then, the intricate question of how one was to check reflexiveness and marry the mind to the world. That process began as it had for Pound and Hemingway with an exercise of discipline—for Stevens an exacting, numbing discipline, as in the early poem "The Snow Man" (1921):

> One must have a mind of winter
> To regard the frost and the boughs
> Of the pine-trees crusted with snow;
>
> And have been cold a long time
> To behold the junipers shagged with ice,
> The spruces rough in the distant glitter
>
> Of the January sun; and not to think
> Of any misery of the sound of the wind,
> In the sound of a few leaves,
>
> Which is the sound of the land
> Full of the same wind
> That is blowing in the same bare place
>
> For the listener, who listens in the snow,
> And, nothing himself, beholds
> Nothing that is not there and the nothing that is.
> (54)

There can be no emotion, no self, even, to be distracted by emotion. There actually is no "misery" out there, except what an anthropocentric observer brings to it; one needs to "behold," to "listen," and not "think" or feel. And even at that, the final yield here is just the realization of the two dimensions of "nothing": the one that the numbed observer does not project into the icy boughs and the one the de-peopled place projects in response. It is a demanding program; one must both have the self-discipline necessary to attain this truer view and endure the resultant bleakness of a landscape without anthropomorphic echoes.

How can one identify and counteract one's own innately human tendency toward reflexive perceiving and knowing? It becomes a kind of subgenre of Stevens's lyric, the poem that cites or shows the necessary discipline—early or late, cold or hot, as here in the 1946 "Credences of Summer," part II:

Postpone the anatomy of summer, as
The physical pine, the metaphysical pine.
Let's see the very thing and nothing else.
Let's see it with the hottest fire of sight.
Burn everything not part of it to ash.

Trace the gold sun about the whitened sky
Without evasion by a single metaphor.
Look at it in its essential barrenness
And say this, this is the centre that I seek.
(288)

No metaphors and no generalized, philosophical "anatomy," then, can be allowed into the act of perception. In another version, in "Man Carrying Thing," we learn that all the inferences we have about a perception must be endured, waited out, "a storm of secondary things" like a snowstorm "we must endure all night/ . . . until/ The bright obvious stands motionless in cold." (281) In "The Bed of Old John Zeller" we get a strong counteractive for the mind's habit of projecting its own hopes in its ideas of order:

This structure of ideas, these ghostly sequences
Of the mind, result only in disaster. It follows,
Casual poet, that to add your own disorder to disaster

Makes more of it. It is easy to wish for another structure
Of ideas and to say as usual that there must be
Other ghostly sequences and, it would be, luminous

Sequences, thought of among spheres in the old peak of night:
This is the habit of wishing, as if one's grandfather lay
In one's heart and wished as he had always wished, unable

To sleep in that bed for its disorder, talking of ghostly
Sequences that would be sleep and ting-tang tossing, so that
He might slowly forget. It is more difficult to evade

That habit of wishing and to accept the structure
Of things as the structure of ideas. It was the structure
Of things at least that was thought of in the old peak of night.
(263–264)

By 1949 Stevens was probably the premier poet of epistemological self-awareness and self-restraint, and he tried in "An Ordinary Evening in

New Haven" "to get as close to the ordinary, the commonplace and ugly as it is possible for a poet to get. It is not a question of grim reality but of plain reality. The object of course is to purge oneself of anything false."[35] He even built that poem around a statement of the nature of this lifelong quest, in terms utterly explicit, uncompromisingly proscriptive, and astoundingly, naively idealistic:

> We keep coming back and coming back
> To the real: to the hotel instead of the hymns
> That fall upon it out of the wind. We seek
>
> The poem of pure reality, untouched
> By trope or deviation, straight to the word,
> Straight to the transfixing object, to the object
>
> At the exactest point at which it is itself,
> Transfixing by being purely what it is,
> A view of New Haven, say, though the certain eye,
>
> The eye made clear of uncertainty, with the sight
> Of simple seeing, without reflection. We seek
> Nothing beyond reality.
> (336)

In some of his poems Stevens counted on the basic inherent richness of things-in-themselves to make his hoped-for encounter with reality more than an exercise in discipline and disappointment. It was a faith he had throughout his career that there was something especially rewarding in the otherness of the other.* Entries from his journal of 1899 (age 20) again and again express his preference for unmediated Nature—"no one paints Nature's colors as well as Nature's self. . . . Out in the open air with plenty of time and space I felt how different literary emotions were from natural feelings"[36]—and so forth, in the conventional terms of the Romantic's escape to Nature. But the belief in the richness of the nonhuman world persisted in his mind, in numerous forms. Perhaps, as critic David P. Young suggests, it is relatable to the influence of Santayana, who got from William James that deep respect for the suprarational flux, that complexity of contingencies.[37]

---

*J. Hillis Miller's ingenious *Poets of Reality* examines this motif as manifesting a kind of surrogate religion for Stevens, and, in different ways, for Conrad, Eliot, Williams, Yeats, and Thomas.

At the end of his career in an essay entitled "On Poetic Truth,"* Stevens stated of poetry,

> its function, the need which it meets and which has to be met in some way in every age that is not to become decadent or barbarous is precisely this contact with reality as it impinges on us from the outside, the sense that we can touch and feel a solid reality which does not wholly dissolve itself into the conceptions of our own minds. It is the individual and particular that does this. And the wonder and mystery of art, as indeed of religion in the last resort, is the revelation of something "wholly other" by which the inexpressible loneliness of thinking is broken and enriched. To know facts as facts in the ordinary way has, indeed, no particular power or worth. But a quickening of our awareness of the irrevocability by which a thing is what it is, has such power, and it is, I believe, the very soul of art.[38]

His "Study of Two Pears" takes one sort of approach, reveling, in its purely descriptive, implicit way, in the sensuous otherness of the fruit:

I

Opusculum paedagogum.
The pears are not viols,
Nudes or bottles.
They resemble nothing else.

II

They are yellow forms
Composed of curves
Bulging toward the base.
They are touched red.

III

They are not flat surfaces
Having curved outlines.
They are round
Tapering toward the top.

---

*Published in *Opus Posthumous* (ed. & intro. Samuel French Morse [Knopf, 1957], 235–238) and conjecturally dated 1954, although the first two sentences were taken verbatim from Stevens's 1948 essay, "About One of Marianne Moore's Poems" (*Necessary Angel*, 96).

IV

In the way they are modelled
There are bits of blue.
A hard dry leaf hangs
From the stem.

V

The yellow glistens.
It glistens with various yellows,
Citrons, oranges and greens
Flowering over the skin.

VI

The shadows of the pears
Are blobs on the green cloth.
The pears are not seen
As the observer wills.

(159)

As Stevens represents it, there can be significant rewards, emotional
as well as intellectual, for achieving the dehumanization of knowing. And
these rewards can come from apprehending reality's rich and intercom-
plicated variety as well as the sheer otherness of its specific forms. "The
greatest poverty is not to live/ In a physical world," he claims in the concluding section of "Esthétique du Mal," and he attempts to show that the
act of internalizing the diverse otherness of the world, despite its considerable hazards, has considerable rewards:

And out of what one sees and hears and out
Of what one feels, who could have thought to make
So many selves, so many sensuous worlds,
As if the air, the mid-day air, was swarming
With the metaphysical changes that occur,
Merely in living as and where we live.

(263)

"A poet feels *abundantly* the poetry of everything," he affirms in one of his
"Adagia."[39]

Part of Stevens's disciplining of reflexiveness seems to have followed
from his implicit insight that our cognition naturally and falsely tends (1)
to represent separate objects as having independent existence, absolute
identityhood, and (2) to represent them as timeless, or frozen in time. I

call it "implicit insight" because while he rarely addresses these particular idols of the mind explicitly, he repeatedly writes poems that discover—as if by eluding the normal habits of perception—reality's basic contextuality and flux. The insights are, of course, strikingly Bergsonian/Jamesian, although the degree to which they were actually influenced by either philosopher is undeterminable. In a 1942 essay, "The Noble Rider and the Sound of Words," Stevens cited Bergson and a Dr. Joad, a commentator who posed the issue this way: since external things are made up of vibration and change, "how, then, does the world come to appear to us as a collection of solid, static objects extended in space? Because of the intellect, which presents us with a false view of it." At that point in his career Stevens avers that "the subject matter of poetry is not that 'collection of solid, static objects extended in space' but the life that is lived in the scene it composes; and so reality is not that external scene but the life that is lived in it."[40] Obviously the Bergsonian formulation struck a responsive chord in Stevens at this point; how much it had influenced his poetry of twenty or so years earlier is unknown. At least since the early twenties Stevens had been exploring the themes of contextuality and flux, although they emerge from representations of immediate perception or rectified apprehension, with no traces of Bergsonian or Jamesian principles or terminology, despite the coincidental revelations.

The contextuality of reality is central in "Anecdote of the Jar" (the "round" jar and "slovenly wilderness" modifying and revealing each other, providing an existential arrangement, like Williams' wheelbarrow and chickens); contextuality is implied in "The Idea of Order at Key West" (the sea and the song, the night and the observer comprising a special here-and-nowness); and it is played with in "Sea Surface Full of Clouds" (juxtaposing five seascapes, all using the same props, the same "collection of solid, static objects extended in space," but with radically different colors, tones, and significances—from "chop-house chocolate/And sham umbrellas" to "porcelain chocolate/And pied umbrellas" [90]). Part V of "Thirteen Ways of Looking at a Blackbird" shows the special subtlety of Stevens's contextual sense, a subtlety not at all related to Jamesian concepts of language, but clearly of the same mind-set as James when he decided that "the *feeling* of the thunder is also a feeling of the silence as just gone" (above, pp. 90–91).

> I do not know which to prefer,
> The beauty of inflections
> Or the beauty of innuendoes,

The blackbird whistling
Or just after.
(20)

The time context is process, flux, as Stevens represented it. Reality is in flux, experience is in flux, the self is in flux: this is what one could discover when freed from one's preoccupations with absolute entities. Roy Harvey Pearce characterizes even Stevens's early poetry this way: "the driving concern of the poems in *Harmonium* (1923, 1931) is with the sensuously flowing aspect of reality as we come to know, partake of, and thus to inform it."[41] In the poems Stevens wrote in the late stages of his career he treated this "flowing aspect of reality" explicitly, as a subject in itself, and with a clearer sense of mutability and morality than he had earlier. In "This Solitude of Cataracts" (from *Auroras of Autumn*, 1950) the speaker's reflexive habit of mind is no more than a futile wish to be stable, "in a permanent realization," . . . "released from destruction"; but to have such a realization, Stevens points out, one would have to be an artifact, an antiquity. The poem represents an ultimate stage of Stevens's explorations of the themes of reflexiveness and flux:

He never felt twice the same about the flecked river,
Which kept flowing and never the same way twice, flowing

Through many places, as if it stood still in one,
Fixed like a lake on which the wild ducks fluttered,

Ruffling its common reflections, thought-like Monadnocks.
There seemed to be an apostrophe that was not spoken.

There was so much that was real that was not real at all.
He wanted to feel the same way over and over.

He wanted the river to go on flowing the same way,
To keep on flowing. He wanted to walk beside it,

Under the buttonwoods, beneath a moon nailed fast.
He wanted his heart to stop beating and his mind to rest

In a permanent realization, without any wild ducks
Or mountains that were not mountains, just to know how it would
   be,

Just to know how it would feel, released from destruction,
To be a bronze man breathing under archaic lapis,

Without the oscillations of planetary pass-pass,
Breathing his bronzed breath at the azury centre of time.
(321–322)

At the close of "An Ordinary Evening in New Haven" Stevens in his own voice explains the transitory-in-essence reality he has been trying to discover through the poem (it sounds a great deal like Aiken on the same theme):

These are the edgings and inchings of final form,
The swarming activities of the formulae
Of statement, directly and indirectly getting at,

Like an evening evoking the spectrum of violet,
A philosopher practicing scales on his piano,
A woman writing a note and tearing it up.

It is not in the premise that reality
Is a solid. It may be a shade that traverses
A dust, a force that traverses a shade.
(351)

Even in their form his late meditative poems, like "An Ordinary Evening," move with the rhythm of transitoriness; as Joseph Riddel points out, Stevens's purpose there is "to catch the activity of the mind as it creates and dissolves (decreates) ideas of forms, creating others in the same process. This was the life of the mind, the 'never-ending meditation' (CP 465), and he came to accept it, for better or worse, as what men of imagination do every instant, as well as in formal poems."[42]

In many of Stevens's formulations the message is not only that one needs to discover and keep in check his or her self-projective tendencies in attempting to perceive and relate to the outside world, but also that perceiving and relating are inescapably self-projective: the first and only universal category of knowing is the human self. Santayana's philosophy of critical realism had taught that "the mind affords a true expression of the world," but one that is inescapably "rendered in vital perspectives and human terms."[43] Stevens, ranging more imaginatively into relativity (somewhat like Einstein) truly put knowing into the realm of the hypothetical, the inconclusive, and the viewpoint-determined.

Conglomerating was one of his principal techniques, and as his work explored a variety of subjects and themes, visions and moods and viewpoints, it developed a diverse and heterogeneous "world," an atomic con-

glomeration of verbal-visual as-ifs. Sometimes this conglomeration is itself imitated in particular poems, such as "Thirteen Ways of Looking at a
Blackbird," and "Like Decorations in a Nigger Cemetery," in which there
are many separate visions but (to push the Einsteinian analogy a step
farther) no "specifically privileged coordinate system."* At other times its
relativistic basis is explored in one degree of explicitness or another, as
here in "Of the Surface of Things" from *Harmonium*:

I

In my room, the world is beyond my understanding;
But when I walk I see that it consists of three or four hills and a
    cloud.

II

From my balcony, I survey the yellow air,
Reading where I have written,
"The spring is like a belle undressing."

III

The gold tree is blue.
The singer has pulled his cloak over his head
The moon is in the folds of the cloak.[44]

The reality is never directly accessible, is always shaped and colored and
cloaked with meaning by the perceiving mind, as it is shown to be in a
parable in "Notes Toward a Supreme Fiction": the character Nanzia Nun-
cio, having sought and found Ozymandias, stands bare before him, saying

I am the woman stripped more nakedly
Than nakedness, standing before an inflexible
Order, saying I am the contemplated spouse. . . .

Then Ozymandias said the spouse, the bride
Is never naked. A fictive covering
Weaves always glistening from the heart and mind.
(222)

But in many of Stevens's poems and prose statements, especially later
in his career, there was another phase to his consideration of the problem
of mind and world, a phase in which he attempted to go beyond the

---

*One might just as profitably suggest the analogies of the cubist system of painting,
Melville's whale, Marianne Moore's estridge ("He Digesteth Hard Yron") or another.
This conglomerative habit is strong among nonabsolutists.

seemingly hopeless dilemma of dualism he and Aiken (and others) anatomized so candidly and meticulously, to some synthetic insight that was deeper or higher, some connection-to-reality that was realer than naive knowing. *Imagination* was the term by which he designated the means of attaining this insight-beyond-knowledge, and although its nature and (I would maintain) its several theoretical end products are unexceptional, its method of functioning is not.* Stevens had the intuition that the way out of the reflexiveness problem was through it, by the obvious, intentional, and ingenious application of reflexiveness itself. The operant assumption is that whatever reality is potentially out there can be discovered only in the new reality that is created by the interpenetration of the imagination and the "other." "The Man With the Blue Guitar" provided, as both explanation and exemplum, the culture's most memorable banner of this new literary epistemology:

> The man bent over his guitar,
> A shearsman of sorts. The day was green.
>
> They said, "You have a blue guitar,
> You do not play things as they are."
>
> The man replied, "Things as they are
> Are changed upon the blue guitar."
>
> And they said then, "But play, you must,
> A tune beyond us, yet ourselves,
>
> A tune upon the blue guitar
> Of things exactly as they are."
> (133)

And there was for Stevens more in this designedly reflexive approach than whatever it is that gets a flying bat through a maze of wires. In terms of the discovery of ultimacies, it was the operation of the imagination that could become, Stevens theorized late in his career, the modern age's surrogate for its lost religion:

> in an age in which disbelief is so profoundly prevalent or, if not disbelief, indifference to questions of belief, poetry and painting, and

---

*For an interesting discussion of Stevens's concept of the imagination compared to that of William Carlos Williams and related to the traditions of neoclassism, romanticism, and modernism, see Albert Gelpi, *Wallace Stevens: The Poetics of Modernism* (Cambridge University Press, 1985), 4–8.

the arts in general, are, in their measure, a compensation for what has been lost. Men feel that the imagination is the next greatest power to faith: the reigning prince. Consequently their interest in the imagination and its work is to be regarded not as a phase of humanism but as a vital self-assertion in a world in which nothing but the self remains, if that remains. So regarded, the study of the imagination and the study of reality come to appear to be purified, aggrandized, fateful.[45]

Stevens's explicit definitions of imagination were neither probing, original, nor collectively quite tenable. For him *imagination* was both an absolute entity and a loosely inclusive category that contained virtually all constructive mental functions not narrowly classifiable as reason. He conceived of it, variously, as the capacity that went beyond the mere apprehension of isolated facts, that connected them and established their patterns and contexts and significances; as the capacity that added involvement and feeling to realism; as the expression of the individuality of the poet; as the vessel of both conscious and subconscious intuitions; as the source of consolation and reassurance in a drab and oppressive world; and as the essence of metaphysics, yet the antithesis of reason.

With his concept of imagination Stevens kept all of philosophy at arm's length while he was grappling with some of its questions, classic and modern, in his own very individual way. Whatever interested him about philosophy, it wasn't philosophers' analyses, their methods, or their approaches to mentality; his letters are full of disclaimers such as "I have read a little of Whitehead but not seriously"; "about Santayana[:] I never took any of his courses and I don't believe I ever heard him lecture. But I knew him quite well"; and "I have never studied systematic philosophy and should be bored to death at the mere thought of doing so."[46] When late in his career he did attempt to study and write an essay explicitly about philosophy, he began with a request for help to Jean Wahl, saying "I have in mind ideas that are inherently poetic, as, for example, the concept of the infinity of the world"[47]—thus maintaining the poetic imagination as the governing category of all his philosophy.* Looking back from 1953

---

*A number of Stevens scholars have noted his antidisciplinary approach to philosophy. Frank Doggett (*Stevens' Poetry of Thought*, 213) claims that "he never goes into any of his ideas . . . far enough to relate him [to specific philosophers] other than as an eclectic reader"; Joseph Riddel (*The Clairvoyant Eye*, 37) says "the evidence of Stevens' prose reveals that he had read in almost every modern philosopher and, except in a very general sense, understood almost none." Well worth considering in this context, however, is the careful correlation of Stevens's ideas and practices with Santayana's in David on his own development he wrote to Bernard Heringman, "While, of course, I come down from the past, the past is my own and not something marked Coleridge, Wordsworth, etc. I know of no one who has been particularly important to me. My reality-imagination complex is entirely my own even though I see it in others."[48]

Stevens saw the product of imagination as poetry, just as philosophy was the product of reason. The speculative problems with which the two dealt were the same: "the point is that poetry is to a large extent an art of perception and that the problems of perception as they are developed in philosophy resemble similar problems in poetry."[49] Santayana had years before insisted that there was just such an essential similarity between poetry and philosophy, an advocacy that cost him dearly in the estimations of fellow philosophers, especially the scientifically oriented. Stevens, while denying all philosophical influences, focused his approach on the poet's relation to his own subjective imagination:

> Professor Eucalyptus said, "The search
> For reality is as momentous as
> The search for god." It is the philosopher's search
>
> For an interior made exterior
> And the poet's search for the same exterior made
> Interior: breathless things broodingly abreath
>
> With the inhalations of original cold
> And of original earliness.[50]

Thus although philosophy was Stevens's preoccupation, it was rarely his endeavor; in his poetry philosophical ideas are glimpsed or shadowed but not relied upon or derived.

While the imagination could flirt with philosophy, it needed to be married to reality to do its fullest and most rewarding job. Poetry is "an interdependence of the imagination and reality as equals,"[51] Stevens said. Although he acknowledged that the precise balance of the mix would (and should) vary, what mattered the most about his poems, he reflected in 1953, was that they were, quite literally, grounded:

> *The Planet on the Table*
>
> Ariel was glad he had written his poems.

P. Young, "A Skeptical Music: Stevens and Santayana," *Criticism* 7 (Summer 1965), 263–283.

They were of a remembered time
Or of something seen that he liked.

Other makings of the sun
Were waste and welter
And the ripe shrub writhed.

His self and the sun were one
And his poems, although makings of his self,
Were no less makings of the sun.

It was not important that they survive.
What mattered was that they should bear
Some lineament or character,

Some affluence, if only half-perceived,
In the poverty of their words,
Of the planet of which they were part.
(386)

It would seem then that for Stevens the poetic imagination was (among other things) an instrument of knowing and the finest that humankind had. Its finest employment involved the conscious application of a complex discipline: certified knowledge had to be excluded, philosophical thinking limited to a resonance; inherent human reflexiveness exposed for what it was and used to produce only avowedly relativistic visions, and the internal stream of image and insight carefully bent to the contours of the outside world.

Sometimes—more frequently in the latter part of his career—Stevens employed his carefully disciplined imagination to attain to some sort of ultimacy of knowing. When he did, the result was something like the "lesson of inherency" Whitman learned in contemplating his favorite yellow poplar tree (pp. 20–21, above), but with a special quality that made it even more intricately abstract than Emerson's Platonism. It was no ideal-form-within-things nor even a transcendental God, but an abstract essence that was more like a quality, half from the real world and half from the informing imagination of the disciplined intuiter. Whereas for Whitman the naming words themselves had had the magic to evoke the inherency of things, for Stevens "the imagination is the only genius. It is intrepid and eager and the extreme of its achievement lies in abstraction."[52]

Santayana had espoused a "realm of essence" that resembled in several important respects the plane of abstraction to which Stevens aspired.

Santayana's particular brand of critical realism identified *essences* as the ultimate data of perception and understanding: "The realm of essence . . . is simply the unwritten catalogue, prosaic and infinite, of all the characters possessed by such things as happen to exist, together with the characters which all different things would possess if they existed."[53] Stevens's realm of abstraction was less clear in its conceptual and verbal boundaries, and he had various ways of referring to it throughout his career. If we simplify their categorization, we can identify three basic ways in which he conceived of his realm of abstraction: (1) as a kind of ur-poetry within certain poems and ideas and things; (2) as a "fiction"—in its most abstract, inclusive form, a "supreme fiction"; and (3) as a "first idea." Let us consider each of these in turn to discover the importance of abstraction in Stevens's works.

The idea of an inherent ur-poetry was predominantly an idea from his early career. As articulated in "A Primitive Like an Orb," it was "the essential poem at the centre of things," an essence manifested fitfully, imperfectly, transiently, as were the Platonic pure forms—"something seen and known in lesser poems," as

> in the instant of speech,
> The breadth of an accelerando moves,
> Captives the being, widens—and was there.
> (317)

The concept is a refinement in abstraction of a very Emersonian-Whitmanesque insight he had had as a young man of twenty when he wrote in his journal, "I'm completely satisfied that behind every physical fact there is a divine force. Don't, therefore, look *at* facts, but *through* them."[54] He was following the same tack when over fifty years later he asserted in an essay, "The Relations between Poetry and Painting," that "there is a universal poetry that is reflected in everything. . . . We find the poetry of mankind in the figures of the old men of Shakespeare, say, and the old men of Rembrandt."[55] The aforementioned search through philosophy for "ideas that are inherently poetic" (p. 258) was part of that same impulse. Sometimes he defined that abstract quality-essence as "pure poetry," and sometimes he elevated its pursuit to a status even higher (because it is more abstract, more quintessential) than the pursuit of the idea of God; as Stevens explained in a 1940 letter to Hi Simons about his poem "The Greenest Continent": "The idea of God is a thing of the imagination. We no longer think that God was, but was imagined. The idea of pure poetry, essential imagination, as the highest objective of the poet, appears to be, at least potentially, as great as the idea of God, and, for that matter, greater, if the idea of God is only one of the things of the imagination."[56]

Stevens's second kind of approach to the realm of abstraction, his concept of a "fiction," is none too precise,* but he seems to have used that term to refer to a construct of the imagination, a hypothetical model of some aspect of that abstract ultimacy that underlies all reality and informs specific poems only fitfully. He shared with Santayana the premise that the ultimate realm of meaning is fictive or hypothesized.[57] ("Does not modern philosophy teach that our idea of the so-called real world is also a work of the imagination?" Santayana had queried.)[58]

Stevens's idea of a "fiction" was more like a positivistic scientific hypothesis than a religious belief insofar as it was avowedly projected, gratuitously and virtually experimentally; yet it was more like a religious intuition insofar as its objective referent was supposedly an ultimate, all-pervasive inherency. The use of the "fiction" was Stevens's grand affirmation of the constructive use of reflexiveness at the same time that it was also an exercise of existentialistic religious faith: "The final belief is to believe in a fiction, which you know to be a fiction, there being nothing else. The exquisite truth is to know that it is a fiction and that you believe in it willingly."[59] A "supreme fiction," then, was a meta-fiction comprised of a broad, possibly exhaustive, combination of all conceivable fictions. His "Notes Toward" such a colossal abstraction were necessarily fragmentary: "As I see the subject, it could occupy a school of rabbis for the next few generations. In trying to create something as valid as the idea of God has been, and for that matter remains, the first necessity seems to be breadth."[60]

Stevens's third approach to the realm of abstraction, the concept of the "first idea," emphasizes the element of otherness in his ultimacy-abstraction. "There is a huge abstraction, venerable and articulate and complete, that has no reference to us, accessible to poets . . . ," he explained in a letter to Hi Simons,[61] elucidating these lines from "Notes Toward a Supreme Fiction":

---

*For example, in attempting to explain "Notes toward a Supreme Fiction" in a 1943 letter, he said: "I ought to say that I have not defined a supreme fiction. A man as familiar with my things as you are will be justified in thinking that I mean poetry. I don't want to say that I don't mean poetry; I don't know what I mean. The next thing for me to do will be to try to be a little more precise about this enigma. I hold off from even attempting that because, as soon as I start to rationalize, I lose the poetry of the idea. In principle there appear to be certain characteristics of a supreme fiction *and the NOTES is confined to a statement of a few of those characteristics* (*Letters of Wallace Stevens*, 435).

But the first idea was not to shape the clouds
In imitation. The clouds preceded us

There was a muddy centre before we breathed.
There was a myth before the myth began,
Venerable and articulate and complete.

(210)

Thus "the first idea was not our own," and although in its pure and primal and eternal actuality it is unconceptualizable by humankind, still "The poem refreshes life, so that we share,/ For a moment, the first idea" (209). That sharing is possible because the first idea is some part of our own makeup as well, he seems to infer at times (even highly memorable times in his own poetry of the thirties):

Oh! Blessed rage for order, pale Ramon,
The maker's rage to order words of the sea,
Words of the fragrant portals, dimly-starred,
And of ourselves and of our origins,
In ghostlier demarcations, keener sounds.[62]

Not just the rage for order, but something of the primal, ultimate order itself is inherent in us and is occasionally glimpsed through our words. Thus, at the farthest reaches of his metaphysical imagination, at the deepest moments of his absorption in the felt abstraction, Stevens knew a reassurance utterly unlike the despairing, rootless relativism of Aiken and so many other modernist contemporaries. The playfulness, the audacity, the iconoclasm of his other poetic moods could expand freely and unthreateningly in a consciousness firmly, religiously anchored in an overarching, indwelling secular abstraction. It was like the fulfillment of Santayana's promise:

Thus a mind enlightened by scepticism and cured of noisy dogma, a mind discounting all reports, and free from all tormenting anxiety about its own fortunes or existence, finds in the wilderness of essence a very sweet and marvellous solitude. The ultimate reaches of doubt and renunciation open out for it, by an easy transition, into fields of endless variety and peace, as if through the gorges of death it had passed into a paradise where all things are crystallised into the image of themselves, and have lost their urgency and their venom.[63]

Thus abstraction, in various forms and contexts, was at the heart of Stevens's poetic creativity.* And he knew this was the case; the measure of a poet, he avowed in an essay in the early forties, "is the measure of his power to abstract himself, and to withdraw with him into his abstraction the reality on which the lovers of truth insist. He must be able to abstract himself and also to abstract reality, which he does by placing it in his imagination."[64] The result was to be a purified knowledge, as near to absolute as could be.

The consequences in Stevens's poetic practice that followed from his program of abstraction gave it many of its defining characteristics. Its impersonality, for one thing: what Stevens often gives us is generic meditation —deeply involved in the meditator's experience with perceived objects, landscapes, and tones, with the interplay of epistemological vistas, but rarely (unlike Aiken) with his individual cares, fears, or relationships. Its characteristic diction, for another thing: the language of the poems is a generalized literary language with nothing like Williams's striving for individual particularity or actual vernacular. Thus, at their most concrete level his poems represent generalized trees and clouds, men and meditations, and they often reveal or build to even more abstract levels of realization. As Louis Martz remembers, Stevens mused about his generalizing process in admitting how "An Ordinary Evening in New Haven" developed from a set of specific impressions to what it finally became:

> "I just fixed on this idea of a poem about a walk in New Haven, but then branching out." He said it really got so far away from the base that New Haven hardly appears in it. "It's only the title, really, but," he said, "that's the way things happen with me. I start with a concrete thing, and it tends to become so generalized that it isn't any longer a local place. I think that puzzles some people."[65]

Much of Stevens's originality stems from this impersonal generation and manipulation of abstractions. The standard sort of knowledge that he has put aside is replaced, at least in higher realms, by abstraction-pyramids that produce not only ultimacies like "first ideas," but generalities like "imagination," "self," "harmony," and "reality," which are likewise unique combinations of reification and indeterminacy—"fictions," in effect. And predictably enough, he works the whole process in the

---

*Joseph Riddel makes the point that "one phase of the history of Stevens's development has been his jockeying of attitudes toward abstraction, the abstracting imagination, and the reality of language that is by definition abstract" (Clairvoyant Eye, 166).

other direction too, embodying generalizations in (relatively) more concrete symbols. In a 1953 letter he cites a pair of salient examples in explaining the process:

> It is difficult for me to think and not to think abstractly. Consequently,
> in order to avoid abstractness, in writing, I search out instinctively
> things that express the abstract and yet are not in themselves abstrac-
> tions. For instance, the STATUE about which I am doing a great deal
> of writing now-a-days was, in the poem which appeared in the
> SOUTHERN REVIEW a symbol for art, art being a word that I have
> never used and never can use without some feeling of repugnance.
> In MR. BURNSHAW, etc., the same statue is also a symbol, but not
> specifically a symbol for art; its use has been somewhat broadened
> and, so far as I have defined it at all, it is a symbol for things as they
> are.[66]

Abstraction is his will and his way, then, the pinnacle of his achievement in that line being his own personal twentieth-century secular
transcendentalism.

But in all of Stevens's transmuting of abstractions into symbols and
symbols into abstractions there is another element than reality probing,
and that is his sheer linguistic virtuousity. His word choices are bizarre,
surprising, figuratively offbeat—to the point of obscurity, at times—and
they seem to indicate at one and the same time an absolute antipathy to
direct and ordinary ways of saying ordinary things, and a thoroughgoing
faith that genuine insight can be generated by verbal means. Stevens is
the modern master of both periphrasis and verbal epiphany.

In his earlier poetry much of the periphrasis, the verbalistic transmutation, is pure play. Take, for example, this rather gratuitous passage
that serves as an invocation to part VI of "The Comedian as the Letter
C":

> Portentous enunciation, syllable
> To blessed syllable affined, and sound
> Bubbling felicity in cantilene,
> Prolific and tormenting tenderness
> Of music, as it comes to unison,
> Forgather and bell boldly Crispin's last
> Deduction. Thrum with a proud douceur
> His grand pronunciamento and devise.
> (72)

The relish of language, the ornately artificial pose, and the clangor are virtually Elizabethan—even euphuistic; only the radicalness of the self-satire and the near-nihilistic sense that language can be almost entirely referentless mark it as modernist. It is a self-aware extreme of the habit of elegant indirection; as Herbert J. Stern stated, "Stevens *does* frequently choose uncommon words as elegant substitutes for plain terms, and he chooses them because of his acute dissatisfaction with the plainness which even in 1900 seemed to him characteristic of our time and place." As Stern shows, Stevens identified the philosophy behind his predilection for euphuism in saying "Euphuism had its origin in the desire for elegance" and in linking elegance to a basic "desire to enjoy reality."* We might also cite Stevens's statement in his appreciation of Marianne Moore's poetic transmutations: "To confront fact in its total bleakness is for any poet a completely baffling experience."[67]

In his later poetry Stevens's elegant indirection is often less exuberant, more an effort to approach the truth through successive approximations while still avoiding twentieth-century plainness. Here in "Description Without Place" (1945) he tries to get at what must have been the quality of Nietzsche's introspections:

Nietzsche in Basel studied the deep pool
Of these discolorations, mastering

The moving and the moving of their forms
In the much-mottled motion of blank time.

His revery was the deepness of the pool,
The very pool, his thoughts the colored forms,

The eccentric souvenirs of human shapes,
Wrapped in their seemings, crowd on curious crowd,

In a kind of total affluence, all first,
All final, colors subjected in revery

To an innate grandiose, an innate light,
The sun of Nietzsche gildering the pool,

Wallace Stevens: Art of Uncertainty (University of Michigan Press, 1966), 43–44. See too David P. Young, "A Skeptical Music," 263–283, which interestingly connects Stevens with Santayana on the subject of Euphuism.

Yes: gildering the swarm-like manias
In perpetual revolution, round and round.
(273–274)

The indirection here is at times forced, a metaphorist's straining not to say the obvious thing, and at times ("the deep pool/ Of these discolorations," "The eccentric souvenirs of human shapes/ Wrapped in their seemings") an access of new insight.

It was indeed Stevens's faith that energy and radical ingenuity applied to language could produce new insight, consolation, even excitement. The dictionary was a great resource and fascination for him: when his insurance company coworkers marshaled their recollections of him they were likely to remember how he loved it, referring to it, reading it, relishing it.[68] And Stevens himself could say of language in "Esthétique du Mal," "Natives of poverty, children of malheur,/ The gaiety of language is our seigneur" (260). J. Hillis Miller has very aptly likened Stevens's linguistic virtuousity to modern painters, who

> have used various techniques (cubism, abstractionism, multiple simultaneous perspectives, fauve color, and so on) to destroy stale ways of seeing reality. . . . The poet seeks unusual ways of speaking which will nevertheless strike the reader as fitting. This is achieved by rhythm, rhyme, alliteration, manipulation of syntax, and above all by diction. The most salient quality of *Harmonium* is the elegance, the finicky fastidiousness, even sometimes the ornate foppishness, of the language. Again and again strange words like "spick," "girandoles," "quirky," "clippered," "lacustrine," "princox," "alquazil," or "chirr" turn out, as R. P. Blackmur and others have seen, to be most exact in sound, texture, and meaning. These words, rescued from oblivion in the dictionaries or sometimes coined by the poet, cooperate with the words around them to create an atmosphere as rich and strange as that of a painting by Matisse or Dufy, and as much a new revelation of reality.

Miller's study goes on to specify how Stevens's linguistic techniques reveal a new sense of time and process: "the flittering of single words or phrases, a sequence of metamorphoses or of phrases in apposition, the expression of the nuances of secondary things, the presentation of a world of swarming plentitude—these are Stevens's means of expressing the mobility of the moment."[69]

In a sense, then, we can see Stevens as a poet more playful than profound—or, more precisely, one who is often more profound through his playfulness than through his profundity. His intricate and various epistemological insights—the idea-foci of his work, in fact—were, though he virtually created them himself, very much in the air in the teens and twenties and thirties, through the work of Santayana and William James, Einstein, Wittgenstein and Duchamp, Stephen Crane, Gertrude Stein and Conrad Aiken. What Stevens did with words, however, was and continues to be puzzling, challenging, unique. Confronted by the whipping of "concupiscent curds" by "the roller of big cigars" or the "exchequering from piebald fiscs unkeyed," we lose a good deal of confidence in the absoluteness of our interpretive bearings; we sense—rather than know or recognize—what it means if "the only emperor is the emperor of ice-cream" or if a search for metaphor comes up against "the vital, arrogant, fatal, dominant X"; and at times we can feel a new sense of realization in the relationship of imagination, mind, and world in the imagery, the sound, and the virtuousity of Stevens's words, as here, in the last of his published poems:

Of Mere Being
The palm at the end of the mind,
Beyond the last thought, rises
In the bronze decor,

A gold-feathered bird
Sings in the palm, without human meaning,
Without human feeling, a foreign song.

You know then that it is not the reason
That makes us happy or unhappy.
The bird sings. Its feathers shine.

The palm stands on the edge of space.
The wind moves slowly in the branches.
The bird's fire-fangled feathers dangle down.
(398)

Stevens's art thus maneuvers, wordwise, out of the certified pathways of knowledge and its acquisition to the glimmering of new insight.

By any measure Stevens's achievement is considerable in this vein. Yet there is an ultimate limitation in the preoccupation of his art with epistemology. The drama is almost all the drama of trying to come to know; it is not (by any contraction of the imagination) an entirely cerebral drama, but there are vast and essential ranges of human experience that are absent. Love or bereavement, courage or betrayal have minor parts, or no parts, to play in his works, while we watch with absorbing intensity the mind watching the mind hunting the real. His is a broader range than Stein's, but if it is the characteristic of the modern-age writer that he or she have an awareness of the limitations of knowledge, of conceptualization, of language, Stevens tends to make this awareness—a preliminary or ancillary one for Faulkner or Williams or Dos Passos, as it had been in the previous century for Whitman, Melville, and Dickinson—into the abiding concern. Thus his poems at times seem finicky, self-absorbed, detached from most human concerns through their absorption in epistemology and their own verbal flamboyance. The age of epistemology had its most dedicated, most talented, most infatuated convert in Wallace Stevens.

13   William Carlos Williams: Thinking a World Without Thought

William Carlos Williams (1883–1963) was one of the writers who carried knowledge destruction to its farthest extremes, canceling out, in certain of his moods, all convention, all tradition, all thought. Not that he was consistent about it; he had other frames of mind in which he was certainly capable of compromise with convention. But his revolt was far-reaching in two special directions: the destruction of the then and elsewhere of tradition in the interest of the here and now; and the destruction of consistency, rationality, and certainty in the interest of heterogeneity, possibility, and empathy. Freed of whatever burdens of conventional thought and invention he could jettison, he attempted to explore and represent his world and himself on his own terms. And, as we shall see, the originality of his accomplishment as a destructionist can be found most notably in his keen appreciation of the otherness and the heterogeneousness of the things and persons depicted in his writing and in his ingenuity in devising various means of dealing with the problem of reflexiveness—especially means involving self-characterization and the processes of creation.

The picture we carry in our minds of Williams in the act of writing is one he himself gave us, of the harried physician snatching a few minutes between patients to scribble a piece of poem or idea or dialogue and sitting up every night well into the night pouring over a literary project that would eventually exhaust his imagination and quiet his mind so he could sleep for the next day. Throughout his productive life—except for a few years near the end—he carried on the two demanding careers simultaneously, and his accumulated literary works reflect the characteristics of restlessness and enthusiasm, as if the mere day's work weren't enough, hadn't taken him far enough after all.

He had a special appetite for the restlessness of the twentieth century, hanging around with Ezra Pound and the whole batch of East Coast experimentalists—with Alfred Kreymborg, Mina Loy, Marianne Moore,

Maxwell Bodenheim, (and later) Louis Zukofsky, and Nathanael West of the literary world; with Alfred Stieglitz, Marcel Duchamp, Walter Arensberg, Charles Demuth, Marsden Hartley, and Charles Sheeler of the art world. He soaked up dada philosophy, Otto Weininger's theories of sex, Einstein's relativity, Kandinsky's aesthetics, Whitehead's *Science and the Modern World*, and the polemics of the Social Credit movement. He was closely and energetically tied in with the little magazines and took a turn editing *Contact* and *New Masses*. He continually battled in print and out against those enemies of modernity, the philistines and the erudite.

His affinities and allegiances certainly got him into the new epistemology, with its problematical visions of perception and representation, of relativity and reflexivity and paint-as-paint. Those were insights that could be of use to him, especially in throwing off the burden of traditional knowledge and form and in suggesting new and original things literature could be and do. But he felt no incentive to take them up as quasi-religious principles or obsessive themes in his works. Unlike Stevens, after recognizing several of the great new ideas of the age of epistemology he went on with his work of representing life and experience in a number of epistemological modes—now imagistic, now naively realistic; now reflexively self-aware, now presumptively objective.

Restlessness, indeed: he felt no need to develop a coherent position in his works. The individual imagination and its freedom were what was important, not any specific track or regulation of their operation. When Stevens objected to Williams's book of poems, *Al Que Quiere!*, on the basis that it lacked a "fixed point of view" ("to fidget with points of view leads always to new beginnings and incessant new beginnings lead to sterility"), Williams replied publicly in his Prologue to *Kora in Hell*, "*What would you have me do with my Circe, Stevens, now that I have double-crossed her game, marry her? It is not what Odysseus did.*"*

In matters of literary form, too, Williams's restlessness and enthusiasm prevailed. Throughout his career he experimented with improvising and composing, compiling and imagining; he tried different styles and forms of poetry and prose; he ventured into modes that were metaphorical or literalistic, rationalistic or fantastic. As was wholly likely, he thereby sacrificed consistency of quality, producing now a minor masterpiece, now a foolish failure. But then consistency of any kind was the other person's game.

Imaginations, ed. Webster Schott (New Directions, 1970), 15, 16. This collection contains *Kora*, *The Great American Novel*, all the prose and poetry of *Spring and All* and *The Descent of Winter*, *A Novelette*, and a number of essays and other prose pieces. Parenthetical page numbers in the present chapter refer to this volume.

Williams's idea of the destruction of knowledge was explicit, fervent, and all-comprehending. As he put it in *In the American Grain*, "however hopeless it may seem, we have no other choice: we must go back to the beginning; it must all be done over; everything that is must be destroyed."[1] Early in his career he had announced his idea of the poet's job: "to tear down, to destroy life's lies, to keep the senses bare, to attack."[2] Wallace Stevens acknowledged in his preface to Williams's *Collected Poems, 1921–1931* that: "the man has spent his life in rejecting the accepted sense of things"—and then he went on, speaking from his own more carefully modulated persona: "In that, most of all, his romantic temperament appears."[3]

In many ways Williams's attack on tradition is pure Whitman: traditional ideas and forms confine the individual and keep him weak; "each age wished to enslave the others"; and "while we are imbibing the wisdom of the ages, we are at the same time imbibing the death and the imbecility, the enslaving rudeness of the ages."[4] The fixed, conventional forms he saw as authoritarian and indigenous to Europe, not to America.[5] In the very earliest stages of his career Williams was at his most tolerant of tradition, but even in such frames of mind he was an incipient destructionist: in 1917, after affirming that "all we have receives its value from that which has gone before," and "in the end all verse is built upon one ground," he went on to insist that the particular forms of traditional poetry were "forms representing other temperaments, other emotional fibers, other adjustments of sense."[6]

Williams's campaign against the tyranny of the past had many aspects, but it found a notable central target in T. S. Eliot. Eliot's literary neo-scholasticism seemed to be urging literature, and very persuasively, in a regressive direction. Looking back in 1951 on his anti-Eliot campaign Williams still showed signs of the bitterness of his struggle. Of the publication of *The Waste Land* he says,

> To me especially it struck like a sardonic bullet. I felt at once that it had set me back twenty years, and I'm sure it did. Critically Eliot returned us to the classroom just at the moment when I felt that we were on the point of an escape to matters much closer to the essence of a new art form itself—rooted in the locality which should give it fruit. I knew at once that in certain ways I was most defeated.[7]

His antitraditionalism also separated him from his early supporter and mentor, Pound, although not with any such public vehemence. The difference between Pound's and Williams's aesthetics, less publicized though nonetheless fundamental, is effectively focused in this comparison by Karl Malkoff of the *Cantos* and *Paterson*: "For Pound, the literary tradition can take root and flower in one's own consciousness, and can be legitimately used to break down the rigidity of the mind; for Williams, the literary tradition remains the product of other consciousnesses—however liberating the original act of creation may have been—and therefore is in itself a check to the imagination."[8] For Williams novelty had to be the watchword: "Nothing is good save the new. If a thing have novelty it stands intrinsically beside every other work of artistic excellence. If it have not that, no loveliness or heroic proportion or grand manner will save it. It will not be saved above all by an attenuated intellectuality" (23–24). As he had said in one of his earliest critical writings, "the only way to be like Whitman is to write *unlike* Whitman."[9] Later he would borrow the statement of Juan Gris: "the way to resemble the classics is to have performed work like them in nothing."[10] For Williams artists should not be conservative, but exploratory: "the processes of art, to keep alive, must always challenge the unknown and go where the most uncertainty lies."[11]

To "go where the most uncertainty lies" would involve repudiating not just standard wisdom itself, but the means by which it had been acquired. Indeed, Williams's ideal seems to be a world without thought in any conventional sense. Certainty—spurious, artificial, and confining—grew, as he saw it, from all the habits and reflexes by which the mind ordered experience; and certainty inevitably became, in the course of time and tradition, certainty purely about the ordering and not about the experience. Williams consequently put himself at odds with the very processes of ordering, the very techniques of arriving at knowledge.

One approach was to destroy or dispense with those fetishes of rationalism, unity and coherence. In most of his works of the twenties—including *Kora in Hell*, *Spring and All*, and *The Great American Novel*, there is a studied, at times explicit, attempt to be randomly inclusive, disjunctive. As with some of Stein's writing, discontinuity seems to be its purpose; *nothing*, at times, seems to account for the arrangement. We see a similar randomness in the structure of Williams's late epic poem *Paterson*, to which critic Henry M. Sayre has applied the term "the aesthetics of heterogeneity," pointing out that the growing inclusiveness of Part II led Williams to abandon even the shaping principles that prevailed in Part I.*

The Visual Text of WCW (University of Illinios Press, 1983), 104. Sayre explains (note 1, p. 115) that the term "aesthetic of heterogeneity" comes from Lawrence Alloway, *Robert Rauschenberg* (Smithsonian Inst., 1976), 5.

Disgusted with Pound's opinion of his Improvisations in *Kora in Hell* (that they were a repeat of Rimbaud, forty years after), Williams exclaimed (interestingly, in a disconnected moment in *A Novelette*) "he's all wet. Their excellence is, in major part, the shifting of category. It is the disjointing process" (285). *Kora* explicitly attacks the kind of mentality that builds a structure of knowing out of the discovery of apparent similarities: "the coining of similes is a pastime of very low order, depending as it does upon a nearly vegetable coincidence. Much more keen is that power which discovers in things those inimitable particles of dissimilarity to all other things which are the peculiar perfections of the thing in question" (18). Ironically enough, Williams's attack could also be leveled against the let-me-tell-you-what-literature-this-work-is-reminiscent-of kind of criticism Pound applied to this very work.

As Williams saw it, rationality itself—that foundation of unity and coherence—was essentially exclusionary in its operation and would have to fall if literature were to try to go "where the greatest uncertainty lies." Near the end of his career Williams was still sounding the note, here in a letter to Sister Bernetta Quinn, who had written an essay on *Paterson* he greatly admired: "one fault in modern compositions such as——(name it yourself) is that the irrational has no place. Yet in life (you show it by your tolerance of things which you feel no loss at not understanding) there is much that men exclude because they do not understand. The truly great heart *includes* what it does not at once grasp, just as the great artist includes things which go beyond him."[12]

Williams attacked "the various categories of intelligence,"—by which he seems to have meant science, philosophy, history, and so forth, as well as their major subconcepts—as especially distorting embodiments of rationality. Intervening between human beings and what there was to be known, they introduced a whole array of distortions and limitations. Categories tended to block out even the knowledge contained in other categories. They were absolutistic too: "obsessed with the convolutions of thought in one segment of the whole, the mind loses touch with the rest and makes the very serious error of believing it has achieved conclusions which govern the others"; especially could it be seen with science, "whose unrelated conclusions are falsely applied to every situation in life whether they are alien or otherwise."[13] In "going nowhere but to gross and minute codification of the perceptions," he claimed, rationalistic inquiry soon produced a situation in which "every common thing has been nailed down, stripped of freedom of action and taken away from use" (303, 295–296) and "the senses witnessing what is immediately before them in detail see a finality which they cling to in despair, not knowing which way to turn. Thus the so-called natural or scientific array becomes fixed, the walking devil of modern life" (14).

In this matter of destroying the habits of thought, Williams consciously and openly used Gertrude Stein's particular scapegoats, philosophy and science, in trying to develop the idea of a literature with greater autonomy and closer relationship to experience.[14] The influence of the Bergson-William James epistemology is conceivably involved too, especially its insight into the way conceptual processes form and freeze an indeterminate and flowing reality. Dada destructionism is more than likely an influence, especially in the fervor and ingenuity of its assault. As his good friend Marsden Hartley presented its credo in his 1921 book, *Adventures in the Arts* (with quotations from Tzara),

> Dada is irritated by those who write "Art, Beauty, Truth," with capital letters, and who make of them entities superior to man. "Dada scoffs at capital letters, atrociously." "Dada ruining the authority of constraints, tends to set free the natural play of our activities." "Dada therefore leads to amoralism and to the most spontaneous and consequently the least logical lyricism. . . . Dada scrapes from us the thick layers of filth deposited on us by the last few centuries." "Dada destroys, and stops at that."[15]

Williams yearned for an indigenous American equivalent to dadaism; the same year that Hartley's book was published, he wrote, "Well America is a bastard country where decomposition is the prevalent spectacle but the contour is not particularly dadaesque and that's the gist of it. We should be able to profit by this French orchid but only on condition that we have the local terms."[16]

In all his repudiation of the cultural tradition and the habitual ways the educated mind "discovered" order, Williams tried to maintain basic values which were not so much epistemological as they were humane. The following explanation occurs in his essay, "The Basis of Faith in Art":

> . . . All the arts have to come back to something.
> And . . . that thing is human need. When our manner of action becomes imbecilic we breed dada, Gertrude Stein, surrealism. These things seem unrelated to any sort of sense UNTIL we look for the NEED of human beings. Examining that we find that these apparently irrelevant movements of art represent mind saving, even at moments of genius, soul saving, continents of security for the pestered

and bedeviled spirit of man, bedeviled by the deadly, lying repeti-
tiousness of doctrinaire formula worship which is the standard work
of the day.[17]

To Williams's mind human need bred the outré, developing it as a survival mechanism, a salvation from the culture's pervasive lies.

While the whole ferment of modernism stimulated and gave substance to his revolt against cultural dogma, that revolt's focus seemed to
him in retrospect to have been initially and fundamentally a matter of
language and technique, with its philosophies and movements evolving
later. Remembering in his autobiography the early, heady days, he says,

> What were we seeking? No one knew consistently enough to formu-
> late a "movement." We were restless and constrained, closely allied
> with the painters. Impressionism, dadaism, surrealism applied to both
> painting and the poem. What a battle we made of it merely getting
> rid of capitals at the beginning of every line! The immediate image,
> which was impressionistic, sure enough, fascinated us all. We had
> followed Pound's instructions, his famous "Don'ts," eschewing inver-
> sions of the phrase, the putting down of what to our senses was
> tautological and so, uncalled for, merely to fill out a standard form.[18]

The destruction of all that was conventional in the language of literature was the quintessential spadework of the saving of minds and souls.
First of all it involved for Williams the repudiation of *English* English and
of English literary forms. "We've got to *begin*," he insisted in one of many
polemics on the subject, "by stating that we speak (here) a distinct, separate language in a present (new era) and that it is NOT English."[19] That
was Whitman's point about language too, and Williams knew it and gave
Whitman credit for making his greatest contribution in denying "the English language as taught in England": "he just leapt off, and he was driven
to find a way for himself, like the American pioneers, we'll say."[20] James
Joyce provided Williams with a model for another sort of destructionist
language; Williams found, in the difficult ingenuity of Joyce's prose-stream,
"a reaffirmation of the forever-sought freedom of truth from usage."[21]

Prosody too needed destroying and reconstituting in the mold of the
here and now: "we have to invent for ourselves . . . , whether we like it or
not, a new prosody based on a present-day world, and real in a present-day
world which the English prosody can never be for us."[22] Poetic forms would
follow the language and prosody; they had to grow out of our own indigenous contemporary experience rather than being artily imposed on it.

Williams repudiated poetic diction too: "there can no longer be serious work in poetry written in 'poetic' diction. It is a contortion of speech to conform to a rigidity of line."[23] Indeed the whole category of "the poetic" gave Williams headaches. He seems to have regarded most usages of the term as spuriously honorific, exclusionary nonsense. Yet when Wallace Stevens in his preface to Williams's *Collected Poems, 1921–1931* recommended him as a poet of the antipoetic,[24] Williams carried a grudge against him for it for the rest of his life. For him, apparently, the category was ambivalent, and Stevens' statement seemed to deny him some aspect he felt was precious. He was still insisting in 1950 that there was *nothing* that was categorically antipoetic:

> The commonest situations in the world have the very essence of poetry if looked at correctly. If I take a dirty old woman in the street, it is not necessary to put her in the situation of a princess. All poets have a tendency to dress up an ordinary person, as Yeats does. It has to be a special treatment to be poetic, and I don't acknowledge this at all. . . . I think that what Stevens said was nonsense.[25]

Along with repudiating the inherent Anglophilia, formalism, and aestheticism of American literary technique, Williams went to work on its figurative bent. "That is what they think a poem is: metaphor," he said, and "they don't live, they metaphorize." Worst of all, "there is for them only one metaphor: Europe—the past."[26] (There is no explicit grammatical referent of "they" in this passage, but we are free to imagine that it includes Eliot and other European-oriented neo-symbolists as well as the traditional American literati.) In an extended meditation in *Spring and All*, spontaneous and disjunctive, he inveighed against the "demoded meanings" that clutter our language and impede our perceptions. "The man of imagination who turns to art for release and fulfilment of his baby promises contends with the sky through layers of demoded words and shapes," he claims. "Crude symbolism is to associate emotions with natural phenomena such as anger with lightning, flowers with love." "Such work is empty," he insists, and candidly admits that almost all his own earlier works (prior to *Spring and All* [1923]) "have that quality about them" (100).

Although it sometimes sounds like such, his attack is not on figurativeness per se. Strict literalness is certainly one kind of antidote to flaccid figurativeness—"no ideas but in things," cold plums, wet wheelbarrows, and so forth. But another antidote is "expansion of imagination" which could in a writer produce the same kind of "residual contact between life and the imagination which is essential to freedom," that would be characteristic (his *Spring and All* meditation asserts) of the farmer and fisherman looking at the sky who "read their own lives there" rather than perceiving "demoded meanings" (100). Only a relatively few of Williams's writings rely on the literalistic antidote. The ultimate enemy is not figurativeness but fixity:

> Language is the key to the mind's escape from bondage to the past. There are no "truths" that can be fixed in language. It is by the breakup of the language that the truth can be seen to exist and that it becomes operative again. Such reasoning as Spengler's depends on the fixities of language which it is the purpose of such writers as Joyce and Stein —fail tho' they may in detail—to blast. In language lodge the prejudices, the compulsions by which stupidity and ineptitude rule intelligences superior to their own.[27]

A reconstituted language, then, would be an indispensable weapon in the struggle against fixity, and Williams seems to have had high regard for Stein's act of reconstitution:

> Stein has gone systematically to work smashing every connotation that words have ever had, in order to get them back clean. It can't be helped that it's been forgotten what words are made for. It can't be helped that the whole house has to come down. . . . It's got to come down because it has to be rebuilt. And it has to be rebuilt by unbound thinking. And unbound thinking has to be done with straight, sharp words.[28]

That Steinian sense of words and language as arbitrary and as culturally bound or unbound—that amazing discovery of language as language —struck Williams as crucial to avoiding the Spenglerian (or Eliotic) syndrome of mistaking a conceptual wasteland for a real civilization in decay. At times he outrightly celebrates language as language and relishes the overthrow of demoded philosophizing:

VI

No that is not it
nothing I have done
nothing
I have done

is made up of
nothing
and the diphthong

ae

together with
the first person
singular
indicative

of the auxiliary
verb
to have

everything
I have done
is the same

if to do

is capable
of an
infinity of
combinations

involving the
moral
physical
and religious

codes

for everything
and nothing
are synonymous
when

energy in vacuo
has the power
of confusion

which only to
have done nothing
can make
perfect
(103–105)

Williams's destructions accomplished what they were supposed to: they gave him both liberation and justification to experiment and invent, to play at the writing game on a field with the broadest possible boundaries. His destructions freed him even from conventional standards of quality and consistency and sanctioned his running of risks in any given direction—incomprehensibility, prosaicness, whatever—in any given work. His innovative writings have a number of special characteristics that constitute his own contributions to the twentieth century's developing sense of literary possibility. Several of them are certainly widely recognized as such: his sense of radical particularity ("no ideas but in things"), his rediscovery of the power of locality and nationality, his explorations of extremes in literalistic language, and the democratic, virtually indiscriminate empathy that infuses his works. There are other characteristics worth exploring along with these: his derivation of literary structure and cadence from the outside world, his imaginative inhabitation of his subjects and their inhabitation of him, his experimentation with the nonfictional persona and with the representation of the process of creation in the created work, and, strangest of all, the conscious opting in some of his works for a naive epistemological perspective in order to achieve other ends. (We should note in passing that many of his innovations are strategies for dealing with that abiding problem of twentieth-century epistemology, reflexiveness, and that many of them are closely analogous to William Jamesian epistemological principles.) His innovations come in various forms, and they are neither fully consistent among themselves nor easy to categorize. For convenience of discussion here (although even these very basic categories are not entirely separable) we might distinguish two basic types of invention Williams used: one to attune to the outside world and the other to attune to his own stream-of-creating-consciousness.

Williams is best known for attunement to the outside world. The slogan "no ideas but in things" and the simple pseudo-visual insistence of that red wheelbarrow have given him his identity in American literature. As his colleague Marianne Moore would have it, "with the bee's sense of polarity he searches for a flower, and that flower is representation."[29] At its most extreme that representation is strictly denotative, the words merely pointing: this thing-to-be-seen, right now, right here.

Between Walls

the back wings
of the

hospital where
nothing

will grow lie
cinders

in which shine
the broken

pieces of a green
bottle. [30]

As Williams himself recalled, "there's nothing subtle about the poem; all
it means, as far as I know, is that in a waste of cinders loveliness, in the
form of color, stands up alive."[31] It's not just a random word-photograph
—his "sense of polarity" has drawn him toward an unexpected "loveliness" "standing up alive" in the place you'd least expect it. The carefully
disciplined diction and the strict objectivity of presentation make the poem
seem like this is what would be left after the destruction of knowledge, of
interposing intellect, and of cultural convention: not nothingness or un-
differentiated anythingness, but pure and primal value. And if an inanimate loveliness can be found standing up alive, so certainly can a complex
human yearning and its simple fulfillment:

To a Poor Old Woman

munching a plum on
the street a paper bag
of them in her hand

They taste good to her
They taste good
to her. They taste
good to her

You can see it by
the way she gives herself
to the one half
sucked out in her hand

Comforted
a solace of ripe plums
seeming to fill the air
They taste good to her.[32]

As in Hemingway's prose, there is a strict accounting of statement and detail—so strict here, in fact, that the physical evidence ("You can see it by/ the way she gives herself") has to be offered immediately for the inference "They taste good to her"; and only thereafter can the woman *reliably* be said to be "Comforted/ a solace of ripe plums/ seeming to fill the air."

The culture around Williams obviously offered a good deal of potential support in the form of models and ideas for an imagination inclined toward literalism. The scientific empiricism of his medical education, the fictional realism and documentary reportage of much of his reading, the "straight photography" of Alfred Stieglitz and his friends at the 291 gallery,* the realism and precisionism of some of his painter friends—all in their various ways conveyed a message of the significance of unadorned, unmanipulated particularities. Williams's friend and collaborator, Louis Zukofsky even raised literalism to an apotheosis of sorts in his objectivism, in which the literalist impulse struggled its way through virtually impenetrable terminology to a footing in untenable dogma. "*Impossible* to communicate anything but particulars," Zukofsky insisted, "—historic and contemporary—things, human beings as things their instrumentalities of capillaries and veins binding up and bound up with events and contingencies."**

Is Williams's literalism the sign of a naive realist, an evolutionary throwback in this age of epistemology? It would seem not to be, first because he does so many other things in his work that a confirmed realist would not do. His imagism and his objectivism like his several other literary modes come and go, relating more to his sense of vantage and value in particular cases than to the sort of consistent epistemology or metaphysic that would give his scholars their handle. Then too, as we shall see later in this chapter, he clearly (at times) recognizes that there is no unmediated perception, no purely mimetic word-combinations. His literalism thus seems an approach he takes under certain circumstances (one way of seeing what hadn't quite been seen before), yet one that is admittedly arbitrary, relative, personally

---

*According to Bram Dijkstra, "if Stieglitz was a pioneer in American art, it was primarily because he established the basis for a non-metaphoric art in America." (*Hieroglyphics of a New Speech* [Princeton University Press, 1969], 105.)

**"An Objective," *Prepositions* (Horizon, 1968), 24. For an account of the Williams-Zukofsky friendship, especially describing the help Zukofsky gave Williams in making a number of his poems more direct and concise, see Neil Baldwin, "Zukofsky, Williams and *The Wedge*," in Carroll F. Terrell, ed., *Louis Zukofsky, Man and Poet* (National Poetry Foundation, 1987).

opted. A particularly fresh and perceptive metaphor could do the same sort of thing, as in "Flowers by the Sea":*

When over the flowery, sharp pasture's
edge, unseen, the salt ocean

lifts its form—chicory and daisies
tied released seem hardly flowers alone

but color and the movement—or the shape
perhaps—of restlessness, whereas

the sea is circled and sways
peacefully upon its plantlike stem.[33]

Williams thought of the specificity of focus of so many of his works as a function of imagination, and imagination in this mode was a refocusing of perception away from ego and categories of knowledge and mind and toward an *other*—an object, a person, or a moment. As he says in *Spring and All*, "To refine, to clarify, to intensify that eternal moment in which we alone live there is but a single force—the imagination. This is its book" (89). And in his earlier book *Kora in Hell* he had lamented "the thing that stands eternally in the way of really good writing is always one: the virtual impossibility of lifting to the imagination those things which lie under the direct scrutiny of the senses, close to the nose" (14). He then set forth an experiment in poetic representation in which the give-and-take of imagination would substitute for the traditional reflexiveness of lyric self-projection: "A poet witnessing the chicory flower and realizing its virtues of form and color so constructs his praise of it as to borrow no particle from right or left. He gives his poem over to the flower and its plant themselves, that they may benefit by those cooling winds of the imagination which thus returned upon them will refresh them at their task of saving the world" (19).

Like Stevens, Williams saw ego-suppression as a prime necessity and essentially an act of imagination: "The associational or sentimental value is false. Its imposition is due to lack of imagination, to an easy lateral sliding" (14). Also like Stevens, he felt that the exploratory imagination had a higher calling, his particular version cherishing "the moment when the consciousness is enlarged by the sympathies and the unity of under-

*Henry M. Sayre makes the point that Williams's antimetaphoricalness has been exaggerated. See his discussion of metaphor in Williams's presumably most directly descriptive poems, like "Primrose," in *The Visual Text of WCW*, 24.

standing which the imagination gives." "Only through the agency of this force [imagination]," he asserts, "can a man feel himself moved largely with sympathetic pulses at work" (120, 105). (Williams's *imagination* begins to sound like a version of Bergson's *intuition* in such moments.) Unlike Stevens, Williams seems to feel himself under no compunction to stop short of the gap between the knower and the known, but rushes forward to embrace things as if reality were independent and apprehensible after all, and not a mere show-window composite of projecting-imagination-and-other. He yearns for the farmer's or the fisherman's "residual contact between life and the imagination which is essential to freedom" (100) and urges that "Some exposure to the sharp edge of the mechanics of living—such as blindness, political exile, a commercial theater to support and be supported by, a profession out of necessity, dire poverty, defiance of the law, insanity—is necessary to the poet."[34] He reminisces appreciatively about the attitude of direct imaginative commitment that made him effective both as doctor and as poet and fiction writer: "I lost myself in the very properties of their [the patients'] minds: for the moment at least I actually became *them*, whoever they should be, so that when I detached myself from them at the end of a half-hour of intense concentration over some illness which was affecting them, it was as though I were reawakening from a sleep."[35]

The attitude toward particulars—a striving toward uncategorical empathy—is very like William James's. Both men are too cagey to be naive realists, yet they see all those people and things out there, waiting to be discovered, animated, understood by our imaginations. Recall James's urging to "place yourself at the point of view of the thing's interior *doing*, . . . get at the expanding center of a human character, the *élan vital*, as Bergson calls it, by living sympathy."[36]

Williams's restless and fervent imagination-realism expanded both the subject boundaries of literature and its possibilities of perspective. Cinders or parsley or slippers or goats—nothing was too ordinary or ugly, nothing too domestic to be aesthetically, humanly significant; "Everything/ is a picture/ to the employing eye/ that feeds restlessly to/ find peace":[37]

The Nightingales

My shoes as I lean
unlacing them
stand out upon
flat worsted flowers
under my feet.

Nimbly the shadows
of my fingers play
unlacing
over shoes and flowers.[38]

In perspective too, this projected, empathetic imagination could find vantage points for poems in the most likely or unlikely places (widow or
farmer, sea elephant or bowl of flowers), just as in fiction it could show
again and again how an observer-narrator comes to an understanding of
another person's (often a patient's) sense of things: the doctor in "Mind
and Body," listening to a middle-aged woman's rambling, unfocused account of her malaise, suggests "Perhaps your trouble is that you need
some woman to love./ I have always loved women more than men, she
agreed."[39]

In his imagination-realist's approach to literary creation, Williams put
great emphasis on concepts he designated as *contact* and *locality*. The periodical he edited in the early twenties he called *Contact*, explaining that
"contact always implies a local definition of effort with a consequent taking on of certain colors from the locality by the experience, and these
colors or sensual values of whatever sort are the only realities in writing
or, as may be said, the essential quality in literature."[40] In his own approximate way he defines the basic human approach to reality in terms very
close to William James's. Here, from *A Pluralistic Universe*, is what James
regards as a basic "methodological postulate," "the principle of pure
experience": "Nothing shall be admitted as fact, it says, except what can
be experienced at some definite time by some experient; and for every
feature of fact ever so experienced, a definite place must be found somewhere in the final system of reality. In other words: Everything real must
be experienceable somewhere, and every kind of thing experienced must
somewhere be real."[41] In a philosophical mood Williams invokes what he
calls "the pluralism of experience" this way: "Quickly, it is this: that every
individual, every place, every opportunity of thought is both favored and
limited by its emplacement in time and place."[42] The concept of contact is
like a methodological postulate for Williams, an epistemological/aesthetic
principle that (like James's) embodied the American sense of the primacy
of individual experience while it accommodated easily to post-Einsteinian
relativity.

Williams's predilection for *locality*, although certainly squarely in the
tradition of nineteenth- and twentieth-century American literary realism,
can also be seen as part of his campaign to destroy conceptual generalities

and discover realities relativistically. Locality is a kind of trademark of much of his work and has been much remarked by his commentators. He loved the paradox that the local, which ought to breed provinciality, really was the entry to universality:

> I wanted, if I was to write in a larger way than of the birds and flowers, to write about the people close about me: to know in detail, minutely what I was talking about—to the whites of their eyes, to their very smells.
>
> That is the poet's business. Not to talk in vague categories but to write particularly, as a physician works, upon a patient, upon the thing before him, in the particular to discover the universal. John Dewey had said (I discovered it quite by chance), "The local is the only universal, upon that all art builds." Keyserling had said the same in different words.[43]

"Place is the only universal," he asserts elsewhere[44] (as part of another assault on Eliot, by the way); in a letter to Marianne Moore he revels in "its releasing quality";[45] in an essay on French painting he insists that "the local in a full sense *is* the freeing agency to all thought, in that it is everywhere accessible to all."[46] Whatever our feeling about the logic of this, Williams is running with an American modernist current. The Dewey reference is to a widely influential article in *The Dial* in 1920 (and, just possibly, to *Democracy and Education*) in which Dewey stressed the universality of the local. Stieglitz made an important contribution to this stream too, with many of his realistically local photographs, with his theoretical predilections, and even with the naming of his gallery, "An American Place," which Williams thought was a capital idea.*

Williams was fascinated and bemused by what he felt was the *communicability* of locality and of its peculiar universality. Whereas Stein essentially denied the possibility of communication between inhabitants of different personal/local worlds (see p. 98, above), Williams (again like Whitman) saw a way to achieve commonality through the true representation of the local:

---

*"Axioms," *A Recognizable Image*, ed. Bram Dijkstra (New Directions, 1978), 175. Williams's connections to Dewey and Keyserling are succinctly covered in James Guimond, *The Art of WCW* (University of Illinois Press, 1968), 55. His connections to Stieglitz are covered in several of Bram Dijkstra's works, but in this context see especially *Hieroglyphics of a New Speech*, 99–100.

If I succeed in keeping myself objective enough, sensual enough, I can produce the factors, the concretions of materials by which others shall understand and so be led to use—that they may the better see, touch, taste, enjoy—their own world *differing as it may* from mine. . . .

That—all my life I have striven to emphasize it—is what is meant by the universality of the local. From me where I stand to them where they stand in their here and now—where I cannot be—I do in spite of that arrive!*

Locality in Williams's works is virtually a constant presence, from the "filthy Passaic" in the first of his collected poems, "The Wanderer," to the presence of that same river (its pollution much reduced, its signification vastly augmented) in the sixth book of *Paterson*, left uncompleted at his death. His biographer Paul Mariani repeatedly points us toward this theme of locality, noting, for example, how the sixteen poems published in the November 1916 issue of *Others* "managed to generate a sense of Williams' locality, a vortex with its own center at 9 Ridge Road," and how Williams's 1938 enthusiasm for the Depression photographs of Walker Evans was linked to his "painting his own portraits of Depression America, composing a book of objectivist details of his environs in an attempt to get the *Paterson* thing finally under way."[47] (Some of these works appeared as *The Broken Span*.)

Williams's idea of locality and how it could be worked up into universality can be seen from his poem "The Source." It opens in a specifically identifiable location,

a pasture which begins

where silhouettes of scrub
and balsams stand uncertainly

On whose green three maples
are distinctly pressed
beside a red barn

with new shingles in the old.

Moving along like an amble over well-recognized ground, the poem discovers the "source" in the final third:

*"Against the Weather," *Selected Essays* (Random House, 1954), 197–198. Linda Welsheimer Wagner in *Interviews with WCW* (New Directions, 1976) offers further constructive discussion of this communication theme; see xv, ff.

the uneven aisles of
the trees

rock strewn a stone
half-green

A spring in whose depth
white sand bubbles
overflows

clear under late raspberries
and delicate-stemmed touch-me-nots

Where alders follow it marking
the low ground
the water is cast upon

a stair of uneven stones
with a rustling sound

An edge of bubbles stirs
swiftness is moulded
speed grows

the profuse body advances
over the stones unchanged.[48]

The "source" is thus threefold: the stream's, the poet's, and the poem's, with deeper resonances of all human lives, how they spring and flow.

Williams's Americanism was, of course, wholly consistent with his attraction to contact, locality, and the discovery of the universality of what lies "under the direct scrutiny of the senses, close to the nose." He was inspired by the Americanness of his experience, exploring the national heritage and trying to make it vividly current in his book of biographies, *In the American Grain*. Also, many of his values—his high regard for heterogeneity, classlessness, democracy, individuality, autonomy, and the pragmatic solving of life's real problems—have a characteristically American flavor.*

When the outside world preoccupied Williams's imagination, it was

---

*The topic has been widely and effectively discussed in the Williams scholarship. See, for example, James E. Breslin, *WCW: An American Artist* (Oxford University Press, 1970); James Guimond, *The Art of WCW: A Discovery and Possession of America* (University of Illinois Press, 1968); and Reed Whittemore, *WCW: Poet from Jersey* (Houghton Mifflin, 1975).

primarily by means of the unique individualities of the things and people out there. The attempt to explore and to capture in words and literary forms those individualities was perhaps the major concern of his entire writing career.

> To be an artist, . . . a man . . . must possess that really glandular perception of their [his materials'] uniqueness which realizes in them an end in itself, each piece irreplaceable by a substitute, not to be broken down to other meaning. Not to pull out, transubstantiate, boil, unglue, hammer, melt, digest, and psychoanalyze, not even to distill but to see and keep what the understanding touches intact—as grapes are round and come in bunches.[49]

The perception of uniqueness, of wholeness is of course the job of imagination and not of thought; Williams critic Rod Townley calls the process "possession by surrender, . . . self abnegating submission to the wisdom of astonishment."[50] The approach is clearly relatable to Bergson's idea that what characterized artists is that "when they look at a thing, they see it for itself, and not for themselves";[51] Bram Dijkstra relates it to Stieglitz's statement "When I am no longer thinking, but simply *am*, then I may be said to be truly affirming life. Not to *know*, but to let exist what is, that alone, perhaps, is truly to know."[52] The dedication to disciplined observation, to contact, to locality came together for Williams in the object's *individuality*:

10/28

in this strong light
the leafless beechtree
shines like a cloud

it seems to glow
of itself
with a soft stript light
of love
over the brittle

grass

But there are
on second look
a few yellow leaves
still shaking

> far apart
> just one here one there
> trembling vividly.[53]

It is well worth noting, though, that as the poet's imagination animates the simple physical facts, not only does it employ the figurative resources of language to vivify the impression—the tree "shines like a cloud/ it seems to glow/ of itself"—but it invests human feeling in the exploration as well—"with a soft stript light/ of love" the tree shines, its sparse leaves "trembling vividly." The poet's imagination is there, responding feelingly to the singularity of this tree. Whitman's relation to his yellow poplar and his striving for the "ultimate vivification" of his subjects by "the imaginative faculty" are direct-line forerunners of this aspect of Williams's creativity. Here Williams presents a later version of the imaginatively realized inherency, although without Whitman's abiding sense of a transcendent referent.

Williams's referent was human, and with a few exceptions in his work a subject's individuality tended to be completed, fulfilled, only when it reached some point of human significance. Thus even his eight-page, nearly microscopic descriptive tour-de-force, "The Crimson Cyclamen" (dedicated "To the Memory of Charles Demuth"), has passages such as this, revealing what it is to be a cyclamen from the perspective of what it is to be a human being:

> the young leaves
> coming among the rest
> are more crisp
> and deeply cupped
> the edges rising first
> impatient of the slower
> stem—the older
> level, the oldest
> with the edge already
> fallen a little backward—
> the stem alone
> holding the form
> stiffly a while longer—.[54]

Thus that tantalizingly absolute otherness of things remains unreachable. An individuality is inevitably, irreducibly an individuality-as-experienced. Imagination remains innately, ineluctably self-reflexive.

With human subjects Williams's fascination for individuality was naturally and profoundly appropriate. He is the creator of a great gallery of originals, a kind of completion of Whitman's democratic dream in vivid particularity:

> On the way
>
> we passed a long row
> of elms, she looked at them
> awhile out of
> the ambulance window and said,
>
> What are all those
> fuzzy looking things out there?
> Trees? Well I'm tired
> of them and rolled her head away.[55]

Individuality is the great theme of Williams's fiction, many narratives existing principally or even solely to present its avatars—Doc Rivers, Jean Beicke, Gurlie Stecher (*The White Mule*), the girl with the pimply face, the "savage brat" ("The Use of Force"), the farmers' daughters, and so forth —all of them fascinating to Williams in the personal peculiarity of their inner drives and outer accommodations. Against the grain of modernist fiction, Williams's exploration of their individualities is done objectively for the most part, the inner self manifested behaviorally in the characters' actions and words: the oddity embodies the quiddity, with the whole personal world behind it to be inferred. There is no mistaking the objective presentation for neutrality, though: Williams's observer-narrators delight in the individuality of their subjects, as in this passage from "Life Along the Passaic River":

> Take for instance the one in the derby hat who was coming up the street just now—a six-footer, looking like the usual bum in vaudeville shows you'd think might be leaning down any minute to get his hooks onto a cigar stub. No hurry. And as he gets near the 1927 open car parked at the curb with the two wooden-faced guys sitting in the front seat staring off into space, loafing, suddenly he gives a hoarse yell at them as much as to say, To hell with you! without looking up, and goes on slowly by, a kind of threatening, cursing growl with plenty of lung power behind it as if he might be chasing kids he'd caught stealing peanuts from a stand. The two hardly noticed him, didn't even move. And he didn't even raise his face either but went

on by as if he'd never said a word. Looked drunk. What are you going to do with a guy like that. Or why want to do anything with him. Except not miss him.[56]

The spontaneity of that man's gesture is the evidence of individuality that makes him interesting to Williams. It's a theme Williams returns to frequently in his fiction and poetry, the fresh unpredictability of things. One time it's in the strange look the observer-narrator gets from a murderer's little daughter ("Why has she chosen me/ for the knife/ that darts along her smile?").[57] Another time it comes from the unexpected and wordless offer of snuff he gets from the elderly non-English-speaking husband of a patient: it gives him a sneezing fit, and then "finally, with tears in my eyes, I felt the old man standing there, smiling, an experience the like of which I shall never, in all probability, have again in my life on this mundane sphere."[58] Another time it leaps out before him as he's looking meditatively at yet another field, "that brilliant field/ of rainwet orange," at another (familiar sort of) tree, "a white birch/ with yellow leaves/ and few/ and loosely hung,"

> and a young dog
> jumped out
> of the old barrel.
> (238)

And so many of his stories and poems are about spring, beginnings, and birth—about love and caring too—all gratuitous, causeless boons. His appetite for experiential novelty seems endless, the living counterpart of his quest for aesthetic novelty. Bergson had insisted that a fundamental characteristic of the universe was "the continuous creation of unforseeable novelty"; in his most metaphysical mode he claimed that "The impetus of life . . . consists in a need of creation. It cannot create absolutely, because it is confronted with matter, that is to say with the movement that is the inverse of its own. But it seizes upon this matter, which is necessity itself, and strives to introduce into it the largest possible amount of indetermination and liberty."[59] Williams seems to have lived in a Bergsonian world and to have immensely enjoyed such manifestations of "the impetus of life" as it offered.

Occasionally, spontaneity and individuality came together in his works in such a way as to produce a kind of Joycean epiphany. In such works, we sense someone or something revealing its essence in its own very particular way:

A Portrait of the Times

Two W.P.A. men
stood in the new
sluiceway

overlooking
the river—
One was pissing

while the other
showed
by his red

jagged face the
immemorial tragedy
of lack-love

whereas an old
squint-eyed woman
in a black

dress
and clutching
a bunch of

late chrysanthemums
to her
fatted bosoms

turned her back
on them
at the corner.[60]

It's a somewhat self-conscious, proletarian portrait, perhaps, but the sudden insight it gives into the counterpoint of indecorousness and decorousness, of lack-love and romance, strikes us as reality speaking its own language to us. "The essence," Williams says in discussing Charles Sheeler's precisionist painting, "lies in the thing, and shapes it, variously, but the sensual particularization is the proof, the connection which proves that the senses see a reality."[61] Interestingly, in this outer-directed mode Williams's sense of seeing and knowing is also very like Hemingway's groping for "the sequence of motion and fact which made the emotion," using the same process of intuitive divining and the same techniques of imagistic representation to discover a relationship between fact and significance. For both writers the surface of the resulting writing is simple, but very deceptively so—and not very amenable to figurative interpretation or expository analysis, since the world to which it refers is made up of neither symbolic correspondences nor general truths.

Quite often in Williams's work reality's epiphanies come through language. The doctor-writer was fascinated with exploring that moment when, as he explained in his autobiography, "we see through the welter of evasive or interested patter, when by chance we penetrate to some moving detail of a life. . . . When the inarticulate patient struggles to lay himself bare for you, or with nothing more than a boil on his back is so caught off balance that he reveals some secret twist of a whole community's pathetic way of thought." There is a subtext to their words, and it is the subtext that is the pure, real thing:

> the underlying meaning of all they want to tell us and have always failed to communicate is the poem, the poem which their lives are being lived to realize. No one will believe it. And it is the actual words, as we hear them spoken under all circumstances, which contain it. It is actually there, in the life before us, every minute that we are listening, a rarest element—not in our imaginations but there, there in fact. It is that essence which is hidden in the very words which are going in at our ears and from which we must recover underlying meaning as realistically as we recover metal out of ore.[62]

Williams's interpreters have been very interested in his sense of language and very astute at studying it. Hugh Kenner concluded that "his ear for compelled speech was nearly absolute."[63] J. Hillis Miller interestingly connected Williams's sense of words with Marcel Duchamp's ready-mades, showing that "sometimes words are taken as *objets trouves*."[64] Linda Welsheimer Wagner stressed the vitality of Williams's relationship to the real speech around him and highlighted his statement in his "Introduction" to *The Wedge*: "When a man makes a poem, makes it, mind you, he takes words as he finds them interrelated about him and composes them . . . that they may constitute a revelation in the speech that he uses."[65]

The use of the self-revealing characteristics of vernacular is a feature of all types of Williams's work, from "poems which were simply fragments of idiom"[66] (or "fieldwork note[s]")[67] to stories that "consist almost entirely of 'auditory scraps from the language'"[68] to *Paterson* and *In the American Grain*, in which the varied individual vernaculars are subjects in themselves. Here is an example from the novel *The White Mule*; a group of mothers in the park are discussing the behavior, the "spirit," of their small children. The passage does not further the narrative, but stands as a thing in itself, a complex inherency, a "moment" of life. Note the vernacular quality of the dialogue and the way that Williams is able to suggest worlds of character and individual feeling beneath the clichés and near-clichés of ordinary talk:

> I got one too. Always up to something, a regular rip. But he hasn't slept so good for the last couple of nights.
> They're down like a stone, up like a cork.
> No, I sez. There was no money born with ye and there'll be none buried with ye.
> Now he's this way—he's good in some ways. If I brought him here and you told him to take the nastiest medicine, he'd take it. But if his father or I tried to make him take it, nothing doing.
> You got nothing to kick at, said the rosy faced woman to the one who had last spoken, with that angel out of heaven you're holdin' there to keep you company.
> Oh she's all right, the woman replied. But that other blister . . . ! Oh my! It's a wonder he's still alive. I could kill him sometimes.
> He wants to sit up and he's fresh—he's a sassy boy—but he hasn't slept so good for the last couple of nights.
> Oh Jesus, Mrs. H! Don't let her get started crying.
> Well, they're here and you got to do the best for them. But I'll tell you the truth, it's a thankless job sometimes.
> You're right it's a thankless job, said a heavy-browed woman who had not spoken until then. My youngest was that kind. He was a wicked one. She paused. I'm ashamed to tell it.[69]

There is an aggressive commonplaceness about a great deal of Williams's writing, and this despite his sometime philosophy of "make it new"; but once we have gone into and through the commonplace surface to what he called "the radiant gist" beneath, we may well feel that our own firsthand experiential world is similarly readable. There is a kind of renewal in the experience of reading what Williams creates when he "takes words as he finds them interrelated about him and composes them." It can put us on a different footing in our own everyday worlds.

The cadence of literary utterance was for Williams an important part of its capacity to manifest inherency. He was consciously, at times painstakingly careful about aural aspects—rhythm, sound, and phrasing—principally striving to make his printed words take on the physical or aural imprint of the outer world. He would have little to do with Gertrude Stein's sort of thing with rhythm invented out of an independent drive or the clicking along of verbal association. For Williams the rhythms of external things were expressive of their reality, and linguistic cadence was a means of discovery. The destruction of conventional poetic meter and patterning left him with the opportunity to follow other, more natural contours.

The rhythm of vernacular speech was one obvious sort of contour: "the rhythmic construction of a poem was determined for me by the language as it is spoken," he once recalled.[70] Several critics have pointed out that his sense of vernacular was not merely a matter of diction but, as Paul Mariani says (paraphrasing Williams), of "variations in the alignment of emphasis, . . . not cracker-barrel vulgate but the pace and pauses and risings and fallings of speech heard every day."[71] In the "Conclusion" part of the short poem "Invocation and Conclusion," for example, the speaker speaks with this vernacular cadence:

> I was married at thirteen
> My parents had nine kids
> and we were on the street
> That's why the old bugger—
>
> He was twenty-six
> and I hadn't even had
> my changes yet. Now look at me![72]

The rhythm of movement of people and things in the outside world was another natural contour he sought to make his verse follow. He occasionally tried the simple trick of imitation of sounds (like that of a freight train in The Descent of Winter [246]); sometimes he attempted visual imitation (like that of the vertical visual shape of "The Locust Tree in Flower").* At his most profound he attains to something more complicated, more an ensemble of suggestive effects, as in "The Cod Head," where the line breaks, the dashes, the onomatopoeia, the basic rhythms and their counterpoints enforce the back-and-forth, raising-lifting of the teeming sea:

---

*Collected Earlier Poems (New Directions, 1951), 93. Henry B. Sayre has recently focused attention on the visual rather than the aural aspect of Williams's metrics (The Visual Text of WCW, 3), and Hugh Kenner earlier pointed out "an audio-visual counterpoint" in many of Williams's poems (A Homemade World [Knopf, 1975], 86).

Miscellaneous weed
strands, stems, debris
oscillate—

firmament to fishes
where the yellow feet
of gulls dabble—

oars whip
ships churn to bubbles—
at night agitate

wildly phosphores-
cent midges but by day
gellatinous

moons in whose
discs sometimes a red
cross lives—four

fathom the bottom
skids a mottle of green
sands backward—

Clearer—three fathom
amorphous
wavering rocks darkly [—]*

two fathom—the
vitreous body
through which the oar tips—

small scudding fish
deep down—and now a
lulling

lift and fall
red stars—
a severed cod-head

*The University of Delaware autographed copy has *darkly* canceled and a dash added in
the same penstroke as the autograph.

between two
green stones—lifting
falling.[73]

As Williams wrote to Kay Boyle in 1932, "I have been watching speech in
my own environment, . . . watching how words match the act, especially
how they come together."[74] At that point he was close to Zukofsky's mystic objectivism, which would insist that "the sound and pitch emphasis of
a word are never apart from its meaning."[75]

Williams himself discussed his metrics often in terms of the "variable
foot"[76] and sometimes in terms of "musical pace."[77] His concepts aren't extraordinarily analytical, referring basically to a kind of cadence that is neither
fixed nor free, a line as loose as Whitman's, as relativistic as Einstein's
physics,[78] yet constituting some sort of intuitive, "musical" configuration.

The architecture of his writing too was frequently determined by the
contours of the external world or at least by his experience of them. Denying intellectual categories, constantly courting chaos and meaninglessness, he would often go so far as to try to translate the structure of an
experience directly into literary form:

XI

In passing with my mind
on nothing in the world

but the right of way
I enjoy on the road by

virtue of the law—
I saw

an elderly man who
smiled and looked away

to the north past a house—
a woman in blue

who was laughing and
leaning forward to look up

into the man's half
averted face

and a boy of eight who was
looking at the middle of

the man's belly
at a watchchain—

The supreme importance
of this nameless spectacle

sped me by them
without a word—

Why bother where I went?
for I went spinning on the

four wheels of my car
along the wet road until

I saw a girl with one leg
over the rail of a balcony.
(119–120)

In the course of his career he would write a great many conventionally focused poems, but he considered this open-to-all-signals kind of form characteristically his own. The opening lines—"In passing with my mind/ on nothing in the world / but the right of way"—became a prescription for the writing of a poem, and its main ingredients are spontaneity and randomness.

Williams felt that a writer-perceiver needed to be as subtly and as miscellaneously attentive to the particularities of experience as possible, and he associated that attentive set with doctoring. In the random, unpredisposed flashes of understanding that came through patients' unconscious self-revelations, "It is then we see, by this constant feeling for a meaning, from the unselected nature of the material, just as it comes in over the phone or at the office door, that there is no better way to get an intimation of what is going on in the world."[79] And the miscellaneousness of things, coming into the mind "just as it comes in over the phone or at the office door" has its own deep significance, as he semi-reveals in this passage from a piece significantly entitled "The Simplicity of Disorder": "The firemen—unlike the cops—have six silver buttons three on each side down the slit at the back and bottom of their coats—of which the lining, as they walk, shows red. This is the essence of literature. And the concrete replica of the Palazzo Vecchio cupid in the frozen fountain hugs still his dolphin."[80] And what might that essence be? The biggest, best, and most authentic of all: as he says in a similar passage in *A Novelette*, "These and other things have a relationship with each other simply because both are actual" (297). It's like Cézanne, Williams said in a late interview: "He put it down on the canvas so that there would be a meaning without saying anything at all. Just the relation of the parts to themselves."[81] We might note the Williams-James connection again, however, and James's idea that

> The real world as it is given objectively at this moment is the sum total of all its beings and events now. But can we think of such a sum? Can we realize for an instant what a cross-section of all existence at a definite point in time would be? While I talk and the flies buzz, a sea-gull catches a fish at the mouth of the Amazon, a tree falls in the Adirondack wilderness, a man sneezes in Germany, a horse dies in Tartary, and twins are born in France. What does that mean? Does the contemporaneity of these events with one another, and with a million others as disjointed, form a rational bond between them, and unite them into anything that means for us a world? Yet just such a collateral contemporaneity, and nothing else, is the real order of the world.[82]

That same kind of collateral contemporaneity was something to which Williams could give himself over with a deep enthusiasm, with a gusto for the multifarious surfaces and details of the world and of life. It seems as if Williams felt it was a profitable exchange: the whole range of intellectual and egocentric concerns for the beautifully indiscriminate and ready (and *meaningful*) particularities of the world. Not quite like Hemingway, preoccupied with a man's inner equilibrium and capacity to survive an alien actuality, or Stevens, so attentive to his own mind's agency reflected in what he saw, Williams, in experimenting so extensively with the aesthetics of heterogeneity, shows a basic commitment to a knowable, trustworthy, love-worthy world. His sense of the invalidity of our categories of form and order thus did not, for the most part, carry with it a sense that our specific perceptions did not represent reality reliably.

Then too, almost paradoxically, Williams found he could discover himself in the very details of the world he had put himself aside to study. This was the conscious premise of his magnum opus *Paterson*: that from a relative point of view (which was all anyone could have) a person's own collateral contemporaneity, if it were represented with maximum linguistic authenticity, could stand not only for the world but for the person. *Paterson*'s sprawling, inconclusive, five-part-plus conglomeration is a kind of model of the city and the world, and of the doctor and the poet too. "That is why I started to write *Paterson*," he said, "a man is indeed a city, and for the poet there are no ideas but in things."[83] Thus are the elements of poetry recreated out of the very effort to destroy and negate them: structure and symbol growing out of conglomerated nominalism and literalness, self-reflection out of the strictest focus on the otherness of the other.

There are a number of excellent studies of *Paterson*, and I do not mean to reduplicate them here,* but let one of his far more modest and conventional examples show how externally guided conglomeration can result in self-depiction. The poem is "Simplex Sigilum Veri," written when Williams was well into his *Paterson* project; the poet-speaker seems to be randomly surveying the clutter on his desk, beginning by noticing "an american papermatch packet/ closed . . . ," and ending the nine-stanza poem like this:

> . . . surfaces of all sorts
> bearing printed characters, bottles
> words printed on the backs of
>
> two telephone directories, titles
> for poems, The Advertising Biographical
> Calendar of Medicine, Wednesday 18
> Thursday 19, Friday 20, papers
>
> of various shades sticking out
> from under others, throwing
> the printing out of line: portrait
> of all that which we have lost,
>
> a truncated pyramid, bronzed
> metal (probably the surface
> only) to match the tray, to which
> a square, hinged lid is fixed,
>
> the inkstand, from whose
> imagined top the Prince of Wales
> having climbed up, once with all
> his might drove a golf ball.**

---

*See, for example, Joel Conarroe, *WCW's Paterson: Language and Landscape* (University of Pennsylvania Press, 1970); Charles Doyle, *WCW and the American Poem* (St. Martin's, 1982); James Guimond, *The Art of WCW*; and Henry M. Sayre, *The Visual Text of WCW*.
**I use Williams's revised version from *Collected Earlier Poems*, 463–464, because it slightly enhances the senses of miscellaneousness, indeterminacy, and flux.

The whole poem has rattled along like this, its punctuation loose and at times too indeterminate for us to decide what goes with what, in constant restless motion like the eye scanning a clutter, coming to a full stop only when the scanning is finished. The focus gradually tightens on relatively more personal concerns for Williams, though, moving from matchflap bank-picture, pencil and primrose in the beginning to printed characters, words, titles, signifiers, off-kilter printed lines, and a "portrait of all that which we have lost." Does that latter thought go with the preceding jumbled elements of language or with the succeeding truncated pyramid, incomplete and probably cheaply bronzed, actually an inkstand, a source of word-characters and symbol of literary creation? Or perhaps with the (conceivably real) triumphant act of the Prince of Wales on the top of a real pyramid, imaginatively superimposed by the poet over this topless metal one on his desk? Either or all of these could stand as a "portrait of all that which we have lost," especially in depicting the self-doubt of a person trying to produce poetry. The implied self-doubt is doubly ironic and humorously so: the action of the Prince of Wales is a mock heroic thing; it is done triumphantly, "with all his might," yet all the conquest and ingenuity it represents is subverted by the vanity and foolishness of the endeavor itself (a golf ball? from off a pyramid??!). But that is exhilaration and accomplishment, while here a would-be writer only sits, facing a clutter of broken, lost, and wasted phrases and his truncated-pyramid-inkstand. Which man then is the greater fool?

The poem is an externally guided conglomeration, its images and their connections dictated by physical presences and relationships, its rhythms and structure by the movement of a perceiving eye, yet it is self-depiction too and in a much deeper way than by merely implying that, yes, I am the person who is identified by the possession of all these things. It also implies a complex sense of the speaker-poet's relation to his art, a subtle portrait of a self-image.

The ambiguous presence of the Prince of Wales is an element of nonliteralism, though. Whether his epic tee-shot is a recollection from the newspaper or a dadaesque fabrication, it comes into the poetic meditation not from the cluttered desktop but from the imagination of the poet. Whatever "simple seal of truth" ("Simplex Sigilum Veri") the poem offers is an internal as well as an external thing, and it can serve to remind us again that to Williams pure literalism is not ultimately achievable.

In exploring Williams's efforts to attune his compositions to his own creating consciousness, let us start with several more of his general postulates. Although he was a good intuitive epistemologist, his general formulations—mostly groping improvisations—were often ungainly and confused. But through the conceptual murk and bad writing we can divine the lineaments of a modernist, postrealist sense of the complex subjective aspects of simple perception. This is a 1920 statement from *Kora in Hell*:

> *In the mind there is a continual play of obscure images which coming between the eyes and their prey seem pictures on the screen at the movies. Somewhere there appears to be a mal-adjustment. The wish would be to see not floating visions of unknown purport but the imaginative qualities of the actual things being perceived accompany their gross vision in a slow dance, interpreting as they go. But inasmuch as this will not always be the case one must dance nevertheless as he can.* (67)

I take this to mean that although we might wish to apprehend "the imaginative qualities of the actual things," we are unable to get beyond a "dance" of "obscure images" which are part internal and part external in their makeup. Here is another formulation, written in the late twenties, part of a discussion of French painters in *The Embodiment of Knowledge*:

> Well, what does one see? to paint? Why the tree, of course, is the facile answer. Not at all. The tree as a tree does not exist literally, figuratively or any way you please—for the appraising eye of the artist—or any man—the tree does not exist. What does exist, and in heightened intensity for the artist is the impression created by the shape and color of an object before him in his sensual being—his whole body (not his eyes) his body, his mind, his memory, his place: himself—that is what he sees.[84]

So for Williams the quest for authentic knowledge leads back to an individual person's experiences, sense of relevance, self. And "since," as he says in *Paterson I*, "we know nothing, pure/ and simple, beyond/ our own complexities,"[85] the writer might just as productively focus on the "dance" of "obscure images" and "imaginative qualities" as on the presumptive "actual things" behind them: thus the obvious inner directedness of much of Williams's writing.

At times it takes the form of an imagined image, such as this one in "To a Solitary Disciple," which by metaphorically extending the lines of a steeple enlarges the possibilities of perceptual reality as well:

Rather grasp
how the dark

converging lines
of the steeple
meet at the pinnacle—
perceive how
its little ornament
tries to stop them—

See how it fails!
See how the converging lines
of the hexagonal spire
escape upward—
receding, dividing!
—sepals
that guard and contain
the flower!

Observe
how motionless
the eaten moon
lies in the protecting lines.[86]

In a similar fit of invention, he had, in the second chapter of *Spring and All* (entitled "Chapter 19"), imagined the destruction of the entire population of the world (that *could* be a kind of joke back in 1923), only to have the whole of evolution repeat itself with the coming of spring in the fourth chapter (entitled "Chapter VI"). "Yes," he proclaims, "the imagination, drunk with prohibitions, has destroyed and recreated everything afresh in the likeness of that which it was. Now indeed men look about in amazement at each other with a full realization of the meaning of 'art'" (93). The episode is no more than a minor dada enactment with a forced moral, but it shows Williams's use of an inventing, synthetic imagination, different from the objectifying, empathizing imagination for which he is so famous. His use of the inventing imagination in the image-concocting mode cannot approach Stevens's in subtlety, ingenuity, or persistence, though.

Frequently Williams would structure a work along lines dictated by his subjective, synthetic imagination, sometimes with interesting and prophetic results. He produced a spate of these works from the late teens to the early thirties—*Kora in Hell, Spring and All, The Great American Novel, The Descent of Winter, A Novelette,* and other shorter works—as well as *Paterson* in the 1940s and 1950s. As the epistemological revolution rolled on, these works influenced or at least anticipated subsequent developments in American literature in the directions of greater spontaneity of composition, more explicit reflexiveness of presentation, and more personal self-revelation. Allen Ginsberg, John Barth, Robert Lowell, and others were soon to make these trends dominant characteristics.

Williams classified *Kora* and *Spring and All* as "improvisations," used actual diary structure for *The Descent*, and called *A Novelette* "automatic writing." Structurally in each he was making an attempt to catch things as they came to him, to make an authentic representation of the creating imagination at work. In *The Great American Novel* he attempted "a satire on the novel form" that would break down conventions of coherence and representation by spontaneously following the moving moment of its own creation. In introducing the work Webster Schott calls it "one of the first anti-novels written in the U.S." (155). Let us look at it in some detail as an example of a subjectively driven composition and a harbinger of literary things to come.

The "novel" begins by confronting its own paradox—"If there is progress then there is a novel," but "Words. Words cannot progress" (158–159), it says. Although these statements are two pages apart, they are explicit points of self-aware reflexiveness acting to channel a diverse stream of recollections and associations, fantasies and self-contradictions:

> Words are not permanent unless the graphite be scraped up and put in a tube or the ink lifted. Words progress into the ground. One must begin with words if one is to write. But what then of smell? What then of the hair on the trees or the golden brown cherries under the black cliffs. What of the weakness of smiles that leaves dimples as much as to say: forgive me—I am slipping, slipping, slipping into nothing at all. Now I am not what I was when the word was forming to say what I am. I sit so on my bicycle and look at you greyly, dimpling because it is September and I am older than I was. (158)

The time imagery is like Aiken's—the smile itself is lost in the very moment of perceiving it as a smile—although Williams's embodiment of this unremitting transience has less the character of a literary set piece, more the character of a Bergsonian meditation, aware of itself at the moment of meditating and of all the flickers of experience, idea, and intuition that make up a moment.

Since this work is meant to give the impression that a writer is improvising it, its structure is inner-driven, developing according to an associational flux—conceptual, imagistic, and at times very conspicuously linguistic:

I'm new, said she, I don't think you'll find my card here. You're new; how interesting. Can you read the letters on that chart? Open your mouth. Breathe. Do you have headaches? No. Ah, yes, you are new. I'm new said the oval moon at the bottom of the mist funnel, brightening and paling. I don't think you'll find my card there. Open your mouth—Breathe—A crater big enough to hold the land from New York to Philadelphia. New! I'm new, said the quartz crystal on the parlor table—like glass—Mr. Tiffany bought a car load of them. Like water or white rock candy—I'm new, said the mist rising from the duck pond, rising, curling, turning under the moon—Unknown grasses asleep in the level mists, pieces of the fog. Last night it was an ocean. Tonight trees. Already it is yesterday. Turned into the wrong street seeking to pass the power house from which the hum, hmmmmmmmmmm—sprang. Electricity has been discovered for ever. I'm new, says the great dynamo. I am progress. I make a word. Listen! UMMMMMMMMMMMMMMMMMM—

Ummmmmmmmmmmmm—Turned into the wrong street at three A.M. lost in the fog, listening, searching—Waaaa! said the baby. I'm new. A boy! A what? Boy. Shit, said the father of two other sons. Listen here. This is no place to talk that way. What a word to use. I'm new, said the sudden word. (162)

Unlike many of Gertrude Stein's improvisational word-streams, that of *The G.A.N.* does not thwart coherence and destroy meaning word by word, but it does conglomerate nonrationally. It even includes embedded narratives of a very conventionally focused sort: "Leaving the meeting room where the Mosquito Extermination Commission had been holding an important fall conference they walked out on to the portico of the County Court House Annex where for a moment they remained in the shadow cast by the moon" (160). Some of the narratives recount the doctor's ordinary or extraordinary experiences; others (since this is after all the Great American Novel) imagine episodes from America's history. Improvisation is the law of this work, not Bergsonism, and its sequence conforms only to the willfulness of a liberated imagination. Here the prose writer is "passing with my mind/ on nothing in the world/ but the right of way," but it's his own whimsically unordered brain he's driving through. "On sped the little family all crowded into one seat, the two children sleeping," he says in one extended passage:

In the Dutch church on the old Paramus Road Aaron Burr was married to Mrs. Prevost, Jataqua! It is near Ho-ho-kus, cleft-in-the-rocks, where the Leni Lenapes of the Delaware nation had their village from time immemorial. Aaron, my darling, life begins anew! It is a new start. Let us look forward staunchly together—

The long, palm-like leaves of the ailanthus trees moved slowly up and down in the little wind, up and down.

And along this road came the British. Aaron, the youth from Princeton, gathered his command together and drove them back. Mother I cannot sleep in this bed, it is full of *British soldiers*. Why so it is! How horrid.

And he too, on his memorable retreat, that excellent judge of horseflesh, George Washington, he too had passed over this road; and these trees, the oldest of them, had witnessed him. And now the wind has torn the finest of them in half. (190)

And the sequence continues through pear tree images, newspaper pictures of women "in very short skirts," jargon from fashion advertisements, Mrs. Prevost's imagined voice flattering Burr, Hamilton's death, the fall of a pear that's eaten by pigs, and a woman's musing on a plan to go to Europe to let her bobbed hairdo grow out. Throughout this passage the writer's imagination thusly overflows with the mental features of a (purportedly) remembered drive.

There is a kind of self-revelation going on in *The G.A.N.* too, with feelings (and flirtations) freely acknowledged—for example an episode in which the narrator recalls having made a rendezvous with a high-school girl, "a pretty pair of legs in blue stockings." But he stands her up—"off he goes in search of a word"—and the consequences, real or imagined, haunt him. His own foolish romanticism on the one hand, and his lack of nerve on the other; his marital infidelity and his habit of escaping from life into literature—all are evoked by this musing:

What do you think! He has left his wife, and a child in the high school has been ill a week, weeping her eyes out and murmuring his name. Is it not terrible?

It is the wind! The wind is in the poplars twiddling the fading leaves between his fingers idly and thinking, thinking of the words he will make, new words to be written on white paper but never to be spoken by the lips to pass into her ear.

Quietly he goes home to his wife and taking her by the shoulder wakes her: Here I am. (180)

This is not quite the confessional stuff of subsequent writers—the work doesn't seem to exist for the purpose of exploring the writer's special instabilities—but the self in it is not the generic self or the remotely implied self of earlier writers either.

In *The G.A.N.* Williams maintains a wryly satirical, self-consciously reflexive approach to the whole welter, personal and impersonal, real and imagined, historical and experiential. The book seems to be saying "Here is America through one American imagination"; and it gives its last words to a rag merchant delivering a long and detailed explanation of the making of shoddy out of discarded woolen rags.

In many ways, of course, Williams's relatively early prose improvisations were clear forerunners of the late epic *Paterson*. In that work he would use a number of the same materials and approaches, especially the inner-imagination-driven structure, and the new style of reflexiveness, with the author making us explicitly aware of the process of constructing the work. In a surge of ambition he would define his subject, his world, more broadly, and employ a more varied array of tones and approaches, but the whole *Paterson* endeavor was implicit in works like *Spring and All* and *The Great American Novel*.

In groping after aesthetic and epistemological frameworks by which to understand the nature and function of his writing, Williams early discovered the idea that the literary work is an independent created object in itself and thus at a stroke put all of his literary productions, however imagined, into the category of subjective. Oddly, considering the realistic specificity of so many of his works, and his notion of "no ideas but in things," he claimed at times that true works of art were not at all mimetic or representational, "not 'like' anything but transfused with the same forces which transfuse the earth" (121); "you do not *copy* nature, you make something which is an *imitation* of nature, . . . you *make* a natural object."[87]

The idea was highly (and variously) derivative. Williams himself cites these sources: Stein's regarding words as real rather than as symbols;[88] the surrealists' distortion of content, thus calling attention to the medium;[89] Virginia Woolf's idea of the work of the imagination that goes into the artistic product;[90] Zukofsky's and the objectivists' theory of the poem as an object;[91] and the painters—Gris, Cézanne and others—who dispensed with the illusion of simple depiction (117). He especially liked the remark a painter-acquaintance made to a woman art gallery customer who had asked "'what is all that down in this left hand lower corner?' . . . 'That, Madam,' said he, 'is paint.'"[92] However derivative the idea was to Williams, there is good evidence that he thoroughly internalized it and worked it over in his own mind. For example, in *The Embodiment of Knowledge* he makes this connection between realism, the nature of language, and the artifactuality of the literary work:

> "Realism" has one inevitable catch in it: it is not susceptible to writing, to being written as a transcription of events or even facts. . . . To transcribe the real creates, by the same act, an unreality, something besides the real which is its transcription, since the writing is one thing, what it transcribes another, the writing a fiction, necessarily and always so.
> The only real in writing is writing itself.[93]

The idea encourages writers to free themselves from bondage to a spurious realism, and makes them conscious of the essential arbitrariness of subjects, language, and techniques. For an aesthetician's purpose it short-circuits the complex relationship between art and experience, although for Williams it seems to have acted as a talisman to liberate and sanction his restless imagination.

In the course of this long study we have observed that writers deeply involved in aesthetic and epistemological concerns tend to be not much involved directly with social or humanistic concerns. Williams is an exception. Not only did he have a humane bias and an occupation that kept him in constant touch with people and their problems, but he seems to have perceived that a world better suited for these people could be attained only through infrapolitical revolution: revolution of the word and the process of conceptualization. Williams felt he needed to think a world without thought because thought was corrupt, an instrument of distraction, reductionism, control. Like those dadaists whose aesthetic revolt began as a revolt against mind-sets such as had produced war and exploitation and regimentation, Williams's version of knowledge destruction had a basically humanistic, infrapolitical thrust. "The fight is on," he proclaimed in *Spring and All* in 1923, "These men who have had the governing of the mob through all the repetitious years resent the new order. Who can answer them? . . . Those who led yesterday wish to hold their sway a while longer. It is not difficult to understand their mood. They have their great weapons to hand: 'science,' 'philosophy' and most dangerous of all 'art' " (98). *Williams* can answer them, and in *Spring and All* he answers with spring and a spontaneous, antirational flux of prose and poems. Much later he could still argue for the social basis of his art, here in a 1950 letter: "The poem to me (until I go broke) is an attempt, an experiment, a failing experiment, toward assertion with broken means but an assertion, always, of a new and total culture, the lifting of an environment to expression. Thus it is social, the poem is a social instrument —accepted or not accepted seems to be of no material importance. It embraces everything we are."[94]

Williams was no social thinker, but in a very nuts-and-bolts way his literary approach forced an attention to the democratic detail, to the individual human being and her or his way of thinking and talking and living. "I was impressed by the picture of the times, depression years, the plight of the poor," he later recalled about the writing of *The Knife of the Times*; "I felt it very vividly."[95] He picked up lingo with great precision and used it with great delight—people's sayings were "found objects" with depth of meaning and the flavor of actuality. Likewise in many of his works with Whitman-like conglomerative structures a great appreciation of the variety of people and their ways comes through as a subtheme, as in this moment of appreciation of the Capitol's mural in "It Is a Living Coral":

> this scaleless
>
> jumble is superb
>
> and accurate in its
> expression
>
> of the thing they
> would destroy—.[96]

Williams is modern America's great defender of heterogeneity, and his destruction of knowledge worked primarily to that end.

14   John Dos Passos: Actuality Montage
(the Real Event and the Speech of the People)

John Dos Passos (1896–1970) was the writer who brought out the political and sociopsychological potentials of the destruction of knowledge, and he did it by way of some striking innovations in language and narrative technique. He had no specific aesthetic or epistemological program and not even much inclination for such concerns, yet the works of his prime —*Manhattan Transfer* (1925) and the trilogy *U.S.A.* (1930, 1932, 1936)—are strikingly original achievements that are monumental products of the destructionist's bent. Two of his greatest cultural preoccupations were politics and art: he grew into (and later through) a period of radical political dissent, and he was deeply fascinated with modernist experiments in the arts in Paris in the late teens and in New York in the twenties. He was also a careful observer of language and its social and psychological effects. The works he concocted out of those preoccupations developed new approaches to perceiving, to knowing, and to fictional representation. So deeply inherent were the epistemological concerns in the art, the politics, and the awareness of language of the age that he became an innovative epistemologist almost inadvertently. Nevertheless, by becoming such he was able to assault American social and political inequities on both the ideological and the subideological levels.

It is revealing to see him come into his artistic and intellectual prime as this process is revealed in his letters, diary entries, and early novels. Before the process began Dos Passos was a highly literate, highly literary undergraduate at Harvard, steeped in the classics and the contemporaries. The English poets, the Russian novelists, Shaw, Henry James, Verlaine, Byron, Cicero, Masefield: his early correspondence cites a vast variety. (Although one of the few non-belletrist writers he recommended back in 1916 was William James, whose writings he with some surprise found "not a bit dry," and "the most interesting books on psychology I know.")[1] Later in his life he tended to make a great deal of the influence of Whitman on his early thinking,[2] of Dreiser, who "had already transferred Zola's naturalism to the American scene,"[3] and of Stephen Crane, who had "a terribly good ear for conversation and the way people put things."[4]

His 1916 opinions about contemporary American literature showed a strong bias toward the ideas of the realists. In his first remunerated piece of writing, an essay, "Against American Literature" (in the October 14, 1916, *New Republic*), he inveighed against the prevailing literature of "gentle satire," backhandedly complimenting it as "sincere, careful, and full of shrewd observation of contemporary life," but criticizing its lacks of "passion and profound thought," of "unconscious intimacy with nature," of "vivid tangibility," and of "dramatic actuality." Referring to Edith Wharton, Robert Herrick, and Mary S. Watts (*The Legacy*), he lamented that "the tone of the higher sort of writing in this country is undoubtedly that of a well brought up and intelligent woman, tolerant, versed in the things of this world, quietly humorous, but bound tightly in the fetters of 'niceness,' of the middle-class outlook."[5] Whitman provided a model of liberation from the genteel: deeply connected, no-holds-barred, vividly candid. Dos Passos was only twenty then, and in his enthusiasm to be one of the promoters of a deeper and more vital literature he took a position that was tautological, built on gender-based critical stereotypes, and, as Townsend Ludington recently pointed out, embarrassingly close to plagiarizing Van Wyck Brooks's *America's Coming of Age*, published just a year earlier.[6]

Like Whitman and the earlier realists, the young Dos Passos also especially venerated raw experience: acquiring it was both a yearning and a duty. "I approve of your manual labor scheme," he wrote to a friend; "How does one do it? I have for years been wanting to do something of the sort, but have never got to anything more strenuous than gardening." Another time he complained, "It is so hard to get away from the lingo, from the little habits of speech and action, from the petty snobberies of ones own class."[7] He was about to get away and into something strenuous indeed:

> In three or four weeks I expect to sail for France—either as an Ambulance Driver with the Norton-Harjes people, or in some other capacity with the Red Cross.
>
> I have been for a long while very anxious to see things at first hand —but circumstances have in every case interfered. This time, however, along with the rest of America—I think I shall get my taste of the war.[8]

The young Dos Passos had a radical social philosophy too. In 1917 he identified fervently with pacifistic and socialistic causes, bitterly opposing

Woodrow Wilson's shift away from neutrality, identifying capitalism as the cause of the war, and, inspired by the speeches of Emma Goldman and Max Eastman, beginning to talk revolution.[9] From the midst of the crackdowns on pacifist opinions, the jailings of "draft obstructors," and the banning of *The Masses* from the mails, he was heading abroad—to look for signs of revolution over there, he would tell himself or his radicalized friends; to help America put an end to that bloody mess, he would say on other occasions. Perhaps; but most of all it was his quest for firsthand experience that was driving him. As he would later recall, "my father died in January of 1917, and I went ahead into the ambulance service. I suppose that World War I then became my university," admitting too that, "like Charlie Anderson in 42nd Parallel, I wanted to go over before everything 'went bellyup.'"[10]

The experience he got in the ambulance corps in France in 1917–1918 was almost enough for him in its awesomeness and specificity: as his diary records for August 26, 1917,

> I want to be able to express, later—all of this—all the tragedy and hideous excitement of it. I have seen so very little. I must experience more of it, & more—The grey crooked fingers of the dead, the dark look of dirty mangled bodies, their groans & joltings in the ambulances, the vast tomtom of the guns, the ripping tear shells make when they explode, the song of shells outgoing, like vast woodcocks—their contented whirr as they near their mark—the twang of fragments like a harp broken in the air—& the rattle of stones & mud on your helmet.[11]

That sort of detached, experience-soaking reaction was only one of his reactions. Witnessed firsthand, the war was brutally absurd, an utter mind- and mouth-stopper, a blank dead end for all the philosophies, categories, and mind-sets one could conceivably bring to it. At times it seemed that all one had that could be saved in words was a stream of sensations and a recoil of bitterly ironic bafflement:

> The stream of sensation flows by—I suck it up like a sponge—my reactions are a constant weather vane—a little whimsical impish—giggling—sneering at tragedy—Horror is so piled on horror that there can be no more—Despair gives place to delirious laughter—
>
> How damned ridiculous it all is! The long generations toiling—skimping, lashing themselves screwing higher and higher the tension of their minds, polishing brighter and brighter the mirror of in-

telligence to end in this—My God what a time—All the cant and hypocrisy, all the damnable survivals, all the vestiges of old truths now putrid and false infect the air, choke you worse than German gas—The ministers from their damn smug pulpits, the business men —the heroics about war—my country right or wrong—oh infinities of them! Oh the tragic farce of the world. Hardy's Arch satirist is more a bungling clown than an astute and sinister humorist.[12]

Typical of American writers caught up in World War I, of Hemingway, Cummings, and others, Dos Passos developed a keen sensitivity to the disparity between the meaningless brutality he personally experienced and the "cant and hypocrisy" by which it was being rationalized. It fit his social philosophy, too, and gave it new colorations, new urgency. As he wrote from the front to his protégé, Rumsey Marvin,

The war is utter damn nonsense—a vast cancer fed by lies and self seeking malignity on the part of those who don't do the fighting.

Of all the things in this world a government is the thing least worth fighting for.

None of the poor devils whose mangled dirty bodies I take to the hospital in my ambulance really give a damn about any of the aims of this ridiculous affair—They fight because they are too cowardly & too unimaginative not to see which way they ought to turn their guns—

For God's sake, Rummy boy, put this in your pipe and smoke it —everything said & written & thought in America about the war is lies—God! They choke one like poison gas.[13]

The language of lies was juxtaposed in Dos Passos's imagination with the more authentic, more human language of the men around him. "The linguistic stimulation of being immersed in the ways of speaking of common soldiers from all sorts of countries" he later cited as a crucial element of his war experience that helped make him a novelist.[14] In his first novel, *One Man's Initiation—1917* (written during and after the war, and first published in 1920), we see the protagonist, Martin Howe, beginning to learn his social philosophy very empirically by listening:

"It is funny," said the little doctor suddenly, "to think how much nearer we are, in state of mind, in everything, to the Germans than to anyone else."

"You mean that the soldiers in the trenches are all further from the people at home than from each other, no matter what side they are on."

The little doctor nodded.

"God, it's so stupid! Why can't we go over and talk to them? Nobody's fighting about anything. . . . God it's so hideously stupid!" cried Martin, suddenly carried away, helpless in the flood of his passionate revolt.

"Life is stupid," said the little doctor sententiously.

Suddenly from the lines came a splutter of machine-guns.[15]

Later in his initiation Martin Howe arrives at this diagnosis of the war: it is a conspiracy by the powers of money and "the phrases, the phrases" of publicity against humanity:

> "What terrifies me rather is their power to enslave our minds," Martin went on, his voice growing louder and surer as his idea carried him along. "I shall never forget the flags, the menacing, exultant flags along all the streets before we went to war, the gradual unbaring of teeth, gradual lulling to sleep of people's humanity and sense by the phrases, the phrases. . . . America, as you know, is ruled by the press. And the press is ruled by whom? Who shall ever know what dark forces bought and bought until we should be ready to go blinded and gagged to war? . . . People seem to so love to be fooled. Intellect used to mean freedom, a light struggling against darkness. Now the darkness is using the light for its own purposes. . . . We are slaves of bought intellect, willing slaves."[16]

The political paradigm Dos Passos brought away from the war would stay with him in nearly the same form well into the late 1930s. As he saw it, humankind was victimized not only by warmongering, profiteering, and patriotic cant, but by a subtler exploitation and brainwashing, too, by "this all pervading spirit of commerce—this new religion of steel and stamped paper!"[17] The lesson he learned about language at the same time was to be even longer lasting: language could be an instrument of victimization or it could be a connection to actuality. It needed to be attended to with care, precision, and vigilance against manipulation and self-delusion. Unguarded, language—especially educated, intellectual language, the language of knowledge—tended to rationalize—to hallow, even—the operations of the social machinery. And to a person deeply within that machinery and at risk, such rationalizing language was not merely hollow but physically revolting. As Dos Passos wrote in his diary on the front in 1917,

At present America is to me utter anathema—I cant think of it without belching disgust at the noisiness of it, the meaningless chatter of
its lying tongues.

I've been trying to read a copy of the New Republic that has come
over—honestly I couldn't get through it. Its smug phraseology, hid-
ing utter meaninglessness—was nauseous.

And away off the guns roar & fart & spit their venom & here I lie
spitting my venom in my fashion.[18]

Get the language clear: like Stein, Pound, Hemingway, Aiken, Stevens, and Williams (and others), Dos Passos was to spend his career as a
writer struggling against debased language and the cultural, emotional,
and intellectual enslavement it brought with it. Dos Passos's special contribution to American literature would be his revelation of the sociopolitical potential of this aspect of the destruction of knowledge.

His first three novels can be seen as attempts to repudiate the politics
and social philosophies of the past and to find a language and a literary
form authentic enough to accomplish that repudiation. *One Man's Initiation:
1917* (1920), *Three Soldiers* (1921), and *Streets of Night* (1923) express their
ideological-level audacities clearly enough: war and conventional politics
are senseless, society is (like the army) a machine for stifling and exploit-
ing the individual, and the cultural heritage of the modern age is no more
than a set of dangerous inhibitions of insight and psyche. The technical
approaches of these novels constitute some destruction of narrative conventions, but they are nowhere near as radical as those of the later *Manhattan Transfer* and *U.S.A.* and of the emerging norms of their own modernist milieu.

In *One Man's Initiation: 1917* Dos Passos confronts us with narrative
discontinuity and a kind of prose imagism in his attack against sociopolitical ideals and assumptions. These antinarrative techniques seem to flow
from the book's basic intent to represent the factors, however unconventional or trivial, that would produce an extreme psychological and political revolution in consciousness. In keeping with his own revelation that
the experience of warfare destroyed one's senses of the relevance and
coherence of experience, he built this book out of a series of moments,
complete but often slight firsthand impressions. The novel is like a string
of expanded diary entries—as a matter of fact it *is* to some extent a string
of diary entries, and some of them not so very much expanded or elaborated at that. (Compare, for example, Dos Passos's diary record of the
men on the troop ship singing "God Help Kaiser Bill" with its descendent

episode from Chapter I of the novel.)[19] Visual impressions and conversational vignettes are the principal materials of this novel, and they have none of the usual sort of narrative coherence. Some of them substantially affect the radicalization of the witnesser-protagonist, so there is a thematic direction to their accumulation, but the episodes interconnect infrequently, their secondary characters (all of the characters but the protagonist, that is) come and go randomly and situationally, and the images in the various episodes are representative details rather than symbols of a more remote unifying truth. The muddy road, the dying mule, the sharing of a bottle of wine in the sunshine, the comments of a cynical doctor, the scorning of the roadside cross, the smell of mustard gas—they're connected by being part of this character's kaleidoscope of education and despair, but they remain essentially discreet details.

Dos Passos presents the novel's moments in a fashion that is nearly imagism. Care has obviously been taken to maximize the vividness and to minimize the mental processing of impressions. Like Williams striving to let the "otherness" of people and things speak through his writings, and like Dos Passos himself later trying to capture the works and ways of people in their own terms in *U.S.A.*, some of the moments in *One Man's Initiation: 1917* seem attempts at unelaborated epiphany:

> There is a new smell in the wind, a smell unutterably sordid, like the smell of the poor immigrants landing at Ellis Island. Martin Howe glances round and sees advancing down the road ranks and ranks of strange grey men whose mushroom-shaped helmets give an eerie look as of men from the moon in a fairy tale.
>
> "Why, they're Germans," he says to himself; "I'd quite forgotten they existed."
>
> "Ah, they're prisoners." The doctor gets to his feet and glances down the road and then turns to his work again.
>
> The tramp of feet marching in unison on the rough shell-pitted road, and piles and piles of grey men clotted with dried mud, from whom comes the new smell, the sordid, miserable smell of the enemy.
>
> "Things going well?" Martin asks a guard, a man with ashen face and eyes that burn out of black sockets.
>
> "How should I know?"
>
> "Many prisoners?"
>
> "How should I know?" (135–136)

Dos Passos was well aware of the principles and practices of imagism: he had reviewed Pound's *Des Imagistes* for the *Harvard Monthly*, and later recommended that a friend read the works of Amy Lowell.* In *One Man's Initiation: 1917* he directly presents the sights, sounds, and smells, along with some of the protagonist's feelings, without interpretation, comment, or even Stephen Crane's kind of narrator's irony. Some interpretation of significances is provided in the dialogue, as Martin Howe learns to articulate his felt radicalism; some is provided in the accounts of his thoughts, as he gropes toward radical understanding; but principally interpretation comes out through the imagery, as if the causes of radicalism were implicitly out there for him (or for anybody) to feel. For example, the following passage shows how Dos Passos could put forth radical politics (pacifistic internationalism) by imagistic means. Martin Howe is observing a wounded German prisoner of war who is being used to help carry wounded Frenchmen:

> The prisoner wiped the sweat from his grime-streaked forehead, and started up the step of the dugout again, a closed stretcher on his shoulder. Something made Martin look after him as he strolled down the rutted road. He wished he knew German so that he might call after the man and ask him what manner of a man he was.
>
> Again, like the snapping of a whip, three shells flashed yellow as they exploded in the brilliant sunlight of the road. The slender figure of the prisoner bent suddenly double, like a pocket-knife closing, and lay still. Martin ran out, stumbling in the hard ruts. In a soft child's voice the prisoner was babbling endlessly, contentedly. Martin kneeled beside him and tried to lift him, clasping him round the chest under the arms. He was very hard to lift, for his legs dragged limply in their soaked trousers, where the blood was beginning to saturate the muddy cloth, stickily. Sweat dripped from Martin's face, on the man's face, and he felt the arm-muscles and the ribs pressed against his body as he clutched the wounded man tightly to him in the effort of carrying him towards the dugout. The effort gave Martin a strange contentment. It was as if his body were taking part in the agony of this man's body. At last they were washed out, all the hatreds, all the lies, in blood and sweat. Nothing was left but the quiet friendliness of beings alike in every part, eternally alike.

*Letter to Rumsey Marvin, March 1920, in Townsend Ludington, ed., *The Fourteenth Chronicle* (Gambit, 1973), 282. Dos Passos's connections to imagism are surveyed in Ludington's, *JDP: A Twentieth Century Odyssey* (E. P. Dutton, 1980), 75, and Linda Welsheimer Wagner, *Dos Passos: Artist as American* (University of Texas Press, 1979), 4–5.

Two men with a stretcher came from the dugout, and Martin laid the man's body, fast growing limper, less animated, down very carefully.

As he stood by the car, wiping the blood off his hands with an oily rag, he could still feel the man's ribs and the muscles of the man's arm against his side. It made him strangely happy. (147–148)

Stephen Crane and Hemingway have scenes of similar imagistic power, but Dos Passos's ability to focus humane political concerns by such means in 1920 is well worth appreciating.

Three Soldiers is similarly set in wartime France; its innovative increments consist of a broader social range, further experimentation with narrative continuity and discontinuity, and an increased emphasis on historiography. Dos Passos departed from the diary-discontinuity of the earlier novel and represented the characters more conventionally and more subjectively, but his choice of protagonists with three very different backgrounds and temperaments gave the book some of its larger scope and some of its own special discontinuity. Private Dan Fuselli is a hard-boiled, son-of-an-immigrant city kid, whose ambitions and smarts are shaped by the system, social and military. He wants to be rich some day, but he very much wants to be a corporal right away, and he schemes and fawns, insinuates and toughs it out, all to that purpose. He admires the self-confidence and easygoing veniality of his superiors, and he outspokenly hates revolutionaries. His eagerness to oblige the system has little success: after the Armistice he's still a private, and he gets assigned to a labor battalion (although we later hear a rumor that he's made corporal at last); meanwhile his supposedly faithful girl back home is reported to have married another man. "Chris" Chrisfield is a kid from an Indiana farm, a little guy with some (unconvincingly homespun) reveries about Mom's cooking and the fresh landscape of "God's country" and a seething, uncontrollable resentment of personal mistreatment. He identifies that urge as sinful, but it drives him to assassinate the officer who had singled him out for abuse. Although Chrisfield gets away with the battlefield assassination (*he* is made a corporal!), he's unable to contain his guilt or his indomitable feeling of oppression in the army, so we last see him down-and-out in Paris, having "flown the coop" from the comparatively easy duty with the army of occupation. Fuselli and Chrisfield have few and inconsequential points of contact. They are thematic complements in terms of natural reactions to oppression (and of that problematical corporalship), but Dos Passos's main intent in building the novel around them seems to have been to represent diversity—psychological, political, and even geographic.

Quite naturally the third soldier would be something like a college-educated Virginian and a musician. John Andrews, having joined the army in a desire to abandon the freedom that was then a terrible burden for him, soon learns to loathe "the mud of common slavery."[20] He sees the war as brutal meaninglessness, and struggles with his soldier status; after the Armistice his creative inspiration seems to be flooding back at the same time the military (perhaps because it has less justification) tightens its control over his life in response to his resistance. In an escalating spiral of spontaneous but self-thwarting rebellions, Andrews demurs, disobeys, and eventually deserts, only to be betrayed and captured at the novel's end. The Andrews story adds to the novel the scope of a different level of society and a more self-aware and socially aware consciousness.

Andrews connects with Chrisfield a bit—they become buddies and tent-mates and later help each other when they meet after both have deserted—but he connects with Fuselli only very incidentally. In this novel Dos Passos is beginning to have a feeling for the random discontinuity of social interaction: characters each have intensely personal lives that bypass, brush, or collide with each other like molecules in one of the old mechanistic systems. He is well behind Conrad in his depiction of the mutually alien individuality of people (*Nostromo* was 1904, *The Secret Agent* 1907), but Dos Passos's innovation is that these life-molecules aren't mutually involved in some single event or "affair" that binds them into a unity, however ironic. There is only the war and the Armistice—the whole military and civilian milieu of urban and rural France that was experienceable by Americans in 1918 and 1919. That and the theme of oppression and revolt are what define this novel as a unit.

Thus the outermost frame of *Three Soldiers* suggests the influence of historiographical rather than purely aesthetic ambitions, an early manifestation of that "passion for history" that Alfred Kazin would later identify as Dos Passos's special gift as a novelist.[21] Indeed Dos Passos himself, in the period between *Three Soldiers* and *Manhattan Transfer*, identified the historical aims of his writing clearly enough, as in this "Statement of Belief" he contributed to a set of credos published in the *Bookman* of September 1924:

> The only excuse for a novelist, aside from the entertainment and vicarious living his books give the people who read them, is as a sort of second-class historian of the age he lives in. The "reality" he misses by writing about imaginary people, he gains by being able to build a

reality more nearly out of his own factual experience than a plain historian or biographer can. I suppose the best kind of narrative would combine the two like Froissart or Commines, or Darwin in "The Voyage of the Beagle". I think that any novelist that is worth his salt is a sort of truffle dog digging up raw material which a scientist, an anthropologist or a historian can later use to permanent advantage. Of course there's Chaucer and Homer and the Edda, but that's all way over our heads.[22]

Looking back from 1932 in an introduction to a reissue of *Three Soldiers*, he stressed the continuing need for the destruction of illusions and the facing up to history:

> Today, though the future may not seem so gaily colored or full of clanging hopes as it was thirteen years ago . . . , we can at least meet events with our minds cleared of some of the romantic garbage that kept us from doing clear work then. Those of us who have lived through have seen these years strip the bunting off the great illusions of our time, we must deal with the raw structure of history now, we must deal with it quick, before it stamps us out.[23]

Thus the interest in history which was to become one of the major characteristics of his work was incipient and slowly emerging, right from the beginning of his career. But after *Three Soldiers* he had another novel to finish before what he would characterize as the "desperate experiment" of *Manhattan Transfer* got under way.

Streets of Night is a novel Dos Passos had started in his Harvard days, and his finishing it in 1923 left him free to pursue new possibilities in the art of fiction, although in itself it is not very venturesome. In terms of our inquiry here its most relevant features are aspects of its inside-outside characterization: its three central characters are presented with a strong message of their being psychologically determined—crippled, really—by their pasts and their social situations and with a very vivid sense of their isolation from each other, despite shared experiences and yearnings. The narrative is somewhat impressionistically constructed, with little or no exposition supporting its wealth of dialogue, reverie, and meditation, but with none of the studied discontinuities of the two war novels. The main characters are closely involved with each other, and this serves to unify the novel in the conventional way, while at the same time making more poignant the depiction of their inability to respond to each other humanly or satisfyingly. The three are young adults, and the streets of night they walk together are literally the streets of Boston where they live and study. Fanshaw is an aesthete Harvardian, always dreaming escapist dreams of wealth and living in the long ago. Torn between his mother's strong hold and the pull of an indeterminate future, and lacking any strong sense of conviction or desire, he will let an opportunity, a friend, or a world slip away. Wenny, his Harvard chum, is impulsive and negligent, likable and full of animal energy, yet terribly sexually inhibited. Nan is living a liberated life on her own and studying for a career as a performing musician, but she is torn between her rational goals and her sexual urges. The first of Dos Passos's many complex female portrayals, she fights good-humoredly and determinedly to find the path that will bring her a successful musical career, love, independence, and integrity, but caught between patterns of all-for-love and all-for-self-determination, she falters and loses it all. Rebuffing Wenny's desperate sexual advance (so desperately hoped-for!) in the interest of self-possession and career, she precipitates his suicide and is left with only a waning hope for success in music.

The past strangles these characters' hopes. Wenny is haunted and defeated by his minister-father's pious antisexuality; Fanshaw is stifled by his possessive and respectability-minded mother; Nan is set in her future spinster-aunt pattern partly by the example and conventional expectations of her own beloved spinster aunt. Class and position play their part too, as Gentility and Mediocrity, toyed with by Fanshaw, outraged by Wenny, and sweetly but firmly managed by Nan, triumph over them all in the end. Our conventions need to be destroyed because they are destroying us, and from the inside, Dos Passos seems to be saying in *Streets of Night*.

Dos Passos's forays into the further reaches of literary experimentation came as a result of his exposure to the milieu of modernism, but not through especially direct influences. Scholars have been able to connect him with a number of specific approaches in modernist painting, theatre, literature, and film, but probably it was the broadly general impetus to innovate, especially by manipulating the arbitrary, relative epistemological factors of perception and representation, that made the most difference in the radicalization of his art. The best introduction to the particular modernism Dos Passos experienced is his own statement in his 1931 foreword to his translation of Blaise Cendrars' *Panama, or the Adventures of My Seven Uncles*:

> The poetry of Blaise Cendrars was part of the creative tidal wave that spread over the world from the Paris of before the last European war.

Under various tags: futurism, cubism, vorticism, modernism, most of the best work in the arts in our time has been the direct product of this explosion, that had an influence in its sphere comparable with that of the October revolution in social organization and politics and the Einstein formula in physics. Cendrars and Apollinaire, poets, were on the first cubist barracades with the group that included Picasso, Modigliani, Marinetti, Chagall; that profoundly influenced Maiakovsky, Meyerhold, Eisenstein; whose ideas carom through Joyce, Gertrude Stein, T. S. Eliot (first published in Wyndham Lewis's "Blast"). The music of Stravinski and Prokofieff and Diaghileff's Ballet hail from this same Paris already in the disintegration of victory, as do the windows of Saks Fifth Avenue, skyscraper furniture, the Lenin Memorial in Moscow, the paintings of Diego Rivera in Mexico City and the newritz styles of advertizing in American magazines.[24]

Dos Passos had been in Paris in the midst of that postwar explosion/ disintegration for periods of months at various times in the late teens and early twenties. He did some studying, some adventuring, and much writing there. He took an avid interest in the modernist painting, theatre, ballet, and poetry being produced and performed there, and he was acquainted with a number of Parisian-based artists. His friendship with Gerald Murphy, for example, introduced him to many members of Murphy's vast circle of artistic friends and colleagues, providing him with such adventures as a visually stimulating walk along the Seine with Murphy and Fernand Léger and a week's work painting and assembling the bizarre stage sets Natalya Goncharova was designing for the premier of the Stravinsky-Balanchine ballet *Les Noces*.[25]

The modernist arts that had political as well as aesthetic significance seemed especially to attract Dos Passos—those that challenged and rearranged not only perceptual sets but social perceptions and attitudes. Thus the modernism of the Futurists, in its attempts to incorporate imagery of contemporary technology and to be both accessible to and critical of contemporary culture had a special appeal for him, as Townsend Ludington recently pointed out.[26] Modernist film too interested him, especially the work of Eisenstein—so much so that he made a special point to search out the great pioneer and a number of his colleagues in Russia in 1928. Part of his fascination with Russian film was with the technique of montage. As he recollected thirty-five years later, "I suspect I got interested in Eisenstein's montage while I was working on *Manhattan Transfer*, though I can't remember exactly. Anyway montage was in the air."[27] But another part of the fascination had to be with the social basis of Russian films. The techniques as Eisenstein conceived of them were primarily means of social depiction with the intent of producing useful social action. "The sphere of work of the new cinematographic possibilities," he insisted, "seems to be the *direct screening of class-useful conceptions*, methods, tactics and practical watchwords, not having recourse for this purpose to the aid of the suspect trappings of the dramatic and psychological past."[28]

It was the modernist theatre with which Dos Passos was most involved, however, and which likely influenced him the most deeply. As he admitted in a blurb for a dramatization of *U.S.A.*, it seemed appropriate that his novels of that period should result in drama, since drama had contributed a great deal to their inspiration: "as I look back with the advantage of thirty years of hindsight at the writing of these three novels, it seems fairly obvious that my excitement over the 'expressionist' theatre of the Nineteen-twenties had a good deal to do with shaping their style."[29] The kind of theatre he had been able to observe in the Paris of the late teens and early twenties was typified (if such bizarre works could be regarded as typifiable at all) by such works as *Parade*, a collaboration of Diaghilev, Picasso, and Cocteau (1917), and *La Creation du Monde*, by Cendrars and Darius Milhaud (1923). In Moscow there were Meyerhold's "constructionist" productions—like *Mystery Bouffe* (1918) and *Give Us Europe* (1924)—which Dos Passos certainly knew about. In discussing the experimental drama of this period, J. Garrett Glover characterizes it as "cubist theatre," relating its formal qualities explicitly (as did many of its practitioners) to cubist painting, which intended "to eliminate the distinction between substance and form, background and foreground, and scene and figure."[30] Especially interesting in connection with Dos Passos's techniques of characterization and narration in *Manhattan Transfer* and *U.S.A.* is the cubist practice by which, as Glover explains, "each geometric plane had its own nucleus, its own gravitational pull to a central point in its interior";[31] Glover demonstrates that the "cubist" dramas achieved this relativistic quality by presenting simultaneous and discontinuous actions, thereby destroying any conventional sense of dramatic focus. Structurally, too, the "cubist" plays can be seen as intimations of Dos Passos's experimental narrative technique: essentially they were assemblages —conglomerations of dance and mime and conventional acting, of shouts and poetry and advertising slogans, of titles, headlines, and nonsense.

Dos Passos's own involvement with this theatre went far beyond his painting of the *Les Noces* sets. He had long conversations with Gerald Murphy while Murphy was working on *Within the Quota*, a ballet curtain-raiser for *La Creation du Monde*.[32] Back in New York he joined up with John Howard Lawson (whom he had met on a boat to Paris) in a group called the New Playwrights, who were attempting to radicalize American theatre in both senses. In a number of introductions, reviews, and manifestos, Dos Passos urged that "explosions of fresh vitality in any art necessarily destroy the old forms";[33] what was needed were plays like Lawson's *Processional* in which "instead of the illusion of 'reality', its aim is to put on a show which creates in a hall full of people its own reality of glamor and significance,"[34] a theatre that is revolutionary in every sense:

> By revolutionary I mean that such a theatre must break with the present theatrical tradition, not with the general traditions of the theatre, and that it must draw its life and ideas from the conscious sections of the industrial and white-collar working classes which are out to get control of the great flabby mass of capitalistic society and mold it to their own purpose. In an ideal state it might be possible for a group to be alive and have no subversive political tendency. At present it is not possible.[35]

The play Dos Passos wrote (and rewrote) out of these impulses reads today very much like an embarrassing piece of Marxist Dada. He began it in 1918 as *The Moon is a Gong* and had it produced by the New Playwrights in 1923 as *The Garbage Man*. As he was writing it he described it as a "historical pastoral comical realistical fantastic lyrical tragical farcical morality."[36] It aggressively and knowingly conglomerates American cultural, political, and artistic clichés, along with elements of sheer fantasy and surrealism. At its climax the hero escapes the police and a "Radiophone" blaring slogans of materialism, patriotism, and intolerance, to climb a skyscraper and ring the gong of the moon ("the moon . . . swollen to bursting with all the dreams of the people of the city")[37] for his sweetheart, who is thereupon carried away by the Garbage Man, death.

The New Playwrights' Theatre foundered for a number of interconnected reasons, not the least of which, according to literary historians George A. Knox and Herbert M. Stahl,[38] was its impossible hope of fusing political radicalism with expressionism in some very dynamic and appealing way. Dos Passos failed along with the rest, but he learned to build literary works out of found objects such as songs and slogans and to work subideologically with techniques that destroyed conventional focus and continuity along with their ideological subjects. He dreamed of a theatre of national consciousness, but despite its context of Marxian inevitability, the dream seemed hopelessly utopian, given the reality that he found

around him in 1923 America: "Something approximating a national theatre is the most direct organ of group consciousness and will come into
being, inevitable with the welding of our cities into living organisms out
of the junk heaps of boxed and predatory individuals that they are at
present."[39]

Unpredictably, the political message of *Manhattan Transfer* (1925) is
studiously inexplicit, a matter of innuendo and implication, a thematic
enrichment but not a limiting purpose or parameter of the narrative. This
Manhattan is indeed, in certain ways, a junk heap of boxed and predatory
individuals, but it is also much more than that, and its characters are
much more than that. Dos Passos's radical political views were intermixed
in the novel with an array of purely infrapolitical destructionist narrative
techniques and a number of uncategorizable human concerns; the result
was a literary work that seems far more an exploration of contemporary
culture, perception, and personality and far less a self-conscious contrivance (like *The Garbage Man*) for the advocacy of an a priori social philosophy.

The inception of *Manhattan Transfer* (again according to the recollections of a much older, politically conservative Dos Passos) was a kind of
convergence of a strong and particular ambition, a fascination with experimental method, and the discovery of a fortuitous subject. Characterizing
his state of mind in the period after his tour of duty in the ambulance
corps and the writing of his first three novels, he cites this ambition: "I
found myself under a compulsion to set down in human terms the panorama of history that roared past my ears. The method was desperately
experimental. As I worked I used to reassure myself with the thought that
at least some of the data I collected might prove useful for the record." His
interest in experimentation he remembers being keyed by the terms *simultaneity, reportage,* and *montage*:

> I had done a lot of reading knocking around the war-wracked world.
> Some of the poets who went along with the cubism of the painters of
> the School of Paris talked about simultaneity. There was something
> about Rimbaud's poetry that tended to stand up off the page. Imag-
> ism. Direct snapshots of life. Reportage was a great slogan. The artist
> must record the fleeting world as sharply as the motion picture film
> recorded it. By contrast and juxtaposition he could build his own
> vision into reality: montage.

And the subject he discovered was one that could unify and focus the
"desperate experiment" at the same time it allowed plenty of latitude for
the panorama of history and the play of literary montage: "New York was

the first thing that hit me when I got back home. I started a reportage on New York. Some of the characters out of abandoned youthful narratives got into the book, but there was more to the life of a great city than you could cram into any one hero's career. The narrative must stand up off the page. Fragmentation. Contrast. Montage. The result was 'Manhattan Transfer.'"[40]

Looked at his way, then, the novel had been intended as a new, mixed literary form: a type of "reportage," a specific representation of "the fleeting world," significant as a part of "the panorama of history." Its substance is a matter of "data I collected," "direct snapshots of life"; its presentation is like "Imagism," concrete and uninterpreted; its structure is a process of "fragmentation," "contrast," "juxtaposition": "montage." If conventional literary continuity and protagonism were destroyed in the process so much the better, for they limited and biased our understanding of our experience.

Within the novel Dos Passos visualizes Manhattan scenically, his particular technique producing effects of vividness and fragmentation, verisimilitude and fabulation. It is imagism and not naive realism, however: as Blanche Gelfant has pointed out, "his is a technique of abstraction which proceeds through an impressionistic method," its "smallest unit of structure" being "the fleeting aesthetic impression."[41] Dos Passos's observer-narrator's words describe *experienced* things. A number of critics have noted the similarity of the novel's scenic techniques to contemporary painting,[42] so I won't labor that point here. I will remark however on the way that the descriptive passages—most notably those used as chapter prologues—in their great variety, apparent randomness, and sometimes unexpected angles of vision provide a sense of environmental verisimilitude for the characters and events and a dense and rich sense of the city as an entity, a whole that is somehow more than the sum of its parts. Some of the narrator's "fleeting aesthetic impressions" are also insistently metaphorical and/or allusive, especially to classical or biblical places, and these linkages serve also to establish Manhattan's special legendary quality. Chapter titles also contribute to this end. Notice, for example, the beginning of the second section, part I: "Great Lady on a White Horse." The title refers to a long-haired girl who is riding a horse through Manhattan, advertising shampoo, although it also evokes resonances of legend and nursery rhyme. The prologue follows, rife with impressions, evoking morning and a good deal more, sensuously as well as thematically:

> *Morning clatters with the first L train down Allen Street. Daylight rattles through the windows, shaking the old brick houses, splatters the girders of the L structure with bright confetti.*
>
> *The cats are leaving the garbage cans, the chinches are going back into the walls, leaving sweaty limbs, leaving the grimetender necks of little children asleep. Men and women stir under blankets and bedquilts on mattresses in the corners of rooms, clots of kids begin to untangle to scream and kick.*
>
> *At the corner of Riverton the old man with the hempen beard who sleeps where nobody knows is putting out his picklestand. Tubs of gherkins, pimentos, melonrind, piccalilli give out twining vines and cold tendrils of dank pepperyfragrance that grow like a marshgarden out of the musky bedsmells and the rancid clangor of the cobbled awakening street.*
>
> *The old man with the hempen beard who sleeps where nobody knows sits in the midst of it like Jonah under his gourd.**

In relation to the novel's principal actions, then, such passages provide counterpoint and irony, reinforcement and reverberation, illustration and irrelevancy, tending to make the Manhattan mise-en-scène both lifelike and larger than life.

The fragmented montage that is the narrative results from two specially innovative interrelated characteristics: the diversity of its materials and the relativity of its perspective. *Manhattan Transfer* is, of course, constructed out of a great variety of linguistic materials, many of them "found objects" such as pop songs, slogans, advertisements, news stories, book quotations and allusions, and references to celebrities, places, and historical events. By this technique the effect of verisimilitude is deepened by literal actuality, at the same time that the fragmentation and the reverberation are enhanced.

The things that happen do so wholly within the contexts of the individual characters. Thus the attentive sets and even the language of the narrative segments tend to shift relative to the preoccupations of their protagonists, and this tends to further fragment the novel. There is no really common concern, no general reality but the kaleidoscopic whirl; the overriding concern of one character is only an inconvenience or irrelevancy to another. Meanings and understandings are generally unstated; the narrator signifies each character's concerns, often from the inside, but, like a narrative imagist, doesn't elaborate. The narrative moves from one event to the next relativistically, like time rearranging particles—

**Manhattan Transfer* (Houghton Mifflin, 1925), 129. Parenthetical page numbers in the discussion of this novel refer to this edition.

gaining or losing connections, gaining or losing characters. When something happens, the "why" is of little concern, as the characters try to cope with the new situation and we are hurried on to what will happen next. It is a potentially very powerful style of narration if we learn to read Dos Passos as we read Hemingway, for the two-thirds beneath the surface. And the surface is so much more complicated here.

It takes an extended passage to reveal the book's very specific relativistic fragmentation and its power. Take, for example, the fifth and sixth chapters of the second section, "Went to the Animals' Fair" and "Five Statutory Questions" (217–248). After an epigraph describing traffic returning to Manhattan on a sticky summer Sunday night, we see Ellen Oglethorpe and George Baldwin in a taxi, making desultory comments about the coming of war to Europe and then arriving at a roadhouse that "oozed pink light and ragtime through every chink" (218). By chance they meet Gus McNeil and his wife and exchange greetings with them. We know from previous events in the novel that Baldwin began his very notable legal career by winning an accident claim for McNeil. He seduced McNeil's wife at the time and carried on a passionate affair with her; although he will soon admit this fact to Ellen, no recognition is made of it during this greeting. We merely see what a camera would see: "Why hello Gus! . . ." and so forth. Ellen too, we know, has other concerns than the war and the McNeils; the preceding chapter has just ended with another zany, passionate, and troubling encounter between her and Stan Emery, her lover, whose determined and self-destructive drunkenness tends to override all his other loyalties. The narrative does nothing to explore this at the roadhouse, though. We can imagine what she feels—indeed we *must* imagine what she feels, because none of it is explained in the narrative. Baldwin begins to urge his longing for her, she remains remote, polite but distracted, the McNeils have been filed away for later in the chapter, and the band makes the only comment on this welter of motive and desire, playing "Everybody's Doing It."

Looking across the room, Ellen "caught sight of Tony Hunter's oval pink and white face. . . . Oglethorpe was not with him. Stan's friend Herf sat with his back to her" (220). As simple and matter-of-fact as that seems, it too conceals depths that are never to be explained. Actor Jojo Oglethorpe is her husband, she is hurting him deeply with her affair with Stan, and although she does not feel malice toward him, her behavior pushes him ever further into the detestable role of injured tragedian. Now here she is, seen by his friends, dining and dancing with George Baldwin. And Jimmy Herf—to her merely "Stan's friend, . . . a long rumpled black head poised a little askew on a scraggly neck"—when he recognizes her across the room "felt something glittering go off in his chest like a released spring" (223) and fights to keep up with a fellow newspaperman's conversation. The conversation is about the "Santa Claus" murder—a white-whiskered man and his daughter both found dead just down the street; whether it was an incest-rape and suicide or a double murder is the point under debate. Indeed, everybody is doing it.

What Dos Passos gives us is just a sequence of impressions: George tritely declares his love for Ellen ("I'd do anything in the world for you"), and Ellen sends her lobster back to the kitchen ("I don't think it's terribly good" [221]); across the room Herf drinks a whiskey and soda, talking about the little old white-whiskered man and the murder of the French socialist Juares, although he is momentarily stunned by seeing Ellen at the bar. Under a picture of the Lusitania, the bartender Congo Jake is "vibrating a shaker between his hairy hands" (223). The narrative is merely an inventory of events—interspersed, juxtaposed—with no explanations or readily recognizable thematic coherence. Life simply goes on, and Dos Passos's camera is grinding. "Funny ting a man's life," says Congo Jake (226), giving us another atom, a philosophical tag.

Conversation is various, desultory, trite, pointless. The characters say the sorts of things people do say. About the war: "What gives me gooseflesh is the armies mobilizing, Belgrade bombarded, Belgium invaded . . . all that stuff. I just can't imagine it." "Those goddam French are so degenerate all they can do is fight duels and sleep with each other's wives. I bet the Germans are in Paris in two weeks" (222–223). "Well maybe when the Germans have licked the pants off her England will give Ireland her freedom" (238). Certainly Dos Passos can't feel that his readers will gain any insight by learning what these characters know. In the discussion about the Santa Claus murder a cabbie boasts, "I seen the bodies laid out stiff before dey took em to de morgue" (218); Bullock, Herf's journalist friend insists, "Canarsie's full of the Black Hand, full of anarchists and undesirable citizens. It's our job to ferret em out and vindicate the honor of this poor old man and his beloved daughter"; and Herf himself responds, "Of course everybody admits he's been crazy for years" (222). This exchange too goes no place, but we can infer some of the reasons why it doesn't. Bullock is an overdramatizing journalist, somewhat drunk, and much impressed with his own powers of expression. Also, he has a stake in making this story turn out to be a big story, since it's his assignment, and he is miffed because the piece he submitted that day was overshadowed and cut down to half a column by the war news. Herf has no such involvement and can mix his disengagement with a bit of satirical egging-on of his fellow journalist.

Dos Passos's narrative—an accumulation of fragments, of relativistic moments—is really an experiment in indirection, a kind of photographic synecdoche. Like many of Stieglitz's pictures, Dos Passos's scenes and details seem to have complex stories around them. Baldwin's yearning, Ellen's yearning, Jimmy Herf's yearning are all figured in, and muted by, the details of the roadhouse, the pointless gossip about murder and war. "Look Herf, have you seen Stan today?" Ellen asks, "He didn't turn up when I expected him" (227), but her concern is quickly overlayered by the barroom conversation. When she attempts to leave without George, he desperately draws a gun, only to have it calmly taken away by the "big red hand" of Gus McNeil. "Didn't nutten happen. . . . Gentleman's a little nervous" (229), McNeil announces to the crowd, and almost as if nothing has happened, Ellen and Jimmy leave the roadhouse to have a meaning-less look at the murder cottage nearby. "Honestly Herf haven't you seen Stan?" she asks again.

Jimmy dutifully sends Ellen home in a taxi, as she requested; earlier when he danced with her, "High ashy walls broke and crackled within him. He was soaring like a fireballoon on the smell of her hair" (228). There is no explicit continuity in the narrative between these events. Dos Passos is like a cubist painter in portraying his characters, getting at his subject not by projecting an ideal wholeness but by constructing an accu-mulation of partial, temporary, surface perceptions.

It is a reality of "simultaneous" surfaces, but Dos Passos is able to suggest a good deal of the depth and complexity of experience thereby. On Jimmy's own long walk home, "an arm hooked in his" (232) and he's joined by Tony Hunter. Tony's "oval pink and white face" and arm-hooking approach are of course twenties-ish signals of homosexuality, and Jimmy gets the full (and nearly explicit) confession from Tony who's lonely, dis-traught, ashamed of himself, and considering suicide. Another surface, another dimension of the human predicament. Jimmy's first reaction is not callous, but it certainly reinforces the theme of the lack of real connec-tion between people: "But it all may be an idea. You may be able to get over it. Go to a psychoanalyst." "Buck up for Heaven's sake," he contin-ues, "they're lots of people in the same boat" (234). But this time in the novel the predicament of one character gets through to another.

"Gosh it's horrible," [Jimmy] shouted suddenly.
"What?"

"All the hushdope about sex. I'd never realized before tonight, the
full extent of this agony. God you must have a rotten time . . . .

"We all have a rotten time." (235)

Jimmy can give Tony nothing but unstructured sympathetic anger, but it
is a point of contact. And after Tony has departed, Jimmy is left with the
weight of all the night contains—his personal longing, Tony's and everybody's sexual agony, his suspicions of a self-slain incestuous Santa, the
declaration of war, and the seething rain; his chapter-closing stream-of-
consciousness meditation explains nothing and interprets nothing, but
envisions all these strains in a state of suspended irresolution. "'Golly
I'm wet,' Jimmy Herf said aloud," and "desperately he walked on," the
narrative leaving behind that fragment too.

The chapter "Five Statutory Questions" is framed by Joe Harland,
cousin of Jimmy Herf and formerly a prosperous businessman, now ru-
ined, alcoholic, and feeling very much down on his luck. First we see him
humiliated by being thrown out of the home of an acquaintance by the
man's mother, who sees Harland as a drunken bum who will corrupt her
children. By the end of the chapter we see him on a park bench, driven to
panhandling from his own cousin Jimmy. What happens in between is all
Ellen's story. She is haunted by Stan's absence, and she receives a deep
shock in the course of the chapter, but the presentation is consistently
atomistic and understated. She wakes to the sound of sparrows on the
window ledge and a sewing machine running upstairs—all the meaningless details of the mundane world—but soon "the pain that has been
teasing all night wells up and bursts. 'Stan, Stan for God's sake,'" she says
aloud (241).

Once she is down on the street, "walking without looking to the
right or left," we get a stream of impressions that might be mere miscellany if it weren't for their negative slanting and the fact of Ellen's loneli-
ness and anxiety, which color and finally overwhelm them:

> The sun already hot simmers slatily on the pavements, on plate-
> glass, on dustmarbled enameled signs. Men's and women's faces as
> they pass her are rumpled and gray like pillows that have been too
> much slept on. After crossing Lafayette Street roaring with trucks
> and delivery wagons there is a taste of dust in her mouth, particles of
> grit crunch between her teeth. Further east she passes pushcarts;
> men are wiping off the marble counters of softdrink stands, a grind-
> organ fills the street with shiny jostling coils of the *Blue Danube*; acrid
> pungence spreads from a picklestand. In Tompkins Square yelling

children mill about the soggy asphalt. At her feet a squirming heap of small boys, dirty torn shirts, slobbering mouths, punching, biting, scratching; a squalid smell like moldy bread comes from them. Ellen all of a sudden feels her knees weak under her. She turns and walks back the way she came.

The sun is heavy like his arm across her back, strokes her bare forearm the way his fingers stroke her, it's his breath against her cheek. (241)

That fragment finished, the narrative then cuts to a conversation Ellen is having with a friend, explaining the divorce she has just gotten. We never knew she was planning a divorce, and this, the only discussion of it we are offered, is almost immediately interrupted by the arrival of producer Harry Goldweiser, his sister, and a friend. Such is Dos Passos's technique, but it has excellent justification. It implies the idea that Ellen's divorce was not a very important thing to her—certainly not as important as the stream of street impressions that sustained her anxious yearning for Stan. Also, in using the device of interruption, it develops the technique of fragmentation into a social theme: these people constantly obtrude into each other's lives. It is in fact surprisingly rare when an action or a conversation is completed in *Manhattan Transfer*. Typically it is diverted or interrupted by someone coming athwart it, full of their own concerns. Harry here wants to sign Ellen for a part in "The Zinnia Girl" and, if he were to get all of his wishes, to marry her too. His sister wants to meet an actress and always say the Right Thing ("Oh yes New York is really pleasanter in midsummer than any other time; there's less hurry and bustle" [244]). Ellen's friend Dick Snow wants to deliver some avuncular advice about the seriousness of divorce and some wisdom about the current state of the theatre ("There's no great acting any more: Booth, Jefferson, Mansfield . . . all gone" [243]). Ellen only wants not to have to deal with these other people: "The long day love was crisp in the curls . . . the dark curls . . . broken in the dark steel light . . . hurls . . . high O God high into the bright. . . . She was cutting with her fork in the crisp white heart of a lettuce. She was saying words while quite other words spilled confusedly inside her like a broken package of beads" (244; Dos Passos's ellipses).

What is absolutely vital to one character is merely distracting to another, and this is why their interaction is all obtrusion and interruption. It is the tragedy of personal relativity. It is also why the narrative is a montage-chronicle of their meaningless encounters. Ellen is dancing with Harry, trying to remember how Stan looked, while Harry is tritely confessing to Ellen her great power over him and trying to persuade her to marry him ("I'd do anything for you, you know that" [245]). The moment is a typical one in this novel, and it too is interrupted. Stan is suddenly there telling of his "most extraordinarily spectacular trip" to Canada and Niagara Falls and how as a kind of drunken joke he wound up married to this groggy little girl with him, Pearline.

"Ellen couldn't see his face," (245) the orchestra gets louder, the room spins, but she holds on: "'Good night Stan,' Her voice was gritty in her mouth, she heard the words very clearly as she spoke them" (246); she excuses herself and goes to the ladies' room to faint. Dos Passos's terse objectivity is both the vehicle and the counterpart of her stoicism under this great pressure.

Time's kaleidoscope gives another jiggle and the pieces rearrange: Jimmy Herf and Joe Harland are sitting on a bench, noticing, amidst all their concern to explain and justify their individual plights to each other, a picture of Ellen in the newspaper, under the caption "Talented Young Actress Scores Hit in the Zinnia Girl." Dos Passos has shifted foreground to background, protagonist to ancillary character, as he does continually throughout this novel, and in the act of shifting he shows that the real story of Manhattan, the public, objective reality is an agglomeration of private realities that relate to each other only transiently, tangentially. Objectivity is made up of an infinitude of relativistic subjectivities. The universe was made by a perspective realist or a cubist.

John Dewey, in his 1916 *Essays in Experimental Logic*, had made the case that an "exclusively intellectual preoccupation with analytic knowing" produced a distortion of experience. Every event takes place in "an immense and operative world of diverse and interacting elements," he claimed, in which consciousness "is only a very small and shifting portion." The wholeness of experience is undetectable by analysis and perhaps undefinable, he tells us, but nonetheless real, the actuality that we inhabit, just as "being ill with the grippe is an experience which includes an immense diversity of factors, but none the less is the one qualitatively unique experience which it is."[43] Dos Passos's technique in *Manhattan Transfer* is like a novelist's attempt to destroy literary convention in order to realize just such a relation with the world.

Thematically, the world Dos Passos's technique depicts and imitates is a lonely and futile place. Fate is chancy, society is fragmented, relationships are hollow and abrasive, and individuals are too distracted, self-justifying or trapped within the lingo of their time to understand even themselves. Their occasional moments of courage or clarity only serve to deepen the irony. Their society is notably unfair, especially to the poor and underprivileged. People of the lower classes suffer meaningless deprivations and misfortunes, and their travails, juxtaposed with the very different but no less inevitable travails of the upper classes, show the remorseless operation of a class system: one character is driven to headache by the tedious fitting ceremony for the dress for her next vacuous and unfulfilling social occasion, while another, in a sudden accidental fire at her station in the sewing room, is being disfigured for life.

As Dos Passos explained the next (the monumental) stage of his career, "I was thoroughly embarked on an effort to keep up a contemporary commentary on history's changes, always as seen by somebody's eyes, heard by somebody's ears, felt through somebody's nerves and tissues. These were the U.S.A. books. Everything must go in. Songs and slogans, political aspirations and prejudices, ideals, hopes, delusions, frauds, crackpot notions out of the daily newspapers."[44] Fragmentation and montage were to hit their heyday in Dos Passos's work, then, as he broadened the inclusiveness and heterogeneity of his approach to represent the whole nation over a period of several decades. He conceived of the work as an American epic in the Whitman mold, and "it started to be one book, but then there was so much that I wanted to get in that it got to be three books very soon, . . . before *42nd Parallel* was finished."* *U.S.A.* was a considerable increment over *Manhattan Transfer* in technical innovation too, as Dos Passos concocted his famous quadripartite system of narration, with Newsreels, biographies, narratives, and the Camera Eye functioning to produce a fuller and yet more systematic and lucid presentation of a great variety of materials. The trilogy had a new and momentous solution to the problem of narrative voice and objectivity as well, and perhaps most significant of all, it developed the twentieth-century sense of the arbitrary, relativistic, and manifold qualities of language to the point where language became a new sort of instrument for the analysis and representation of society. *U.S.A.* maintained a more explicit political outlook too, and one moreover that interrelated ideally with the trilogy's epistemological and stylistic features. The destruction of political and infrapolitical —literary, linguistic, and epistemological—conventions came together here in a unified, though sprawling, heterogeneous whole.

*Interview with David Sanders, *Writers at Work*, fourth series, ed. George Plimpton (Viking, 1976), 81. For a valuable description of *U.S.A.*'s compositional stages (including photographic reproductions of notes and annotated typescript), see Donald Pizer, *Dos Passos' U.S.A.* (University Press of Virginia, 1988), 86–112.

Dos Passos's intents were conflicting in writing his epic—something like a combination of social satire, historicism, and impressionism: as he later admitted, "I wanted to be objective, satirically objective, like Swift or Fielding," and yet to maintain that deep subjective immersion in events "always as seen by somebody's eyes, heard by somebody's ears, felt through somebody's nerves and tissues."[45] He resolved the conflict principally by a separation of narrative functions, and the key to it was the Camera Eye: "I aimed at total objectivity by giving conflicting views—using the camera eye as a safety valve for my own subjective feelings. It made objectivity in the rest of the book much easier."[46] Some of the "subjective feelings" the Camera Eye presented were the sorts of aesthetic ideas that studded *Manhattan Transfer*'s narrative—bits of imagery artily observed and poetically expressed, the residues of imagism and impressionism in Dos Passos's evolving narrative technique. Some, however, were moral ideas and reactions—some of them quite explicit and of the sort that didn't come into the previous book in any direct way.

The raw materials for the Camera Eye passages were the subjective experience-atoms in Dos Passos's notebooks and memory, and the continuing story they tell, chronologically coordinated with the other types of narrative, is the story of the development of the author's own perceptions and attitudes. In conception a kind of *A Portrait of the Artist as a Young Man*, the Camera Eye functions as a precursor to what would later be called New Journalism: it makes explicit the personal predilections that went into the making of the whole work. Williams had written into *The Great American Novel* his personal experience in doing the writing; Dos Passos in *U.S.A.* includes his personal experience in coming to the point of writing. Both eschewed the conventions of ingenuous objectivity, controlling the writer's inescapable reflexiveness by direct avowal, as if saying "this is me and this is the book I'm producing." The Camera Eye provides not just an interesting subjective correlative to the more public and objective strains of *U.S.A.*, but it adds a new dimension of candor and authenticity, the acknowledged relativistic foundation for the work's relativity.

Its earlier segments are clearly reminiscent of *A Portrait of the Artist* in syntax, imagery, and language; sometimes too they sound the dominant theme of the Camera Eye, the development of the narrator-recorder's social consciousness:

> you were scared
> but now the dark was all black again the lamp in the train and the

sky and everything had a blueblack shade on it and She was telling a
story about

Longago Beforetheworldsfair Beforeyouwereborn and they went to
Mexico on a private car on the new international line and the men
shot antelope off the back of the train and big rabbits jackasses they
called them and once one night Longago Beforetheworldsfair Beforeyouwereborn one night Mother was so frightened on account of all
the rifleshots but it was allright turned out to be nothing but a little
shooting they'd been only shooting a greaser that was all.

that was in the early days.[47]

The language here is basically the standard stream-of-consciousness dialect of modernist fiction, studded with specific childhood locutions
("Longago Beforetheworldsfair Beforeyouwereborn")—it has the sound
of indirect discourse filtered through memory. The "subjective feelings"
come by indirection: the emotional and aesthetic response to the poetic
imagery ("and everything had a blueblack shade on it") and the moral
response to the implicit and ironic lesson of the inconsequentially mur-
dered Mexican.

The strategy of indirection, of implying those subjective feelings and
themes in the arrangement of images is, of course, the practice of imagism, and Dos Passos sometimes fashioned a Camera Eye episode in the
shape of a poem. This one (number 29), for example, quoted in full,
is from the wartime milieu of 1919 and shows the emergence of a very
real and personal sense of mortality. It reads like one of the seeming
journal entries in *One Man's Initiation*, but destabilized and poetically re-
fashioned:

the raindrops fall one by one out of the horsechestnut tree over the
arbor onto the table in the abandoned beergarden and the puddly
gravel and my clipped skull where my fingers move gently forward
and back over the fuzzy knobs and hollows

spring and we've just been swimming in the Marne way off somewhere beyond the fat clouds on the horizon they are hammering
on a tin roof in the rain in the spring after a swim in the Marne with
that hammering to the north pounding the thought of death into our
ears

the winey thought of death stings in the spring blood that throbs
in the sunburned neck up and down the belly under the tight belt

hurries like cognac into the tips of my toes and the lobes of my ears
and my fingers stroking the fuzzy closecropped skull

shyly tingling fingers feel out the limits of the hard immortal skull under the flesh a deathshead and skeleton sits wearing glasses in the arbor under the lucid occasional raindrops inside the new khaki uniform inside my twentyoneyearold body that's been swimming in the Marne in red and whitestriped trunks in Chalons in the spring.[48]

Camera Eye 45 from *The Big Money* shows us the narrator in an artsy Greenwich Village setting. The episode is almost Prufrockian, but with an essential difference: this character fights to preserve his selfhood by asserting alienation and by hastening back to contact with the twin realities of the teeming New York street and the surging of his own blood. In a way this is the story of the building of the aesthetic of the trilogy:

the narrow yellow room teems with talk under the low ceiling and crinkling tendrils of cigarettesmoke twine blue and fade round noses behind ears under the rims of women's hats in arch looks changing arrangements of lips the toss of a bang the wise I-know-it wrinkles round the eyes all scrubbed stroked clipped scraped with the help of lipstick rouge shavingcream razorblades into a certain pattern that implies

this warmvoiced woman who moves back and forth with a throaty laugh head tossed a little back distributing with teasing looks the parts in the fiveoclock drama

every man his pigeonhole

the personality must be kept carefully adjusted over the face . . .

the old brown hat flopped faithful on the chair beside the door successfully snatched . . .

the stairs go up and down

lead through a hallway ranked with bells names evoking lives tangles unclassified

into the rainy twoway street where cabs slither slushing footsteps plunk slant lights shimmer on the curve of a wet cheek a pair of freshcolored lips a weatherlined neck a gnarled grimed hand an old man's bloodshot eye

street twoway to the corner of the roaring avenue where in the lilt of the rain and the din the four directions

(the salty in all of us ocean the protoplasm throbbing through cells growing dividing sprouting into the billion diverse not yet labeled not yet named

always they slip through the fingers
the changeable the multitudinous lives)
box dizzyingly the compass.[49]

Camera Eye 50, the most quoted and celebrated one, makes a direct
and explicit statement of the narrator's sense of social justice as he is faced
with the impending execution of Sacco and Vanzetti, the event that precipitated the social vision of the trilogy:

> they have clubbed us off the streets   they are stronger   they are
> rich   they hire and fire the politicians the newspapereditors the old
> judges the small men with reputations the collegepresidents the
> wardheelers (listen businessmen collegepresidents judges   America
> will not forget her betrayers) they hire the men with guns   the uni-
> forms the policecars the patrolwagons
>   all right you have won   you will kill the brave men our friends
> tonight . . .
>   all right we are two nations . . .
>   we stand defeated America.[50]

Thus the Camera Eye, in presenting immediate, primary, intuitive
experience in the language of modernism, gives Dos Passos's trilogy a
necessary framework of relativity and subjectivity, and yet one that establishes values too.

The trilogy's biographies give it historicity and literalness. They are
sketches of actual people—people who, whether through the consequences of their actions or ideas or through the widely known example of
their lives, were determining factors in American life. Debs and Bryan,
Edison and Wilson, Morgan and Veblen: their thoughts and the principal
events of their lives are made primary subjects in the trilogy, and their
cultural impact can be traced in the Newsreels, the Camera Eye, and the
fictional narratives surrounding their biographies. Dos Passos claimed that
the biographies are "meant as illustrative panels, portraits of typical or
important personalities of the time, intended to interrupt, and by contrast
to give another dimension to the made-up stories, which are the body of
the book, much as the portraits of saints illustrated and reinforced the
narrative in the *retablos* of early church painting."[51]

Whatever their function in the trilogy's heterogeneity, the biographies
tend to advance a very specific view of American society: that of the social
attitudes of the Camera Eye narrator who had experienced the Sacco-

Vanzetti debacle. They vary in form, some in conventional prose, and others separated in single-assertion lines like poetry, but common to them all is a relatively terse expressive mode that sounds like a recitation of the simple facts, albeit facts that are loaded. Big money and political power have very strong negative implications, and the apologists and ideologues of the social system are revealed by means of irony as opportunists or fools. The leftist humanitarians are eulogized, and it is irony again that is used to express the tragic gap between their aspirations and their fate at the hands of a power-hungry and hypocritical society.

There is innovation in the use of language even in the biographies, including the use of linguistic "found objects." The sayings of some of the subjects of the biographies are prominently featured—linguistic tags and formulas that echo through the society. Debs says *"while there is a lower class I am of it, while there is a criminal class I am of it, while there is a soul in prison I am not free"*; Bryan says *"you shall not crucify mankind upon a cross of gold"*; Randolph Bourne says *"war is the health of the state."* Other fragments of actual quotation serve the purposes of specific biographies: part of a Horatio Alger eulogy for Thomas Edison, a study of Paxton Hibben that sounds like straight biographical dictionary, a marshaling of quoted official clichés for the Unknown Soldier. In both subject and language, therefore, the biographies contribute to this unprecedented mixture of actual and fictional that is the trilogy.

Interestingly, Dos Passos's uses of language in the Camera Eye and the biographies run the gamut from personal and subjective (with private usages; cadences that are grammatically free and follow stream-of-consciousness contours; and a "logic" of association, echo, and dream) to absolutely objective (the exact quotation of actual statements). The Newsreels of course further develop this objectivity, this construction of found objects, establishing contexts and points of contact for the narratives, to be sure, but more generally establishing a multithematic (though often satirical) sense of verisimilitude. The Newsreels give us a sense of experience's solidity, its continuity: their subjects—such as the war (to take an obvious example), the prewar establishment's persecution of the iww, the postwar boom of the aircraft industry—are repeatedly and seemingly continuously *there*, like real objects that can be perceived from different standpoints, the kaleidoscopic montage-structure notwithstanding. And not only are their subjects the elements of the American milieu, but so are their lingoes. These are the public voices, the common linguistic objects of the U.S.A.:

MOON'S PATENT IS FIZZLE

insurgents win at Kansas polls. Oak Park soulmates part
Eight thousand to take autoride says girl begged for her husband

PIT SENTIMENT FAVORS UPTURN

Oh you be-eautiful doll
You great big beautiful doll

the world cannot understand all that is involved in this, she said. It appears like an ordinary worldly affair with the trappings of what is low and vulgar but there is nothing of the sort. He is honest and sincere. I know him. I have fought side by side with him. My heart is with him now.

Let me throw my arms around you
Honey ain't I glad I found you

ALMOST MOTIONLESS IN MIDSUMMER LANGUOR
ON BUSINESS SEAS ONE MILLION SEE
DRUNKARDS BOUNCED

JURORS AT GATES OF BEEF BARONS

compare love with Vesuvius emblazoned streets await
tramp of paladins

Honey ain't I glad I found you
Oh you beautiful doll
You great big beautiful doll

TRADES WHITE HORSE FOR RED

Madero's troops defeat rebels in battle at Parral
Roosevelt carries Illinois oratory closes eyelids Chicago pleads for
more water

CONFESSED ANARCHISTS ON BENDED KNEES KISS
U.S. FLAG

THE SUNBEAM MOVEMENT IS SPREADING
BOMB NO. 4 IN LEVEE WAR SPLINTERS
WEST SIDE SALOON

a report printed Wednesday that a patient in a private pavilion in St. Luke's Hospital undergoing an operation for the extirpation of a cancerous

> *growth at the base of the tongue was General Grant was denied by both the hospital authorities and Lieut. Howzes who characterized the story as a deliberate fabrication.*[52]

The Newsreels, the closest things Dos Passos wrote to the Steinese of *Pink Melon Joy*, show piece-by-piece discontinuity, although the pieces themselves are complete enough to be semantic units. They involve some repetitions, continuations, and ironic parallels, to be sure, but their principal effect is that of fragmentation, disparateness—the disparateness extending even to their viewpoint and implied purposes (informative, celebrative, manipulative, gossipy, apologetic, self-righteous, and so forth).

In the introduction he wrote for the reissue of *Three Soldiers* in 1932—while he was writing *U.S.A.*—Dos Passos developed an untechnical term—"straight writing"—for writing that depicted an age through the craftsmanlike shaping and assembling of that age's own linguistic forms:

> I think there is such a thing as straight writing. A cabinet maker enjoys cutting a dovetail because he's a cabinetmaker; every type of work has its own vigor inherent in it. The mind of a generation is its speech. A writer makes aspects of that speech enduring by putting them in print. He whittles at the words and phrases of today and makes of them forms to set the mind of tomorrow's generation. That's history. A writer who writes straight is the architect of history.[53]

"Straight writing" for Dos Passos was an extension of the historian's craft (or at least what he conceived to be the historian's craft) into literary style and language. It was accumulative, directly representational, and, like imagism, another way for the twentieth-century writer to approach the goal of being nonjudgmental.*

Dos Passos rhapsodized "straight writing" in the preface to the one-volume edition of the trilogy. "The young man walks fast by himself through the crowd that thins into the night streets," it begins, and soon develops into a Whitmanesque self-portrait of (probably) the narrator of the Camera Eye. His "blood tingles with wants; mind is a beehive of hopes buzzing and stinging; muscles ache for the knowledge of jobs, for the roadmender's pick and shovel work, the fisherman's knack with a hook when he hauls on the slithery net from the rail of the lurching trawler,

---

*There is no evidence linking Dos Passos's notion of "straight writing" and the concept of "straight photography" of the American photographers (see 162–163, above), although the coincidence of (literalist) intents, (purist) means, and the term itself is striking.

. . . the engineer's slow grip wise on the throttle," and so forth. He hungers for experiences: "he must catch the last subway, the streetcar, the bus, run up the gangplanks of all the steamboats, register at all the hotels, work in the cities, answer the wantads, learn the trades, take up the jobs, live in all the boardinghouses," and so on. Though he's alone, he is linked to life by the speech that he hears:

> the ears are caught tight, linked tight by the tendrils of phrased words, the turn of a joke, the singsong fade of a story, the gruff fall of a sentence; linking tendrils of speech twine through the city blocks, spread over pavements. . . .
>   it was the speech that clung to the ears, the link that tingled in the blood; U.S.A.

"U.S.A. is the slice of a continent," he says, and he says it is a lot of other things as well, "but mostly U.S.A. is the speech of the people."

"Straight writing" was meant to be the linguistic essence of experience and also democracy in prose form (literary technique wedded to politics), but at the same time it is a system of relativity, and the Newsreels have a great deal to do with establishing that. They are constructions in flawed speech, fallible speech, speech with its attitudes and purposes painfully apparent. Conservative or radical, puritan or libertine, the assertions made in these linguistic fragments are equally valid—or equally invalid. There is no surety in the context of this linguistic multifariousness. The authority of all forms of public expression is destroyed. In this respect Dos Passos is waging another battle in the war Melville and Dickinson fought against abstract, ideological language. His author-narrator approximates authenticity not by pretending to have the right words for real truths, but by using the real lingoes and by giving no lingo specially privileged status. His own attitudes about social justice (honestly enough acknowledged and urged in the Camera Eye) come across then only as affecting the selection and arrangement of the Newsreel items and as connotation.

In the fictional narratives the relativity and the fragmentation culminate. The characters are bound and defined each by his or her own individual language, and in the process of creating them Dos Passos was able to develop an overall, politically based theme of the decay of individual potential in American society and to use vernacular-based means to show character as process, changing over time.

Several Dos Passos scholars have pointed out the genius of his characterization by vernacular: Blanche Gelfant said

Dos Passos brings us into an immediate contact with his characters by adapting for each one of them a language directly expressive
of the quality of his mind and sensibility. He writes the narrative
in the idiom of the characters, thus creating them for us by the
very style in which he describes them. His sheer mastery of the language of the people has never been demonstrated so impressively
as in these narrative sections in which he has made successfully
high aesthetic demands upon even the coarsest vulgate speech.
Style can no longer be separated as a vehicle of expression: it has
become character. His purpose is to achieve the highest degree of
objectivity by withdrawing himself as narrator and allowing the
characters to be the medium through which their stories received
expression.[54]

Donald Pizer offers a useful extended discussion of what he calls "this
vast exercise in free indirect discourse,"[55] and Alfred Kazin said of this use
of the characters' own speech styles, "This is the 'poetry' behind the book
that makes the 'history' in it live."[56] It is, in other words, the apotheosis of
"straight writing."

Take, for example, this passage from "Janey," occurring about one-
third of the way into The 42nd Parallel. It shows the level of sexual awareness and the powerfully conditioned gentility of Janey and her homely
friend Alice as they discuss the great tragedy of Janey's life: the accidental
death of Alec, chum of her older brother Joe, and Janey's secret flame:

Graduation came and commencement and she and Alice went out
to parties and even once with a big crowd on one of the moonlight
trips down the river to Indian Head on the Steamboat Charles McAlis-
ter. The crowd was rougher than Janey and Alice liked. Some of the
boys were drinking a good deal and there were couples kissing and
hugging in every shadow; still the moonlight was beautiful rippling
on the river and she and Janey put two chairs together and talked.
There was a band and dancing, but they didn't dance on account of
the rough men who stood round the dancefloor making remarks.
They talked and on the way home up the river, Janey, talking very
low and standing by the rail very close to Alice, told her about Alec.
Alice had read about it in the paper, but hadn't dreamed that Janey
had known him so well or felt that way about him. She began to cry
and Janey felt very strong comforting her and they felt that they'd be
very close friends after that. Janey whispered that she'd never be able
to love anybody else and Alice said she didn't think she could ever

love a man anyway, they all drank and smoked and talked dirty among themselves and had only one idea.[57]

The passage is written as Janey and Alice would write it, with their perceptions ("Some of the boys were drinking a good deal and there were couples kissing and hugging in every shadow") and their insights ("Janey felt very strong comforting her and they felt that they'd be very close friends after that") expressed solely in their language. We are saturated in the world of their speech; as Dos Passos lets the characters (so to speak) take themselves at their own words, the structures and limitations of their minds are revealed in the very diction and syntax of their language. Also revealed, as we move from Janey's story to Mac's to Eleanor's to J. Ward's, is the discreteness of their experiential worlds. Their individual realities are as different and as class-burdened as their lingoes.

Their actions and their interactions, like their perceptions and insights, are inextricable from their language. What they can do seems determined by what they can say, and this is why so often in the trilogy the resounding public clichés are such powerful motivational forces. In the following passage, for example, a climactic moment in the life and mind of Eleanor Stoddard, the confusing and conflicting impulses and possibilities of the moment seem to rush into the preset molds of the language of a romantic (and thoroughly bogus) self-sacrifice. Eleanor and J. Ward are confronting Ward's wife Gertrude, who, vindictive because of the alienation of her husband's affection, has persuaded her mother, the principal investor in Ward's business, to take financial retribution. Outside, the newspapers are announcing world war. Not incidental to the language and perceptions of this passage is the fact that Eleanor is an interior decorator:

Gertrude Moorehouse held out her hand without getting up. "Excuse me for not getting up, Miss Stoddard," she said, "but I'm absolutely prostrated by the terrible news."

"Civilization demands a sacrifice . . . from all of us," said Eleanor.

"Of course it is terrible what the Huns have done, cutting the hands off Belgian children and all that," said Gertrude Moorehouse.

"Mrs. Moorehouse," said Eleanor, "I want to speak to you about this unfortunate misunderstanding of my relations with your husband. . . . Do you think I am the sort of woman who could come out here and face you if there was anything in these horrible rumors? Our relations are pure as driven snow."

"Please don't speak of it, Miss Stoddard. I believe you."

When J.W. came in they were sitting on either side of the fire talking about Gertrude's operation. Eleanor got to her feet. "Oh, I think it's wonderful of you, J.W."

J.W. cleared his throat and looked from one to the other.

"It's little less than my duty," he said.

"What is it?" asked Gertrude.

"I have offered my services to the government to serve in whatever capacity they see fit for the duration of the war."

"Not at the front," said Gertrude with a startled look.

"I'm leaving for Washington tomorrow. . . . Of course I shall serve without pay."

"Ward, that's noble of you," said Gertrude. He walked over slowly until he stood beside her chair, then he leaned over and kissed her on the forehead. "We must all make our sacrifices. . . . My dear, I shall trust you and your mother. . . . "

"Of course, Ward, of course. . . . It's all been a silly misunderstanding." Gertrude flushed red. She got to her feet. "I've been a damn suspicious fool . . . but you mustn't go to the front, Ward. I'll talk mother around." . . . She went up to him and put her hands on his shoulders. Eleanor stood back against the wall looking at them. He wore a smoothfitting tuxedo. Gertrude's salmon-colored teagown stood out against the black. His light hair was ashgray in the light from the crystal chandelier against the tall ivorygray walls of the room. His face was in shadow and looked very sad. Eleanor thought how little people understood a man like that, how beautiful the room was, like a play, like a Whistler, like Sarah Bernhardt. Emotion misted her eyes.

"I'll join the Red Cross," she said. "I can't wait to get to France."[58]

The passage is highly satirical, but the judgment of the characters is wholly implicit in their own language. The speech of the people both justifies and damns the reality it manifests.

With Dos Passos committed to the technique of describing the characters in their own words, change becomes a strange and ambiguous thing. Change is constant and inevitable in the lives of these characters, but causally discontinuous. Causes and meanings aren't significantly explored in the characters' languages, so when changes occur we get only new sets of reactions and rationalizations. Consistency and continuity are not important as characters age, alter, find new interests and terms of expression; experiences, it seems, are transitory atoms.

Take, for example, the career of Richard Ellsworth Savage, spread out as it is across the whole of *1919* and the conclusion of *The Big Money*. The stages in his development, like a series of still photographs, are frozen in the specific vernacular of each phase. When he was a child, "he held on to Dad's back and punched his arm and the muscle was hard like a chair or a table and when Dad laughed he could feel it rumble in his back"; once when Dad "whaled him" for being a nuisance, "Mummy had picked Dick up and carried him upstairs crying in her evening dress all lacy and frizzly and with big puffy silk sleeves; touching silk put his teeth on edge, made him shudder all down his spine." Later the minister, Doctor Atwood, tells him of his acceptance as a scholarship student at Kent and "Then he told him a few things a growing boy ought to know and said he must avoid temptations and always serve God with a clean body and a clean mind, and keep himself pure for the lovely sweet girl he would some day marry, and that anything else led only to madness and disease. Dick went away with his cheeks burning." After his sexual initiation by Hilda Thurlow, the bored young wife of another minister, she ended the affair saying "bygones must be bygones" and Dick "stalked up and down and ran his hands through his hair and talked darkly about death and hellonearth and going to the devil as fast as he could, but Hilda just laughed and told him not to be silly, that he was a goodlooking attractive boy and would find many nice girls crazy to fall in love with him. Before he left they had a long talk about religion and Dick told them, with a bitter stare at Hilda, that he'd lost his faith and only believed in Pan and Bacchus, the old gods of lust and drink." Years later in France during the war, "Fred Summers had bought himself a prophylactic kit and a set of smutty postalcards. He said the last night before they left he was going to tear loose. When they got to the front he might get killed and then what? Dick said he liked talking to the girls, but that the whole business was too commercial and turned his stomach. Ed Schuyler, who'd been nicknamed Frenchie and was getting very continental in his ways, said that the streetgirls were too naive." Later Dick puts his reaction to the war itself in a letter: "in urging young men to go into this cockeyed lunatic asylum of war [Rev. Thurlow's] doing everything he can to undermine all the principles and ideals he most believes in. . . . It's crooked from A to Z. If it wasn't for the censorship I could tell you things that would make you vomit." He meets J. Ward in France and writes home "I've been promised a position in J. Ward Moorehouse's office here in Paris; he's a dollar-a-year expert, but as soon as peace is signed he expects to start his business up again. He's an adviser on public relations and publicity to big corporations like Standard Oil. It's the type of work that will allow me to continue my real work on the side. Everybody tells me it's the opportunity of a lifetime." We see little more of him until the end of *The Big Money*, where, after having been an executive in J. Ward's public relations organization for some time, he deals with the cases of Reggie Talbot, a personal friend whom he had promised to help in the company, and Myra Bingham, naive daughter of a wealthy client:

> As Ed was leaving the office he turned and said, "Say, Dick, I wish you'd give that youngster Talbot a talking to. . . . I know he's a friend of yours so I don't like to do it, but Jesus Christ, he's gone and called up again saying he's in bed with the grippe. That's the third time this month."
>
> Dick wrinkled up his brows. "I don't know what to do about him, Ed. He's a nice kid all right but if he won't knuckle down to serious work . . . I guess we'll have to let him go. We certainly can't let drinking acquaintance stand in the way of the efficiency of the office. These kids all drink too much anyway."
>
> After Ed had gone Dick found on his desk a big lavender envelop marked Personal. A whiff of strong perfume came out when he opened it. It was an invitation from Myra Bingham to come to the housewarming of her studio on Central Park South. He was still reading it when Miss Hilles' voice came out of the interoffice phone. "There's Mr. Henry B. Furness of the Furness Corporation says he must speak to Mr. Moorehouse at once." "Put him on my phone, Miss Hilles. I'll talk to him . . . and, by the way, put a social engagement on my engagement pad . . . January fifteenth at five o'clock . . . reception Miss Myra Bingham, 36 Central Park South."[59]

There is a frightening logic to the development in lingoes and in life from naïveté to idealism to disillusionment to glib opportunism, and it is the actuality of the linguistic forms that gives this development much of its disturbing power. People *have* said those things and still *do* say those things.

Each of the things Dick Savage says or thinks is true to his sense of reality at the time. The passage of time changes his truth: none of the phases or fashions of his lingo has any permanent authority, despite the fact that each seems profoundly permanent when he's in it. Character—to consider it in more general terms—isn't essence but process. Dos Passos is clearly of the Bergson/William James school of psychology, and the linguistic minutiae out of which he constructs his characters manifest this.

The specific direction of Dick Savage's evolution from victim of hypocrisy to its perpetrator is paralleled by the development of the other fictional protagonists of the trilogy, for the unifying theme of all their stories is the souring of potential. Take as examples the increasing point-lessness of the lives of Daughter and Joe Williams and Charlie Anderson, culminating in their meaningless deaths; the descent of Mary French into ideological unreality and unpersonhood; the grandiose self-deception of J. Ward, who becomes an isolated and out-of-touch product of his own image building; or the devolution of Janey from the scared, humane, loyal little sister of her big brother Joe to the proper and genteel young woman who is too ashamed of Joe's lower-class ways to leave a bridge game to be with him, who becomes, finally, the dutiful, worshipful secretary charac-terized by J. Ward as "a treasure." In every case what is most valuable in a character tends to be what is sold out or simply spoiled. And it happens to each of them in his or her own words—the idealism, the yearning, the compromise, the rationalization, the cynicism, or the self-delusion. Not unjustifiably, critic John Lydenberg has offered the suggestion that the words and their corruption might really be what *U.S.A.* is about. The politically motivated manipulation of words by politicians, businessmen, and public relations men like the fictional J. Ward and the actual apolo-gists for the Sacco-Vanzetti decision emerges as the most serious of can-cers on the democracy.[60]

Whatever "poetry" and authenticity "straight writing" contributes to the fictional narratives, there is no ignoring some of its literary disadvan-tages. For one thing it can be very flat writing. Dos Passos's code of verisi-militude seems to mitigate against his flavoring the cast with especially salty characters or even with characters whose perceptiveness or articu-lateness we could admire and enjoy. The characters are all relatively lim-ited people who generally have the conventional insights and reactions we'd expect them to have, and long stretches of their experiences in their own language do not make for fascinating reading. The shifting among stories and interspersed Newsreels, biographies, and Camera Eye passages —like the vaudevillian variety that clangs through *The Garbage Man*—helps vary the flatness, but also can dismayingly disrupt our involvement. *U.S.A.* is clearly a book one can put down, and since its first publication critics have complained of a lack of involvement with the characters. "Straight writing" can also put great demands on the virtuosity of the writer, who needs to move the plot along and at the same time maintain his saturation in the language and thought processes of the character. Sometimes Dos Passos slips: Joe Williams has just deserted from the navy, and as he walks idly along the shore, his language shifts from something like his own to something like the Camera Eye's: "With the box tucked right under his arm, feeling crummy in the baggy civies, he walked slowly out to the beacon and watched the fleet in formation steaming down the River Plate. The day was overcast; the lean cruisers soon blurred into their trailing smokesmudges."[61] However, although Dos Passos's diction may slip at times in the narratives, his noninterpretive, nonjudgmental stance never does.

The tone of *U.S.A.* is complex, and the trilogy's interpretive possibilities are manifold. Of course. Interpretive ambiguity is one of the characteristics of experience, the reality Dos Passos meant to represent. Whether particular episodes or elements of the trilogy are satirical or pathetic, futilitarian, reformist, humorous, or documentarily realistic in their import can legitimately be the subject of critical debate. A simple schema of the whole trilogy is easy to arrive at but undefinitive. Dos Passos's technique was specifically intended to evade the kinds of intellectual categories that would block our perception of experience with prejudgments that American society is such-and-such or reality is thus-and-so.

This is not to deny that *U.S.A.* has a more political, class-conscious outlook than Dos Passos's previous books. It resounds with the words and deeds of Debs and Haywood, Bourne and Veblen and Hibben, and those men's visions of society tend to prevail in the caustic portraits of Ford and Wilson, Taylor and Keith and all the patriotic capitalistic blather of the Newsreels; the characters in the narratives struggle and adapt, suffer and fail by those same lights, and the Camera Eye records the experiential education of an isolated social radical. Even so, *U.S.A.* is less ideological than it was taken to be by many left-wing critics of the thirties and forties. The biographies also include studies of complex individuals in the midst of conflicting social forces (Hearst and Reed, for example); the narratives present characters (like Mac or Eveline) whose fates are determined by complex mixtures of personal, environmental, biological, and ideological factors; the Newsreels are irreducibly multifarious; and the Camera Eye persona grows through profound challenges to his perception of the world and his relationship to it. Thus, whatever else it might have been, Dos Passos's search for the real America was an epistemological search —the challenge was to perceive, to absorb, and to represent in words a phenomenon infinitely complex and vastly ambiguous; to know at the same time that there was no definitive ordering perspective, and why; and to invent an approach that would mitigate the reflexiveness problem —how can one be both an individual person (biased, emotional, political) and a camera eye?

The fascination—the obsession, practically—of Dos Passos scholarship has been his shifting ideology, from the radical left in *U.S.A.* to the far right in *District of Columbia*. But when Dos Passos himself was long afterward questioned about the political nexus of his novels, he tended to answer not in terms of ideas or ideologies, but in terms of experience: "they have a strong political bent because after all—although it isn't the only thing—politics in our time has pushed people around more than anything else."[62]

The real events of politics absorbed him more and more after *U.S.A.* and experiments in representing experience far less. Newsreels, biographies, the Camera Eye, and "straight writing" were all in the category of things that had been done. We really can't imagine a subsequent novel that would incorporate these approaches without seeming distinctly warmed-over. Probably wisely, Dos Passos didn't even try. But his innovativeness seemed played out too: there were no very ambitious experiments after *U.S.A.*, as he focused his "contemporary chronicles" on the political turmoil of the late thirties, the forties, fifties, and sixties, and its effect on the private lives and the characters of its participants and its victims, fictional and fictionalized. Dos Passos always did dialogue well, so there is always some of the speech of the people, and locutions continue to give character and actuality to passages of reflection and indirect discourse, but the later narratives are not saturated with the characters' speech and thought patterns.

Dos Passos wrote his most challenging, most enduring works while the fit of epistemological experimentation was upon him. These works, in their convention-subverting, knowledge-destroying, infrapolitical mode, managed to touch more levels of experience and to reveal or imply more of its implications than his more traditional creations. Those traditional works, early and late, tended to be limited by his conscious understanding of society and psychology, history and politics. Somehow, destructionism more than maximized his potential as a writer, as if the power of a more randomized intuition, working in and around the channels of his very capable, concentrated, and politically oriented intelligence multiplied the power of his perception substantially.

As was the case with Stein and Williams, the randomizing, the liberation of his intuition came with fragmentation, separating moments of experience from their conventional, logical, chronological, and even associational connections and assembling them in new contextual structures. Dos Passos had a fine sense of words and vernaculars, a wonderful "ear," and a vast talent for verbal imitation. The moments that were his building blocks were moments of real event and the speech of the people, which, focused in his vision of American society, what it had become and what it ought to be, became his montage of actuality.

Notes

■ Preface

1 "Add This to Rhetoric," *The Palm at the End of the Mind* (Vintage, 1972), 161.
2 *In the American Grain* (New Directions, 1925), 215.
3 "Argument," *The Pilgrimage of Festus* (Knopf, 1923).
4 *Lectures in America* (Random House, 1935), 11.
5 *Literary Essays of Ezra Pound*, ed. and intro. T. S. Eliot (New Directions, 1954), 267.
6 *Final Harvest*, ed. Thomas H. Johnson (Little, Brown, 1961), 46.
7 Quoted in Jayne L. Walker, *The Making of a Modernist* (University of Massachusetts Press, 1985), 149.
8 Townsend Ludington, ed., *The Fourteenth Chronicle: Letters and Diaries of John Dos Passos* (Gambit, 1973), 89–90.
9 (Horizon, 1967), 16.

■ 1 The Emersonian Myth of Knowledge in the New World

1 1840 journal entry quoted in Francis Otto Matthiessen, *American Renaissance* (Oxford University Press, 1941), 35.
2 Quoted in David Porter, *Emerson and Literary Change* (Harvard University Press, 1978), 145.
3 Hershel Parker and others, eds., *Norton Anthology of American Literature*, vol. 1 (Norton, 1985), 424.

■ 2 Walt Whitman and the World Beyond Rationalism

1 (Small, Maynard, 1904), 32–33.
2 1855 Preface to *Leaves of Grass*, quoted by Paul A. Bové in his discussion of the deconstructive intentions of Whitman's poetics in *Destructive Poetics* (Columbia University Press, 1980), 149.
3 (Small, Maynard, 1904), 18.
4 *American Primer*, 16–17.
5 *A Backward Glance O'er Travelled Roads, Leaves of Grass and Selected Prose*, ed. John Kouwenhoven (Modern Library, 1950), 548.

■ 3   Herman Melville and the Failure of Higher Truth

1   Reprinted in *White-Jacket*, ed. Harrison Hayford, Hershel Parker, and G. Thomas Tanselle (Northwestern University Press and Newberry Library, 1970), 487.
2   *White-Jacket*, 15.
3   *White-Jacket*, 74–75.
4   *The Letters of HM*, ed. Merrill R. Davis and William H. Gilman (Yale University Press, 1960), 143.
5   Letter to Hawthorne, June, 1851, *The Letters*, 129.
6   *Ishmael's White World* (Yale University Press, 1965), 27.
7   *Ishmael's White World*, 128.
8   Reviews from *New York Literary World* and *Harper's New Monthly Magazine*, reprinted in *Moby-Dick*, 613–616.
9   (New York: W.W. Norton, 1970).
10 From "Hawthorne and His Mosses," *Moby-Dick*, 541–542.
11 *Ishmael's White World*, 87.
12 "Pebbles," III and VII, *The Collected Poems of HM*, ed. Howard P. Vincent (Packard, 1947), 205, 206.

■ 4   Emily Dickinson and the Destruction of the
Language of Knowledge

1   "Sumptuous Destitution," in Richard H. Rupp, *Critics on ED* (University of Miami Press, 1972), 48.
2   "The Poetic Tradition," in Rupp, *Critics*, 24.
3   Quoted in Richard Benson Sewall, *The Life of ED* (Farrar, Straus & Giroux, 1974) vol. 2, 675.
4   Emily Dickinson, *Final Harvest*, ed. Thomas H. Johnson (Little, Brown, 1961), 115 (Johnson poem no. 475).
5   *Final Harvest*, 248 (Johnson poem no. 1129).
6   *Final Harvest*, 21 (Johnson poem no. 193).
7   *Final Harvest*, 184–185 (Johnson poem no. 742).
8   *Final Harvest*, 305 (Johnson poem no. 1624).
9   *Final Harvest*, 112, 85 (Johnson poems nos.184, 141).
10 *Final Harvest*, 74 (Johnson poem no. 345).
11 *Final Harvest*, 45–46 (Johnson poem no. 285).
12 *ED's Poetry: Stairway of Surprise* (Holt, Rinehart & Winston, 1960), 130.
13 *ED's Poetry* (University of Chicago Press, 1975).
14 *Lyric Time: Dickinson and the Limits of Genre* (Johns Hopkins University Press, 1979).
15 *The Life of ED*, 2 vols. (Farrar, Straus & Giroux, 1974).
16 *Final Harvest*, 229 (Johnson poem no. 986).
17 *Final Harvest*, 50–51 (Johnson poem no. 293).
18 *Final Harvest*, 126 (Johnson poem no. 512).
19 *ED's Poetry: Stairway of Surprise*, 3, 32–33, 285.
20 *The Nightingale's Burden: Women Poets and American Culture before 1900* (Indiana University Press, 1982), 114–15.

21   *Lyric Time*, 45, 51, 143.

22   *Final Harvest*, 101 (Johnson poem no. 435).

■ 5   Scientists and Their Knowledge

1   Don C. Rawson, "The Process of Discovery: Mendeleyev and the Periodic Law," *Annals of Science* 31, no. 3 (May 1974), 190, 197, 199.

2   Rawson, 195–196.

3   Quoted in James Campbell Brown, *A History of Chemistry* (J. A. Churchill, 1913), 404.

4   Quoted in Rawson, 203.

5   Quoted in Milič Čapek, *The Philosophical Impact of Contemporary Physics* (D. Van Nostrand, 1961), 319.

6   *The Logic of Modern Physics* (Macmillan, 1927), 5.

7   Albert Einstein, *The World as I See It*, trans. Alan Harris (John Lane, 1935), 156–157, 136.

8   Niels Bohr, *Atomic Theory and the Description of Nature* (Cambridge University Press, 1934), 4–5, 96.

9   *The World as I See It*, 138.

■ 6   Science and the Epistemologists

1   (Dover, [1953]), 13.

2   Quoted in H. S. Thayer, "Pragmatism," in D. J. O'Connor, ed., *A Critical History of Western Philosophy* (Free Press, 1965), 456.

3   *The Influence of Darwin upon Philosophy and Other Essays* (Henry Holt, 1910), 98.

4   Quoted in Morris Weitz, "Analysis," in Paul Arthur Schlipp, ed., *The Philosophy of Bertrand Russell* (Northwestern University Press, 1944), 106.

5   Quoted in Roderick M. Chisholm, *Realism and the Background to Phenomenology* (Free Press, 1960), 231.

6   *Our Knowledge of the External World* (Open Court, 1915), 88.

7   "Logical Atomism," in A. J. Ayer, ed., *Logical Positivism* (Free Press, 1959), 48.

8   "Logical Atomism," 34.

9   Weitz, "Analysis," 104, 106.

10   "Logical Atomism," 38.

11   "Logical Atomism," 38–39.

12   *Bertrand Russell and the British Tradition in Philosophy* (Random House, 1967), 268.

13   See, for example, *The Problems of Philosophy* (Henry Holt, 1929), 245–250.

14   *The Logical Syntax of Language* (Kegan Paul, Trench, Trubner, 1927), 279.

15   Ludwig Wittgenstein, *Tractatus Logico-Philosophicus*, ed. & trans. C. K. Ogden (Kegan Paul, Trench, Trubner, 1922), 187, 189.

16   *The Logical Structure of the World* (University of California Press, 1967), 108n.

17   *The Logical Structure*, 292–293.

18   *The Logical Structure*, 215.

19   *The Logical Structure*, 335.

20.   In Harold Stearns, ed., *Civilization in the United States* (Harcourt Brace, 1922), 152–153, 172.

21   *Time and Free Will*, trans. F. L. Pogson (Harper & Row, 1960), 128.

22   William James, *Principles of Psychology* (Henry Holt, 1923), vol. 1, 239.

23   (Henry Holt, 1911), ix.

24   *Bergson and Modern Physics* (D. Reidel, 1971), 56.

25   *Creative Evolution*, trans. Arthur Mitchell (Henry Holt, 1911), xi–xii.

26   Quotes in this paragraph are from *A Pluralistic Universe* (Longmans, Green, 1920), 249, 212, 218–219, 215.

27   (Harvard University Press, 1976), 46, 45.

28   1: 225.

29   *Principles of Psychology* 2: 7.

30   *Principles of Psychology* 2: 76.

31   *Collected Essays and Reviews* (Longmans, Green, 1920), 55.

32   *Creative Evolution*, 176.

33   *Creative Evolution*, 177, xii.

34   *The Creative Mind*, trans. Mabelle L. Andison (Greenwood Press, 1968), 162–163.

35   *Creative Evolution*, 171.

36   *A Pluralistic Universe*, 262.

37   *Principles of Psychology* 1: 241–242.

38   *Principles of Psychology* 1: 225.

39   "Stream of Consciousness and 'Durée Réelle,'" *Philosophy and Phenomenological Research* 10, no.3 (March 1950), 352.

40   *Principles of Psychology* 1: 240–241.

41   *A Pluralistic Universe*, 284.

42   *Principles of Psychology* 1: 241.

43   *Principles of Psychology* 1: 245–246.

44   *Principles of Psychology* 1: 263.

45   *The Creative Mind*, 49.

46   Thomas English Hill's concise account of Whitehead's epistemology in his *Contemporary Theories of Knowledge* (Ronald Press, 1961), esp. pp. 265–270, was useful in helping me formulate my summary.

47   *Symbolism, Its Meaning and Effect* (Macmillan, 1927), 27.

48   Quoted in Craig R. Eisendrath, *The Unifying Moment* (Harvard University Press, 1971), 99.

49   *The Philosophical Impact of Contemporary Physics* (D. Van Nostrand, 1961), 398.

50   *Science: A New Outline* (Thomas Nelson & Sons, 1935), 114.

51   *Thematic Origins of Scientific Thought* (Harvard University Press, 1973), 368.

52   *Mind and the World Order* (Scribner's, 1929), 402, 403.

■ 7   Uncertain Paths Toward Certainty

1   *The Responsibilities of the Novelist* (Doubleday, Page, 1903), 11.

2   *Editor's Study*, ed. James W. Simpson (Whitson, 1983), 22.

3   *Editor's Study*, 22.

4   From *Realism: A Study in Art and Thought* (1918), quoted in George J. Becker *Realism in Modern Literature* (Ungar, 1980), 88.

5   *Editor's Study*, 22.

6   *Editor's Study*, 22.

7   *Criticism and Fiction and Other Essays,* ed. Clara Marburg Kirk and Rudolph Kirk (New York University Press, 1959), 14.

8   *Criticism and Fiction,* 13.

9   See my *American Literature and the Universe of Force* (Duke University Press, 1981).

10 *Criticism and Fiction,* 66, 217, 9–10.

11 *Criticism and Fiction,* 216, 66, 51, 66.

12 Durant Drake and others, *Essays in Critical Realism* (Peter Smith, 1920), 5.

13 In Edwin B. Holt and others, *The New Realism* (Macmillan, 1912), 474.

14 R. J. Hirst, *Perception and the External World* (Macmillan, 1965), 226–227.

15 Quoted in Thomas English Hill, *Contemporary Theories of Knowledge* (Ronald Press, 1961), 132.

16 Holt, *The New Realism,* 10.

17 Hill, *Contemporary Theories,* 157.

18 Holt, *The New Realism,* 2–3.

19 Quoted in William Henry Werkmeister, *A History of Philosophical Ideas in America* (Ronald, 1949), 412.

20 Hill, *Contemporary Theories,* 102–103.

21 Werkmeister, *A History,* 413.

22 Hill, *Contemporary Theories,* 103.

23 Holt, *The New Realism,* 353, 360, 352.

24 Werkmeister, *A History,* 380, 462.

25 Drake, *Critical Realism,* 20-21n.

26 Drake, *Critical Realism,* 30, 28.

27 Drake, *Critical Realism,* 210.

28 Quoted in Hirst, *Perception,* 239.

29 Quoted in Werkmeister, *A History,* 268.

30 *Scepticism and Animal Faith* (Dover, 1955), 179, 125.

31 Quoted in Werkmeister, *A History,* 450, 376.

32 Drake, *Critical Realism,* 226–227.

33 Holt, *The New Realism,* 472.

34 Drake, *Critical Realism,* 212–213.

35 Drake, *Critical Realism,* vii.

36 Holt, *The New Realism,* 359.

37 *A History,* 370.

38 Drake, *Critical Realism,* 105.

■ 8   Stephen Crane and Robert Frost

1   *SC and Literary Impressionism* (Pennsylvania State University Press, 1981), 86.

2   "SC, an English View," in Robert Weatherford, ed., *SC: The Critical Heritage* (Routledge, Kegan & Paul, 1973), 274.

3   To John Northern Hilliard (January 1896?), *SC: Letters,* ed. R. W. Stallman and Lillian Gilkes (New York University Press, 1960), 108–109, 110.

4   *SC* (Twayne, 1962), 123.

5   *The Passages of Thought* (Oxford University Press, 1969), 6.

6   James Nagle, *SC and Literary Impressionism,* 84.

7   *The Red Badge of Courage,* ed. Fredson Bowers (University Press of Virginia, 1975), 5.

8 From *War Is Kind*, in *Poems and Literary Remains*, ed. Fredson Bowers (University Press of Virginia, 1975), 52.

9 *Tales of Adventure*, ed. Fredson Bowers (University Press of Virginia, 1970), 70.

10 *Tales of Adventure*, 82.

11 *The Palm at the End of the Mind*, ed. Holly Stevens (Vintage, 1972), 98.

12 *Tales of Adventure*, 85.

13 *Tales of Adventure*, 92.

14 *Tales of Adventure*, lxvii–lxviii.

15 *SC's Artistry* (Columbia University Press, 1975), 66.

16 To John Northern Hilliard (1897?), *SC: Letters*, 158–159.

17 *Tales, Sketches, and Reports*, ed. Fredson Bowers (University Press of Virginia, 1973), 333–334.

18 *Bowery Tales*, ed. Fredson Bowers (University Press of Virginia, 1969), 66.

19 *The Passages of Thought*, 134.

20 *Selected Prose of RF*, ed. Hyde Cox and Edward Connery Lathem (Holt, Rinehart, Winston, 1966), 1.

21 *RF: The Work of Knowing* (Oxford University Press, 1977), 222, 201.

22. "The Need of Being Versed in Country Things," *The Poetry of RF*, ed. Edward Connery Lathem (Holt, Rinehart, & Winston, 1969), 242.

23 Quoted in Richard Poirer, *RF: The Work of Knowing*, 30.

24 *Interviews with RF*, ed. Edward Connery Lathem (Holt, Rinehart & Winston, 1966), 64.

25 *Selected Prose*, 59.

26 "Pod of the Milkweed," *The Poetry*, 412.

27 "The White Tailed Hornet," *The Poetry*, 279.

28 "Why Wait for Science," *The Poetry*, 395.

29 *RF: The Early Years* (Holt, Rinehart & Winston, 1966), 536, 239–240, 372, and 383–386.

30 *RF: The Work of Knowing*, 25–26, xii, 264, and xvi.

31 *Selected Letters*, ed. Lawrance Thompson (Holt, Rinehart & Winston, 1964), 419.

32 *Selected Prose*, 61.

33 "The Figure a Poem Makes," *Selected Prose*, 20.

34 *RF: The Work of Knowing*, 26–27.

35 "Education by Poetry," *Selected Prose*, 39.

36 *Selected Prose*, 38.

37 "The Constant Symbol," *Selected Prose*, 24.

38 *Selected Prose*, 13–14.

39 *Selected Letters*, 110.

40 *Selected Letters*, 80.

41 *Selected Letters*, 140.

42 *Selected Letters*, 158–159.

43 *Selected Letters*, 140.

44 *Selected Letters*, 191–192.

■ IV   The Revolution in Visual Arts

1 Edward Fry, *Cubism* (Thames and Hudson, 1966), 134.

2 Quoted in Daniel-Henry Kahnweiler, *Juan Gris: His Life and Work*, trans. Douglas

Cooper (Valentin, 1947), 144–145.

3 Victor H. Miesel, *Voices of German Expressionism* (Prentice-Hall, 1970), 108.

4 *Flight Out of Time* (Viking, 1974), 7.

5 "In War's Purifying Fire" (1915), in Meisel, *Voices*, 160–161.

6 Quoted in John D. Erickson, *Dada: Performance, Poetry, and Art* (Twayne, 1984), 127.

7 Umbro Apollonio, *Futurist Manifestoes*, trans. Brain, Flint, Higgitt, and Tisdall (Viking, 1973), 219.

8 Roland Rood writing in *Camera Work*, quoted in Dickran Tashjian, *Skyscraper Primitives* (Wesleyan University Press, 1975), 17.

9 Fry, *Cubism*, 91.

10 "Preliminary Notice," in Daniel-Henry Kahnweiler, *The Rise of Cubism*, trans. Henry Aronson (Wittenborn, Schultz, 1949), vi.

11 *Cubism: A History and an Analysis, 1907–1914* (George Wittenborn, 1959), 15.

12 William Innes Homer, *Alfred Stieglitz and the American Avant-Garde* (New York Graphic Society, 1977), 45.

13 (Whitney Museum, 1963), 19.

14 Homer, *Alfred Stieglitz*, 86.

15 Homer, *Alfred Stieglitz*, 165.

16 Lloyd Goodrich, *The Decade of the Armory Show* (Whitney Museum, 1963), 36.

■ 9 The Artistic Process and the Wider Event

1 Edward Fry, *Cubism* (Thames and Hudson, 1966), 64.

2 Fry, *Cubism*, 60.

3 *The Futurist Moment* (University of Chicago Press, 1986), 81, 90.

4 Umbro Apollonio, ed. *Futurist Manifestoes*, trans. Brain, Flint, Higgitt, and Tisdall (Viking, 1973), 24–26.

5 Apollonio, *Futurist Manifestoes*, 111.

6 Bruno Corradini and Emilio Settimelli in Apollonio, *Futurist Manifestoes*, 146.

7 Apollonio, *Futurist Manifestoes*, 29.

8 Trans. M. T. H. Sadler (Houghton Mifflin, 1914), 24.

9 Victor H. Miesel, *Voices of German Expressionism* (Prentice-Hall, 1970), 182.

10 "The Problem of Form," Meisel, *Voices*, 50, 52.

11 Robert Motherwell, ed., *The Dada Painters and Poets* (G. K. Hall, 1981), 250.

12 Motherwell, *The Dada Painters*, 43.

13 Quoted in John D. Erickson, *Dada: Performance, Poetry, and Art* (Twayne, 1984), 43.

14 Dore Ashton, *Twentieth Century Artists on Art* (Pantheon, 1985), 50, and Motherwell, *The Dada Painters*, 266.

15 "The Problem of Form," Meisel, *Voices*, 47.

16 "Foreword," Motherwell, *The Dada Painters*, xiii.

17 *291*, nos. 7–8 (Arno Press, 1972), 1.

18 Quoted in Beaumont Newhall, *The History of Photography from 1839 to the Present* (Museum of Modern Art, 1982), 168.

19 Quoted in John Pultz and Catherine B. Scallen, *Cubism and American Photography, 1910–1930* (Sterling and Francine Clark Art Institute, 1981), 25.

20 *The Precisionist View in American Art* (Walker Art Center, 1960), 28, 13.

21 Fry, *Cubism*, 166.

22   Marjorie Perloff, *The Futurist Moment* (University of Chicago Press, 1986), 47.

23   Daniel-Henry Kahnweiler, *The Rise of Cubism*, trans. Henry Aronson (Wittenborn, Schultz, 1949), 14.

24   *Cubism*, trans. Stuart Gilbert (Skira, 1959), 76.

25   Quoted in Bernard Noël, *Matisse*, trans. Jane Brenton (Universe Books, 1987), 77, 80.

26   Ashton, *Twentieth*, 35.

27   Apollonio, *Futurist Manifestoes*, 90, 44, 89, 28, 47.

28   Quoted in Willy Rotzler, *Constructive Concepts*, trans. Stanley Mason (ABC Edition, 1977), 60.

29   *The Art of Spiritual Harmony*, trans. M. T. H. Sadler (Houghton Mifflin, 1914), 40.

30   Fry, *Cubism*, 117.

31   Quoted in Rotzler, *Constructive*, 38, 42.

32   Quoted in Alfred H. Barr, *Cubism and Abstract Art* (Harvard University Press, 1986), 122.

33   Quoted in Ashton, *Twentieth*, 83.

34   Jack D. Flam, *Matisse on Art* (E. P. Dutton, 1978), 66.

35   Fry, *Cubism*, 111.

36   Fry, *Cubism*, 53.

37   Fry, *Cubism*, 132. See also Fry's own discussion of these connections on pp. 132–133.

38   Apollonio, *Futurist Manifestoes*, 50, 49.

39   Motherwell, *The Dada Painters*, 248.

40   *Surrealism and Painting*, trans. Simon Watson (Macdonald, 1972), 70.

41   Quoted from Herschel Chipp, *Theories of Modern Art* (University of California Press, 1975), 421–422, and Breton, *Surrealism and Painting*, 134.

42   *Languages of Revolt* (Duke University Press, 1983), 33.

43   Quoted in Chipp, *Theories*, 414.

44   Quoted in Wolf-Dieter Dube, *Expressionism*, trans. Mary Whittall (Praeger, 1973), 21.

45   *Kandinsky* (G. Wittenborn, 1959), 4.

■ V   The American Writer in the Age of Epistemology

1   (Harcourt, Brace, 1922), vii.

■ 10   Gertrude Stein and the Splendid Century

1   *Selected Writings of GS*, ed. Carl Van Vechten (Random House, 1962), 73.

2   *Picasso* (B. T. Batsford, 1939), 49, 50.

3   *GS in Pieces* (Oxford University Press, 1970), xv.

4   *The Geographical History of America* (Random House, 1936), 198.

5   *Lectures in America* (Random House, 1935), 11.

6   "Composition as Explanation," *Selected Writings*, 513.

7   *GS and the Literature of Modern Consciousness* (Frederick Ungar, 1970), 57.

8   *Selected Writings*, 495.

9   (Harcourt, Brace, 1921), 10.

10   *What Are Masterpieces* (Conference Press, 1940), 86.

11   *Geography and Plays* (Four Seas, 1922), 189.

12   *GS: Her Life and Work* (Harper, 1957), 76.

13   *Narration* (Greenwood Press, 1969), 25–26.

14   *Narration*, 17.

15   *Narration*, 20.

16   *Everybody's Autobiography* (Random House, 1937), 71.

17   *What Are Masterpieces*, 88, 90–91.

18   "GS: Her Escape from Protective Language," *Fiction and the Figures of Life* (Alfred A. Knopf, 1970), 79–96.

19   *Selected Writings*, 198–199.

20   *Everybody's Autobiography*, 317.

21   "American Language and Literature" (1944, unpub.), quoted in Jayne L. Walker, *The Making of A Modernist* (University of Massachusetts Press, 1985), 149.

22   Introduction, *Geography and Plays*, 5, 8.

23   "A 1 Pound Stein" (1934), *Selected Essays of William Carlos Williams* (Random House, 1954), 163; and "The Work of Gertrude Stein" (1930), *Imaginations*, ed. Webster Schott (New Directions, 1970), 348.

24   *Geography and Plays*, 355–356.

25   *What Are Masterpieces*, 53–54.

26   *The Autobiography of Alice B. Toklas, Selected Writings*, 70.

27   *Selected Writings*, 496.

28   *Selected Writings*, 112.

29   *Axel's Castle* (Charles Scribner's Sons, 1932), 243–244.

30   "Poetry and Grammar," *Lectures in America*, 236–237.

31   *Lectures in America*, 241.

32   "Portraits and Repetition," *Lectures in America*, 191–192.

33   From Wilder's "Introduction" to Stein's *Four in America* (Yale University Press, 1947), xi–xii.

34   "Portraits and Repetition," *Lectures in America*, 202.

35   *Exact Resemblance to Exact Resemblance* (Yale University Press, 1978), 48–49.

36   "Portraits and Repetition," *Lectures in America*, 178, 183.

37   "Portraits and Repetition," *Lectures in America*, 198.

38   "Henry James," *Four in America*, 119.

39   *Four in America*.

40   *Portraits and Prayers* (Random House, 1934), 63–64.

41   Quoted in Thornton Wilder, "Introduction" to Stein's *Four in America*, xi.

42   *The Development of Abstractionism in the Writings of GS* (University of Pennsylvania Press, 1965), 78, 131.

43   *The Development*, 116.

44   *GS: Her Life and Work*, 94.

45   "A Transatlantic Interview 1946," quoted in Walker, *The Making of a Modernist*, 13.

46   *Picasso*, 12, 11.

47   "Composition as Explanation," *Selected Writings*, 513.

48   *The Structure of Obscurity* (University of Illinois Press, 1984), 19.

49   "Composition as Explanation," *Selected Writings*, 522.

50   *Everybody's Autobiography*, 21–22.

■ 11 Ezra Pound and Ernest Hemingway

1 Herbert N. Schneidau, *EP: The Image and the Real* (Louisiana State University Press, 1969), 152–153.
2 "The Wisdom of Poetry," (1912), *Selected Prose 1909–1965*, ed. William Cookson (New Directions, 1973), 362.
3 *Literary Essays of EP*, ed. & intro. T. S. Eliot (New Directions, 1954), 6.
4 Letter to Harriet Monroe (October 1912), *Letters 1907–1941*, ed. D. D. Paige (Harcourt, Brace, 1950), 11.
5 *Literary Essays*, 3.
6 Letter to Harriet Monroe (January 1915), *Letters*, 48–49.
7 "The Serious Artist," *Literary Essays*, 46.
8 "A Retrospect," *Literary Essays*, 9.
9 "EP," quoted in K. L. Goodwin, *The Influence of EP* (Oxford University Press, 1966), 128.
10 From a letter to Lady Gregory, quoted in Noel Stock, *The Life of EP* (Random House, 1970), 130.
11 "The Wisdom of Poetry," *Selected Prose*, 360.
12 *Literary Essays*, 5.
13 "I Gather the Limbs of Osiris" (1911–12), *Selected Prose*, 41.
14 *EP and the Visual Arts*, ed. Harriet Zinnes (New Directions, 1980), 166.
15 *The Matrix of Modernism* (Princeton University Press, 1985), 115–124.
16 "Axiomatica" (1921), *Selected Prose*, 50.
17 "The Wisdom of Poetry," *Selected Prose*, 361.
18 "A Few Don'ts," *Literary Essays*, 4.
19 *EP and the Visual Arts*, 8.
20 Stock, *The Life*, 64–65, 106; also Richard Sieburth, *Instigations* (Harvard University Press, 1978), 10.
21 (New Directions, 1952), 7–8.
22 "Aeschylus" (1919), *Literary Essays*, 267.
23 *EP and the Visual Arts*, 151.
24 *Gaudier-Brzeska: A Memoir* (1916) (New Directions, 1970), 92.
25 (City Lights, 1936), 9, 12, and 13.
26 *The Spirit of Romance* (New Directions, [1952]), 14.
27 "How to Read," *Literary Essays*, 36.
28 *Literary Essays*, 25.
29 Bell, *Critic as Scientist* (Methuen, 1981), 243; see Sieburth, *Instigations*, 120–121.
30 "I Gather the Limbs of Osiris," *Selected Prose*, 21.
31 Both quotations are from Canto XXXVIII, *Selected Poems* (New Directions, 1957), 129–130, 134.
32 *A Farewell to Arms* (Scribner's, 1949), 191, 241.
33 *The Young Hemingway* (Basil Blackwell, 1986), 183.
34 *The Green Hills of Africa* (Scribner's, 1935), 69–70.
35 *A Moveable Feast* (Scribner's, 1964), 13, 69.
36 *The Young Hemingway*, 158.
37 *The Green Hills*, 70.
38 See Michael Reynolds, *Hemingway's Reading, 1910–1940* (Princeton University Press, 1981).

39 "The Cult of Experience in American Writing," *Image and Idea* (New Directions, 1949).
40 Grace Hall Hemingway to EH, December 4, 1926, quoted in Reynolds, *The Young*, 53.
41 *The Snows of Kilimanjaro* (Scribner's, 1970), 4.
42 *In Our Time* (Scribner's, 1970), 98–99.
43 *The Short Stories of EH* (Scribner's, [1953]), 440.
44 "Hemingway," in Morton Dauwen Zabel, ed. *Literary Opinion in America* (Harper, 1962), 445–446.
45 "From Detective Story to Detective Novel," *MFS* 29 (Autumn 1983), 484.
46 "EH's Unhurried Sensations," *The Hemingway Review* 1, no. 2 (Spring 1982), 28.
47 Warren, "Hemingway," 449; Kenner, "Small Ritual Truths," *A Homemade World* (Knopf, 1975), 140–141.
48 *A Moveable*, 132.
49 *Death in the Afternoon* (Scribner's, 1932), 19.
50 *Death in the Afternoon*, 53.
51 *A Moveable*, 17–18.
52 *The Green Hills*, 20.
53 *A Moveable*, 132.
54 *The Apprenticeship of EH* (Farrar, Straus & Young, 1954), 229–236.
55 "Hemingway," 452.
56 (Scribner's, 1926), 186–187.
57 *Death in the Afternoon*, 192.
58 *Death in the Afternoon*, 17, 20.
59 Quoted in Jeffrey Meyers, *Hemingway: A Biography* (Harper & Row, 1985), 138.
60 1945; quoted from Larry W. Phillips, *EH on Writing* (Scribner's, 1984), 77.
61 *Death in the Afternoon*, 2.
62 *The Green Hills*, 26–27.
63 *In Our Time*, 110.
64 *A Moveable*, 17.
65 "A 1 Pound Stein," *Selected Essays of William Carlos Williams* (Random House, 1954), 163.
66 "Hemingway's Tutor, Ezra Pound," *MFS* 17, no. 4 (Winter 1971), 477.
67 *The Young Hemingway*, 213–214.
68 *In Our Time*, 103.
69 *Death in the Afternoon*, 14.
70 "EH's Unhurried Sensations," 21.
71 *The Sun Also Rises*, 104.

■ 12   Conrad Aiken and Wallace Stevens

1 *The Continuity of American Poetry* (Princeton University Press, 1961), 349.
2 Letter to Huston Peterson (June 8, 1928), *Selected Letters of CA*, ed. Joseph Killorin (Yale University Press, 1978), 145.
3 (March, 1913), *Selected Letters*, 29, 30.
4 *Ushant: An Essay* (Duell, Sloan & Pearce, 1952), 168.
5 (Knopf, 1923).

6   *Collected Poems*, 2d ed. (Oxford University Press, 1970), 668–669.

7   Letter to G. B. Wilbur (January 2, 1931), *Selected Letters*, 166–167.

8   "LX" (from *Time in the Rock*), *Collected Poems*, 722–723.

9   *Ushant*, 322–323.

10 *The Collected Stories of CA* (World, 1960), 276.

11 *Collected Poems*, 499.

12 "XIX" (from *Preludes to Memnon*), *Collected Poems*, 520.

13 "XLVIII" (from *Time in the Rock*), *Collected Poems*, 712.

14 Quotes are from *Great Circle* (Scribner's, 1933), 308, 309.

15 "IX" (from *Time in the Rock*), *Collected Poems*, 672.

16 "LIX" (from *Preludes to Memnon*), *Collected Poems*, 568.

17 "V" (from *Preludes to Memnon*), *Collected Poems*, 503.

18 *Ushant*, 166.

19 *Ushant*, 167, 246.

20 "Adagia," *Opus Posthumous*, ed. and intro. Samuel French Morse (Knopf, 1957), 172.

21 *Stevens' Poetry of Thought* (Johns Hopkins University Press, 1966), 1.

22 *Letters of WS*, ed. Holly Stevens (Knopf, 1967), 255.

23 *Parts of a World* (Random House, 1983), 165n.

24 *Letters of WS*, 742–743.

25 *Poets of Reality* (Harvard University Press, 1965), 259.

26 *Destructive Poetics* (Columbia University Press, 1980), 186, 187.

27 "Effects of Analogy," *The Necessary Angel* (Random House, 1951), 130.

28 *Scepticism and Animal Faith* (Dover, 1955), 40–41.

29 To Ronald Lane Latimer (January 10, 1936), *Letters of WS*, 305.

30 *Opus Posthumous*, 66.

31 *The Clairvoyant Eye* (Louisiana State University Press, 1965), 72.

32 *Opus Posthumous*, 67–68.

33 (February 18, 1942), *Letters of WS*, 402.

34 Letter to Henry Church (December 8, 1942), *Letters of WS*, 431.

35 *Letters of WS*, 636–637.

36 *Letters of WS*, 27.

37 "A Skeptical Music: Stevens and Santayana," *Criticism* 7 (Summer 1965), 264–265.

38 *Opus Posthumous*, 237.

39 *Opus Posthumous*, 164.

40 *The Necessary Angel*, 25.

41 *The Continuity of American Poetry*, 382.

42 *The Clairvoyant Eye*, 228–229.

43 *Skepticism and Animal Faith*, 98.

44 *The Collected Poems of WS* (Knopf, 1954), 57.

45 "The Relations between Poetry and Painting," *The Necessary Angel*, 171.

46 Letters to Sister M. Bernetta Quinn (December 28, 1950) and Bernard Heringman (May 3, 1949), *Letters of WS*, 704, 637, 636.

47 "A Collect of Philosophy" (1951), *Opus Posthumous*, 183–202; the quote is on p. 183.

48 *Letters of WS*, 792.

49 "A Collect of Philosophy," *Opus Posthumous*, 191.

50   "An Ordinary Evening in New Haven," *The Palm*, 345.

51   *The Necessary Angel*, 27.

52   "Imagination as Value," *The Necessary Angel*, 139.

53   *Scepticism and Animal Faith*, 77.

54   *Letters of WS*, 32.

55   *The Necessary Angel*, 160, 159.

56   *Letters of WS*, 369.

57   Young, "A Skeptical Music," 272–274.

58   "A Brief History of My Opinions," *The Philosophy of Santayana*, ed. Irwin Edman (Scribner's, 1953), 6.

59   *Opus Posthumous*, 163. I have corrected the *Opus Posthumous* text's "friction" to "fiction."

60   *Letters of WS*, 435.

61   *Letters of WS*, 444.

62   "Idea of Order at Key West," *The Palm*, 98–99.

63   *Scepticism and Animal Faith*, 76.

64   "The Noble Rider and the Sound of Words," *The Necessary Angel*, 23.

65   Peter Brazeau, *Parts of a World*, 175.

66   To Ronald Lane Latimer, *Letters of WS*, 290.

67   *The Necessary Angel*, 95.

68   See, for example, Brazeau, *Parts of a World*, 23, 25, 40.

69   *Poets of Reality*, 237, 274.

■ 13   William Carlos Williams

1   (New Directions, 1956), 215.

2   "Notes from a Talk on Poetry," *Poetry* (July 1919), 211. Quoted in Paul Mariani, *WCW: A New World Naked* (McGraw Hill, 1981), 159.

3   Stevens, *Opus Posthumous*, ed. & intro. Samuel French Morse (Knopf, 1957), 255.

4   *The Embodiment of Knowledge*, ed. & intro. Ron Loewinsohn (New Directions, 1974), 107.

5   *The Embodiment*, 9.

6   "America, Whitman, and the Art of Poetry," *Poetry Journal* 8 (November 1917), 27–29.

7   *The Autobiography of WCW* (New Directions, 1967), 174.

8   *Escape from the Self* (Columbia University Press, 1977), 77.

9   "America, Whitman and the Art of Poetry," 31.

10   *The Embodiment*, 52.

11   "Preface," *Selected Essays of WCW* (Random House, 1954), xvii.

12   (August 23, 1951), *Selected Letters*, ed. John C. Thirlwall (McDowell, Oblensky, 1957), 309.

13   *The Embodiment*, 122–123.

14   See his essay "The Work of Gertrude Stein," *Imaginations*, esp. 347.

15   (Boni & Liveright, 1921), 252.

16   *Contact* 1 (1920); reprinted in *A Recognizable Image*, ed. Bram Dijkstra (New Directions, 1978), 66.

17   *Selected Essays*, 178–179.

18 *The Autobiography*, 148.

19 Letter to Jean Starr Untermeyer (October 1948), *Selected Letters*, 268–269.

20 Interview with Walter Sutton, 1961; reprinted in Linda Welsheimer Wagner, *Interviews With WCW* (New Directions, 1976), 42.

21 "Comment" from *Contact* 1 (1921), *Selected Essays*, 28.

22 *Selected Letters*, 269.

23 Letter to Kay Boyle (n.d. 1932), *Selected Letters*, 134.

24 Stevens, *Opus Posthumous*, 255.

25 Comment from an interview, quoted in Wagner, *Interviews*, 60–61.

26 *Autobiography*, 385.

27 *The Embodiment*, 20.

28 "A 1 Pound Stein," *Selected Essays*, 163–164.

29 Marianne Moore, *Predilections* (Viking, 1955), 138.

30 *Collected Earlier Poems* (New Directions, 1951), 343.

31 Letter to Babette Deutsch (May 25, 1948), *Selected Letters*, 265.

32 *An Early Martyr and Other Poems* (Alcestis Press, 1935), 22; also in *Collected Earlier Poems*, 99.

33 *An Early Martyr*, 14.

34 *Selected Essays*, 238.

35 *Autobiography*, 356.

36 *A Pluralistic Universe* (Longmans, Green, 1920), 117; quoted above, p. 89.

37 "The Fault: Matisse," unpub. ms. quoted in Dickran Tashjian, "William Carlos Williams and the American Scene," brochure from Whitney Museum of American Art, 1978.

38 *Sour Grapes* (Four Seas, 1921), 70.

39 *The Farmers' Daughters* (New Directions, 1961), 46.

40 "Yours, O Youth," from *Contact* 4 (1922), *Selected Essays*, 32.

41 *A Pluralistic Universe*, 372.

42 *The Embodiment*, 149.

43 *The Autobiography*, 391.

44 "Axioms," *A Recognizable Image*, 175.

45 (June 2, 1932), *Selected Letters*, 123.

46 *The Embodiment*, 23.

47 *WCW: A New World Naked*, 134, 417.

48 *Collected Earlier Poems*, 347–348.

49 "Charles Sheeler," *A Recognizable Image*, 143.

50 *The Early Poetry of WCW* (Cornell University Press, 1975), 152–153.

51 *The Creative Mind*, trans. Mabelle Andison (Greenwood Press, 1968), 162; quoted above, p. 88.

52 *The Hieroglyphics of a New Speech* (Princeton University Press, 1969), 102–103.

53 *Descent into Winter*, *Imaginations*, 244–245.

54 *Collected Earlier Poems*, 399.

55 "The Last Words of My English Grandmother," *The Broken Span* (New Directions, 1941) [n.p.].

56 *Farmers' Daughters*, 111–112.

57 "Sympathetic Portrait of a Child," *Collected Earlier Poems*, 155.

58 "Ancient Gentility," *Farmers' Daughters*, 275.

59   *The Creative Mind*, 123; *Creative Evolution*, trans. Arthur Mitchell (Henry Holt, 1911), 251.

60   *The Broken Span* [n.p.].

61   *A Recognizable Image*, 144.

62   *Autobiography*, 359, 362.

63   *A Homemade World* (Knopf, 1975), 85.

64   *Poets of Reality* (Harvard University Press, 1965), 293.

65   *Interviews with WCW*, xiv.

66   Wagner, *Interviews with WCW*, xi.

67   Kenner, *A Homemade World*, 85.

68   Miller, *Poets of Reality*, 294.

69   (MacGibbon & Kee, 1965), 120–121.

70   *I Wanted to Write a Poem*, reported & ed. by Edith Heal (Beacon Press, 1967), 74–75.

71   *WCW: A New World Naked*, 365.

72   *An Early Martyr*, 30; also *Collected Earlier Poems*, 105.

73   *The Cod Head* (Harvest Press, 1932).

74   *Selected Letters*, 129–130.

75   "An Objective," *Prepositions* (Horizon, 1968), 25.

76   *I Wanted to Write a Poem*, 82.

77   *Selected Letters*, 136, 326.

78   "America, Whitman, and the Art of Poetry" 30–31; also *Selected Letters*, 335–336.

79   *Autobiography*, 360.

80   *Selected Essays*, 94.

81   Wagner, *Interviews*, 53.

82   "Reflex Action and Theism," *Essays on Faith and Morals*, ed. Ralph Barton Perry (Longmans, Green, 1949), 118–119.

83   *Autobiography*, 390.

84   *The Embodiment*, 24.

85   (New Directions, 1945–58), 3.

86   *Al Que Quiere!* (Four Seas, 1917), 67–68; also *Collected Earlier Poems*, 167–168.

87   "A Beginning on the Short Story (Notes)," *Selected Essays*, 303.

88   *The Embodiment*, 18; *Autobiography*, 265.

89   *The Embodiment*, 18–19.

90   *Selected Essays*, 303; *Autobiography*, 241.

91   *Autobiography*, 264–265.

92   *Autobiography*, 240.

93   *The Embodiment*, 13.

94   *Selected Letters*, 286.

95   *I Wanted to Write a Poem*, 49.

96   *Collected Earlier Poems*, 326.

■ 14   John Dos Passos

1   Letter to Rumsey Marvin (December 4, 1916), *The Fourteenth Chronicle*, ed. Townsend Ludington (Gambit, 1973), 57.

2   Letter to William H. Bond (March 26, 1938), *The Fourteenth*, 516.

3 "What Makes a Novelist," *National Review* 20 (January 16, 1968), 30.

4 Interview with David Sanders, *Writers at Work*, fourth series, ed. George Plimpton (Viking, 1976), 76.

5 8: 270.

6 *JDP: A Twentieth Century Odyssey* (E. P. Dutton, 1980), 93.

7 To Rumsey Marvin (April 10, 1917 and September 28, 1916), *The Fourteenth*, 70, 48.

8 Letter to George St. John (May 5, 1917), *The Fourteenth*, 72.

9 Virginia Spencer Carr, *JDP: A Life* (Doubleday, 1984), 119–120.

10 Interview with David Sanders, 72.

11 *The Fourteenth*, 95.

12 From the diary entry for July 31, 1917, *The Fourteenth*, 89–90.

13 (August 23, 1917), *The Fourteenth*, 92.

14 "What Makes a Novelist," 29.

15 *One Man's Initiation* (Cornell University Press, 1969), 71. Ellipsis is Dos Passos's.

16 *One Man's*, 159. Ellipses are Dos Passos's.

17 Letter to Rumsey Marvin (June [n.d.] 1919), *The Fourteenth*, 254.

18 Entry for August 24, 1917, *The Fourteenth*, 94.

19 Compare *The Fourteenth*, 85–86, with *One Man's*, 44–50.

20 *Three Soldiers* (George H. Doran, 1921), 22.

21 "JDP: Inventor in Isolation," *Saturday Review* 52 (March 5, 1969), 16.

22 68: 26.

23 (Modern Library), ix.

24 Quoted in *The Fourteenth*, 378.

25 Carr, *JDP: A Life*, 196, 197.

26 *JDP: A Twentieth Century Odyssey*, 145.

27 Quoted in David Sanders, "*Manhattan Transfer* and 'the Service of Things,'" in Ray B. Brown and Donald Pizer, eds., *Themes and Directions in American Literature* (Purdue University Studies, 1969), 180.

28 "The New Language of Cinema," trans. Winifred Ray, in Sergei Eisenstein, *Film Essays: and a Lecture*, ed. Jay Leyda (Praeger, 1970), 34.

29 "Looking Back on *USA*," *New York Times*, Sunday, October 25, 1959, sec. 2, 5.

30 *The Cubist Theatre* (UMI Press, 1983), 39.

31 *The Cubist Theatre*, 6.

32 Ludington, *JDP: A Twentieth Century Odyssey*, 226.

33 Foreword to John Howard Lawson, *Roger Bloomer* (Thomas Seltzer, 1923), vi.

34 "Is the 'Realistic' Theatre Obsolete?," *Vanity Fair* 24 (May 1925), 114.

35 "Towards a Revolutionary Theatre," *New Masses* 3 (December 1927), 20.

36 Quoted in Carr, *JDP: A Life*, 193.

37 *The Garbage Man* (Harper, 1926), 47.

38 *Dos Passos and "The Revolting Playwrights"* (A.-B. Lundequistska, 1964).

39 Forward to Lawson, *Roger Bloomer*, v.

40 "The Desperate Experiment," *Book Week* (September 15, 1963), 3.

41 *The American City Novel* (Oklahoma University Press, 1954), 142, 143.

42 Notably Gelfant, *The American City Novel*, 143–144; Ben Stoltzfus, "JDP and the French," in Ailen Belkind, ed. *JDP, the Critics, and the Writer's Intention* (Southern Illinois University Press, 1971), 198–99, 202; and Ludington, *JDP: a Twentieth Century Odyssey*, 145.

43 (Dover [1953]), 5, 6 and 7.
44 "The Desperate Experiment," 3.
45 "The Desperate Experiment," 3.
46 Interview with David Sanders, 81.
47 Camera Eye 3, *42nd Parallel, U.S.A.* (Random House, 1937), 25.
48 *1919, U.S.A.*, 71–72.
49 *The Big Money, U.S.A.*, 125–126.
50 *The Big Money*, 461–462, 464.
51 Quoted from an interview in Melvin Landsberg, *Dos Passos' Path to U.S.A.* (Associated University Press, 1972), 192.
52 Newsreel X, *42nd Parallel*, 148–149.
53 (Modern Library), vii–viii.
54 *The American City Novel*, 173.
55 *Dos Passos' U.S.A.* (University Press of Virginia, 1988), 66–71.
56 "JDP: Inventor in Isolation," 19.
57 *42nd Parallel*, 146–147.
58 *42nd Parallel*, 360–361. Ellipses are Dos Passos's.
59 *1919*, 72, 73, 78, 87, 98, 200, 393–4; *The Big Money*, 519. Ellipses are Dos Passos's.
60 John Lydenberg, "Dos Passos's *USA*: The Words of the Hollow Men," in Belkind, *Dos Passos, the Critics, and the Writer's Intention*, 94, 104.
61 *1919*, 5.
62 Interview with David Sanders, 74.

Bibliography

Aiken, Conrad. *Collected Poems*, 2nd ed. New York: Oxford University Press, 1970.

———. *The Collected Short Stories of Conrad Aiken*. Cleveland: World, 1960.

———. *Great Circle*. New York: Scribner's, 1933.

———. Interview in *Paris Review, Writers at Work*, fourth series, ed. George Plimpton. New York: Viking, 1976, 21–44.

———. *The Pilgrimage of Festus*. New York: Knopf, 1923.

———. *A Reviewer's ABC: Collected Criticism of Conrad Aiken from 1916 to the Present*, ed. & intro. Rufus A. Blanshard. [New York]: Meridan Books, 1958.

———. *Selected Letters of Conrad Aiken*, ed. Joseph Killorin. New Haven: Yale University Press, 1978.

———. *Ushant: An Essay*. New York: Duell, Sloan and Pearce, 1952.

Anderson, Charles. *Emily Dickinson's Poetry: Stairway of Surprise*. New York: Holt, Rinehart & Winston, 1960.

Apollonio, Umbro, ed. *Futurist Manifestos*, trans. Brain, Flint, Higgitt, and Tisdall. New York: Viking, 1973.

Ashton, Dore, ed. *Twentieth Century Artists on Art*. New York: Pantheon, 1985.

Ayer, A. J., ed. *Logical Positivism*. Glencoe, Ill.: Free Press, 1959.

Baker, Houston A., Jr. *Modernism and the Harlem Renaissance*. Chicago: University of Chicago Press, 1987.

Ball, Hugo. *Flight Out of Time*, ed. John Elderfield, trans. A. Raines. New York: Viking, 1974.

Barr, Alfred H. *Cubism and Abstract Art*. Cambridge, Mass.: Harvard University Press, 1986.

Barry, Elaine. *Robert Frost on Writing*. New Brunswick, N.J.: Rutgers University Press, 1973.

Becker, George J. *Realism in Modern Literature*. New York: Ungar, 1980.

Belkind, Allen. *Dos Passos, the Critics, and the Writer's Intention*. Carbondale, Ill.: Southern Illinois University Press, 1971.

Bell, Ian F. A. *Critic as Scientist: The Modernist Poetics of Ezra Pound*. New York: Methuen, 1981.

Benfey, Christopher E. G., *Emily Dickinson and the Problem of Others*. Amherst, Mass.: University of Massachusetts Press, 1985.

Bergon, Frank. *Stephen Crane's Artistry*. New York: Columbia University Press, 1975.

Bergson, Henri. *Creative Evolution*, trans. Arthur Mitchell. New York: Henry Holt, 1911.

———. *The Creative Mind*, trans. Mabelle L. Andison. New York: Greenwood Press, 1968.

————. *Matter and Memory*, trans. Nancy M. Paul and W. Scott Palmer. New York: Macmillan, 1911.

————. *Time and Free Will*, trans. F. L. Pogson. New York: Harper & Row, 1960. (Reprint of Macmillan 1910 ed.)

Bohr, Niels. *Atomic Theory and the Description of Nature*. Cambridge: Cambridge University Press, 1934.

Bové, Paul A. *Destructive Poetics: Heidigger and Modern American Poetry*. New York: Columbia University Press, 1980.

Brazeau, Peter. *Parts of a World: Wallace Stevens Remembered*. New York: Random House, 1983.

Breton, André. *Surrealism and Painting*, trans. Simon Watson Taylor. London: Macdonald, 1972.

Bridgman, P[ercy] W. *The Logic of Modern Physics*. New York: Macmillan, 1927.

Bridgman, Richard. *Gertrude Stein in Pieces*. New York: Oxford University Press, 1970.

Brodtkorb, Paul, Jr. *Ishmael's White World: A Phenomenological Reading of Moby Dick*. New Haven: Yale University Press, 1965.

Brown, James Campbell. *A History of Chemistry*. London: J.A. Churchill, 1913.

Cady, Edwin H. *Stephen Crane*. New York: Twayne, 1962.

Cameron, Sharon. *Lyric Time: Dickinson and the Limits of Genre*. Baltimore: Johns Hopkins University Press, 1979.

Čapek, Milič. *Bergson and Modern Physics*. Boston Studies in the Philosophy of Science, Vol. 7, ed. Robert S. Cohen and Marx W. Wartofsky. Dordrecht-Holland: D. Reidel, 1971.

————. *The Philosophical Impact of Contemporary Physics*. Princeton, N.J.: D. Van Nostrand, 1961.

————. "Stream of Consciousness and 'Durée Réelle,'" *Philosophy and Phenomenological Research* 10, no. 3 (March 1950), 331–353.

Carnap, Rudolph. *The Logical Structure of the World*. Berkeley: University of California Press, 1967.

————. *The Logical Syntax of Language*. London: Kegan Paul, Trench, Trubner, 1937.

Carr, Virginia Spencer. *Dos Passos: A Life*. Garden City, N.Y.: Doubleday, 1984.

Cendrars, Blaise. *Panama or the Adventures of My Seven Uncles*, trans. John Dos Passos, in *Selected Writings of Blaise Cendrars*, ed. Walter Albert. New York: New Directions, 1966, 100–137.

Chipp, Herschel. *Theories of Modern Art*. Berkeley: University of California Press, 1975.

Chisholm, Roderick M. *Realism and the Background to Phenomenology*. Glencoe, Ill.: Free Press, 1960.

Cook, Charles H., Jr. "Ahab's 'Intolerable Allegory,'" *Boston U. Studies in English* 1 (1955–56), 45–52.

Cox, James Melville. *Robert Frost: A Collection of Critical Essays*. Englewood Cliffs, N.J.: Prentice-Hall, 1962.

Crane, Stephen. *Bowery Tales*, ed. Fredson Bowers. Charlottesville: University Press of Virginia, 1969.

————. *Poems and Literary Remains*, ed. Fredson Bowers. Charlottesville: University Press of Virginia, 1975.

————. *The Red Badge of Courage/An Episode of the American Civil War*, ed. Henry Binder. New York: W. W. Norton, 1979.

——. *The Red Badge of Courage/An Episode of the American Civil War*, intro. J. C. Levenson, ed. Fredson Bowers. Charlottesville: University Press of Virginia, 1975.

——. *Stephen Crane: Letters*, ed. R. W. Stallman and Lillian Gilkes. New York: New York University Press, 1960.

——. *Tales of Adventure*, ed. Fredson Bowers. Charlottesville: University Press of Virginia, 1970.

——. *Tales, Sketches, and Reports*, ed. Fredson Bowers. Charlottesville: University Press of Virginia, 1973.

Dembo, L. S. *Conceptions of Reality in Modern American Poetry*. Berkeley: University of California Press, 1966.

Dewey, John. *Essays in Experimental Logic*. New York: Dover [1953].

——. *The Influence of Darwin upon Philosophy and Other Essays in Contemporary Thought*. New York: Henry Holt, 1910.

Dickinson, Emily. *Final Harvest*, ed. Thomas H. Johnson. Boston: Little, Brown, 1961.

——. *Poems*, 3 vols., ed. Thomas H. Johnson. Cambridge: Harvard University Press, 1955.

Dijkstra, Bram. *The Hieroglyphics of a New Speech: Cubism, Stieglitz and the Early Poetry of William Carlos Williams*. Princeton, N.J.: Princeton University Press, 1969.

Doggett, Frank A. *Stevens' Poetry of Thought*. Baltimore, Md.: Johns Hopkins University Press, 1966.

Donley, Carol C. "'A little touch of/Einstein in the night—': Williams' Early Exposure to the Theories of Relativity," *WCWN* 4, no. 1 (Spring 1978), 10–13.

Donoghue, Denis. *Connoisseurs of Chaos: Ideas of Order in Modern American Poetry*. New York: Macmillan, 1965.

Dos Passos, John. "Against American Literature," *New Republic* 8 (October 14, 1916), 269–271.

——. "The Desperate Experiment," *Book Week* (September 15, 1963), 3.

——. *District of Columbia*, trilogy, comprising *Adventures of a Young Man, Number One*, and *The Grand Design*. Boston: Houghton Mifflin, 1952.

——. Forward to John Howard Lawson, *Roger Bloomer*. New York: Thomas Seltzer, 1923.

——. *The Garbage Man/A Parade with Shouting*. New York: Harper, 1926.

——. Interview with David Sanders in *Paris Review*, *Writers at Work*, fourth series, ed. George Plimpton. New York: Viking, 1976, 67–89.

——. "Introduction" to *Three Soldiers*. New York: Modern Library, 1932.

——. "Is the 'Realistic' Theatre Obsolete?" *Vanity Fair* 24 (May 1925), 64, 114.

——. "Looking Back on *USA*," *New York Times*, Sunday, October 25, 1959, ii, 5.

——. *Manhattan Transfer*. Boston: Houghton Mifflin, 1925.

——. *One Man's Initiation: 1917*. Ithaca, N.Y.: Cornell University Press, 1969.

——. "Statement of Belief," *Bookman* 68 (September 1924), 26.

——. *Streets of Night*. New York: George H. Doran, 1923.

——. *Three Soldiers*. New York: George H. Doran, 1921.

——. "Towards a Revolutionary Theatre," *New Masses* 3 (December 1927), 20.

——. *U.S.A.*, trilogy, comprising *42nd Parallel, 1919*, and *The Big Money*. New York: Random House, 1937.

——. "What Makes a Novelist," *National Review* 20 (January 16, 1968), 29–32.

Drake, Durant, and others. *Essays in Critical Realism*. New York: Peter Smith, 1920.

Dube, Wolf-Dieter. *Expressionism*, trans. Mary Whittall. New York: Praeger, 1973.

Dubnick, Randa. *The Structure of Obscurity: Gertrude Stein, Language, and Cubism*. Urbana: University of Illinois Press, 1984.

Eames, Elizabeth R. *Bertrand Russell's Theory of Knowledge*. New York: George Braziller, 1969.

Eddington, A. S. *The Nature of the Physical World*. New York: Macmillan, 1928.

Einstein, Albert. *The World as I See It*, trans. Alan Harris. London: John Lane, 1935.

Eisendrath, Craig R. *The Unifying Moment: The Psychological Philosophy of William James & Alfred North Whitehead*. Cambridge, Mass.: Harvard University Press, 1971.

Eisenstein, Sergei. *Film Essays: And a Lecture*, ed. Jay Leyda. New York: Praeger, 1970.

Emerson, Ralph Waldo. *Essays and Lectures*, ed. Joel Porte. New York: Library of America, 1983.

Erickson, John D. *Dada: Performance, Poetry, and Art*. Boston: Twayne, 1984.

Fenollosa, Ernest. *The Chinese Written Character as a Medium for Poetry*, ed. Ezra Pound. San Francisco: City Lights, 1936.

Fenton, Charles A. *The Apprenticeship of Ernest Hemingway*. New York: Farrar, Straus & Young, 1954.

Fiedelson, Charles Jr. *Symbolism and American Literature*. New Haven: Yale University Press, 1965.

Flam, Jack D. *Matisse on Art*. New York: E.P. Dutton, 1978.

Friedman, Martin L. *The Precisionist View in American Art*. Minneapolis: Walker Art Center, 1960.

Frost, Robert. *Interviews with Robert Frost*, ed. Edward Connery Lathem. New York: Holt, Rinehart & Winston, 1966.

———. *The Poetry of Robert Frost*, ed. Edward Connery Lathem. New York: Holt, Rinehart & Winston, 1969.

———. *Selected Letters*, ed. Lawrance Thompson. New York: Holt, Rinehart & Winston, 1964.

———. *Selected Prose of Robert Frost*, ed. Hyde Cox and Edward Connery Lathem. New York: Holt, Rinehart & Winston, 1966.

Fry, Edward. *Cubism*. London: Thames & Hudson, 1966.

Gass, William H. "Gertrude Stein: Her Escape from Protective Language," in *Fiction and the Figures of Life*. New York: Knopf, 1970, 79–96.

Gates, Henry Louis, Jr. *The Signifying Monkey*. New York: Oxford University Press, 1988.

Gelfant, Blanche. *The American City Novel*. Norman: University of Oklahoma Press, 1954.

Gelpi, Albert. *Wallace Stevens: The Poetics of Modernism*. New York: Cambridge University Press, 1985.

Glover, J. Garrett. *The Cubist Theatre*. Ann Arbor, Mich.: UMI Press, 1983.

Golding, John. *Cubism: A History and an Analysis, 1907–1914*. New York: George Wittenborn, 1959.

Goodrich, Lloyd. *The Decade of the Armory Show*. New York: Whitney Museum, 1963.

Goodwin, K. L. *The Influence of Ezra Pound*. London: Oxford University Press, 1966.

Greenberg, Robert M. "Cetology: Center of Multiplicity and Discord in *Moby-Dick*." *ESQ* 27, 1st Quart. (1981): (1[102]), 1–13.

Guimond, James. *The Art of William Carlos Williams: A Discovery and Possession of America*. Urbana: University of Illinois Press, 1968.

Habasque, Guy. *Cubism*, trans. Stuart Gilbert. [Paris?]: Skira, 1959.

Hartley, Marsden. *Adventures in the Arts*. New York: Boni & Liveright, 1921.

Hedges, Inez. *Languages of Revolt: Dada and Surrealist Literature and Film*. Durham, N.C.: Duke University Press, 1983.

Hemingway, Ernest. *Death in the Afternoon*, New York: Scribner's, 1932.

————. *A Farewell to Arms*. New York: Scribner's, 1949.

————. *The Green Hills of Africa*. New York: Scribner's, 1935.

————. *In Our Time*. New York: Scribner's, 1970.

————. *A Moveable Feast*. New York: Scribner's, 1964.

————. *The Short Stories of Ernest Hemingway*. New York: Scribner's, [1953].

————. *The Snows of Kilimanjaro and Other Stories*. New York: Scribner's, 1970.

————. *The Sun Also Rises*. New York: Scribner's, 1926.

Hill, Thomas English. *Contemporary Theories of Knowledge*. New York: Ronald Press, 1961.

Hirst, R.J. *Perception and the External World*. New York: Macmillan, 1965.

Hoffman, Daniel, ed. *Ezra Pound and William Carlos Williams*. Philadelphia: University of Pennsylvania Press, 1984.

————. *The Twenties: American Writing in the Postwar Decade*. New York: Viking, 1955.

Hoffman, Michael J. *The Development of Abstractionism in the Writings of Gertrude Stein*. Philadelphia: University of Pennsylvania Press, 1965.

Holt, Edwin B[issell], and others. *The New Realism*. New York: Macmillan, 1912.

Holton, Gerald. *Thematic Origins of Scientific Thought*. Cambridge, Mass.: Harvard University Press, 1973.

Homer, William Innes. *Alfred Stieglitz and the American Avant-Garde*. Boston: New York Graphic Society, 1977.

Howard, Leon. *Herman Melville: A Biography*. Berkeley: University of California Press, 1951.

Howe, Irving. *The Idea of the Modern in Literature and the Arts*. New York: Horizon, 1967.

Howells, William Dean. *Criticism and Fiction and Other Essays*, ed. Clara Marburg Kirk and Rudolph Kirk. New York: New York University Press, 1959.

————. *Editor's Study*, ed. James W. Simpson. Troy, N.Y.: Whitson, 1983.

Hurwitz, Harold M. "Hemingway's Tutor, Ezra Pound," *MFS* 17, no. 4 (Winter 1971): 469–482.

Hutchisson, James M. *Paper Wars: The Literary Manifesto in America*. Unpublished Ph.D. Dissertation, University of Delaware, 1987.

James, William. *Collected Essays and Reviews*. New York: Longmans, Green, 1920.

————. *Essays on Faith and Morals*, ed. Ralph Barton Perry. New York: Longmans, Green, 1949.

————. *Essays in Radical Empiricism*. Cambridge, Mass.: Harvard University Press, 1976.

————. *A Pluralistic Universe*. New York: Longmans, Green, 1920.

————. *Principles of Psychology*, 2 vols. New York: Henry Holt, 1923.

————. *The Writings of William James*, ed. John J. McDermott. New York: Modern Library, 1968.

Kahnweiler, Daniel-Henry. *Juan Gris: His Life and Work*, trans. Douglas Cooper. New York: Valentin, 1947.

————. *The Rise of Cubism*, trans. Henry Aronson. New York: Wittenborn, Schultz, 1949.

Kandinsky, Wassily. *The Art of Spiritual Harmony*, trans. M. T. H. Sadler. Boston: Houghton, Mifflin, 1914.

Kazin, Alfred. "John Dos Passos: Inventor in Isolation." *Saturday Review* 52 (March 5, 1969), 16–19.

————. *On Native Grounds*. Garden City, N.Y.: Doubleday, 1956.

Kellner, Bruce, ed. *A Gertrude Stein Companion*. New York: Greenwood, 1988.

Kenner, Hugh. *A Homemade World: The American Modernist Writers*. New York: Knopf, 1975.

Knox, George A., and Herbert M. Stahl. *Dos Passos and "The Revolting Playwrights"*. Upsala: A.-B. Lundequistska, 1964.

Kuenzli, Rudolf E., ed. *New York Dada*. New York: Willis Locker & Owens, 1986.

Landsberg, Melvin. *Dos Passos' Path to USA: A Political Biography*. Boulder, Colo.: Associated University Press, 1972.

Leitch, Thomas. "From Detective Story to Detective Novel," *MFS* 29 (Autumn 1983), 475–484.

Levin, Gail. "Wassily Kandinsky and the American Literary Avant-Garde," *Criticism* 21 (1979), 347–361.

Levinson, Ronald Bartlett. "Gertrude Stein, William James, and Grammar," *American Journal of Psychology* 54 (January 1941), 124–128.

Lewis, Clarence Irving. *Mind and the World Order: Outline of a Theory of Knowledge*. New York: Scribner's, 1929.

Ludington, Townsend, ed. *The Fourteenth Chronicle: Letters and Diaries of John Dos Passos*. Boston: Gambit, 1973.

————. *John Dos Passos: A Twentieth Century Odyssey*. New York: E.P. Dutton, 1980.

Lydenberg, John. "Dos Passos's USA: The Words of the Hollow Men," in Allen Belkind, ed. *Dos Passos, the Critics and the Writer's Intention*. Carbondale, Ill.: Southern Illinois University Press, 1971, 93–105.

MacGowan, Christopher J. *William Carlos Williams's Early Poetry: The Visual Arts Background*. Ann Arbor, Mich.: UMI Press, 1984.

Malkoff, Karl. *Escape from the Self: A Study in Contemporary American Poetry and Poetics*. New York: Columbia University Press, 1977.

Mariani, Paul. *William Carlos Williams: A New World Naked*. New York: McGraw, Hill, 1981.

Marling, William. *William Carlos Williams and the Painters, 1909–1923*. Athens, Ohio: Ohio University Press, [c. 1982].

Martin, Ronald E. *American Literature and the Universe of Force*. Durham, N.C.: Duke University Press, 1981.

Matthiessen, Francis Otto. *American Renaissance*. New York: Oxford University Press, 1941.

Melville, Herman. *Collected Poems of Herman Melville*, ed. Howard P. Vincent. Chicago: Packard, 1947.

————. *The Confidence-Man: His Masquerade*, Norton Critical Edition, ed. Hershel Parker. New York: W.W. Norton, 1971.

————. *The Letters of Herman Melville*, ed. Merrell R. Davis and William H. Gilman. New Haven: Yale University Press, 1960.

————. *Moby-Dick*, Norton Critical Edition, ed. Harrison Hayford and Hershel Parker. New York: W.W. Norton, 1967.

————. *Pierre, or The Ambiguities*, ed. Harrison Hayford, Hershel Parker, and G. Thomas Tanselle. Evanston and Chicago: Northwestern University Press and Newberry Library, 1971.

——. *Redburn, White-Jacket,* and *Moby-Dick,* ed. Harrison Hayford, Hershel Parker, and G. Thomas Tanselle. New York: Library of America, 1983.

——. *White-Jacket; or The World in a Man-of-War,* ed. Harrison Hayford, Hershel Parker, and G. Thomas Tanselle. Evanston and Chicago: Northwestern University Press and Newberry Library, 1970.

Meyers, Jeffrey. *Hemingway: A Biography.* New York: Harper & Row, 1985.

Middlebrook, Diane Wood. *Walt Whitman and Wallace Stevens.* Ithaca, N.Y.: Cornell University Press, 1974.

Miesel, Victor H. *Voices of German Expressionism.* Englewood Cliffs, N.J.: Prentice-Hall, 1970.

Miller, J. Hillis. *Poets of Reality: Six Twentieth-Century Writers.* Cambridge, Mass.: Harvard University Press, 1965.

——, ed. *William Carlos Williams: A Collection of Critical Essays.* Englewood Cliffs, N.J.: Prentice-Hall, 1966.

Moore, Marianne. *Predilections.* New York: Viking, 1955.

Motherwell, Robert, ed. *The Dada Painters and Poets,* forward by Jack D. Flam. Boston: G.K. Hall, 1981.

Nagel, James. *Stephen Crane and Literary Impressionism.* University Park: Pennsylvania State University Press, 1981.

Newhall, Beaumont. *The History of Photography from 1839 to the Present.* New York: Museum of Modern Art, 1982.

Noël, Bernard. *Matisse,* trans. Jane Brenton. New York: Universe Books, 1987.

Norman, Dorothy. *Alfred Steiglitz: An American Seer.* New York: Random House, 1973.

Norris, Frank. *The Responsibilities of the Novelist and Other Literary Essays.* New York: Doubleday, Page, 1903.

O'Connor, D.J., ed. *A Critical History of Western Philosophy.* Glencoe, Ill.: Free Press, 1965.

Parker, Hershel, ed. *The Norton Anthology of American Literature.* Vol. 1. New York: W.W. Norton, 1985.

——and Harrison Hayford, eds. *Moby-Dick as Doubloon: Essays and Extracts (1851–1970).* New York: W.W. Norton, 1970.

Pearce, Roy Harvey. *The Continuity of American Poetry.* Princeton, N.J.: Princeton University Press, 1961.

——. *Whitman: A Collection of Critical Essays.* Englewood Cliffs, N.J.: Prentice-Hall, 1962.

Pears, D.F. *Bertrand Russell and the British Tradition in Philosophy.* New York: Random House, 1967.

Peckham, Morse. *Man's Rage for Chaos: Biology, Behavior and the Arts.* New York: Schocken, 1965.

Perloff, Marjorie. *The Futurist Moment: Avant-garde, Avant-guerre and the Language of Rupture.* Chicago: University of Chicago Press, 1986.

Phillips, Larry W. *Ernest Hemingway on Writing.* New York: Scribner's, 1984.

Pizer, Donald. *Dos Passos' U.S.A.* Charlottesville: University Press of Virginia, 1988.

Poirer, Richard. *Robert Frost: The Work of Knowing.* New York: Oxford University Press, 1977.

Porter, David. *Emerson and Literary Change.* Cambridge, Mass.: Harvard University Press, 1978.

Pound, Ezra. *Ezra Pound and the Visual Arts*, ed. Harriet Zinnes. New York: New Directions, 1980.

———. *Gaudier-Brzeska: A Memoir*. New York: New Directions, 1970.

———. *Letters 1907–1941*, ed. D. D. Paige. New York: Harcourt, Brace, 1950.

———. *Literary Essays of Ezra Pound*, ed. & intro T. S. Eliot. New York: New Directions, 1954.

———. *Selected Poems*. New York: New Directions, 1957.

———. *Selected Prose 1909–1965*, ed. William Cookson. New York: New Directions, 1973.

———. *The Spirit of Romance*. New York: New Directions, [1952].

Pultz, John, and Catherine B. Scallen. *Cubism and American Photography, 1910–1930*. Williamstown, Mass.: Sterling and Francine Clark Art Institute, 1981.

Rahv, Philip, "The Cult of Experience in American Writing," in Morton Dauwen Zabel, *Literary Opinion in America*. New York: Harper, 1962, 550–560.

Rawson, Don C. "The Process of Discovery: Mendeleev and the Periodic Law," *Annals of Science* 31, no. 3 (May 1974), 181–204.

Read, Herbert. *Kandinski*. New York: G. Wittenborn, 1959.

Reynolds, Michael. *Hemingway's Reading, 1910–1940: An Inventory*. Princeton, N.J.: Princeton University Press, 1981.

———. *The Young Hemingway*. Oxford: Basil Blackwell, 1986.

Riddel, Joseph H. *The Clairvoyant Eye: The Poetry and Poetics of Wallace Stevens*. Baton Rouge: Louisiana State University Press, 1965.

Rogers, Rodney O. "Stephen Crane and Impressionism," *Nineteenth Century Fiction* 24, no. 3 (December 1969), 292–304.

Rosenberry, Edward. *Melville and the Comic Spirit*. Cambridge, Mass.: Harvard University Press, 1955.

Rosenfeld, Paul. *Port of New York*. Urbana: University of Illinois Press, 1961.

Rotzler, Willy. *Constructive Concepts*, trans. Stanley Mason. Zurich: ABC Edition, 1979.

Rupp, Richard H. *Critics on Emily Dickinson*. Coral Gables, Fla.: University of Miami Press, 1972.

Russell, Bertrand. "Logical Atomism," in A. J. Ayer, ed., *Logical Positivism*. Glencoe, Ill.: Free Press, 1959, 31–50.

———. *Our Knowledge of the External World*. Chicago: Open Court, 1915.

———. *The Problems of Philosophy*. New York: Henry Holt, 1929.

Sanders, David. "*Manhattan Transfer* and 'the Service of Things,'" in Ray B. Brown and Donald Pizer, eds., *Themes and Directions in American Literature: Essays in Honor of Leon Howard*. Lafayette, Ind.: Purdue University Studies, 1969, 171–188.

Santayana, George. *The Philosophy of Santayana*, ed. Irwin Edman. New York: Scribner's, 1953.

———. *Skepticism and Animal Faith*. New York: Dover, 1955.

Sapir, Edward. *Language*, New York: Harcourt, Brace, 1921.

Sayre, Henry M. *The Visual Text of William Carlos Williams*. Urbana: University of Illinois Press, 1983.

Schlipp, Paul Arthur, ed. *The Philosophy of Bertrand Russell*. Chicago: Northwestern University Press, 1944.

Schneidau, Herbert N. *Ezra Pound: The Image and the Real*. Baton Rouge: Louisiana State University Press, 1969.

Scholnick, Robert J. "The 'Password Primeval': Whitman's Use of Science in 'Song of Myself,'" *Studies in the American Renaissance* (1986), 385–425.

Schwartz, Sanford. *The Matrix of Modernism: Pound, Eliot, and Early Twentieth Century Thought*. Princeton, N.J.: Princeton University Press, 1985.

Sewall, Richard Benson. *The Life of Emily Dickinson*, 2 vols. New York: Farrar, Straus & Giroux, 1974.

Sieburth, Richard. *Instigations: Ezra Pound and Remy de Gourmont*. Cambridge, Mass.: Harvard University Press, 1978.

Simpson, Louis. *Three on the Tower: The Lives and Works of Ezra Pound, T. S. Eliot, and William Carlos Williams*. New York: Morrow, 1975.

Smitherman, Geneva. *Talkin and Testifyin: The Language of Black America*. Boston: Houghton Mifflin, 1977.

Sprigge, Elizabeth. *Gertrude Stein: Her Life and Work*, New York: Harper, 1957.

Stearns, Harold, ed. *Civilization in the United States: An Inquiry by Thirty Americans*. New York: Harcourt, Brace, 1922.

Stein, Gertrude. *Everybody's Autobiography*. New York: Random House, 1937.

———. *Four in America*, Intro. Thornton Wilder. New Haven: Yale University Press, 1947.

———. *The Geographical History of America: Or, the Relation of Human Nature to the Human Mind*. New York: Random House, 1936.

———. *Geography and Plays*. Boston: Four Seas, 1922.

———. *Lectures in America*. New York: Random House, 1935.

———. *Narration*. New York: Greenwood Press, 1969.

———. *Picasso*. London; B.T. Batsford, 1939.

———. *Portraits and Prayers*. New York: Random House, 1934.

———. *Selected Writings of Gertrude Stein*, ed. Carl Van Vechten. New York: Random House, 1962.

———. *What Are Masterpieces*. Los Angeles: Conference Press, 1940.

Steiner, Wendy. *Exact Resemblance to Exact Resemblance; The Literary Portraiture of Gertrude Stein*. New Haven: Yale University Press, 1978.

Stern, Herbert J. *Wallace Stevens: Art of Uncertainty*. Ann Arbor, Mich.: University of Michigan Press, 1966.

Stevens, Wallace. *The Collected Poems of Wallace Stevens*. New York: Knopf, 1954.

———. *Letters of Wallace Stevens*, ed. Holly Stevens. New York: Knopf, 1967.

———. *The Necessary Angel: Essays on Reality and the Imagination*. New York: Random House, 1951.

———. *Opus Posthumous*, ed. & intro. Samuel French Morse. New York: Knopf, 1957.

———. *The Palm at the End of the Mind: Selected Poems and a Play*, ed. Holly Stevens. New York: Random House, 1972.

Stewart, Allegra. *Gertrude Stein and the Present*. Cambridge, Mass.: Harvard University Press, 1967.

Stock, Noel. *The Life of Ezra Pound*. New York: Random House, 1970.

Stoltzfus, Ben. "John Dos Passos and the French," in Allen Belkind, ed., *John Dos Passos, the Critics, and the Writer's Intention*. Carbondale, Ill.: Southern Illinois University Press, 1971, 197–218.

Sullivan, J. W. N. *Gallio: Or the Tyranny of Science*. New York: E.P. Dutton, 1928.

———. *Science: A New Outline*. New York: Thomas Nelson & Sons, 1935.

Tanner, Tony. "Ernest Hemingway's Unhurried Sensations," *The Hemingway Review* 1, no. 2 (Spring 1982), 20–38.

Tapscott, Stephen. *American Beauty: William Carlos Williams and the Modernist Whitman.* New York: Columbia University Press, 1984.

Tashjian, Dickran. *Skyscraper Primitives: Dada and the American Avant-Garde, 1910–1925.* Middletown, Conn.: Wesleyan University Press, 1975.

———. *William Carlos Williams and the American Scene 1920–1940.* New York: Whitney Museum, 1978.

Taylor, Gordon O. *The Passages of Thought: Psychological Representation in the American Novel, 1870–1900.* New York: Oxford University Press, 1969.

Terrell, Carroll F., ed. *William Carlos Williams: Man and Poet.* Orono, Maine: National Poetry Foundation, 1987.

Thompson, Lawrance. *Robert Frost,* 3 vols. New York: Holt, Rinehart & Winston, 1966–76.

Townley, Rod. *The Early Poetry of William Carlos Williams.* Ithaca, N.Y.: Cornell University Press, 1975.

Turner, Frederick Jackson. *The Frontier in American History.* Philadelphia: Franklin Library, 1977.

291: Nos. 1–12, 1915–1916, intro. Dorothy Norman. New York: Arno Press, 1972.

Wagner, Linda Welshimer. *Dos Passos: Artist as American.* Austin: University of Texas Press, 1979.

———, ed. *Interviews with William Carlos Williams.* New York: New Directions, 1976.

———. *The Prose of William Carlos Williams.* Middletown, Conn.: Wesleyan University Press, 1970.

———. *"The Sun Also Rises*: One Debt to Imagism," *Journal of Narrative Technique* 2, no. 2 (May 1972), 88–98.

Walker, Cheryl. *The Nightingale's Burden: Women Poets and American Culture before 1900.* Bloomington: Indiana University Press, 1982.

Walker, Jayne L. *The Making of a Modernist: Gertrude Stein from "Three Lives" to "Tender Buttons."* Amherst, Mass.: University of Massachusetts Press, 1985.

Warren, Robert Penn, "Hemingway," in Morton Dauwen Zabel, ed., *Literary Opinion in America.* New York: Harper, 1962, 444–463.

Weatherford, Robert, ed. *Stephen Crane: The Critical Heritage.* Boston: Routledge & Kegan Paul, 1973.

Weinstein, Norman. *Gertrude Stein and the Literature of Modern Consciousness.* New York: Frederick Ungar, 1970.

Weisbuch, Robert. *Emily Dickinson's Poetry.* Chicago: University of Chicago Press, 1975.

Werkmeister, William Henry. *A History of Philosophical Ideas in America.* New York: Ronald, 1949.

Westbrook, Max. "Whilomville: The Coherence of Radical Language," in Joseph Katz, ed., *Stephen Crane in Transition: Centenary Essays.* De Kalb, Ill.: Northern Illinois University Press, 1972, 86–105.

Whitehead, Alfred North. *The Concept of Nature.* Cambridge: Cambridge University Press, 1920.

———. *Symbolism, Its Meaning and Effect.* New York: Macmillan, 1927.

Whitman, Walt. *An American Primer.* Boston: Small, Maynard, 1904.

———. *Complete Poetry and Collected Prose,* ed. Justin Kaplan. New York: Library of America, 1982.

———. *Leaves of Grass and Selected Prose*, ed. John Kouwenhoven. New York: Modern Library, 1950.

———. *Specimen Days and Collect*. Philadelphia: David McKay, 1882–1883.

Williams, William Carlos. *Al Que Quiere! A Book of Poems*, Boston, Four Seas, 1917.

———. "America, Whitman, and the Art of Poetry," *Poetry Journal* 8 (November 1917), 27–36.

———. *The Autobiography of William Carlos Williams*. New York: New Directions, [1967].

———. *The Broken Span*. Norfolk, Conn.: New Directions, 1941.

———. *The Cod Head*. San Francisco: Harvest Press, 1932.

———. *Collected Earlier Poems*. New York: New Directions, 1951.

———. *An Early Martyr and Other Poems*. New York: Alcestis Press, 1935.

———. *The Embodiment of Knowledge*, ed. & intro. Ron Loewinsohn. New York: New Directions, 1974.

———. *The Farmers' Daughters: Collected Stories*. Norfolk, Conn.: New Directions, 1961.

———. *I Wanted to Write a Poem*, reported & ed. Edith Heal. Boston: Beacon Press, 1967.

———. *Imaginations*, ed. Webster Schott. New York: New Directions, 1970.

———. *In the American Grain*. New York: New Directions, 1956.

———. *Paterson*, 5 vols. New York: New Directions, 1945–58.

———. *A Recognizable Image: William Carlos Williams on Art and Artists*, ed. Bram Dijkstra. New York: New Directions, 1978.

———. *Selected Essays of William Carlos Williams*. New York: Random House, 1954.

———. *Selected Letters*, ed. John C. Thirlwall. New York: McDowell, Obolensky, 1957.

———. *Sour Grapes*. Boston: Four Seas, 1921.

———. *A Voyage to Pagany*. New York: Macaulay, 1928.

———. *White Mule*. London: MacGibbon & Kee, 1965.

Wilson, Edmund. *Axel's Castle*. New York: Scribner's, 1932.

Wittgenstein, Ludwig. *Tractatus Logico-Philosophicus*, ed. & trans. C. K. Ogden. London: Kegan Paul, Trench, Trubner, 1922.

Wolford, Chester L. *The Anger of Stephen Crane: Fiction and the Epic Tradition*. Lincoln: University of Nebraska Press, 1983.

Young, Daniel P. "A Skeptical Music: Stevens and Santayana," *Criticism* 7 (Summer 1965), 263–283.

Zukofsky, Louis. *Prepositions*. New York: Horizon, 1968.

Index

■ About the Author

Ronald E. Martin is Professor in the Department of English and the Center for Science and Culture, University of Delaware. He is the author of *The Fiction of Joseph Hergesheimer* and *American Literature and the Universe of Force*.

Library of Congress Cataloging-in-Publication Data
Martin, Ronald E., 1933–
American literature and the destruction of knowledge : innovative writing in the age of epistemology / by Ronald E. Martin.
Includes bibliographical references and index.
ISBN 0-8223-1125-9
1. American literature—History and criticism.   2. Literature, Experimental—United States—History and criticism.
3. Knowledge, Theory of, in literature.   4. Philosophy in literature.   I. Title.
PS169.K45M37   1991
810.9—dc20   90-21088   CIP